Martin Luther and the Arts

# Studies in Medieval and Reformation Traditions



VOLUME 236

The titles published in this series are listed at *brill.com/smrt*

# Martin Luther and the Arts

*Music, Images, and Drama to Promote the Reformation*


*By*

Andreas Loewe
Katherine Firth



BRILL

LEIDEN | BOSTON

Cover illustration: Lucas Cranach the Younger, Epitaph-altarpiece of Johann Friedrich the Magnanimous [central panel], 1555, painting on lime wood, 360 × 311 cm, Herder-Kirche, Weimar (FR434). Photograph by Wolfgang Sauber, shared under CC-BY-SA 4.0 on commons.wikimedia.org

The Library of Congress Cataloging-in-Publication Data is available online at https://catalog.loc.gov
LC record available at https://lccn.loc.gov/2022043630

Typeface for the Latin, Greek, and Cyrillic scripts: "Brill". See and download: brill.com/brill-typeface.

ISSN 1573-4188
ISBN 978-90-04-52742-3 (hardback)
ISBN 978-90-04-52743-0 (e-book)



This book is printed on acid-free paper and produced in a sustainable manner.

Printed by Printforce, United Kingdom

*For our family*
*and our Melbourne friends*

# Contents

# Acknowledgements


This book has been more than a decade in the making, and research for it took place on two continents—Europe and Australia. In Australia, much of the research and writing took place in Narrm (Melbourne), on the traditional lands of the Wurundjeri People of the Kulin Nation, sovereign lands that were never ceded. We pay our respects to their Elders past and present.

We would like to thank the institutions that helped make this book possible: the staff and students at the University of Melbourne where we both research and teach, in particular colleagues at the Faculty of Culture and Communications and the Faculty of Fine Art and Music. At La Trobe University, Melbourne, we thank our colleagues at the Research Education and Development team, and at the University of Divinity, Melbourne, our colleagues at Trinity College Theological School. Thank you to the librarians and collections that supported our research: the State Library of Victoria, Melbourne; the Baillieu Library of the University of Melbourne; and the Dalton McCaughey Library at the University of Divinity. Thank you also to the libraries that created digital images of works in their repositories, and for granting us the rights to reproduce them.

This book builds on our previous work, together and individually, on Luther, the arts, and the influence of the Reformation. We would like to thank the editors of the series and journals in which previous versions of some of the chapters appeared, for helping us shape and explore our ideas then, and for the opportunity to expand them in this volume. Earlier versions of these chapters were published as: '"Musica est optimum": Martin Luther's Theory of Music', *Music and Letters*, 94.4 (2013), 'Why do Lutherans sing? Lutherans, Music and the Gospel in the First Century of the Reformation', *Church History*, 82 (2013), 'Martin Luther's "Mighty Fortress"', *Lutheran Quarterly*, 32.2 (2018), and 'Proclaiming the Passion: Popular Drama and the Passion Tradition in Luther's Germany', *Renaissance and Reformation Review*, 12.2 (2010). They are reproduced here with permission.

We acknowledge the following image permissions: Wolfgang Sauber for permission to reproduce the image of Cranach's *Herderaltar* on the front cover of the book, Dr Avishai Teicher for permission to reproduce figure 8, the British Museum for permission to reproduce figure 1, the Metropolitan Museum of Art for permission to reproduce figure 2, the Bayerische Staatsbibliothek München for permission to reproduce figures 3, 6, 7, the Universitäts- und Landesbibliothek Sachsen-Anhalt Halle an der Saale for permission to reproduce figure 4, the Universitäts- und Landesbibliothek Münster for permission to reproduce figure 5, and the Staatsbibliothek zu Berlin—Preußischer Kulturbesitz for permission to reproduce figure 9.

In 2019, we spent Michaelmas term at our Colleges at the University of Cambridge. We would like to thank the Principal and Fellows of Newnham College, and the Master and Fellows of Selwyn College, for the opportunity to return to a familiar pattern of research and sharing of ideas within their academic Fellowships. A particular thanks to colleagues at the Faculty of Divinity, the Centre for Research in the Arts, Social Sciences and the Humanities, and the staff at the Cambridge University Library.

We would like to thank our commissioning editor, Ivo Romein and our series editor, Prof. Chris Ocker, and the two anonymous readers who made many helpful comments on our manuscript. Many colleagues contributed directly to the development of the book: Sam Allchurch, Dr Sam Barrett, Dr Alistair Clark, Dr Leofranc Holford-Strevens for his translation of the Latin text of Luther's *Praefatio zu den Symphoniae Iucundae, 1538,* Prof. Dorothy Lee, Dr Grantley McDonald, Prof. Michael Marissen, Philip Nicholls, Prof. Markus Rathey, Prof. Lyndal Roper, Prof. Paul Rorem, and Dr Daniel Trocmé-Latter. Thank you in particular to Canon Dr Ruth Redpath AO for proofreading our manuscript, and Dr Elizabeth Culhane for preparing the manuscript for publication.

Thank you to our wonderful colleagues both at St Paul's Cathedral Melbourne, in particular the Venerable Heather Patacca, Archdeacon of Melbourne, who served as Acting Dean of St Paul's Cathedral during Michaelmas term 2019; and at International House, the University of Melbourne. Thank you to our families—the Revd Dr Jill and the Revd Len Firth, Bob and Laura Firth with Lucy, Molly, Sam and Emily; Susan and Nicholas Firth-McCoy with Elena and Maya; Dr Brigitte Loewe; Eva Loewe and Klaus Sigl with Leopold and Lucia; and our lockdown family during the coronavirus pandemic of Khang Chiem, Zane Gaylard, Dr Christina McLeish, Anne Shea with Lucy and Mika, Ana Torres Ramirez and, of course, the Deanery Cat, who helped with some of the edits.

*The Deanery, Melbourne, 2022*

# Figures and Tables

## Figures

## Tables

# Abbreviations

| | |
|---|---|
| AWA | Archiv zur Weimarer Ausgabe der Werke Martin Luthers (Köln: Böhlau, 1985) |
| BBKL | *Biographisch-Bibliographisches Kirchenlexikon* (Herzberg: Traugott Bautz, 1993) |
| CCSL | *Corpus Christianorum Series Latina*, ed. by L. Jocqué (Turnhout: Brepols, 1977–) |
| CCCM | *Corpus Christianorum Continuatio Mediaevalis*, ed. by T. Denecker, B. Janssens, and L. Jocqué (Turnhout: Brepols, 1967–) |
| CR | Philipp, Melanchthon, *Corpus Reformatorum*, ed. by Karl Gottlob Bretschneider and others (Halle: C. A. Schwetschke & Sohn, 1834–1946) |
| CSM | *Corpus Scriptorum de Musica*, ed. by Roger Bragard (Rome: American Institute of Musicology, 1950–73) |
| ES | *Evangelische Schulordnungen, I: Die evangelischen Schulordnungen des Sechzehnten Jahrhunderts*, ed. by Reinhold Vormbaum (Gütersloh: Bertelsmann, 1860) |
| FR | Max J. Friedländer and Jakob Rosenberg, *Die Gemälde von Lukas Cranach*, rev. by G. Schwartz (Basel: Birkhäuser Verlag, 1979) |
| GS | *Scriptores ecclesiastici de musica sacra potissimum ex variis Italiae, Galliae et Germaniae codicibus manuscriptis collecti et nunc primum publica luce donati*, ed. by Martin Gerbert, 3 vols (St Blasien: Typis San Blasianis, 1784; repr. Hildesheim: Georg Olms, 1963) |
| KF | Dieter Koepplin and Tilman Falk, *Lukas Cranach: Gemälde, Zeichnung, Druckgraphik*, 2 vols (Basel: Birkhäuser, 1974–76) |
| KG | Arno Weber, *Geschichte der Kantorei-Gesellschaften im Gebiete des ehemaligen Kurfürstentums Sachsen*, Publikationen der Internationalen Musikgesellschaft: Beihefte IX (Leipzig: Breitkopf und Härtel, 1902) |
| KS | Johannes Rautenstrauch, *Luther und die Pflege der kirchlichen Musik in Sachsen: Ein Beitrag zur Geschichte der katholischen Brüderschaften, der vor- und nachreformatorischen Kurrenden, Schulchöre und Kantoreien Sachsens* (Leipzig: Breitkopf und Härtel, 1907) |
| LW | Martin Luther, *Luther's Works: American Edition*, ed. by Jaroslav Pelikan, Helmut T. Lehmann, and others (St Louis, MO: Concordia, 1955–) |
| MGG | *Die Musik in Geschichte und Gegenwart: Allgemeine Enzyklopädie der Musik*, ed. by Friedrich Blume, 17 vols (Kassel: Bärenreiter, 1949–68) |
| MGG² | *Die Musik in Geschichte und Gegenwart: Allgemeine Enzyklopädie der Musik*, ed. by Ludwig Finscher, Andreas Jaschinski, Ilka Sühring, 29 vols (Kassel: Bärenreiter, 1994–2008) |

PG *Patrologiae Cursus Completus, Series Graeca*, ed. by Jacques-Paul Migne, 161 vols (Paris: Imprimerie Catholique, 1857–66)

PLMA Publications of the Modern Languages Association

W[1] *D. Martin Luthers sowol in Deutscher als Lateinischer Sprache verfertigte und aus der letztern in die erstere übersetzte Sämtliche Schriften*, ed. by Johann George Walch (Halle: Johann Justinus Gebauer, 1740–53)

WA Martin Luther, *D. Martin Luthers Werke: Kritische Gesamtausgabe*, ed. by Joachim Karl Friedrich Knaake and others, 120 vols (Weimar: Hermann Böhlau, 1883–1985)

WA Br *Briefwechsel*, Luther's *Letters*

WA DB *Deutsche Bibel*, Luther's *German Bible*

WA Tr *Tischreden*, Luther's *Table Talk*

# Introduction

Martin Luther was the architect and engineer of the Protestant Reformation, which transformed Germany five hundred years ago and lives on in the global denomination that continues to bear his name. Luther's fascinating life story is often told, and has been told in great detail:[1] from cloistered monk in Erfurt struggling with the demands of the doctrine of salvation, to university lecturer in Wittenberg; from academic questioning the practice of indulgences, to outspoken opponent of the Papacy; from excommunicated outcast under house arrest on the Wartburg, to instigator of an entirely new branch of the Christian faith that still takes its name from his protests—'Protestantism'.

It has been well documented that the fact that Luther taught and wrote at the time of a communication revolution substantially bolstered the success of his Reformation message.[2] However, what has particularly fascinated us was the reformer's strategic use of so many different art-forms to promote his message. Because of his effective use of the arts, more people were able to access and understand Luther's ideas, which made his Reformation such a successful movement. This book tells the story of how Luther used many disciplines of the arts available to him to communicate Reformation thoughts among the literate, illiterate, and semiliterate alike.

This book builds on our previous work, together and individually, on Luther, the arts, and the influence of the Reformation: on Luther's use of the arts to promote his Reformation message by Loewe and Firth; on propaganda images and collaboration by Firth; drama, music theory, the Lutheran choral tradition and Reformation polemics by Loewe; and the ongoing ramifications of anti-Semitism and hate speech in German history by Loewe and Firth.[3] New

1 For instance, by Lyndal Roper, *Martin Luther: Renegade and Prophet* (New York: Random House, 2017), Heiko Augustinus Oberman, *Luther: Man between God and the Devil*, trans. by Eileen Walliser-Schwartzbart (London: Harper Collins, 1993), or Martin Brecht, *Martin Luther*, trans. by James L. Schaaf, 3 vols (St Louis, MO: Augsburg Fortress, 1985–99).

2 Most notably by Elizabeth Eisenstein, *The Printing Press as an Agent of Change* (Cambridge: Cambridge University Press, 1980), and Mark U. Edwards, Jr, *Printing, Propaganda and Martin Luther* (Berkeley: University of California Press, 1994), and Andrew Pettegree, 'Books, Pamphlets and Polemic', in *The Reformation World*, ed. by Andrew Pettegree (London: Routledge, 2002), pp. 109–26.

3 Andreas Loewe, '"Musica est optimum": Martin Luther's Theory of Music', *Music and Letters*, 94.4 (2013), 573–605, Andreas Loewe, 'Why do Lutherans sing? Lutherans, Music and the Gospel in the First Century of the Reformation', *Church History*, 82 (2013), 69–89, Andreas Loewe, 'Proclaiming the Passion: Popular Drama and the Passion Tradition in Luther's Germany', *Renaissance and Reformation Review*, 12.2 (2010), 235–82, Andreas Loewe and Katherine Firth, 'Martin Luther's "Mighty Fortress"', *Lutheran Quarterly*, 32.2 (2018), 125–45.

 | DOI 10.1163/9789004527430_002

material considers Luther's theory of visual art, the analysis of his polemical images, and Hans Sachs' Reformation poetry and plays. We draw on our academic backgrounds in church history, theology, cultural history, musicology, art history, and literary and performance studies. In this one volume, we therefore consider Luther's engagements across the arts: through hymns, song, poetry, painting, engravings, sculpture, drama, architecture, and rhetoric. We explore church, civil, political, and educational settings. We draw on many previously unpublished primary sources in German, provide new complete translations, as well as extensively use German secondary literature less commonly consulted in English-language scholarship of the field.[4] This cross-disciplinary survey aims to be the most comprehensive study to date of Luther's theoretical, practical and theological engagement with different forms of art, in ways that will be useful to both established scholars and researchers new to the fields.

This volume supports, on the one hand, the many deeper engagements with one or perhaps two of these art-forms, while, on the other, addressing the close-analysis gaps in some of the major survey studies. In the run-up to the 2017 quincentenary of the publication of Luther's *Ninety-Five Theses on Indulgences*, a wealth of new works on Luther saw the light of day, especially in Germany. This book engages with recent German research on the reformer, and on the artistic genres he fostered and employed to spread his message. While some of the findings of German scholars, especially in the area of Luther and the Image, have been made available to English-speaking readers through works such as Werner (2016) and Roper (2021), much research, especially from the 1980s and 1990s, still remains untranslated.[5] This work will enable English-speaking readers to access German research published since the quincentenary, as well as more established German research on Luther and the arts.

As was typical in his time, Luther studied all seven liberal arts, including music theory and rhetoric, as part of his university education at Erfurt and Wittenberg. In his mature work, he consistently developed theories about the various arts, though these are scattered across his letters, pamphlets, and other writings. This work brings together these disparate sources in outlining the systematic framework that underpins Luther's thinking. While Luther was himself a competent artist—particularly as a singer and hymn writer—he was first of all a theologian and polemicist. Our book, therefore, uses the theological lens of the polemical interchanges of the Reformation to look at the ways

4 All translations are by the authors unless otherwise credited.

5 Elke Anna Werner, 'Martin Luther and Visual Culture', in *Oxford Research Encyclopedia, Religion* (Oxford: Oxford University Press, 2016), Lyndal Roper, *Living I Was Your Plague: Martin Luther's World and Legacy* (Princeton, NJ: Princeton University Press, 2021).

in which Luther directly engaged in commissioning or creating artworks in music, visual arts, rhetoric, and drama. It both examines the belief systems that give expression to his writings, and the polemical rhetoric used in his collaborations with other artists to advance his message.

Our work continually refers back to Luther's own writings. In our analysis we let the reformer speak and explain his rationale. We thoroughly survey Luther's writings and sayings on each of the artistic fields considered, which has made it possible for us to point to the theoretical framework Luther held on the arts. This is particularly true for our examination of his theology of music (Chapter 1) where we show that, while he did have a 'passionate love affair with music', Luther also had a highly developed theoretical approach to music.[6] The same holds true in our consideration of Luther's theory of the image (Chapter 4) where we show for the first time that, in addition to having a 'vivid visual imagination', Luther also held a systematic theory of the image.[7] Wherever possible, we refer back to Patristic or medieval sources, such as Augustine and Plotinus, who influenced Luther's theology of the image, and Boethius who shaped his theology of music. Where there is contemporary theoretical work that closely matches Luther's own, such as the work of Matthäus Herbenus (*c.*1445–1538) which directly influenced Luther's theology of music, we cross-reference these sources.[8] Our book makes it possible for students of Luther's approach to the arts to explore both Luther's art theory and the Patristic or late-medieval philosophical landscapes that nurtured it. In this way, readers will be able to judge for themselves whether claims, such as that made by modern scholars such as Block (2002), that 'Luther did not use any music-theoretical treatise to confront and approach music', are justified.[9]

In his use of the arts to share his message, Luther was building on well-established cultural and religious artistic conventions. During Luther's lifetime, community was maintained by the communal performance of art. Communal festivals and fairs were often centred on shared theatrical performances, and music-making. Singing together in guilds, public houses or public

---

6 Johannes Block, *Verstehen durch Musik: Das gesungene Wort in der Theologie—Ein hermeneutischer Beitrag zur Hymnologie am Beispiel Martin Luthers*, Mainzer Hymnologische Studien, 6 (Tübingen/Basel: Francke, 2002), p. 40: 'leidenschaftliche[s] Verhältnis der Liebschaft'.

7 For instance, Elke Anna Werner, 'Pictorial Concepts of Law and Grace: Relations between the Lutheran Reformation and the Anthropology of the Image', in *Anthropological Reformations: Anthropology in the Era of Reformation*, ed by Anne Eusterschulte and others (Göttingen: Vandenhoek & Ruprecht, 2015), pp. 134–53 (p. 42).

8 Matthäus Herbenus, *De natura cantus ac miraculis vocis*, ed. by Joseph Smits van Waesberghe, Beiträge zur Rheinischen Musikgeschichte, 22 (Köln: Staufen, 1957).

9 Block, *Verstehen durch Musik*, p. 42, 'Luther bedient sich keines musiktheoretischen Traktates, um sich der Musik zu stellen und sich ihr zu nähern'.

squares strengthened the fabric of society.[10] Highly decorated church and civic buildings included carved, painted and mosaic images. With the expansion of the printing press, more ephemeral visual images were widely distributed and displayed, for example in broadsheets and pamphlets. Academic debates between scholars at the university took place in front of a public audience and were announced on the doors of public buildings, as was anecdotally the case for the inciting event of the Protestant Reformation, Luther's ninety-five theses.

Similarly, the Luthers' Wittenberg home was both a domestic space and a residential theological training community for up to forty students at any one time. Fascinating archaeological work on Luther's domestic setting at the Black Cloister has shed light on how even the decorations of everyday objects such as tiled stoves and ceramic handwashing basins used in the Luthers' home were designed to contribute to the spread of his message.[11] A more formal study of architectural decorations in domestic and public spaces was considered for inclusion in this volume but excluded for reasons of length.

## 1 Structure and Scope of This Book

We have structured our examination of how Luther's thought was widely diffused in popular culture and disseminated in Protestant artistic practice by art-form. Each section develops Luther's theory of that art-form, gives a historical account of his use of the art-form, and provides a close reading of one or more significant exemplars of the art-form.

### 1.1 *Music*

In the first section of this volume, we consider Luther's use of music. Luther thought extensively about the importance and function of music; he also wrote hymns and directly incorporated music into his theological and proselytising strategies. In Chapter 1, we outline Luther's theoretical approach to music and

---

10 Documented extensively by Dorothea Freise, *Spiele und Spielinitiativen in spätmittelalterlichen Städten*, Veröffentlichungen des Max-Plancks-Instituts für Geschichte, p. 178 (Frankfurt a.M.: Vandenhoeck und Ruprecht, 2002).

11 Mirko Gutjahr, 'Wie protestantisch ist Luthers Müll: Die Konfessionalisierung und ihre Auswirkungen auf die materielle Alltagskultur des 16. Jahrhunderts', in *Religiosität in Mittelalter und Neuzeit*, ed. by Matthias Untermann and others, Mitteilungen der Deutschen Gesellschaft für Archäologie des Mittelalters und der Neuzeit, 23 (Heidelberg: Neumann, 2011), pp. 43–50, Louis D. Nebelsick and Tomoko Emmerling, '"Finding Luther": Toward an Archaelogy of the Reformer and the Earliest Reformation', *Church History*, 86.4 (2017), 1155–1207.

show how he successfully drew on a medieval Boethian model of classifying music to make his case that music was 'next to theology' in enabling the proclamation of God's goodness and praise. At university, Luther played the lute and sang in ensembles but also acquired a detailed understanding of late-medieval musical theory. Unlike many modern commentators, who ground their analysis on the effect music and singing had on Luther, we first look at the theories that give shape to the framework by which Luther describes the different origins, aspects, and applications of music.

This book endeavours to take up the challenge by Leaver (2007) to present a detailed assessment of the reformer's music theory.[12] Few other works apply a systematic lens to enable meaningful distinction between the different forms of musical expression in Luther's work.[13] Indeed, most works on Luther and music suggest that the reformer's approach to music was one of sentiment: they emphasise how for Luther music was principally a personal passion and a profound comfort in times of his *Anfechtungen* (spiritual trials or religious crises). For example, a comprehensive German study on the hermeneutics of Luther's music by Block (2002) proposes that 'Luther's way of understanding music is not limited to an objective, externally measured approach' but that 'it is the passionate love affair that determines Luther's approach to music'.[14] In contrast, in Chapter 1, we demonstrate that Luther has a highly developed theory of music that is firmly rooted in classical and late-medieval philosophy, which goes far beyond a 'passion for music' and 'comfort in adversity' or, indeed, the recognition of its use as a vehicle to communicate his gospel.[15]

One of the most significant contributions to the arts has been the strong musical tradition established by the reformer. In Chapter 2, we look at how Luther made use of hymns and songs to ensure that his message was heard across Germany, and how singing was deliberately fostered in schools and parishes by the establishment of school choirs and *Kantoreien*. Through historical analysis, we demonstrate how Luther used music to spread his message across class and national boundaries, and how that message was reinterpreted in his own time and continues up to the present day.

In Chapter 3, we focus on Luther's most popular hymn, 'A Mighty Fortress' (*Ein feste Burg*). Through close textual and musicological analysis, we demonstrate that Luther's hymns mirror his other work—such as, for instance, Bible

12 Robin A. Leaver, *Luther's Liturgical Music: Principles and Implications*, Lutheran Quarterly Books (Grand Rapids: Eerdmans, 2007), pp. 19–20.

13 Ibid., pp. 65–103 (pp. 97–102).

14 Block, *Verstehen durch Musik*, p. 40: 'Luthers Verstehensweise der Musik beläuft sich nicht auf einen objektiven, auf einen von außen abmessenden Zugang. Es ist vielmehr das leidenschaftliche Verhältnis der Liebschaft, das Luthers Zugang zur Musik bestimmt'.

15 Block, *Verstehen durch Musik*, p. 38.

translation—to make his message accessible. We further trace the influence of 'A Mighty Fortress' in promoting the idea of a triumphant Protestant *Reich*, blessed by God and founded on the theology of Martin Luther, into the nineteenth and twentieth centuries.

### 1.2 *Images*

In the second section of the volume, we consider Luther's close collaboration with image makers, particularly Lucas Cranach the Elder and Younger and the printer Hans Lufft, as well as his engagement with pre-existing church artworks. In Chapter 4, we establish a new account of Luther's theory of the image, examining how, in his opposition to the Iconoclast movement, he provided a systematic philosophical and theological framework to determine which kinds of images were to be retained, destroyed, adapted or, indeed, promoted. While Luther's theoretical approach to the visual arts is significantly less organised than his theoretical approach to music, he nonetheless has a coherent theological and artistic theory about visual art, which he deploys in images that promote his views and condemn his opponents.

Exploring Luther's theory of the image requires a careful close study of Luther's writings across all his publications and sermons, including his extensive *Table Talk*. Unfortunately, only the most obvious of his systematic underpinnings, the *Merkbild* (Image of Remembrance), has been widely identified. By classifying too many images as *Merkbilder*, the distinctiveness of this category of image is lost. Werner (2016) is right in saying that *Merkbilder* is 'a status [...] too commonly attributed in a sweeping way to Protestant images in general'.[16] Even though she also contributed an article on the concept of the *Feindbild* (Image of Enmity), frustratingly, she did not follow up on her suspicion that Luther's theology might provide a more nuanced theory of the image than these two broad categories.[17]

It is noteworthy that in their analysis of Luther's use of the visual arts, recent German commentators have increasingly resorted to a false dichotomy between the aural and visual arts. Following Koepplin (1983), Nipperday (1983), and Koerner (1993), Friedrich (2007) and Wegmann (2011) affirmed a hierarchy of communication in which the image was subservient to the word.[18] In

16 Werner, 'Pictorial Concepts of Law and Grace', p. 151.

17 Elke Anna Werner, 'Feindbild', in *Handbuch der politischen Ikonographie*, ed. by Uwe Fleckner, Martin Warnke, and Hendrik Ziegler (München: Beck, 2011), I, pp. 301–305.

18 Dieter Koepplin, 'Kommet her zu mir alle. Das tröstliche Bild des Gekreuzigten im Verständnis Luthers', in *Martin Luther und die Reformation in Deutschland. Vorträge zur Ausstellung im Germanischen Nationalmuseum Nürnberg 1983*, ed. by Kurt Löcher (Schweinfurt: Weppert, 1983), pp. 153–99 (p. 190); Thomas Nipperday, 'Luther und die Bildung der Deutschen', in *Luther und die Folgen. Beiträge zur sozialgeschichtlichen*

support of their theory, they drew on a single sermon preached at the very end of Luther's life, in which he spoke about the nature of Christ's kingdom as a 'listening kingdom, not a visual kingdom' (*ein hőr Reich, nicht ein Sehe-Reich*).[19] Luther explained then that 'the eyes direct and lead us not to the kingdom, where we may find Christ and come to know him, but the ears have to do that'.[20] However, it is important to emphasise that Luther here did not comment on a dichotomy between different art-forms but on his understanding of the two realms, as he made clear in the introduction to his sermon: 'in this way the realm of Christ is distinguished from the secular realm'.[21] Unfortunately, Friedrich's and Wegmann's distinction was taken up by subsequent researchers, who developed their erroneous distinction further. Thus Eusterschulte (2012) postulated that Luther

> transfers the experience of a spiritual presence, which in the pictorial-theological tradition of the image is brought to the visual-visionary effectiveness of the image and is founded in certain rhetorical categories, and at the same time suspends one dimension of spiritual pictorial rhetoric—the real presence of the Logos in pictorial visual form.[22]

---

*Bedeutung der lutherischen Reformation* ed. by Hartmut Löwe and Claus-Jürgen Roepke (München: Christian Kaiser Verlag, 1983), pp. 13–27 (p. 15): 'Protestant culture is no longer a culture of the eye, but a culture of the ear. Meaning is conveyed through words, not through regarding' (*Protestantische Kultur ist nicht mehr Kultur des Auges, sondern Kultur des Ohres. Sinn ist durch Wort, nicht durch Anschauung vermittelt*). Joseph L. Koerner, *The Moment of Self-Portraiture in German Renaissance Art* (Chicago: University of Chicago Press, 1993), p. 379. Susanne Wegmann, Der reformatorische Blick. Sehen oder Hören—welche Sinneswahrnehmung führt zu Gott?', in *Sehen und Sakralität in der Vormoderne*, ed. by David Ganz and Thomas Lentes, Kultbild, 4 (Berlin: Reimer Verlag, 2011), pp. 292–301, Markus Friedrich, 'Das Hör-Reich und das Sehe-Reich. Zur Bewertung des Sehens bei Luther und im frühneuzeitlichen Luthertum', in *Evidentia. Reichweiten visueller Wahrnehmung in der Frühen Neuzeit*, ed. by Gabriele Wimböck, Karin Leonhard, and Markus Friedrich, Pluralisierung & Autorität, 9 (Berlin: LIT, 2007), pp. 425–50.

19 Martin Luther, *Predigt, in Merseburg gehalten 6 August 1545*, WA 51: 11, 29.

20 Ibid., 11, 29–33: 'Und ist Christi Reich ein hőr Reich, nicht ein sehe Reich. Denn die augen leiten und fůren uns nicht dahin, da wir Christum finden und kennen lernen, sondern die ohren můssen das thun'.

21 Ibid., 11, 19–20: 'scheidet bald das Reich Christi von dem Weltlichen Reich'. For a theological reading of the sermon, see: Andrea Grün-Oesterreich and Peter Oesterreich, '*Dialectica docet, rhetorica movet*: Luthers Reform der Rhetorik', in *Rhetorica Movet: Studies in Historical and Modern Rhetoric in Honour of Heinrich F. Plett*, ed. by Peter Oesterreich and Thomas Sloane (Leiden: Brill, 1999) pp. 25–42 (pp. 36–39).

22 Anne Eusterschulte, 'Der reformulierte Bilderstreit—Grundlagen einer reformierten Theorie der Imago', in *Philosophie der Reformierten*, ed. by Günter Frank and H. J. Selderhuis, Melanchthon-Schriften der Stadt Bretten, 12 (Stuttgart-Bad Cannstadt: Frommann-Holzboog, 2012), pp. 113–67 (p. 148): 'überträgt er die in der bildtheologischen

Mis-readings of Luther's theological intent such as this are as regrettable as they are far reaching. Bridget Heal (2013) was among the first to set out 'to re-evaluate the role of the visual in Lutheran piety, and to debunk the myth'—introduced twenty years earlier—of the Reformation as an essentially non-visual event'.[23] Von Rosen (2018), also affirmed 'that Luther ascribes significant importance to the sense of sight for religious practice and, in doing so, aims both at material paintings and at the powerful evocative images of the imagination'.[24] Nevertheless, it is clear that insufficient theological understanding or insufficient consultation of Luther's wider output, has led to serious misrepresentations of the reformer's viewpoint that, independent from their amplification by words, images served 'for witness, remembrance, and as signs'.[25]

We find that the widely held theory that the reformer introduced a 'hierarchy of reading arts', in which aural culture had a higher standing than visual culture, is not tenable. In our reflection on the entire gamut of Luther's theology of the image—imaginative and figurative, deceptive and defamatory, idolatrous, fearful and comforting—we show that Luther used both the 'listening arts' and the 'visual arts' equally widely, to equal effect. We further show that he used both words and image in combination with one another in promoting his message, for example in the many comic-strip-like woodcuts of the Reformation. In this way, Luther bolstered their effect.[26] As Spinks (2021), commenting on Heal (2017), explains: Luther 'did not merely tolerate images and visual environments, but celebrated them in dazzling, multi-sensory ways

---

Tradition an die visuell-visionäre Wirkkraft der Bilder herangetragene, mit rhetorischen Kategorien begründete, geistige Präsenzerfahrung auf das Wort und setzt damit zugleich eine Dimension der geistlichen Bildrhetorik, die Realpräsenz des Logos in bildlicher Visualgestalt, außer Kraft'.

23 Bridget Heal, 'The Catholic Eye and the Protestant Ear: The Reformation as a Non-Visual Event?', in *The Myth of the Reformation*, ed. by Peter J. Opitz, Refo500 Academic Studies, 9 (Göttingen: Vandenhoeck & Ruprecht, 2013), pp. 321–55 (p. 322), a point she elaborated at greater length in her later monograph *A Magnificent Faith: Art and Identity in Lutheran Germany* (Oxford: Oxford University Press, 2017).

24 Valeska von Rosen, 'Gibt es "das reformatorische Bild"? Zur Revision essentialistischer und dichotomer Medienvorstellungen in der deutschen und niederländischen Reformation', in *Reformation Heute: Band IV—Reformation und Medien: Zu den intermedialen Wirkungen der Reformation*, ed. by Johann Anselm Steiger (Leipzig: Evangelische Verlagsanstalt, 2018), pp. 9–34 (p. 12): 'dass Luther dem Sehsinn für die religiöse Praxis durchaus bedeutenden Stellenwert zuschreibt und hierbei sowohl auf materielle Gemälde abzielt, als auch auf die wirkmächtigen evokativen Bilder der Phantasie'.

25 Luther, *Wider die himmlischen Propheten, von den Bildern und Sakrament* (*Against the Heavenly Prophets in the Matter of Images and the Sacraments*), LW 40/2: 92, WA 18: 80, 7–8: 'zum zeugnis, zum gedechtnis, zum zeychen'.

26 See, for instance, Andrew Pettegree, *Reformation and the Culture of Persuasion* (Cambridge: Cambridge University Press, 2005), p. 120.

that at key moments became central to the expression of Lutheran identity'.[27] In our close reading of the image of *Law and Grace*, we apply the successful use of a combination of word and image to one of Luther's most popular collaborations with Lucas Cranach the Elder and Younger and their workshops. As with his 'A Mighty Fortress' (*Ein feste Burg*) in Chapter 4, we focus on the promotion of the most iconic of Reformation images to further his theology of justification by grace alone.

In Chapter 5, we build on more established ground, by concentrating on the use of images to ridicule and condemn Luther's adversaries by depicting them as monstrous and abject Others.[28] Our examination centres on two spiteful polemical writings created both in the early years of the Reformation and towards the end of Luther's life: two anti-Catholic cartoons created in 1523 by Lucas Cranach, *Papstesel* (*Pope Donkey*) and *Mönchskalb* (*Monk Calf*) and Luther's virulently anti-Semitic *Vom Schem Hamphoras* (*Of the Ineffable Name*), along with the reformer's description of the Wittenberg *Judensau*, a thirteenth-century sculpture embedded in the walls of his own parish church that explicitly likens the 'Ineffable Name of God' to pig shit.[29] We draw on Kristeva's paradigm of abjection, and aesthetic theories of race, to examine the way in which Luther and his artistic collaborators used the visual arts—images, woodcuts, even sculptures—to teach his followers to hate his adversaries.[30] We acknowledge how, following Luther's death, this strong condemnation of Jews and Jewish culture was used by later German administrations to justify systematic anti-Semitism.[31]

## 1.3 *Drama*

In the third and final section of this volume, we explore Luther's support of religious drama, and his active commissioning of new religious plays to communicate his message. Specifically, in Chapter 6, we explore the development of a Lutheran tradition of school and educational religious drama in objection to existing forms of popular and religious drama. Civic confraternities performed plays and organised processions to mark the festivals of the church's year: Passion plays, play processions on the feast of Corpus Christi,

27 Jennifer Spinks, 'After Luther: Visual Culture, Materiality and the Legacy of 1517', *Journal of Ecclesiastical History*, 72.4 (2021), pp. 822–27 (p. 827).

28 Following on from works like R. W. Scribner, *For the Sake of Simple Folk: Popular Propaganda for the German Reformation* (Oxford: Clarendon Press, 1994).

29 See Roper, *Living I Was Your Plague*, pp. 162–63.

30 Julia Kristeva, *Powers of Horror: An Essay on Abjection*, trans. by Leon S. Rodiez (New York: Columbia University Press, 1980; repr. 1982).

31 See Andreas Loewe and Katherine Firth, 'The Debate about Interpreting and Identifying anti-Judaism and anti-Semitism in Bach's *John Passion*', forthcoming.

and re-enactments of the lives of the saints, such as on St Martin's and St Nicholas' Day.[32] Luther worked together with educators such as Joachim Greff (1510–1552) to develop new Protestant forms of drama that made the actors into proclaimers of the Passion and audiences into congregations who were moved to faith. Luther's influence on drama has been generally neglected and has not previously been included in surveys of his use of the arts.

In our consideration of each art-form, we show how Luther was able to see both the strengths and problems of existing art-forms. Luther brought his analytical and creative talents to help reform and popularise each art-form, as well as using the art-form to proclaim his Reformation message. Luther worked closely with other artists, craftspeople, teachers, and theologians to create and disseminate the new works; collaborating with princes, burghers and ordinary people, with women and men and children, across Germany and further afield.

Although there are many individual scholars who have examined aspects of Luther's engagements with the arts, we agree with Tacke and Münch (2020) that 'the interplay of image, text and music receives too little interdisciplinary attention in Reformation research'.[33] We hope that this volume, exploring Luther's theory and application of the art-forms that were so successful in promoting his Reformation, will lead to further such cross-disciplinary approaches in the field and that our comprehensive bibliography will enable researchers to dig deeper into areas that are of special interest to them. In letting the reformer speak, by providing extensive translated original sources, we especially wish to enable researchers with little theological knowledge or insufficient linguistic background in German, Hebrew, Greek and Latin, to understand and assess Luther's own thoughts for themselves. We hope that this volume will help our readers to follow the developments and impact of Luther's wide-ranging engagement with the arts—on high art and mass culture, for the next four centuries, across Europe and the globe.

---

32 For the enduring appeal of these re-enactments see Annette Schneider, 'Studie zu Kinderfesten an Martini und Nikolaus. Untersucht am Beispiel ausgewählter Orte des Mansfelder Landes' (unpublished doctoral dissertation, Martin-Luther-Universität Halle-Wittenberg, 1994).

33 Andreas Tacke and Birgit Ulrike Münch, 'Bildende Kunst und Reformation', in *Musik und Reformation—Politisierung, Medialisierung, Missionierung*, ed. by Christiane Wiesenfeldt and Stefan Menzel, Beiträge zur Geschichte der Kirchenmusik im Auftrag der Görres-Gesellschaft, 22 (Paderborn: Ferdinand Schoenigh, 2020), pp. 131–44 (p. 135): 'dem Zusammenspiel von Bild, Text und Musik zu wenig interdisziplinäre Aufmerksamkeit in der Reformationsforschung zukommt'.

CHAPTER 1

# Luther's Theory of Music

An enthusiastic singer, capable lute player, competent composer, and prolific hymn writer, Martin Luther frequently asserted that he 'always loved music'.[1,2] Luther not only loved music but had studied music theory as a part of his liberal arts degree at Erfurt University. In a letter dated 1520, a fellow student and later rector of Erfurt, Crotus Rubeanus (Johannes Jäger), addressed Luther: 'You were, among our group of students, the musician and erudite philosopher', suggesting that among his contemporaries Luther's understanding of music as a philosophical discipline, and his practical skills in monophony, polyphony, and composition, and as a singer and lutenist were highly regarded.[3]

Luther's love of music and his personal accomplishments as a musician have been well documented. While a primary function of music for Luther was undoubtedly the 'preaching' or proclaiming of doctrine 'through sound', it was his profound appreciation of music as an art-form in itself that inspired successive generations of artists to use their craft in the service of God and Luther's Reformation. He encouraged composers to use their skill not merely to create 'sermons in sound', but to enable others to obtain a glimpse of the beauty of God's kingdom: 'by embellishing and ornamenting their tunes in wonderful ways and sounds, and so to lead others (as it were) into a heavenly dance'.[4]

Despite a wealth of hagiographic writings on Luther's appreciation and use of music to further the cause of his Reformation, however, studies on Luther's theology of music remained relatively few until the late twentieth century. It was only in 1988 that one of the first academically rigorous studies on the subject was published: a slender volume entitled *Luther on Music* by the Lutheran

1 An earlier version of this chapter was published as Loewe, '"Musica est optimum"', 573–605.

2 'Musicam semper amavi'; *Tischreden, Tischreden aus den Jahren 1540–44* (*Table Talk*), WA Tr 5: 557, 18, no. 6248: 'And at times, following meals, the Doctor would sing, for he was also a lute player' (*Vnnd nach Tische sang auch Doctor bißweilen, wie er auch ein Lautenist war*), Johannes Mathesius, *Historien von deß Ehrwürdigen in Gott seligen theuren Manns Gottes, D. Martin Luthers, Anfang, Lehre, Leben* (Nürnberg: Kauffmann, 1608), p. 135.

3 Luther, *Briefe 1520–22* (*Letters*), WA Br 2: 91, 141–2: 'Eras in nostro quondam contubernio musicus et philosophus eruditus'.

4 Luther, *Praefatio zu den Symphoniae Iucundae* (*Preface to the Symphoniae Iucundae*), *1538*, LW 53: 321–324, WA 50, 371, 37–8: 'Mit mancherley art vnd klang dieselbe weise wunderbarlich zieren vnd schmücken vnd gleich wie einen Himlischen Tantzreigen füren'. LW does not provide a translation of the German version of Luther's *Preface*. An English translation from the Latin and the German by Dr Leofranc Holford-Strevens is included in Appendix 1.

 | DOI: 10.1163/9789004527430_003

church musician Carl Schalk.[5] Schalk's work significantly updated earlier studies in English of the reformer's understanding of music, in particular by Walter Buzsin and Paul Nettl.[6] While Buszin and Nettl provided a useful oversight of Luther's statements on music in English, as Schalk explained, their works 'caused frustration because of a lack of documentation': where Nettl's slender monograph was entirely unreferenced, Buszin's study 'was restricted because of its brevity'.[7] In addition, both studies subscribed to a now largely outmoded Protestant paradigm of the Reformation and therefore require substantial re-evaluation.[8] Schalk's principal concern was to sketch a thorough overview of the 'relationship between music and [the church's] common life' in the writings of Martin Luther.[9] This he undertook by tracing 'certain paradigms of praise' in Luther's statements on music and relating them to a theological understanding of music that, in his view, has continued to influence music-making in Lutheran churches to the present day.[10]

The work of Johannes Schilling and Robin Leaver significantly extended Schalk's scholarship: the stream of articles on Luther, Lutheranism, and music that the former published between 1997 and 2006 were combined in Leaver's comprehensive study, *Luther's Liturgical Music*, while in 2005 Schilling contributed a thorough survey of Luther's writing on music to the *Luther Handbuch*.[11] Their works concentrate on Luther's practical reforms to liturgical music and the history of the music employed in Lutheran worship and education, especially Luther's hymnody. Neither addresses in any detail the theoretical basis that underpins the reformer's insights into music.[12] Their emphasis on Luther's

5 Carl F. Schalk, *Luther on Music: Paradigms of Praise* (St Louis, MO: Concordia, 1988), p. 19.

6 Walter Buszin, 'Luther on Music', *Musical Quarterly*, 32 (1946), 80–97; Paul Nettl, *Luther and Music* (Philadelphia: Muhlenberg Press, 1948; repr. New York: Russell & Russell, 1967). Where Nettl's work is indebted to Johannes Rautenstrauch, *Luther und die Pflege der kirchlichen Musik in Sachsen* [*KS*] (Leipzig: Breitkopf und Härtel, 1907), Buszin's 'Luther on Music' is based in part on Karl Anton, *Luther und die Musik: Eine Gabe an das deutsche Volk zum Reformations-Jubiläum* (Zwickau: Hermann, 1916). Neither appears to have been aware of the article 'On Luther's Love for and Knowledge of Music', *Musical Times*, 1.11 (1845), 82–87, by an anonymous 'German Student', which provides a first comprehensive English-language compilation of Luther's sayings on music.

7 Schalk, *Luther on Music*, p. 7.

8 In particular, Nettl, *Luther and Music*, pp. 2–6, and pp. 105–12, 'Music in the Catholic Church and in the Reformed Churches'.

9 Schalk, *Luther on Music*, p. 31.

10 Ibid.

11 Robin A. Leaver, 'The Lutheran Reformation', in *The Renaissance from the 1470s to the End of the Sixteenth Century*, ed. by Iain Fenlon (Englewood Cliffs, NJ: Prentice Hall, 1989), pp. 263–85; Johannes Schilling, 'Musik', in *Luther Handbuch*, ed. by Albrecht Beutel (Tübingen: Mohr Siebeck, 2005), pp. 236–243.

12 Schalk, *Luther on Music*, p. 18; Leaver, *Luther's Liturgical Music*, pp. 27–30, pp. 34–5.

practical use of music rather than his theoretical understanding of music should not surprise: previous studies on Luther and music almost universally concentrated on Luther's aptitude as a musician, his enthusiasm for music as an art-form, and his practical use of music to further his Reformation, and so bypassed the subject of his music theory altogether.[13] Indeed, from the outset, Leaver affirms that *Luther's Liturgical Music* is principally dedicated to an exploration of Luther's liturgical music and invites other researchers to undertake the task of revealing 'more about Luther's understanding of music'.[14]

Johannes Block's extensive hermeneutical consideration of Luther's music, *Verstehen durch Musik: Das gesungene Wort in der Theologie*, also comes to the conclusion that Luther did not use a systematic music-theoretical approach.[15] More specialised studies on sixteenth-century German music have focused on the practical uses of music for Lutheran education and the importance of music as an instrument to disseminate Reformation thought, among them Ralph Lorenz's dissertation on specifically Lutheran music; Rebecca Wagner Oettinger's *Music as Popular Propaganda in the German Reformation*; Christopher Brown's *Singing the Gospel*, and Inga Mai Groote's 'Musikalische Katechismen'.[16] Even studies that intentionally set out to investigate Luther's philosophy of musical aesthetics, such as Joe Tarry's 'Music in the Educational Philosophy of Martin Luther', banish the subject of his music theory to a couple of footnotes.[17]

---

13 Rautenstrauch, *KS*, p. vi, comments on Luther's 'theoretical knowledge' (*theoretische Kenntnisse*), although only with reference to his knowledge of the musical genre, in particular his understanding of harmonics and his ability to offer practical advice on how compositions might be improved. Similarly, Nettl, *Luther and Music*, pp. 31–2, offers a brief general overview of the development of a late-medieval philosophy of music but confines his observations on Luther to practical reforms.

14 Leaver, *Luther's Liturgical Music*, pp. 19–20.

15 Block, *Verstehen durch Musik*, p. 42.

16 Ralph Lorenz, 'Pedagogical Implications of Musica practica in Sixteenth-Century Wittenberg' (unpublished doctoral dissertation, Indiana University, 1995); Rebecca Wagner Oettinger, *Music as Propaganda in the German Reformation* (Aldershot: Ashgate, 2001); Christopher Brown, *Singing the Gospel: Lutheran Hymns and the Success of the Reformation* (Cambridge, MA: Harvard University Press, 2005); Inga Mai Groote, 'Musikalische Katechismen und "kunstreiche Componisten" für Schule und Haus—eine "Sozialisierung" von Musik in lutherischen Kontexten?', in *Musik und Reformation—Politisierung, Medialisierung, Missionierung*, ed. by Christiane Wiesenfeldt and Stefan Menzel, Beiträge zur Geschichte der Kirchenmusik im Auftrag der Görres-Gesellschaft, 22 (Paderborn: Ferdinand Schoenigh, 2020), pp. 201–220 (pp. 201–213).

17 Joe E. Tarry, 'Music in the Educational Philosophy of Martin Luther', *Journal of Research in Music Education*, 21 (1973), pp. 355–65, unfortunately does not follow up on his suspicions that Luther's understanding of music was influenced by Boethius and that he regarded music as one of the quadrivial arts.

This chapter takes on Leaver's challenge to present a detailed assessment of the reformer's music theory. Rather than speculate on what Luther might have written in a projected (but never written) treatise on music, we examine extant sources to establish a theoretical framework for Luther's music theory.[18] Drawing on his sustained systematic reflection on music, the *Praefatio zu den Symphoniae Iucundae* (*Preface to the Symphoniae Iucundae*), 1538, his other writings and *Table Talk*, we outline Luther's theory of music and, wherever possible, identify and follow his own classification of music.[19] We contend that even though Luther had already significantly departed from late-medieval philosophy in many of his theological writings, in his writings on music he remained strongly indebted to a late-medieval understanding of music as a quadrivial art, and therefore continued to draw on essential elements of scholastic philosophy throughout his life.

## 1 Music among the Seven Liberal Arts

By Luther's time music had long been an established part of the Quadrivium—arithmetic, geometry, music, and astronomy—four sciences that were studied alongside the Trivium of grammar, logic, and rhetoric.[20] Together, the quadrivial

---

18 Leaver, *Luther's Liturgical Music*, pp. 85–97, in line with Schilling, 'Musik', p. 240, attempts to construct such a work, using as a basis Luther's brief outline of 1530 for the projected treatise *Peri tes Mousikes* (*On Music, Über die Musik*) against the radical *Schwärmer* (enthusiasts), see WA 30: 2, 696, and a famous letter of October 1530 to composer Ludwig Senfl, *Briefwechsel* (*Letters*), WA Br 5: 639, no. 1727.

19 The original Latin was published by Georg Rhau in 1538, in *Symphoniae iucundae atque adeo breves quatuor vocum* (Wittenberg: Walther, 1538), the German not until 1564, in an edition by Lorenz Schwenck, *Lob vnd Preis, Der Himlischen Kunst MVSICA: Mit einer herrlichen, schönen Vorrede, des seligen, tewren, hochbegabten Mannes, Doctoris Martini Lutheri, vormals deudsch im Drucke nihe ausgegangen durch Johan Walther* (Wittenberg: Walther, 1564), with Luther's *Preface* at sig. 2a–B 2a. The WA editors suggest that the Latin version of the *Preface* is Luther's original yet include the German version that translates and, in some instances, amplifies the Latin; Luther, *Praefatio zu den Symphoniae Iucundae, 1538*, WA 50: 364–74. Walter Blankenburg suggests that the German was Luther's original in his 'Überlieferung und Textgeschichte von Martin Luthers "Encomion musices"', *Lutherjahrbuch*, 39 (1972), 80–104. Since the heading of the German text, 'vormals deudsch im Drucke nihe ausgegangen', allows for the possibility of a previous Latin edition, Appendix 1 presents both versions in parallel.

20 For the role played by musical education in the Quadrivium, see Anja Heilmann, *Boethius' Musiktheorie und das Quadrivium* (Göttingen: Vandenhoek und Ruprecht, 2007), pp. 68–104, and Karl Gustav Fellerer, 'Die Musica in den Artes Liberales', in *Artes Liberales: Von der Antiken Bildung zur Wissenschaft des Mittelalters*, ed. by Joseph Koch and others (Leiden: Brill, 1976), pp. 33–49.

and trivial arts formed the corpus of learning in the arts faculty of the medieval university. At the heart of musical studies from at least the mid-fourteenth century onwards had been Boethius' *De institutione musica libri quinque* (*c.*500) and Johannes de Muris' influential commentary on his work, *Musica speculativa secundum Boetium* (*c.*1323).[21] De Muris' *Musica speculativa* not only provided a commentary on the philosophical and arithmetical foundations of music, but also combined music theory with such strong 'pedagogical qualities that his writings [were assured] a wide diffusion until the end of the Middle Ages'.[22]

An integral part of the Quadrivium, de Muris' work, both in its entirety and more frequently in excerpts, became a set text for students at universities in England, France, and Germany, including the University of Erfurt.[23] As a student at Erfurt from 1501, Luther had a thorough philosophical grounding in the seven liberal arts.[24] The curricular evidence of the continued use of a selection of chapters from Boethius' work and his later commentators, like de Muris, at Erfurt's philosophy faculty support Blankenburg's assertion that Luther

---

21 Anicius Manlius Severinus Boethius, *De institutione musica libri quinque*, in *Anicii Manlii Torquati Severini Boetii De institutione arithmetica libri duo; De institutione musica libri quinque; accedit geometria quae fertur Boetii*, ed. by Gottfried Friedlein, Bibliotheca scriptorum Graecorum et Romanorum Teubneriana (Leipzig: Teubner, 1867); for a comprehensive introduction to Boethius, see Henry Chadwick, *Boethius: The Consolations of Music, Logic, Theology and Philosophy* (Oxford: Clarendon Press, 1990); Johannes de Muris, *Musica speculativa secundum Boetium*, ed. by Christoph Falkenroth, Beihefte zum Archiv für Musikwissenschaft, 34 (Stuttgart: F. Steiner, 1992).

22 Emmanuel Pouelle, 'John of Murs', in *Dictionary of Scientific Biography*, ed. by Charles Goulston Gillispie (New York: Scribner, 1973), VII, 128–33 (p. 128).

23 The 1449 statutes of Erfurt University certainly make provision for the study of 'music for one month' (*musica per 1 mensem*) every year: *Acten der Erfurter Universität*, ed. by J. C. Hermann Weissenborn, Historische Commission der Provinz Sachsen (Halle: Hendel, 1884), II, 134, 13. In addition, Masters and Baccalaureate students in the liberal arts read Boethius 'for four months' (*per quatuor menses*); ibid., II, p. 134, nos. 21–2. The statutes governing the quadrivial examination of Masters students include an examination on 'the *Music* of de Muris' (*musicam Muris*); ibid., II, p. 138, no. 23. For the place of de Muris in the Quadrivium at Paris, see Joseph Dyer, 'Speculative "Musica" and the Medieval University of Paris', *Music and Letters*, 90 (2009), pp. 177–204 (p. 181). The work was used at Oxford from 1431, according to James Weisheipl, 'Curriculum of the Faculty of Arts at Oxford in the Early Fourteenth Century', *Medieval Studies*, 26 (1964), 143–85 (p. 171), probably alongside the anonymous *Commentum Oxoniense in musicam Boethii*: see *Commentum Oxoniense in musicam Boethii*, ed. by Matthias Hochadel, Veröffentlichungen der Musikhistorischen Kommission der Bayrischen Akademie der Wissenschaften, 16 (München: Beck, 2002), pp. lxxix–xc.

24 The Easter term matriculations for 1501 record the admission at Erfurt of 'Martinus Ludher ex Mansfeldt' (Martin Luther from Mansfeld): *Acten der Erfurter Universität*, II, 219, 12.

'successfully completed a regular course in *musica speculativa* as part of the liberal arts'.[25] Although the curricular requirements at Erfurt do not include the study of music practitioners such as Adam von Fulda in the elementary stages of mathematical instruction, Leaver is right in suggesting that his work on *musica practica* influenced the reformer's understanding of music: Luther's *Praefatio zu den Symphoniae Iucundae* (*Preface to the Symphoniae Iucundae*) is clearly dependent on Adam von Fulda's music theory.[26]

Because Luther's systematic reflections on the nature and function of music are few, his *Prafeatio* (*Preface*) affords unrivalled insights into the reformer's understanding of the theory of music.[27] Luther had been asked to provide a preface for a collection of fifty-two motets by nineteen composers, including Ludwig Senfl, Johann Walter, Heinrich Isaac, and Pierre de la Rue, as compiled by Georg Rhau,[28] a former Cantor of St Thomas' Leipzig and composer turned Wittenberg publisher.[29] Luther's reflections on the origin, role, and function of music in the *Praefatio* closely follow those of late-medieval and humanist commentators. Leaver's suggestion, therefore, that 'in his understanding of the *inventio* of music Luther is distinctively different from his medieval predecessors', stands in need of reassessment.[30]

---

25 Ibid., II, 134, 138. 'Ein reguläres und erfolgreiches Studium der Musica speculativa im Rahmen der Artes liberales'; Walter Blankenburg, 'Luther, Martin', in *Die Musik in Geschichte und Gegenwart: Allgemeine Enzyklopädie der Musik* [MGG], ed. by Friedrich Blume, 17 vols (Kassel: Bärenreiter, 1949–68), VIII, 1334–46 (p. 1335). Blankenburg further explained that in addition to de Muris, Luther certainly would also have studied late-medieval commentators such as Johannes Tinctoris; see 'Martin Luther und die Musik', in *Kirche und Musik: Gesammelte Aufsätze zur Geschichte der gottesdienstlichen Musik*, ed. by Erich Hübner and Renate Steiger (Göttingen: Vandenhoek und Ruprecht, 1979), p. 20.

26 For the influence on Luther of Adam von Fulda's *De Musica*, see Leaver, *Luther's Liturgical Music*, pp. 34–5.

27 Modern edition in *Symphoniae jucundae 1538*, ed. by Hans Albrecht, Georg Rhau Musikdrucke, 3 (Kassel: Bärenreiter, 1959).

28 For Georg Rhau, see Marie Schlüter, *Musikgeschichte Wittenbergs im 16. Jahrhundert: Quellenkundliche und sozialgeschichtliche Untersuchungen* (Göttingen: Vandenhoek und Ruprecht, 2010), pp. 170–80; for his *Symphoniae Iucundae*, a collection of church motets, see Wolfram Steude, *Untersuchungen zur mitteldeutschen Musiküberlieferung und Musikpflege im 16. Jahrhundert* (Leipzig: Peters, 1978); for his influence as a publisher of the Lutheran Reformation, see Walter Wölbing, 'Der Drucker und Musikverleger Georg Rhau: Ein Beitrag zur Drucker- und Verlegertätigkeit im Zeitalter der Reformation' (unpublished doctoral dissertation, Friedrich-Wilhelms-Universität Berlin, 1922).

29 'Asked Luther and Melanchthon for prefaces' (*Sich Vorworte von Luther und Melanchthon erbat*), WA 1: 364, 7–10, 22–3. Melanchthon's preface to Rhau's *Selectae Harmoniae quatuor vocum de Passione Christi, 1538*, is reproduced in CR 5: 918–21.

30 Leaver, *Luther's Liturgical Music*, p. 71.

In December 1538, the reformer had told a company of singers that he admired their music-making greatly.[31] In their ensuing discussion about music Luther suggested that music was one of the 'prime matters', a point he reiterated in writing the same year.[32] In speaking about music as a discipline, therefore, Luther drew on a Boethian understanding of music and its place within the created order: 'prime matter', the sixth-century philosopher Boethius held, following Nicomachus of Gerasa and Aristotle, was matter that had never been shaped or formed by human action, and therefore was 'natural' (prevalent in nature), rather than 'artificial' (shaped by artisans or artists), a concept shared by later philosophers and theologians, including Thomas Aquinas and Peter Lombard.[33] In the context of a convivial debate among singers, recorded as such in his *Table Talk*, Luther's reference to 'prime matter' might suggest a casual or imprecise use of the term. However, the fact that he referred to music as 'prima materia' more than once suggests that the reformer used the term intentionally, referring his hearers back to a philosophical school still very much prevalent in the third decade of the sixteenth century.[34]

It is not only Luther's understanding of the order of music within creation that shows that his views on music were underpinned by traditional late-medieval music theory.[35] The reformer consistently classified music in strictly quadrivial terms as part of the study of the mathematical disciplines alongside (and possibly subordinate to) arithmetic.[36] In Boethian terms, music theory had long been regarded as a part of arithmetic:

---

31 Luther, *Tischreden* (*Table Talk*), WA Tr 5: 191, no. 4192, n. 5: 'In the year [15]38, on 17 December, when Dr Martin Luther hosted some singers who sang some pleasing motets, he said admiringly' (*Anno 38, 17. Decembris, cum Doctor Martinus Lutherus apud se haberet cantores egregias motettas canentes, dixit admirans*).

32 *Tischreden* (*Table Talk*), WA Tr 5: 191, 34: 'Est materia prima'. For the Aristotelian understanding of prime matter, see Christopher John Fardo Williams, *Aristotle's De Generatione et Corruptione* (Oxford: Oxford University Press, 2002), p. xv, especially the discussion, 'Prime matter in *De Generatione et Corruptione*', pp. 211–19 (Appendix). For its Boethian adaptation, see Heilmann, *Boethius' Musiktheorie und das Quadrivium*, pp. 305–7.

33 Heilmann, *Boethius' Musiktheorie und das Quadrivium*, p. 306, n. 12.

34 *Tischreden* (*Table Talk*), WA Tr 5: 191, 34, no. 4192; *Praefatio zu den Symphoniae Iucundae* (*Preface to the Symphoniae Iucundae*), 1538, WA 50: 370, 9.

35 For the Aristotelian understanding of music among the prime matters, see Eckhard Roch, 'Zwischen Geist und Materie: Grundlagen des musikalischen Materialbegriffes in Philosophie und Rhetorik', *Archiv für Musikwissenschaft*, 59 (2002), 136–64 (pp. 138–44).

36 For the place of music as a subset of mathematics, see Eva Hirtler, 'Die Musik im Übergang von der scientia mathematica zur scientia media', in *Musik und die Geschichte der Philosophie und Naturwissenschaften im Mittelalter: Fragen zur Wechselwirkung von 'Musica' und 'Philosophia' im Mittelalter*, ed. by Frank Hentschel, Studien und Texte zur Geistesgeschichte des Mittelalters, 62 (Leiden: Brill, 1998), pp. 19–38.

> The four mathematical disciplines of the Quadrivium were paired by Boethius [...] depending on whether the discipline concerned multitude (arithmetic, music) or magnitude (geometry, astronomy). Accordingly, arithmetic is *multitudo per se,* while music is *multitudo ad aliquid* (i.e., one number related to another proportionally).[37]

At German-speaking universities courses in music were frequently taught by mathematicians: in Vienna, the arithmetician Erasmus Heritius (Höritz) taught both music and arithmetic, while in Frankfurt an der Oder Ambrosius Lacher, who held the 'chair in sacred mathematics', undertook the teaching of speculative music from his own influential textbook *Johannes de Muris in musicam Boecii* (1508).[38] Luther very likely read contemporary commentators on Boethius and de Muris such as Lacher, and therefore regarded music in similar terms: in his 1524 *An die Ratsherren aller Städte deutschen Landes* (*Appeal to the Councillors of all Cities of the German Nation*), encouraging town councillors to set up schools and teach a Lutheran curriculum, he expressed the hope that all children should 'learn music alongside the whole of mathematics'.[39] His classification of music as a part of mathematics strongly suggests that, despite the far reaching reforms of his theological opinions, Luther's understanding of music continued to be informed by late-medieval philosophy.

Some forty years after Luther's death, towards the close of the sixteenth century, music would increasingly be defined in terms of its bridge function between the trivial and quadrivial arts, whose centrality among the arts was extolled by Luther. This bridge function of music between the mathematical and rhetorical arts was not only expressed in philosophical writings but also reflected architecturally: in the redevelopment in 1589 of the town hall in the

---

37 Joseph Dyer, 'The Place of Musica in Medieval Classifications of Knowledge', *Journal of Musicology*, 24 (2007), 3–71 (p. 6); John Butt, *Music Education and the Art of Performance in the German Baroque* (Cambridge: Cambridge University Press, 1994), p. 3; Heilmann, *Boethius' Musiktheorie und das Quadrivium*, p. 103: 'Die Subordination der Musiktheorie unter die Arithmetik'.

38 Ambrosius Lacher, *Euclides Elementorum libri VI sumptu et opera Ambrosii Lacher de Merspurgk excussa* (Frankfurt an der Oder: Magister Ambrosius, 1506), frontispiece: 'Sacre Mathematice ... ordinarius'; Ambrosius Lacher, *Epytoma Johannis de Muris in musicam Boecii* (Frankfurt an der Oder: Magister Ambrosius, 1508); for his music-theoretical teaching at Frankfurt, see Klaus Wolfgang Niemöller, 'Deutsche Musiktheorie im 16. Jahrhundert: Geistes- und institutionsgeschichtliche Grundlagen', in *Deutsche Musiktheorie des 15. bis 17. Jahrhunderts*, 1: *Von Paumann bis Calvisius*, ed. by Theodor Göllner (Darmstadt, 2003), pp. 69–98 (p. 78).

39 Luther, *An die Ratsherren aller Städte deutschen Landes, 1524*, WA 15: 46, 15: 'Die musica mit der gantzen mathematica lernen'.

Lutheran Hanseatic town of Lemgo, music took centre place among the seven liberal arts on an outstanding late Renaissance bas-relief.[40] Its central position below the first-floor bay window of the *Kornherrenstube* provided a link in stone of the rhetorical arts—grammar, dialectic, and rhetoric—with the mathematical arts: arithmetic, geometry and astronomy.[41]

## 2 Sources for Luther's Theory of Music

Although it takes up only eighty-three lines in the Weimar edition, Luther's *Praefatio zu den Symphoniae Iucundae* (*Preface to the Symphoniae Iucundae*) provides the most detailed outline of the reformer's theory of music. The *Preface* is framed by his praise of the 'many and great uses' of music.[42] He sets out by extolling 'this most excellent gift of God', which is 'to be commended to all',[43] and ends with an approbation of 'this noble, salutary, and happy creature'.[44] A solemn warning not to abuse the gift of music 'as an enemy of

40 We are grateful to Prof. Markus Rathey for alerting us to this architectural expression of the bridge function of music in the late 16th century on one of the outstanding civic buildings of the *Weser-Renaissance*. For the architectural development of Lemgo's town hall, and the *Kornherrenstube* (Offices of the Supervisors of the Grain Trade), see *Die Stadt Lemgo*, ed. by Otto Gaul and Ulf-Dietrich Korn (Münster: Aschendorff, 1983), pp. 490, 520f., and Max von Sonnen, *Die Weserrenaissance: Die Bauentwicklung um die Wende des XVI. und XVII. Jahrhunderts an der oberen und mittleren Weser und in den angrenzenden Landesteilen* (Münster: Aschendorff, 1969); for the role of music in Lemgo during the Renaissance, see Hans Hoppe, 'Musikalische Renaissance in der alten Hansestadt Lemgo und am Hofe Simons VI. zu Brake', *Heimatland Lippe*, 57 (1964), 93–7.

41 Created in 1589 by Georg and Ernst Crossmann, the ornate sandstone bas-relief of the *Kornherrenstube* is adorned with seven allegorical depictions of 'Grammatica, Dialectica, Rhetorica, Musica, Arithmetica, Geometria, Astrono[mia]', with the Art of Music at its centre, bridging trivial and quadrivial learning. The Art of Music is represented by a trumpeting female figure holding a music manuscript, seated in front of an organ and next to a drum and a harp. The attributes of trumpet and harp refer to 'Jubal, the father of those who play the harp and wind instruments' (Gen. 4.3).

42 Luther, *Praefatio zu den Symphoniae Iucundae* (*Preface to the Symphoniae Iucundae*), *1538*, WA 50: 368, 5–6: 'Multitudine et magnitudine virtutis et bonitatis eius' and 'Viel und grosse nutze'.

43 Luther, *Praefatio* (*Preface*), WA 50: 368, 4–5: 'Omnibus commendatum esse donum illud diuinum et excellentissimum'; 368, 17: 'Schöne vnd köstliche Gabe Gottes', 369, 14: 'Von jederman tewr vnd werd zu achten ist'.

44 Luther, *Praefatio* (*Preface*), WA 50: 373, 8: 'Tu [...] commendatam hanc nobilem, salutarem et laetam creaturam'; and 373, 20–21: 'Darumb wil ich jederman [...] diese Kunst befohlen vnd sie hiemit vermanet haben, das sie jnen diese köstliche, nützliche vnd fröliche Creatur Gottes tewr, lieb vnd werd sein lassen'.

God and an adversary of this most delightful nature and art' concludes his reflection on music.[45] Since the *Preface* was primarily addressed to music lovers and musicians (and not theologians or philosophers), Luther made use of terminology that could easily be understood by those without quadrivial music theory. While this means that the language of the *Preface* is more accessible than many earlier textbooks on music philosophy, the work is neither philosophically lightweight nor unstructured.[46]

Luther made clear at the beginning of the *Preface* that music was 'such a wonderful and noble art' that he found it hard 'to determine where I should begin or stop praising it, let alone to find manner and form to praise it'.[47] Whether or not he really was at a loss as to the proper 'manner and form' for his praise of music, he certainly resorted to a traditional theoretical form of classifying music for his brief treatise, adopting a framework he had studied at university: 'musica Muris' had been part of Luther's philosophical education in Erfurt.[48] There are numerous parallels between de Muris' and Luther's thoughts on the origins of music, which strongly suggest an intellectual dependence on earlier textbooks on *musica speculativa*, such as Lacher's *Johannes de Muris in musicam Boecii*. In addition, Luther drew on scholastic and humanist predecessors; his reflections on the origin, form, and function of music follow a structure common to three humanist music theorists then working in Germany: the Wittenberg music theorist Adam von Fulda (*c.*1445–1505),[49] the Köln theo-

45 Luther, *Praefatio* (*Preface*), WA 50: 370, 9: 'Hostem Dei et aduersarium naturae et artis huius iucundissimae'; and 374, 8–9: 'Ein Feind Gottes, der Natur vnd dieser lieblichen Kunst'.

46 In the *Praefatio* (*Preface*), WA 50: 370, 10, for instance, Luther likened the human voice to prime matter (*prima materia*) and commented that philosophers may have classified and 'observed, but not fully grasped' (*mirantur, sed non complectuntur*) the complexities of the voice, let alone of human emotions.

47 Luther, *Praefatio* (*Preface*), WA 50: 368, 6–7: 'Ein herrliche vnd edle Kunst ist, das ich nicht weis, wo ich dieselbe zu loben anfahen oder auffhören sol, oder auff was weise vnd form ich sie also loben möge', and 368, 6–7: 'to determine where I should begin or stop praising it, let alone to find manner and form to praise it' (*Neque initium neque finem neque modum orationis inuenire queam*).

48 *Acten der Erfurter Universität*, II, 138, 23.

49 For Adam von Fulda, see Peter Slemon, 'Adam of Fulda on Musica plana and Compositio: De musica, Book II, A Translation and Commentary' (unpublished doctoral dissertation, University of British Columbia, 1994), pp. 6–19, incorporating a new edition of part of Adam von Fulda's *De Musica*, also published in *Scriptores ecclesiastici de musica sacra potissimum ex variis Italiae, Galliae et Germaniae codicibus manuscriptis collecti et nunc primum publica luce donati* [GS], ed. by Martin Gerbert, 3 vols (St Blasien: Typis San Blasianis, 1784; repr. Hildesheim, 1963), III, pp. 329–81.

rist Nicolaus Wollick (*c*.1480–1541),[50] and the Maastricht theorist Matthäus Herbenus (*c*.1445–1538).[51]

Though Luther's *Preface* seems to reflect the influence of all three theorists, it shows particular affinity with Herbenus' 1496 *De natura cantus ac miraculis vocis* (*Nature of Singing and the Miracle of the Voice*).[52] Herbenus had dedicated his work to Johannes von Dalberg, Bishop of Worms and Chancellor of the Palatinate Court in Heidelberg. Herbenus' theory of music has very concrete practical implications for voice building and voice production (a characteristic that may well have been attractive to Luther). During his visits to Heidelberg, Herbenus had sought to 'reform the renowned Schola Cantorum at the Palatinate Court [...] in line with his thoughts on music'.[53] In addition

50 For Adam's potential connection with Nicolaus Wollick, see Slemon, 'Adam of Fulda on Musica plana and Compositio', p. 132; for a critical edition of Wollick's seminal *Opus Aureum Musice castigatissimum de Gregoriana et figurativa atque contrapuncto Simplici percommode tractans* (Köln: Quentell, 1501), see *Die Musica Gregoriana des Nicolaus Wollick*, ed. by Klaus Wolfgang Niemöller, Beiträge zur Rheinischen Musikgeschichte, 11 (Köln: Staufen, 1955), pp. 1–80, and *Nicolaus Wollick, 1480–1541, und sein Musiktraktat*, ed. by Klaus Wolfgang Niemöller, Beiträge zur Rheinischen Musikgeschichte, 13 (Köln: Staufen, 1956).

51 For Matthäus Herbenus (Herben), from 1485 rector (*praefectus*) of St Servaas School, gospeller (*evangelarius*) and, following his priesting in 1504, chaplain (*capellanus*) of St Servaas Collegiate Church in Maastricht, see Maastricht, Regionaal Historisch Centrum Limburg MS Collection 14B.002A: Kapittel van St Servaas te Maastricht, 980–1; Kapelanen, p. 14; and Heinrich Hüschen, 'Herbenus (Herben), Matthaeus', in *MGG*, VI, 190, rev. by Klaus-Jürgen Sachs (2002), *MGG*², VIII, 1359–60; H. H. E. Wouters, 'Mattheus Herbenus Trajectensis, een humanist van het eerste uur', in *Miscellanea Trajectensia: Bijdragen tot de geschiedenis van Maastricht*, ed. by Gerard Willem Augustinus Panhuysen (Maastricht: Limburgs Geschied- en Oudheidkundig Genootschap, 1962), pp. 263–329; G. J. M. Bartelink, 'Bemerkungen über die Quellen der Schrift "De natura cantus ac miraculis vocis" von Herbenus Traiectensis', *Humanistica Lovaniensia* 21 (1972), 51–64, and J. IJsewijn, 'The Coming of Humanism to the Low Countries', in *Itinerarium Italicum: The Profile of the Italian Renaissance in the Mirror of its European Transformations, Dedicated to Paul Oskar Kristeller on the Occasion of his 70th Birthday*, ed. by Heiko Augustinus Oberman and Thomas A. Brady Jr (Leiden: Brill, 1975), pp. 193–301.

52 Herbenus, *De natura cantus ac miraculis vocis*, pp. 16–78. The original of the work, completed 'in Maastricht on 27 April 1496' (*Ex Traiecto super Mosam, quinto Kalenda Maias Anni dominici MCCCCXCVI*) and dedicated to Dalberg, is located in Munich, Bayerische Staatsbibliothek, clm 10277, fos. 2ʳ–56ᵛ; a copy produced in Germany and dedicated to Johann II of Baden, Bishop of Trier, is in Berlin, Staatsbibliothek Preußischer Kulturbesitz, MS lat. Quarto 479, fos. 1–37.

53 Peter Walter, 'Johannes von Dalberg und der Humanismus', in *1495—Kaiser, Reich, Reformen: Der Reichstag zu Worms. Ausstellung des Landeshauptarchivs Koblenz in Verbindung mit der Stadt Worms zum 500jährigen Jubiläum des Wormser Reichstags von 1495*, ed. by Claudia Helm and Jost Hausmann (Koblenz: Landeshauptarchivverwaltung Rheinland-Pfalz, 1995), pp. 139–71 (p. 148): 'Durch seine Überlegungen auf die berühmte

to his collaboration with the Kapellmeister of the Palatinate Court, Johannes Susato (von Soest), at Heidelberg Herbenus came into contact with a circle of leading humanists including Rudolf Agricola, Johannes Reuchlin, Jodocus Gallus (Jost Han), Johannes Vigilius, Dietrich von Pleningen, his close friend Johannes Trithemius (von Trittenheim), and the young Philipp Melanchthon.[54] At the end of his life, recalling his own time among the humanists gathered around Dalberg as a youth (*deinde adolescens vidi*), Melanchthon praised the Palatinate Academic Sodality (*sodalitas litteraria Rhenana*) 'not only as an adornment of Germany, but a promoter of learning in Germany'.[55]

Despite the fact that, prior to the publication of a modern critical edition (1957), Herbenus' *Nature of Singing and the Miracle of the Voice* was only ever published in part, he was instrumental in shaping the understanding of the interdependence of rhetoric and music in later humanist writings on music.[56] In addition to the two extant copies in Munich and Berlin, eighteenth-century antiquarian accounts report the existence of two further copies of the work in the 'Zurich library' (*Bibliotheca Tigurina*) and 'in the former library of Raymund Kraft in Ulm'.[57] Herbenus influenced the work of his Heidelberg companion, the Augustinian Rutgerus Sycamber, who in his *Dialogus de musica* (1500) praised both Herbenus and his work: 'so learned a man and so great and incomparable a musician and writer that, without a doubt, he may be said to

---

Sängerkapelle am pfalzgräflichen Hof in Heidelberg Einfluss nehmen wollte'. Herbenus certainly knew and in 1469 had very probably travelled from Maastricht to Rome with the then succentor of St Mary's Maastricht, Johannes Susato (von Soest) who, in 1472, was appointed Kapellmeister of the Heidelberg Schola: see Klaus Pietschmann and Steven Rozenski, Jr, 'Singing the Self: The Autobiography of the Fifteenth-Century German Singer and Composer Johannes von Soest', *Early Music History*, 29 (2010), 119–59 (pp. 130–2).

54 For Johannes Susato, see Pietschmann and Rozenski, 'Singing the Self', pp. 119–21; Heinrich Hüschen, 'Susato, Johannes de', in *Rheinische Musiker*, ed. by Karl Gustav Fellerer (Köln: Volk, 1966), 4, 165–67; Sabine Žak, 'Die Gründung der Hofkapelle in Heidelberg', *Archiv für Musikwissenschaft*, 50 (1993), 145–63.

55 Philip Melanchthon, *Melanchthoniana Paedagogica: Eine Ergänzung zu den Werken Melanchthons im Corpus Reformatorum*, ed. by Karl Hartfelder (Leipzig: Teubner, 1892), p. 71: 'Non solum ornamento Germaniae fuit, sed etiam studijs profuit'.

56 The dedication and preface of Herbenus' work were reproduced in Johann Georg Schelhorn, *Amoenitates Literariae: Quibus Variae Observationes, Scripta item quaedam anecdota & rariora Opuscula exhibentur* (Frankfurt a.M. and Leipzig: Daniel Bartolomäus, 1725), 2, pp. 82–6.

57 Jean-François Foppens, *Bibliotheca Belgica, sive Virorum in Belgio vita, scriptisque illustrium* (Brussels: Petrus Foppens, 1739), 2, p. 867: 'in der ehemaligen Raymund Kraftischen Bibliothek zu Ulm'; Georg Wilhelm Zapf, *Über das Leben und die Verdienste Johann von Dalbergs* (Augsburg: [n. pub.], 1789), pp. 42–3, n. 30. Both collections have been subsumed into larger collections, neither of which appears to hold the manuscripts today.

be most appealing'.[58] Franz Müller-Heuser and Klaus Niemöller suggest that in his *Tetrachordum musices* (1511) Johannes Cochlaeus also 'follows [Herbenus'] opinions'.[59] Similarly, in his *Pandectae* (1548), the Zurich bibliographer Conrad Gesner also refers to Herbenus' work, which implies that it was well known both in Catholic and Protestant humanist circles.[60]

Regardless of whether Luther became acquainted with Herbenus' work through Melanchthon and other members of the Heidelberg humanist sodality, through a widely travelled music theorist and fellow-Augustinian like Sycamber, the Erfurt friends of Abbot Trithemius,[61] or through the pages of a theological opponent like Cochlaeus, his *Praefatio zu den Symphoniae Iucundae* (*Preface to the Symphoniae Iucundae*) shares two key concepts formulated by Herbenus:[62] the insistence on the significance of music as an instrument to communicate God's Word, and a sense of marvel at the power of music to control the human emotions.[63] Since Herbenus also makes use of de Muris' philosophical framework, there is further significant overlap in the understanding of the nature of music, and its place and function in creation, between Herbenus' writings on music and Luther's *Preface*.

---

58 Rutgerus Sycamber de Venray, *Dialogus de musica*, ed. by Fritz Soddemann, Beiträge zur Rheinischen Musikgeschichte, 54 (Köln: Arno Volk, 1963), pp. 1–64 (p. 26): 'Tam docto viro, tam magno et incomparabili musico et scriptori, quod sine dubio dixerim, delectabilissimo'. For Sycamber, see Konrad Wiedemann, 'Rutgerus Sycamber', in *Contemporaries of Erasmus: A Biographical Register of the Renaissance and Reformation*, ed. by Peter Bietenholz and Thomas Deutscher (Toronto: University of Toronto Press, 1987), III, pp. 301–2.

59 Franz Müller-Heuser, *Vox humana: Ein Beitrag zur Untersuchung der Stimmästhetik des Mittelalters*, Kölner Beiträge zur Musikwissenschaft, 196 (Regensburg: Gustav Bosse, 1997), p. 46: 'In dieser Einstellung folgt ihm 1511 Johannes Cochlaeus'; Klaus Wolfgang Niemöller, 'Die musikalische Rhetorik und ihre Genese in Musik und Musikanschauung der Renaissance', in *Renaissance-Rhetorik*, ed. by Heinrich F. Plett (Berlin, 1993), pp. 285–311 (p. 290), supports his view.

60 'Matthaei Herbeni de natura vocis ac ratione Musicae libri 5'; Conrad Gesner, *Pandectae* (Zürich, 1548), no. 100. 'The works of Jean Gerson (nos. 117 and 177) and Mathaeus Herbenus (no. 100) would undoubtedly have passed through Gesner's hands'; Lawrence F. Bernstein, 'The Bibliography of Music in Conrad Gesner's *Pandectae* (1548)', *Acta Musicologica*, 45 (1973), 119–63 (p. 134).

61 For Trithemius' Erfurt connections, see Harald Müller, *Habit und Habitus: Mönche und Humanisten im Dialog* (Tübingen: Mohr Siebeck, 2006), p. 214.

62 Leaver suggests that the works of both Cochlaeus and Wollick influenced the *Compendaria musicae artis* (Leipzig: Stöckel, 1516) of Michael Koswick and, through him, music education at Wittenberg in the first decades of the Reformation: Leaver, *Luther's Liturgical Music*, p. 35.

63 Herbenus, *De natura cantus ac miraculis vocis*, pp. 41, 48; WA 50: 369, 11–371, 12.

## 3 Luther's Theory of Music

Luther believed that it was by praising God in music that humans were enabled to 'relish with amazement (but not understand) God's absolute and perfect wisdom in his marvellous work of music'.[64] In his *Preface*, he presented his readers with a vision of music as an instrument that has the ability to connect the entire created order with its Creator. His *Preface* follows an arc that takes as its origin the very beginning of creation and descends from God to those who have been given a voice, in order to return to heaven through composed music: Luther explained that the praises sung by his readers had the potential to take the singers straight back to heaven, and the ultimate origin and goal of music.

Like the philosophers of music he followed in his *Preface*, Luther adopted a textbook classification of the various forms of music, distinguishing between the music of the natural world (*musica naturalis, natürliche Musica*, WA 50: 368, 10–372, 1) and the music that 'rests in various instruments' (*quae in quibusdam constituta est instrumentis*); that is, music composed through the exercise of skill (*musica artificialis, durch die Kunst gescherfft vnd poliert*; WA 50: 372, 11–373, 6) and performed either by voices, or instruments, or both.[65]

Luther's comments on natural music are subdivided into three further categories. Adopting a categorisation of music outlined in Adam von Fulda's *De musica* (1490) and Nicolaus Wollick's *Opus aureum musice* (1501), Luther in turn addressed the music of the natural world (*musica mundana*), the music of the human voice (*musica vocis humanae, Kunst der Menschlichen Stimme*), and the music of heaven (*musica caelestis*).[66]

---

64 Luther, *Prafeatio* (*Preface*), WA 50: 372, 12–13: 'Hic tandem gustare cum stupore licet (sed non comprehendere) absolutam et perfectam sapientiam Dei in opere suo mirabile Musicae'; and 372, 30–32: 'Da sihet vnd erkennet man erst zu teil (denn gentzlich kanns nicht begrieffen noch verstanden werden) mit grosser verwunderung die grosse vnd volkomene weisheit Gottes in seinem wunderbarlichen werck der Musica'.

65 Boethius, *De institutione musica libri quinque*, 1: ch. 2, in *Boetii De institutione arithemetica*, ed. by Friedlein, 187. 20–3; Ernest T. Ferand, '"Sodaine and Unexpected" Music in the Renaissance', *Musical Quarterly*, 37 (1951), 10–27 (p. 27), provides a helpful schematic overview.

66 Adam von Fulda, GS, III, 333: 'There are two forms of music: natural and artificial music. Natural music is [divided into] universal and human music. Universal music includes that of the heavenly and supernatural bodies that resonate through the motion of the spheres [...] a genre researched by mathematicians. Human [music] exists in body and soul, [...] a genre researched by physicians, about which I shall say nothing at present. Artificial music is a genre researched by musicians that falls into instrumental and vocal music. Instrumental music is the sound created by diverse instruments. Although [this sound] is created by the voice, nevertheless its sounds are musical' (*Musica est duplex, naturalis et artificialis. Naturalis est mundana et humana. Mundana est supercoelestium*

## 4 The Origins of Music

The *Speculum musicae*, a work wrongly attributed to Johannes de Muris in the only complete copy, but now known to be by a certain Jacobus, postulated that music had been at the heart of creation from the time before 'the first substances were separated'.[67] Luther also held that 'music belonged to the transcendental matters' in numbering music among those things that were called into being at the 'very beginning of the world'.[68] The *Speculum* explained that its provenance as both a first fruit of creation and a fruit of the Spirit was attested to by the prophets; indeed, the very 'heavens declare the glory of God' (Ps. 19.1).[69] Luther, in turn, believed that the testimony of the 'prophets'—a term he used to refer to the Psalmists—to the creative gift of music was not only evidence of its essential nature but also proof that the gifts of the Spirit were communicated through music itself.[70] Music, therefore, was both an intrinsic part of creation that dated back to the very beginning of the cosmos and in itself an agent of God's ongoing work in creation. It also had the capacity to communicate the gifts of the Holy Spirit to humankind: 'his gifts are instilled in the prophets through music [i.e., the Psalmists]'.[71] The Psalmists, in turn, used their spiritual gifts to enable others to share in singing the eternal song that lies at the heart of all creation, thereby concluding the arc that links the Creator to humankind, and humankind to its maker.

---

*corporum ex motu sphaerarum resonantia* [...] *et hoc genus considerant mathematici. Humana exstat in corpore et anima* [...] *et hoc genus considerant physici, de quibus nihil ad praesens. Artificialis: hoc genus tenent musici. Est vel instrumentalis vel vocalis. Instrumentalis est sonus per diversa instrumenta causatus, qui cum sit vocalis, tamen eius voces sunt materiales*).

67 *Jacobi Leodiensis Speculum musicae*, ed. by Roger Bragard, CSM, I, 40–1: 'A prima substantias [...] separatas'. From the mid-20th century onwards, the *Speculum* has been reattributed to Jacques de Liège; see Klaus-Jürgen Sachs, 'Zur Funktion der Berufungen auf das achte Buch von Aristoteles "Politik" in Musiktraktaten des 15. Jahrhunderts', in *Musik und die Geschichte der Philosophie und Naturwissenschaften im Mittelalter: Fragen zur Wechselwirkung von 'Musica' und 'Philosophia' im Mittelalter*, ed. by Frank Hentschel, Studien und Texte zur Geistesgeschichte des Mittelalters, 62 (Leiden: Brill, 1998), pp. 269–90 (p. 274), and Frank Hentschel, *Sinnlichkeit und Vernunft in der mittelalterlichen Musiktheorie* (Stuttgart: Frank Steiner Verlag, 2000), p. 14.

68 WA 50: 369, 1; cf., 'rerum transcendencium', *Speculum musicae*, ed. by Bragard, I, 40.

69 *Speculum musicae*, ed. by Bragard, I, 41, 'De quibus dicit Propheta: Coeli enarrant gloriam Dei' (As the prophet says about these things, 'The heavens declare the glory of God' [Ps. 8.1]).

70 In particular, *Praefatio* (*Preface*), WA 50: 371, 10–11, as well as in a letter to Senfl in October 1530, WA Br 5: 639, 18–20, no. 1727.

71 Luther, *Praefatio* (*Preface*), WA 50: 371, 10–11: 'Dona sua [Spiritui Sancti] per eam [musicam] Prophetis illabi'.

Luther's introductory remarks in the *Preface* echo Herbenus' belief that 'God is excellently honoured [...] by the art of music' and that creation itself praised God's 'unbounded joy, utter love, peak of wisdom, and incomprehensible power' through music from the very beginning.[72] While both writers share much common ground, there are differences. Where Herbenus couched his belief in the eternity of music in a rhetorical question—'Who would deny that [...] music exists eternally in God?'—Luther expressed the same insight by a positive affirmation: 'Music existed from the beginning of the world'.[73] Rhetorical preferences notwithstanding, both subscribed to the belief that music existed from the very beginning of creation. Herbenus affirmed that music 'was from eternity before the creation was made from nothing' before it was finished and 'separated from God's nature'.[74] Luther elaborated further that music, both from the moment of creation and as a creature (*creatura*) of it, had been imparted to all creation: 'music was impressed on or created with every single creature, one and all'.[75]

### 4.1 Musica naturalis

Luther's belief in the centrality of music in the created order next led him to consider the various forms of music in the natural world. In his analysis, he followed the philosophical framework set out in Adam von Fulda's *De musica* (1490) and Nicolaus Wollick's *Opus aureum musice* (1501), who, themselves both broadly following Boethius, identified distinctive subgroups of natural music:[76] *musica mundana*, the sounds of the natural world; *musica humana*,

72 Herbenus, *De natura cantus ac miraculis vocis*, p. 36: 'Deus excellentius honoraretur'; cf., WA 50: 368, 10–369, 11.

73 Herbenus, *De natura cantus ac miraculis vocis*, p. 36: 'Quis negaverit ... discantandi aeternaliter in Deo existere?'; 'Musicam esse ab initio mundi'; WA 50: 369, 1–2. His use of 'discantandi' implies polyphonic music.

74 Herbenus, *De natura cantus ac miraculis vocis*, pp. 16–78 (p. 35): 'Ab aeterno antea in Creatore fuisse quam creatura facta ex nihilo'.

75 Luther, *Praefatio* (*Preface*), WA 50: 369, 1–2: 'Inditam seu concreatam creaturis vniuersis, singulis et omnibus'.

76 See the excellent schematic overview provided by Ferand, 'Sodaine and Unexpected Music', p. 27, showing the classification of music into *naturalis* and *artificialis* in both works. Where Adam von Fulda divided *musica naturalis* into *mundana* and *humana*, Wollick divided it into *humana* and 'coelestis aut mundana'. Unlike Wollick, who equated the music of heaven with that of the 'heavenly bodies and sounds of the spheres', Luther, like Herbenus, regarded celestial music in terms of music in praise of God. Almost certainly attracted by its Trinitarian parallels, Luther adopted a threefold subdivision into *mundana, humana,* and *caelestis*. For Luther's strong conviction that the Blessed Trinity could be discerned in similar threefold structures throughout the seven liberal arts, see WA Tr 1: 395, 10–16, no. 815.

the music that humans and animals make when they laugh, cry, or speak; and *musica caelestis*, the music of heaven.[77] Luther adopted their distinctions, addressing first the subject of *musica mundana* (WA 50: 369, 2–11), secondly the subject of *musica humana* (WA 50: 369, 12–370, 12), and lastly the music of heaven (WA 50: 370, 13–372, 10).[78]

### 4.2 Musica mundana

For Luther, *musica mundana* was constituted by the sounds that occurred when things were moved. In his treatise *De musica*, Adam von Fulda explained that '*musica mundana* is comprised of the music of the heavenly and supernatural bodies that resonate by the motion of the spheres [...] a genre researched by mathematicians'.[79] Like Adam and de Muris, Luther believed that there was nothing in existence that when moved (*tamen motus sit, durch was beweget vnd getrieben wird*) did not make a sound.[80] The *Summa musice* stipulated that it was 'not possible for bodies to be moved rapidly and persist without sound'.[81] In the *Preface*, Luther closely followed the language of the *Summa musice*: 'Nothing (*nihil enim, nichten nichts*) is without sound, or sounding number'.[82]

Towards the beginning of his *Musica speculativa*, de Muris had identified three elements requisite for the generation of sound:

> The generation of sound of necessity requires three elements: that which strikes, that which is struck, and the medium through which this percussion occurs. The first rapidly breaks the air, the second is a body with the ability to resound naturally, the third air which is violently struck.[83]

---

77 Boethius, *De institutione musica libri quinque*, ed. by Friedlein, I, ch. 2, 187–9.

78 Luther, *Praefatio* (*Preface*), WA 50: 368, 10: 'first' (*Primum*) and 'first of all' (*erstlichen aber*); 369, 31: 'secondly' (*zum andern*).

79 GS, III, 333: 'Mundana est supercoelestium corporum ex motu sphaerarum resonantia [...] et hoc genus considerant mathematici'.

80 Luther, *Praefatio* (*Preface*), WA 50: 369, 2–369, 36.

81 'Non fuit possibile, tanta corpora tam velociter moveri et tam continue absque sono'. The anonymous *Summa musice*, once erroneously attributed to Johannes de Muris, has been edited by Christopher Page, *The 'Summa musice': A Thirteenth-Century Manual for Singers* (Cambridge: Cambridge University Press, 1991); see p. 150. On the proposed redating to c.1300, see Michael Bernhard, 'La *Summa musice* du Ps.-Jean de Murs: Son auteur et sa datation', *Revue de musicologie*, 84 (1998), 19–25.

82 Luther, *Praefatio* (*Preface*), WA 50: 369, 2–5: 'Nihil enim est sine sono, seu numero sonoro' and 'Da ist nichten nichts in der Welt, das nicht ein Schall vnd Laut von sich gebe'.

83 De Muris, *Musica speculativa*, 79: 'Ad generationem soni necessario tria requiruntur: percutiens, percussum, medium percutiendi. Primum frangens aerem celeriter, secundum corpus sonabile naturaliter, tertium aer fractus violenter'.

De Muris held that music can be noticed in particular when the air moved an inanimate object, 'for sound is the movement of air generated by the impulse of a mover on a moved object'.[84] Luther shared this view and explained to his readers that even entities that were invisible, such as air, could be perceived by the senses: 'the very air, which of itself is invisible and impalpable, and imperceptible to all the senses, and least musical of all things, but utterly mute and of no account, yet in motion sounds and can be heard and even touched'.[85] Unlike de Muris, however, Luther was less interested in providing his readers with a detailed examination of the physical processes required to create sound than in bringing the 'miracle' of sound itself to the attention of his readers. The fact that sound made it possible for human beings to perceive aurally things 'imperceptible to all the senses, and least musical of all things', even things that can neither be seen nor touched (*inuisibilis et inpalpabilis*, *vnsichtbarlich vnd vnbegreifflich*), was nothing short of the miraculous.[86]

For de Muris, the processes through which air was able to generate sound led to a sustained mathematical investigation of musical proportions.[87] Luther, on the other hand, was content in his *Preface* to leave the physics of acoustics unexplored. He did not investigate the subject beyond noting that it was a combination of air (*aer*, *Lufft*) and movement (*motus*, *beweget vnd getrieben*) by, on, or through another entity (*was*: literally 'something', the *tertium quid* of scholastic ontology) that enabled human beings to hear and sense things that they might otherwise not perceive. At the end of his brief reflection on the sounds of the universe and their generation Luther returned to his overarching theme: in *musica mundana* 'the Spirit signifies marvellous mysteries'.[88] He concluded the section by stating that he was unable to elaborate on the mystery of sound and its generation in the universe in this place; unfortunately, he never returned to a detailed exploration of musical proportions in his later writings.[89]

---

84 Ibid.: 'Est igitur sonus fractio aeries ex impulsu percutientis ad percussum'.

85 Luther, *Praefatio* (*Preface*), WA 50: 369, 3–5: 'Et aer ipse per sese inuisibilis et inpalpabilis, omnibusque sensibus [...] tamen motus sit sonorus et audibilis, tunc etiam palpabilis', and 369, 23–29: 'Auch [...] die Lufft, welche doch an jr selbs vnsichtbarlich vnd vnbegreifflich [...] wenn sie durch was beweget vnd getrieben wird, so gibt sie auch jre Musica, jren klang von sich'.

86 Luther, *Praefatio* (*Preface*), WA 50: 369, 4: 'Plane mutus et nihil reputatus' and 'Die zuuor nicht gehöret noch begreifflich war'.

87 De Muris, *Musica speculativa*, pp. 83–9.

88 Luther, *Praefatio* (*Preface*), WA 50: 369, 5–6: 'Mirabilia in hoc significante spiritu mysteria, de quibus hic non est locus dicendi', and 369, 29–30: 'Durch welches der Geist wunderbarliche vnd grosse Geheimnis anzeiget, dauon ich itzund nicht sagen wil'.

89 A projected treatise on music by Luther is outlined in Leaver, *Luther's Liturgical Music*, pp. 85–97.

### 4.3 Musica humana

Since he believed that the sounds and noises of animals were 'even more wonderful' than the way the air created sounds and noises in and through inanimate objects, Luther next explored the concept of *musica humana*.[90] In his *De musica*, Adam von Fulda, following de Muris, had defined *musica humana* as 'the music that exists in body and soul', explaining that 'this genre is explored by natural philosophers'.[91] Where Adam had cut short the debate on *musica humana* and the genre of physics it inspired with a simple 'about which I shall say nothing at present',[92] in his *Book of the Nature of Singing and the Miracle of the Voice*, Matthäus Herbenus reflected at length on the 'voices' that occurred in the natural world. The voice was granted to the 'nobler' creatures: 'those with voices are easily proved superior to mute and inanimate beings'.[93] Luther also believed that the 'music of living beings' was superior to that of inanimate objects in nature: the music of living beings, 'especially birds', were prime examples of *musica humana*.[94] Indeed, the patron of all sacred music, the

> most musical king and divine harpist David, with great amazement and exultant spirit proclaims that wondrous skill and assurance birds have in singing, saying in Ps. 103 [104.12]: 'By them shall the fowls of the heaven have their habitation, which sing among the branches'.[95]

In his first book on the voice, Matthäus Herbenus had explained that it was their *dignitas*, their place and order in creation, which had granted humans the gift of intelligent speech and discourse:[96]

---

90 Luther, *Praefatio* (*Preface*), WA 50: 369, 7: 'Mirabilior' and 369, 32: 'Noch viel wunderbarlicher'.

91 GS, III, 333: 'Humana [musica] exstat in corpore et anima ... et hoc genus considerant physici'.

92 Ibid., 'De quibus nihil ad praesens'.

93 Herbenus, *De natura cantus ac miraculis vocis*, p. 3: 'Quae voces edunt praestantiores et mutis et inanimis facile perhibentur'.

94 Luther, *Praefatio* (*Preface*), WA 50: 369, 7: 'Musica in animantibus, praesertim volucribus'; and 369, 32: 'Der Thieren vnd sonderlich der Vogel Musica'.

95 Luther, *Praefatio* (*Preface*), WA 50: 369, 8–11: 'Vt Musicissimus ille Rex et diuinus psaltes Dauid cum ingenti stupore et exultante spiritu praedicit mirabilem illam volucrum peritiam et certitudinem canendi, dicens Psalmo centesimo tertio [following the numbering of the Vulgate], "Super ea volucres coeli habitant, de medio ramorum dant voces"'; and 369, 32–35: 'Wie denn der König Dauid, der köstliche Musicus, welcher auff seinem Psalter vnd Seitenspiel lauter Göttlichen Gesang singet vnd spielet, selbs bezeuget vnd mit grosser verwunderung vnd freidigem [i.e., 'leidenschaftlichem', passionate] Geist von dem wunderbarlichen Gesang der Vogel am 104. Psalm weissaget vnd singet, da er also spricht: "Auff denselben sitzen die Vogel des Himels vnd singen vnter den Zweigen"'.

96 Herbenus, *De natura cantus ac miraculis vocis*, p. 68: 'The dignity of our nature is manifested in the human voice' (*Ex voce humana manifesta est nobis naturae dignitas*); for

> Human beings stand out from the sensitive creatures on account of their dignity and excellence. [...] Thus they have not only been given a voice, like other creatures, but use discourse and speak with their voice.[97]

Luther shared Herbenus' understanding of discourse and speech in terms of a divine gift: the human voice was a gift graciously bestowed (*begnadet*) on human beings by their Creator in his 'abundant and incomprehensible munificence and wisdom'.[98] While 'music, sound, and song' of animals such as birds were superior to the music of the wind and the air, and as such 'marvellous', the miracle of the human voice was greater still.[99] Since the human voice possessed the capacity for discourse and speech (*articulationem vocis et verborum*) and the gift of emotion (*gemüt*), it was without peer in the natural world: 'the human voice cannot be compared to all other songs, sounds, or noises, for God has blessed it with such music, that it cannot and may not be grasped'.[100]

In the opening chapter of his extensive reflection on the voice, 'On the Nature of Song and the Miracle of the Voice', Herbenus provided a useful overview of the 'descriptions of the voice according to the ancients'.[101] Even the philosophers had been able neither to grasp the innate quality (*ingenium*) of

---

Giovanni Pico della Mirandola and his understanding of *dignitas hominis*, see Giovanni Pico della Mirandola, *Über die Würde des Menschen*, trans. by Norbert Baumgarten, ed. by August Buck, Philosophische Bibliothek, 427 (Hamburg: Felix Meier, 1990), pp. vii–xxvii, and Giovanni Pico della Mirandola, 'Die Rangstellung des Menschen in der Renaissance: Dignitas et miseria hominis', *Archiv für Kulturgeschichte*, 42 (1960), 61–75. For other humanist exponents of the concept, including Lorenzo Valla, Giannozzo Manetti, and Juan Luis Vives, see, for instance, Sven Grosse, 'Renaissance-Humanismus und Reformation: Lorenzo Valla und seine Relevanz für die Kontroverse über die Willensfreiheit in der Reformationszeit', *Kerygma und Dogma*, 48 (2002), 276–300, and Erik de Bom, '"Homo ipse ludus ac fibula": Vives's Views on the Dignity of Man as Expressed in his *Fabula de Homine*', *Humanistica Lovaniensia*, 57 (2008), 91–114.

97 Herbenus, *De natura cantus ac miraculis vocis*, p. 35: 'Sed cum super sensibilem creaturam dignitate atque excellentia emineat homo. [...] Itaque non solum vociferatur ut ceterae animantes, immo vero et sermone utitur et voce loquitur'.

98 Luther, *Praefatio* (*Preface*), WA 50: 369, 14–370, 1: 'Supereffusa et incompraehensibilis munificentia et sapientia'; and 370, 16–17: 'Seine vberschwengliche vnd vnbegreiffliche Güte vnd Weisheit'.

99 Luther, *Praefatio* (*Preface*), WA 50: 369, 21–22: 'Der Vogel Musica, Klang vnd Gesang'.

100 Luther, *Praefatio* (*Preface*), WA 50: 369, 38–370, 18: 'Des Menschen Stimme, gegen welcher alle andere Gesenge, Klang vnd Laut gar nicht zu rechnen sind, denn dieselbigen hat Gott mit einer solchen Musica begnadet [die] [...] nicht kan noch mag verstanden werden', one of a few instances where the German text elaborates on the Latin, rather than the Latin elaborating on the German.

101 Herbenus, *De natura cantus ac miraculis vocis*, p. 22: 'De natura cantus ac miraculis vocis'; 'Descriptiones vocis secundum antiquos'.

the human voice nor to tell precisely how it was that humans were enabled to speak. Some scholars agreed that the place of sound formation (*locus formationis eius*) was 'deep in the chest, for others in the upper regions of the throat, for some between closed teeth, for others by the movement of the tongue against the palate'.[102] Again, Luther's comments appear to have been inspired by Herbenus: 'philosophers and learned folk' had not yet been able to fathom the mysterious art (*mirabile artificium, wunderbarlich Werck*) of how 'words, sounds, song and noise, endowed with force (*gewaltig*)' could be created by the 'mere flow of air and the smallest movement of the tongue and the even smaller movement of throat and windpipe […] directed and steered by the mind'.[103]

Where Herbenus devoted an entire chapter to the different forms of the human voice, Luther, constrained by the overall brevity of his *Preface*, restricted his comments on the subject to a few lines.[104] Both marvel at the different expressions of each voice: for Herbenus, voices 'not only differ specifically and individually, but also from person to person, and individual to individual'; 'each human voice is different according to a manifold variety of factors: age, condition, and status'.[105] Luther shared this view: 'one cannot find two human beings with exactly the same voice, speech, and pronunciation; even if one of them assiduously seeks to follow the other exactly and seeks to ape all the other does'.[106] Furthermore, Herbenus had explained that, in the exercise of their calling and standing, each voice adapts to the office and work of the speaker: '[the voice] of the shepherd herding his flock turns rustic, that of the soldier militaristic, and that of a duke for instance is aristocratic, while

102 Ibid., 'Quidam in imo pectore eam formari arbitrati sunt, quidam in suprema gutturis regione, nonulli intra complexum dentium, alii obiectu linguae ad palatum'.

103 Luther, *Praefatio* (*Preface*), WA 50: 370, 18: 'Philosophi vnd gelerten Leut', 'Gewaltig Wort, Laut, Gesang vnd Klang'; 370, 24: 'quo modo tam leui motu linguae leuiorique adhuc motu gutturis pulsus aer funderet illam infinitam varietatem et articulationem vocis et verborum'; and 370, 20–23: 'Das die Lufft durch eine solche kleine vnd geringe bewegung der Zungen, vnd darnach auch noch durch eine geringere bewegung der kelen oder des halses […] durch das gemüt geregieret vnd gelencket wird'.

104 Herbenus, *De natura cantus ac miraculis vocis*, pp. 29–30: 'Quae appellationes singulis vocibus accidere possint'; cf., WA 50: 372, 5–10; 372, 21–29.

105 Herbenus, *De natura cantus ac miraculis vocis*, p. 29: 'Non solum sunt voces […] discrepantes specifice ac individualiter, immo etiam singillatim ac suppositaliter: […] Vox in eodem homine pro diversitate aetatum, conditionum ac statuum multipliciter mutatur!'.

106 Luther, *Praefatio* (*Preface*), WA 50: 372, 25–28: 'Das man nicht zween Menschen könne finden, welche gantz gleiche stimme, sprach vnd ausrede haben möchten, Vnd ob gleich einer sich auf des andern weise mit hohem vleis gibet, vnd jm gleich sein vnd wie der Aff alles nach thun wil'.

the emperor's is entirely imperious'.[107] Again Luther shared Herbenus' view that human voices reflect each individual's standing and call: the difference in voice, pronunciation, and discourse reflects how 'one marvellously excels another'.[108]

The subject of the human emotions was for Luther more impressive even than the generation of intelligent speech or the immense variety of human voices and their uses for differing purposes. Early modern philosophers of music genuinely appear to have been at a loss to explain the generation of tears beyond stating the obvious: that sadness can lead to tears and that often 'music gladdens the sad'.[109] Even Herbenus, who devoted two chapters of his second book to the theme, restricted his observations to noting that tears could be turned to laughter through the power of song.[110] Luther is therefore right in stating that 'none have yet been found who could determine and establish the nature of that hiss and as it were alphabet or prime matter of the human voice, namely laughter (of weeping I will say nothing)'.[111] Unfortunately, Luther did not venture an explanation of the generation of the human emotions either (although he did consider the effects of music on the human *affectus* in his reflections on *musica caelestis*). He merely noted that the philosophers had not been able to research it fully (*könnens nicht erforschen*) and therefore, 'wonder, but do not comprehend'.[112]

Although they had been unable to offer a comprehensive answer to the subject of the voice, its generation and its place and use in creation, philosophers of music explored the subject in far greater detail than Luther. Where Herbenus had devoted two volumes to the study of the voice, Luther condensed his argument to two paragraphs, one as part of his consideration of

107 Herbenus, *De natura cantus ac miraculis vocis*, p. 29: 'Pastor gregum efectus, pastoralis fuisset. Sin in aliqua insigni urbe editus, vox penitus foret urbana; miles factus, militaris; ducis enim ducalis est. Nam Imperatoris tota imperialis est'.

108 Luther, *Praefatio* (*Preface*), WA 50: 372, 7–8: 'Vt alius alium mirabiliter excellat'; and 372, 25: 'Einer dem anderen also weit vberlegen ist'.

109 For instance, 'Musica laetificat tristes'; Adam von Fulda, *Musica pars prima*, GS, III, 333; and 'Musica tristitiam depellit'; Johannes Tinctoris, *Complexus effectuum musices* (*c.*1474–5), in *Johannes Tinctoris Opera theoretica*, ed. by Albert Seay, CSM, 22, II, 165–77 (pp. 165–6).

110 Herbenus, *De natura cantus ac miraculis vocis*, pp. 48–9.

111 Luther, *Praefatio* (*Preface*), WA 50: 370, 27–29: 'Ja es ist auch noch keiner nicht komen, welcher hette könen sagen vnd anzeigen, wo von das Lachen des Menschen (denn vom Weinen wil ich nichts sagen) kome'; Herbenus, *De natura cantus ac miraculis vocis*, pp. 48–9.

112 Luther, *Praefatio* (*Preface*), WA 50: 370, 10: 'Mirantur, sed non complectuntur' and 'Des verwundern sie sich, darbey bleibts auch, vnd können nicht erforschen'.

*musica humana* (WA 50: 370, 1–9; 370, 18–25), another as part of his reflection on *musica caelestis* (WA 50: 372, 5–10; 372, 21–28). Since the reformer's intended audience would have consisted primarily of singers and music enthusiasts and not (as in Herbenus' case) rhetoricians and philosophers of music, Luther felt that it was sufficient to provide a brief overview of the complex nature and immense gift of the human voice.[113] He summed up his reflection by inviting others to research the subject further: other scholars with 'more time on their hands than we do' would do well to consider (*bedencken*) the complexity of the human voice.[114] He concluded his discussion on *musica humana* by pointing his readers once again to the mysterious nature of the human voice. Recalling the end of his reflection on *musica mundana*, ultimately the sound of the human voice was reason not only for great wonder (*verwunderlich*) but also for gratitude to God for this 'unique creation' bestowed on humankind by 'God's infinite wisdom'.[115]

### 4.4 Musica caelestis

The final category of 'natural music' for Luther was the music of heaven, the rather loosely defined *musica caelestis*. Heavenly music offered humankind a glimpse of heaven in the world around them in the same way in which the scholastic anagogical sense of Scripture revealed something essential about heaven.[116] Just as God's Word was able to direct the human will, so *musica caelestis* also had the capacity to influence people profoundly. For that reason, 'music, after God's Word, deserves and ought to be celebrated'.[117] Earlier commentators such as Petrus dictus Palma ociosa, whose *Compendium de Discantu Mensurabili* (*c*.1336) remains extant in Erfurt University's Bibliotheca Amploniana, had already argued that measured music (*musica mensurabilis*) had the ability to determine the way in which musicians performed, directing 'the voices of all musicians, watching over them, mastering and governing them'. It is nevertheless unlikely that Luther would have been familiar with

113 Luther, *Praefatio* (*Preface*), WA 50: 370, 32–33: 'Den, so mehr zeit, denn wir haben, zu bedencken befehlen, ich habs allein kürtzlich wollen anzeigen'.

114 Ibid., 'So mehr zeit, denn wir haben'.

115 Luther, *Praefatio* (*Preface*), WA 50: 370, 32: 'Vna Creatura'; 'Einigen Creatur'; 'Infinita sapientia Dei'; 'vnmesslichen weisheit Gottes'.

116 For the four *sensus* of Scripture and the gradual shift to the literal sense of biblical interpretation in the mid-16th century, see J. Andreas Loewe, *Richard Smyth and the Language of Orthodoxy: Re-imagining Tudor Catholic Polemicism*, Studies in Medieval and Reformation Traditions, 96 (Leiden: Brill, 2003), p. 94.

117 Luther, *Praefatio* (*Preface*), WA 50: 371, 1–2: 'Musicam esse vnam, quae post verbum Dei merito celebrari debeat' and 'Das nach dem heiligen wort Gottes nichts nicht so billich vnd so hoch zu rhümen vnd zu loben, als eben die Musica'.

Petrus dictus Palma ociosa's work: the manuscript shows little sign of use within the respective fascicle.[118]

Matthäus Herbenus extended this concept significantly, suggesting that heavenly music had not only the capacity to direct and control the manner in which humans performed music, but also the power to influence the human will. The music of the ministers of God (*Dei ministerii*) in heaven could 'faithfully express the will of God within us and [...] open a way to guide the good on the path of virtue, direct the evildoers towards the way of righteousness, console the sad, and assist the afflicted'.[119] Yet even here on earth (*terrena nostra corpora*), by the agency of this divine art (*divina arte*) humans were still able to experience the 'support, guidance, and governance of the divine mind'.[120] The music of heaven was there to enable humans to 'admire and honour the divine goodness and eternal majesty of God in harmony', in heaven as on earth.[121]

Luther shared Herbenus' belief that music could govern the human will. In his *Preface*, he emphasised that music 'rules and governs the human passions [...] by which humans themselves are governed as if by their masters'.[122] The ability to influence the human heart was in itself sufficient praise for Luther: 'than this praise of music none greater can be imagined, at least by us'.[123] Luther's followers, most notably Hermann Finck in his *Practica musica*

118 Petrus dictus Palma ociosa, *Compendium de Discantu Mensurabili*, Erfurt, Bibliotheca Amploniana, MS 94, in Johannes Wolf, 'Ein Beitrag zur Diskantlehre des 14. Jahrhunderts', *Sammelbände der Internationalen Musikgesellschaft*, 15 (1914), 504–34 (p. 507): 'Measured music is the true and perfect science of singing; the empress, mistress and governor of the voices of all musicians' (*Musica mensurabilis est ... omnium musicantium vocum speculatrix, gubernatrix et magistra*; cf., *Musica mensurabilis est vere perfecta quod* [read: *perfecteque*] *cantandi scientia omnium musicalium vocum imperatrix, magistra, et gubernatrix*), in Jan W. Herlinger, 'A Fifteenth-Century Italian Compilation of Music Theory', *Acta Musicologica*, 53 (1981), 90–105 (p. 97). Petrus dictus Palma ociosa contrasts the ordered singing of measured music with the freer flow of plainchant.

119 Herbenus, *De natura cantus ac miraculis vocis*, p. 33: 'Divinam voluntatem fidelissime nobis enuntiant et [...] insinuant, bono in via virtutum custodientes, malos ad iter rectitudinis dirigentes, tristes consolantes, afflictis assistentes'.

120 Herbenus, *De natura cantus ac miraculis vocis*, p. 41, 'Divina mente nostra ferri, dirigi, gubernari'.

121 Ibid., 'Divinam bonitatem atque maiestatem sempiternis concentibus possimus admirari et honorare'.

122 Luther, *Praefatio* (*Preface*), WA 50: 371, 2–4: 'Domina et gubernatrix affectuum humanorum [...] quibus tamen ipsi homines, ceu a suis dominis, gubernantur et saepius rapiuntur'; and 371, 16–18: 'Ein Regiererin, jr mechtig vnd gewaltig ist, durch welche doch offtmals die Menschen, gleich als von jrem Herren [note the singular in the German], regiert vnd vberwunden werden'.

123 Luther, *Praefatio* (*Preface*), WA 50: 371, 4–5: 'Hac laude Musicae nulla maior potest (a nobis quidem) concipi'.

(1556), readily adopted this insight: next to the praise of God the principal use of music was that of being 'the governor of the emotions'.[124] Closely following pseudo-Aquinas, who held that 'sung music had great power to move the souls of its hearers: whether it lightly touches the ears, or steels wills, incites warriors to battle, recalls the lapsed and desperate, disarms bandits, soothes the irate, gladdens the sad and anxious, pacifies those who quarrel, drives away vain thoughts, and tempers frenzied rage',[125] Luther elaborated his theme:[126]

> For whether you wish to cheer the miserable, or deter the cheerful, encourage the despairing, break the proud, calm the lovers, soothe the haters—and who shall count all those masters of the human heart, the affections and impulses or spirits that drive all virtues or vices?—what could you find more efficacious than music herself?[127]

The music of heaven not only was an effective control (*inuenias efficatius*) of human emotions but also fulfilled two further important functions: it was able both to convey the gifts of the Holy Spirit and to drive away evil. Following Herbenus and Adam von Fulda, Luther cited the example of the prophet Elisha in the second book of Kings, who called for a musician to enable him to prophesy and found that 'while the musician was playing, the power of the Lord came on him' (2 Kgs. 3.15).[128] Like his predecessors, Luther interpreted the passage to suggest that the gifts of the Spirit were conveyed through music to prophets

---

124 Hermann Finck, *Practica musica Hermanni Finckii, exempla variorum signorum, proportionum et canonum, iudicium de tonis, ac quaedam de arte suaviter et artificiose cantandi continens* (Wittenberg: Georg Rhau, 1556), sig. A 3r: 'Gubernatrix affectuum'.

125 The quotation by 'Aquinas' certainly goes back to the widely known treatise, *De Musica*, by Johannes of Afflighem (*c.*1100) and is subsequently taken up by many later theorists; see Johannes of Afflighen, *De Musica cum Tonario*, ed. by J. Smits van Waesberghe, CSM, I, 114.

126 Pseudo-Aquinas, *Ars musice*, ed. by Marco di Martino (Napoli: Eugenio di Simone, 1933), pp. 23–39 (p. 27): 'Quam magnam vim commovendi animos auditorum cantus musyce habet: Si quidem aures mulcet, mentes erigit, proeliatores ad bellum incitat, lapsos et desperantes revocat, latrones exarmat, iracundos mitigat, tristes et anxios letificat, discordes pacificat, vanas cogitationes eliminat, freneticorum rabiem temperat'.

127 Luther, *Praefatio* (*Preface*), WA 50: 371, 5–9: 'Siue enim velis tristes erigere, siue laetos terrere, desperantes animare, superbos frangere, amantes sedare, odientes mitigare, et quis omnes illos numeret dominos cordis humani, scilicet affectus et impetus seu spiritus, impulsores omnium vel virtutum vel vitiorum? Quid inuenias efficatius quam ipsam Musicam?'

128 Herbenus, *De natura cantus ac miraculis vocis*, p. 71; 'By the beat of the psaltery Elisha is attended by the Spirit of prophecy' (*Ad tactum psalterii Elisaeus prophetiae spiritum consecutus est*); Adam von Fulda, *Musica Pars Prima*, GS, III, 334.

(a term that included Psalmists and musicians):[129] 'the encouragement and promotion of all kinds of graces and good works is conveyed through music to the prophets'.[130] Heavenly music had the ability to communicate heavenly gifts 'because the Holy Spirit himself praises and honours this fine art as the proper instrument of his office'.[131]

Luther again drew on the historical writings of the Old Testament for his suggestion that the music of heaven had the capacity to drive away evil. Like de Muris and his numerous followers, including Nicolaus Wollick, Adam von Fulda, and Johannes Tinctoris, he cited the famous example of David playing the harp before Saul in 1 Sam. 16.23.[132] However, where his predecessors had interpreted the episode in terms of the power of music to soothe the human temperament and 'recall Saul from his demented fury', he regarded it in much more fundamental terms. Luther's use of the story of David soothing Saul's spirit as evidence of the ability of music to drive away evil closely follows Tinctoris, who explicitly associates music with deliverance from evil: his use marks a sea change in later humanist interpretation.[133] The episode demonstrated (*angezeiget*) that music was even able 'to drive away Satan, who tempts people to all kinds of sins and vices'.[134] While previous interpreters,

---

129 Luther, *Praefatio* (*Preface*), WA 50: 317, 25–31. Luther first explored this concept in his *Dictata super Psalterium* (*Lectures on the Psalms*), *1513–16*, WA 3: 40, 15–17, LW 10, in considering Psalm 4.1: 'It is the function of music to arouse the sad, sluggish, and dull spirit. Thus Elisha summoned a psaltery player so that he might be stirred up to prophesy' (*Habet enim natura Musice, excitare tristem, pigrum et stupidum animum. Sic Heliezeus vocavit psalten, ut excitaretur ad prophetiam*).

130 Luther, *Praefatio* (*Preface*), WA 50: 371, 26–27: 'Das seine Gaben, das ist, die bewegung vnd anreitzung zu allerley tugend vnd guten wercken, durch die Musica den Propheten gegeben werden'.

131 Ibid., 'Ja der heilige Geist lobet vnd ehret selbs diese edle Kunst als seines eigenen ampts Werckzeug'.

132 De Muris, GS, III, 195–6; Wollick, *Die Musica Gregoriana des Nicolaus Wollick*, p. 3; Adam von Fulda, GS, III, 334.

133 Tinctoris marks the relevant section in his treatise 'Musica diabolum fugat'; Tinctoris, *Complexus effectuum musices*, II, 165–77 (p. 171), while Wollick, for instance, only speaks of the power of music to bring Saul back to his senses: 'Saul a furore dementiae refocillabatur'; Wollick, *Die Musica Gregoriana des Nicolaus Wollick*, p. 3.

134 Luther, *Praefatio* (*Preface*), WA 50: 371, 12: 'Per eandem [musicam] expelli Satanam, id est omnium vitiorum impulsorem'; and 371, 31–33: 'Das durch die Musica der Sathan, welcher die Leute zu aller vntugend vnd laster treibet, vertrieben werde'; following Chrysostom, who held that the singing of psalms was a safeguard against evil habits inspired by Satan, such as convivial drinking (*ta polla en symposiois ho diabolos ephedreuei*, τά πόλλα ἐν σύμποσιοις ό διάβολος ἐφέδρέυει) and an antidote to demons (*daimones*, δάιμονες) and the powers of evil (*dunameis*, δύναμεις); *Patrologiae Cursus Completus, Series Graeca* [PG], ed. by Jacques-Paul Migne, 161 vols (Paris: Imprimerie Catholique, 1857–66), LV, 157, 162.

like de Muris and Adam von Fulda, had both identified Saul's evil spirit as demonic, neither interpreted the story in terms of music driving away Satan.[135] Both Luther's interpretation of the ability of music to drive away evil and his identification of Saul's spirit as Satanic is adopted by Lutheran successors like Johannes Lippius, who asserted in his *Synopsis musicae* (1612) that 'Satan is the enemy of God's beautiful and most delightful gift of music'.[136]

For Luther, celestial music was able to accomplish three fundamental things: it conveyed the gifts of the Spirit, encouraged the fostering of a habit of goodness in hearers and performers, and prevented evil and vice. In combination with the Word of God, it was ideally suited to move human hearts (*die hertzen der Menschen bewegen*).[137] Here Luther once more follows the humanist rhetorical tradition. Matthäus Herbenus' work was devoted to exploring the relationship between rhetoric and song, the combination of message and music. He knew 'that the human voice has great power, that the word has great power, and lastly that great and incredible power lies in the mystery of song'.[138] Luther shared his opinion. The capacity to combine Scripture with music (*sermo et vox*), to draw on heavenly music and heavenly words, was what ultimately distinguished human beings from animals:

> Then again humans alone apart from the rest were given the gift of words combined with song, so that he should know that he ought to praise God, that is with loud preaching and words combined with sweet melody.[139]

It was this insight that had led Luther to employ music as an effective practical instrument to further his reforms and that in turn led to the establishment of a distinctive Lutheran choral tradition, in which musicians and theologians

---

135 Adam von Fulda, GS, III, 334; 'That when King Saul was besieged by a demon it put the demon to flight' (*Saule rege obsesso a daemone daemonium effugasse*); de Muris, GS, III, 195.

136 Johannes Lippius, *Synopsis musicae novae omnino verae atque methodicae universae, in omnis sophiae praegustum* [*Parergos*] *inventae disputatae et propositae omnibus philomusis* (Strassburg: Paulus Ledertz, typis Carolus Kieffer, 1612), p. 17: 'Der schönen und herrlichsten Gaben Gottes ist die Musica, der ist der Satan sehr feindt'.

137 Luther, *Praefatio* (*Preface*), WA 50: 371, 39.

138 Herbenus, *De natura cantus ac miraculis vocis*, p. 61: 'Magna igitur in voce humana vis inest, magna in sermone potestas, magnum denique et incredibile pene in cantu mysterium'.

139 Luther, *Praefatio* (*Preface*), WA 50: 372, 2–4: 'Denique homini soli prae caeteris sermo voci copulatus donatus est, vt sciret, se Deum laudare oportere verbo et Musica'; and 372, 16–18: 'Dem Menschen aber ist allein vor den andern Creaturen die stimme mit der rede gegeben, das er solt künnen vnd wissen, Gott mit Gesengen vnd worten zugleich zu loben'.

collaborated in creating musical artworks in order to allow their communities to share in singing and preaching the good news.[140]

### 4.5 Musica artificialis

A final part of Luther's *Praefatio Symphoniae Iucundae* (*Preface to the Symphoniae Iucundae*) explores the concept of 'artificial music'. Composed music had the ability to amplify and shape (*gescherfft vnd poliert*) natural music. By employing their God-given gifts of composition, writers of music were able to 'correct, enhance, and develop' natural music and to create a piece of art that was greater than its component voices or parts.[141] In his *Book of the Nature of Singing and the Miracle of the Voice*, Herbenus had expressed the strong belief that humans were given a mind 'in order to join their voices artfully [...] so that they can honour their Creator by singing, and in artistic partnership with their fellow human beings'.[142]

Luther shared Herbenus' belief: the two principal purposes of artificial music were, firstly, to provide a bridge between the music of heaven and the music of humans by enabling many voices to share in singing God's praises, and secondly, to point beyond itself to God the Creator and giver of music. Whenever human beings used their voice to sing God's praises, *musica humana* and *musica caelestis* were conjoined. In combination, the music of humans and heaven made known 'God's goodness and grace by beautiful words and lovely songs at one and the same time'.[143] This principle held true regardless of whether one or many voices joined in singing God's praises, or whether that praise was sung in unison or multiple musical parts. The skill of composers merely shaped the singing of God's praise, making it possible for more than one part to share in singing or playing to God's glory.

When he praised the combination of word and music, Luther clearly thought of multiple voices in multiple parts singing God's praises. Like Herbenus, who posed the rhetorical question 'what if all the voices before [the throne of] God were single, and were emitted entirely in silence? How much more do we believe them to be in a well-arranged concert of voices by which the heavens

---

140 Ibid., 'Sonora praedicatione'; for Luther's views on music as an essential part of public education, see Chapter 2 below.

141 Luther, *Praefatio* (*Preface*), WA 50: 372, 10–11: 'Musica artificialis, quae naturalem corrigat, excolat et explicet'.

142 Herbenus, *De natura cantus ac miraculis vocis*, p. 36: 'Voces suas artificialiter coniungere possent [...] cantando quoque cum naturae suae consortibus artificialiter Creatorem suum honorare possit'.

143 Luther, *Praefatio* (*Preface*), WA 50: 372, 19–20: 'Gottes güte vnd gnade, darinnen schöne wort vnd lieblicher klang zugleich würde gehöret'.

resound with praise',[144] Luther also envisaged many singers joining voices 'with loud preaching and words combined with sweet melody'.[145] Such 'concerted' singing required the skill of composers. Only where *musica humana* and *musica caelestis* were shaped by *musica artificialis* was it possible for 'three, four, or five separate parts together with [...] the simple melody or tenor' to share on earth in the worship of heaven.[146]

> Where natural music is tempered and polished through artistic endeavour, one is able to see and perceive in part (for one cannot ever comprehend or understand it fully) with great wonder the immense and complete wisdom of God in his wonderful work of music.[147]

Just as Herbenus had foreseen the music of heaven as 'full of unity and perfection where all voices resound together, sung by all, most melodiously without any mistake at all', so Luther also envisaged a heavenly harmony.[148] In heaven, there was a perfect polyphony of voices, 'singing adorned by many voices' that through the art of composition and the skill of artists 'led as it were a heavenly dance' in music, as each part 'plays and moves in sundry ways and tones the same tune is wonderfully ornamented and decorated'.[149] Polyphonic music composed to the glory of God not only had the ability to align performers with the heavenly voices but also to transport hearers to the courts of heaven: 'those who perceive it a little and are moved by it, marvel greatly and believe that there is nothing more wonderful on earth than such polyphonic singing'.[150]

---

144 Herbenus, *De natura cantus ac miraculis vocis*, p. 45: 'Quodsi tanti sunt apud Deum voces singulorum et fere in silentio emissae, quanti tandem credimus eas esse quae in bene disposito concinentium choro caelos conscendunt cum iubilo?'.

145 Luther, *Praefatio* (*Preface*), WA 50: 372, 18–20: 'Mit dem hellen, klingenden predigen vnd rhümen von Gottes güte vnd gnade, darinnen schöne wort vnd lieblicher klang zugleich würde gehöret'; cf., 373, 1–3.

146 Luther, *Praefatio* (*Preface*), WA 50: 372, 34–35: 'Drey, vier oder fünff andere stimmen [...] vmb solche schlechte [i.e., 'schlichte', simple] weise oder Tenor'.

147 Luther, *Praefatio* (*Preface*), WA 50: 372, 29–32: 'Wo aber die natürliche Musica durch die Kunst gescherfft vnd polirt wird, da sihet vnd erkennet man erst zum teil (den gentzlich kans nicht begrieffen noch verstanden werden) mit grosser verwunderung die grosse vnd volkomene weisheit Gottes in seinem wunderbarlichem werck der Musica'.

148 Herbenus, *De natura cantus ac miraculis vocis*, p. 33: 'Summa unitate atque perfectione, ubi omnium voces communes omnibus sine ulla discrepantia melodissime consonant'.

149 Luther, *Praefatio* (*Preface*), WA 50: 373, 15: 'Gesang mit viel stimmen geschmückt'; 372, 38: 'Einen Himlischen Tantzreien füren'; 372, 36–38: 'Spielen vnd springen vnd mit mancherley art vnd klang dieselbige weise wunderbarlich zieren vnd schmücken'.

150 Luther, *Praefatio* (*Preface*), WA 50: 372, 38–373, 3: 'So solches ein wenig verstehen vnd dadurch bewegt werden, sich des hefftig verwundern müssen und meinen, das nichts seltzamers in der Welt sey, denn ein solcher Gesang mit vielen stimmen'.

As suggested by his vision of many human voices joining in the praise of God on earth, mirroring the praises sung in heaven, the greatest quality of *musica caelestis* was its capacity to bridge heaven and earth. Following the publication of his *Preface to the Symphoniae Iucundae*, Luther had told a group of musicians assembled at his home to sing motets in December 1538 that among the 'dross of this life' music was 'a noble gift that our Lord God has granted us'.[151] Its beauty permitted glimpses of God's glory and insights into the nature and wisdom of God (*weisheit Gottes*).[152] The music of heaven was not restricted to the music of the angels in heaven that from time to time (most significantly at the birth of Christ as narrated in Lk. 2.15) could be heard on earth, providing an occasional musical bridge between heaven and earth. Rather, whenever human beings sang the praises of God, they aligned their voices with those of heaven, and so the music of heaven could resound on earth.[153] Conversely, as Luther pointed out in his *Preface*, the unworthy (*non digni sunt*) who have no appreciation of God's gift of music never even perceived the music of heaven. This was not a simple example of 'pearls before swine' (Mt. 7.6), but rather a reflection of the insight formulated by Luther's predecessors that not all creatures had been endowed with the capacity to shape music. As Herbenus had explained in his chapter, 'On the different ways in which angels and humans and certain animals praise God by their voices', God's greatest gift to humankind was the ability to use their talents to give shape and order to music: 'Animals lack art because they have no mind by which they can join their notes in composition'.[154] Luther merely elaborated Herbenus' thought: for the unworthy, the music of heaven remained *musica mundana* at its most base level, remained the song of animals. Because they lacked the mind to perceive God's gift of ordered, composed music, to them 'a Chorale is like the brute, wild braying of donkeys, or the music of dogs and sows'.[155] On the other hand, when humans

---

151 Luther, *Tischreden* (*Table Talk*), WA Tr 4: 191, 31–2, no. 4192: 'So vnser Her Gott in diesem leben in das scheißhaus (literally: 'latrine') solche edle gaben gegeben hat'.

152 Luther, *Praefatio* (*Preface*), WA 50: 372, 3–32.

153 In the same year, Luther expressed the same insight in his famous poem, *Fraw Musica, 1538*, WA 35: 484, 33–40: 'Day and night Music sings and sounds God's praise / Since nothing will tire her in praising him / my own song, too, shall honour him / and give him thanks eternally' (*Dem* [*Gott*] *singt und springt sie* [*Musica*] *tag und nacht, / Seines lobs sie nichts müde macht, / Den ehrt und lobt auch mein gesang / Und sagt jm ein ewigen danck*). See also the discussion of the poem in WA 48: 293–7, and Leaver, *Luther's Liturgical Music*, pp. 73–6.

154 Herbenus, *De natura cantus ac miraculis vocis*, p. 36: 'Arte quidem carent quia mentem, qua voces suas artificialiter coniungere possent, non habent'.

155 Luther, *Praefatio* (*Preface*), WA 50: 373, 5: 'Das wüste, wilde Eselsgeschrey des Chorals, oder der Hunde oder Sewe Gesang vnd Musica'.

offered the gift of *musica humana* to the Giver, by joining their voices in the ordered singing of the praise of God, they were enabled to 'relish with amazement (but not understand) God's absolute and perfect wisdom in his marvellous work of music'.[156] At table with his musician friends in December 1538, Luther reiterated the same conclusion: *musica caelestis* pointed beyond the ephemeral to the eternal; indeed, it was in itself a part of 'eternal life [...] where everything is most perfect and joyous'.[157]

## 5 Music as a 'Habitus' and Model of Goodness and Praise

Luther noted in conclusion that both in its essence (*res, die sach*) and its use (*der nutz*), 'this noble art is far greater and richer than could be recounted in this brief space'.[158] Music pointed beyond itself to the Creator of all things and enabled human beings to recognise glimpses of God in this world (*Creatorem agnoscere*): its beauty could effect a profound response of love in humans, both for the Creator and for his creature music.[159] Music was the principal instrument through which humans were able to express their response of love for God and his gifts, giving voice to human 'laud and praise'.[160] It was also a powerful force to promote goodness and overcome evil, both in society and within the universe: this 'noble, salutary, and happy creature' made it possible for all people, especially the young, to develop a permanent habit (*Gewohnheit*) of 'shunning evil thoughts and the avoidance of evil company as well as sinful behaviour'.[161] Building up such a habit relied both on the individual's recognition (*erkenntnis*) of the salutary function of music and their

156 Luther, *Praefatio* (*Preface*), WA 50: 372, 12–14, 'Gustare cum stupore licet (sed non comprehendere) absolutam et perfectam sapientiam Dei in opere suo mirabili Musicae'; and 272, 31–33: 'Da sihet vnd erkennet man erst zum teil (denn gentzlich kans nicht begrieffen noch verstanden werden) mit grosser verwunderung die grosse vnd volkomene weisheit Gottes in seinem wunderbarlichen werck der Musica'.

157 Luther, *Tischreden* (*Table Talk*), WA Tr 4: 191, 33, no. 4192: 'Ewigen leben [...] ubi omnia erunt perfectissima et iucundissima'.

158 Luther, *Praefatio* (*Preface*), WA 50: 373, 18–20: 'Es ist die sach vnd der nutz dieser edlen Kunst viel grosser vnd reicher, denn das es also in einer kürtze möge erzelt werden'.

159 Luther, *Praefatio* (*Preface*), WA 50: 373, 22: 'Value, love and esteem this [...] Creature of God' (*Diese [...] Creatur Gottes tewr, lieb vnd werd sein lassen*).

160 Luther, *Praefatio* (*Preface*), WA 50: 373, 25: 'Loben vnd preisen'.

161 Luther, *Praefatio* (*Preface*), WA 50: 373, 8–10: 'Nobilem, salutarem et laetam creaturam'; and 373, 22: 'Diese köstliche, nützliche vnd fröliche Creatur Gottes'; 373, 22–24: 'Böse gedancken vertreiben vnd auch böse Geselschafft vnd andere vntugend vermeiden'.

assiduous practice (*vleissige vbung*).[162] Luther here referred to both the strenuous mental effort involved in striving to attain the moral benefits he associated with music-making, as well as the actual practice of voice and instruments, in order to achieve his vision of 'natural music tempered by art' rather than an external work.[163]

Although there is no doubt of his love for music as a discipline, and his firm belief in music as a force for great good, Luther ended his *Preface to the Symphoniae Iucundae* with a resounding note of caution: just like any other gift of God, music had the capacity to be abused by depraved souls (*deprauos animos*) for their own ends:[164]

> Indecent poets, for their own mad loves, certain that the devil seizes them against nature, so that she who wishes and ought by this gift to praise only God its author, is developed by those bastard sons, the raiders of God's gift, as an enemy of God and an adversary of this most delightful nature and art.[165]

---

162 Luther clearly reinterprets the Thomist understanding of the *habitus* in the light of his own Reformation doctrine on justification. One of the most accurate and succinct summaries of Luther's critique of the Thomist role of supernatural habits of grace is still Alister McGrath, *Iustitia Dei: A History of the Christian Doctrine of Justification. The Beginnings to the Reformation* (Cambridge: Cambridge University Press, 1986), p. 154.

163 Luther, *Praefatio* (*Preface*), WA 50: 372, 29: 'Natürliche Musica durch die Kunst gescherfft'.

164 Once more, Luther's opinion finds parallels in a number of earlier writers, not least Vittorino da Feltre's student Sassuolo da Prato (Saxolus Pratensis, *c.*1416–49), mathematician and musician at the court of Alessandro Gonzaga in Mantua, who famously noted in his *De Victorini Feltrensis Vita* that contemporary (*haec huius temporis*) music had the capacity to be 'polluted, indecent, corrupt as well as corrupting' (*iniquinata, impudens, corrupta atque corruptrix*): see Alessandro Gonzaga, *De Victorini Feltrensis Vita*, in *Il pensiero pedagogico dell'Umanesimo*, ed. by Eugenio Garin (Florence: Guintine & Sansoni, 1958), p. 530.

165 Luther, *Praefatio* (*Preface*), WA 50: 374, 1–5: 'Impudici poetae, ad suos insanos amores, et summo studio caueto et vitato, certus, quod Diabolus eos rapiat contra naturam, vt quae hoc dono vult et debet Deum solum laudare autorem, isti adulterini filii, rapina ex dono Dei facta, colunt eodem hostem Dei et aduersarium naturae et artis huis iucundissimae'; and 372, 27–374, 10: 'Die vnzüchtigen Poeten auch mit jrer Natur vnd Kunst thun, zu schendlicher, toller, vnzüchtiger liebe missbrauchen, mit allem vleis fliehen vnd vermeiden vnd gewis wissen sollen, das solche der Teuffel, wider die Natur, also treibet, welche Natur, dieweil sie allein Gott, den Schöpffer aller Creaturn, mit solcher edlen Gabe sol vnd wil ehren vnd loben, so werden diese vngeratene Kinder vnnd Wechselbelge durch den Satan dazu getrieben, das sie solche Gabe Gott dem HERRN nemen vnd rauben vnd damit den Teuffel, welcher ein Feind Gottes, der Natur vnd dieser lieblichen Kunst ist, ehren vnd damit dienen'.

Music was so attractive that it had the inherent potential to be used as much for the promotion of the good news as it could to further selfish, perverted, even evil goals. Ultimately, for Luther, the responsibility to choose wisely and to use music as an instrument to promote goodness lay with each individual. The Reformation had made it possible to sing with understanding, by introducing vernacular church music as well as by providing sound education in literacy and music; the obligation to be discerning in their choice and use of music now lay squarely on the shoulders of each singer and instrumentalist.[166]

Luther knew that such choices required not only the habit of practising one's art as a musician and the continuous conscious effort to turn away from evil but, above all, the free gift of God's grace. Music was '*lieblich*', a word he had parsed in his *German Bible* as 'comforting, most blessed, grace-filled', and was clearly regarded by Luther as an agent, if not a vehicle, of grace.[167] Having commenced his *Preface* by 'wishing all lovers of the liberal art of music [...] grace and peace from God our Father and the Lord Jesus Christ', he concluded the work by commending his readers—'all of you'—to God in the certain hope that they would indeed employ God's gift to his glory.[168]

This survey of Martin Luther's *Praefatio Symphoniae Iucundae* (*Preface to the Symphoniae Iucundae*) has shown that more than twenty years after the beginning of the Wittenberg Reformation, the reformer continued to draw on a traditional late-medieval theoretical understanding of music, its generation and its classification into natural and artificial music. It is clear that for Luther music is the principal among the quadrivial arts: in his writings he continues to relate music to the wider field of mathematics, regarding it as part of arithmetic in his 1524 *An die Ratsherren aller Städte deutschen Landes* (*Appeal to the Councillors of all Cities of the German Nation*)[169] and relating it to the study of the heavens—astronomy—in his consideration of the generation

166 For the concept of 'singing with understanding' (*meta suneseōs psallontes*, μέτα σύνεσεῶς ψαλλόντες), see Chrysostom, *Expositio in Psalmum XLI*, PG, LV, 157; for a brief summary of the debate about 'singing with understanding' among Continental humanists and reformers, see Jonathan P. Willis, *Church Music and Protestantism in Post-Reformation England: Discourses, Sites and Identities* (Farnham: Ashgate, 2010), p. 45.

167 Luther, *Deutsche Bibel* (*German Bible*), WA DB 7: 235: 'Das ist Tröstlichen holdseligen gnadenreichen etc'. (in a marginalium to Col. 3.16).

168 *Praefatio* (*Preface*), WA 50: 368, 14–16: 'Allen Liebhabern der freien Kunst Musica wünsch Ich [...] Gnad vnd Fried von Gott dem Vater vnd vnserm Herrn Jhesu Christ'; 374, 10–11: 'Thus I commend you all to the LORD God' (*Hiemit will ich euch alle Gott dem HERRN befohlen haben*).

169 Luther, *An die Ratsherren aller Städte deutschen Landes, 1524* (*Appeal to the Councillors of all Cities of the German Nation*), WA 15: 46, 15: 'Learn music among the whole of mathematics' (*Die musica mit der gantzen mathematica lernen*).

of music in the *Preface* and his reflections on the creation of the universe in the *Vorlesungen über 1. Mose* (*Lectures on Genesis*).[170] Music not only occupied a chief position among the quadrivial arts. For Luther, it undoubtedly is the first of the four mathematical arts. As he famously observed in a letter to the Bavarian court composer Ludwig Senfl (1530): 'the prophets [Psalmists] did not make use of any [quadrivial] art other than music, attaching their theology neither to geometry, nor arithmetic, nor astronomy, but to music'.[171]

At the same time, for Luther and his followers, music formed an important bridge between the quadrivial and trivial arts.[172] His positioning of music between the three rhetorical arts and the three mathematical arts enabled him to trace distinctive groups of three in the philosophical arts themselves: three mathematical arts, three rhetorical arts, and music, which in itself was based on a number of tripartite units.[173] This buttressed his opinion that the blessed Trinity was all-pervasive in the philosophical arts:[174]

> in astronomy, motion, light, and flux; in music, the three notes re, mi, fa; in geometry, the three dimensions lines, surfaces, and bodies; in grammar, the three parts of an oration; in the Hebrew language, the three-letter root of each word; in arithmetic, three numbers; in rhetoric, disposition, elocution, and action or gesture [...] in dialectic, definition, division, and argument.[175]

170 Luther, *Vorlesungen über 1. Mose von 1535–45* (*Lectures on Genesis*), WA 42: 94, 32–5: 'In the same way in which they no longer marvel at the incredible light the sun gives, because it is given daily, we no longer marvel at the countless other gifts of creation either, for we have become deaf to what Pythagoras aptly called this wonderful and most lovely music coming from the harmonies of the motions that are in the celestial spheres' (*Sic non admirantur illam admirabilem solis lucem, quia quotidiana est, non admirantur alia creationis dona infinita, obsurduimus enim ad hace, sicut Pythagoras bene dixit, mirabilem concentum et suavissimum aedi ab illa harmonia motum, qui sunt in ordibus coelestibus*).

171 Luther to Senfl, October 1530, WA Br 5: 639, 18–20, no. 1727: 'Prophetae nulla sic arte sint usi ut musica, dum suam theologiam non in geometriam, non in arithemeticam, non in astronomiam, sed in musicam digesserunt'.

172 As exemplified by its positioning at the centre of the seven liberal arts in the 1589 bas-relief at Lemgo town hall.

173 For instance, Luther's division of natural music into *musica mundana, musica humana,* and *musica caelestis,* as discussed above in this chapter.

174 A concept taken on by numerous Lutheran musicologists, among them Burmeister: 'That from the one godhead of the triad who would deny you derived / your beginning, O divine music?' (*Abs uno triados, quis te duxisse negaret, / Numine, principium, musica dia, tuum?*); Joachim Burmeister, *Hypomnematum musicae poeticae* (Rostock: Reusner, 1599), in *Joachim Burmeister: Musical Poetics*, trans. and ed. by Benito V. Rivera (New Haven, CT: Yale University Press, 1993), pp. 212–13.

175 Luther, *Tischreden* (*Table Talk*), WA Tr 1: 395, 10–16, no. 815: 'In astronomia motus, lumen ac influentia, in musica re mi fa, tres tantum notae, in geometria tres dimensiones: linea,

Luther's liberal use of ideas common to Matthäus Herbenus, one of the foremost humanist interpreters of the relationship between music and rhetoric, in the compilation of his *Preface* further underlines the importance of music as a connector between the quadrivial and the trivial arts. Music relates as much to rhetoric as it does to arithmetic, to dialectic and geometry, to grammar as well as to the grammar of the universe, astronomy. It therefore forms a natural link between what later came to be classified as 'the sciences' and 'the arts'. Luther highlighted this central function of music in epitomising philosophical learning by naming music as the foremost of the seven liberal arts: 'music is the best of the arts'.[176]

Luther's famous dictum that music was 'next to theology' makes much more sense when understood in terms of his perception of music as the most important of the seven liberal arts.[177] If music epitomised all philosophical learning, it naturally was next to theology: it did, after all, present the sum of all other learning and therefore comes a close second to the queen of sciences; it comes 'next after theology'. Luther affirmed: 'I plainly judge and do not hesitate to affirm that, after theology', not itself one of the seven liberal arts, 'there is no art that can equal music'.[178] In that way, music is akin to theology, but not the same as theology: it remains a philosophical art with its own important function of summing up and unifying the traditional sciences and the arts.

Finally, for Luther music had supernatural qualities: 'it is a great enemy of Satan, and an instrument to drive away temptations (*Anfechtungen*) and evil thoughts'.[179] Because of its ability to enable people to withstand *Anfechtungen*, music for Luther intriguingly also assumed a function akin to that of late-scholastic supernatural habitual grace.[180] Luther's opinion that music enabled people to endure the very *Anfechtungen* that led him to challenge the

---

superficies, corpus, in grammatica tres orationum partes, in dictione apud Ebraeos tres literae substantiales, in arithmetica tres numeri, in rhetorica dispositio, elocutio et actio seu gestus [...] in dialectica definitio, divisio, argumentatio'.

176 Luther, *Tischreden* (*Table Talk*), WA Tr 1: 490, 8, no. 968: 'Musica ist der besten Künsten eine'.

177 Luther, *Tischreden* (*Table Talk*), WA Tr 6: 348, 22–4, no. 7034: 'Ich gebe nach der Theologie der Musica den nähesten Locum und höchste Ehre'.

178 Luther, *Briefwechsel* (*Letters*), WA Br 5: 639, 12–13, no. 1727: 'Et plane iudicio, nec pudet asserere, post theologiam esse nullam artem, quae musicae possit aequari'; WA 50: 371, 1; 25.

179 Luther, *Tischreden* (*Table Talk*), WA Tr 1: 490, 6–7, no. 968: 'Der ist der Satan sehr feind, damit man viel Anfechtunge und böse Gedanken vertreibt'.

180 Luther, *Tischreden* (*Table Talk*), WA Tr 1: 490, 22–3: 'Music is halfway to being a disciplinarian and a mistress of manners that makes humans milder and mellower, more courteous and more sensible, more decent and more reasonable' (*Musica ist eine halbe Disciplin und Zuchtmeisterin, so die Leute gelindert und sanftmüthiger, sittsamer und vernüftiger macht*).

late-medieval doctrine of justification in the first place is theologically significant. Like the scholastic supernatural habit of grace, music also was a free gift (*Gabe, donum*) created by God.[181] Like the habit of grace, music was in itself grace-filled (*gnadenreich*).[182] Like the habit of grace, music had a profound effect on the human soul, encouraging and enabling other habits of goodness and grace.[183] In this way, while it was not in itself an agent of justification, music contributed to the formation of a character or *habitus* that closely resembled the late-scholastic supernatural habit of grace (*gratia creata*). As Luther made clear in his *Marginalia to Peter Lombard's Sentences* (1509–1512), rejecting the scholastic distinction between created and uncreated grace as artificial, 'that habit is the Holy Spirit'.[184]

Despite its close resemblance to a created habit of grace, music was never in itself able to promote justification, a process that could only be accomplished by the uncreated grace of the Holy Spirit. As an instrument of the Holy Spirit, however, music shared in the work of the Spirit, in particular in its function as a communicator of spiritual gifts to humankind.[185] Furthermore, the practice of music for the purposes of God's praise could confirm a habit of goodness that enabled performers and hearers of music alike to believe in their justification and, out of that faith, joyfully sing of it. It is this quality of music to enable humans to sing the story of salvation, 'especially when sung by the entire congregation together', which convinced Luther of the importance of music as a tool for proclamation of his theological message and his Reformation.[186] Music was best employed 'to speak and preach of the promise and grace of God so that others might come to hear of it and partake of it [...] and to incite people to do good, and teach them'.[187] As a result, music education formed the nucleus

---

181 Luther, *Praefatio* (*Preface*), WA 50: 368, 4: 'Donum illud diuinum'; 368, 17–18: 'sehr schöne vnd köstliche Gabe Gottes'; *Tischreden* (*Table Talk*), WA Tr 1: 490, 6, no. 968: 'Der schönsten und herrlichsten Gaben Gottes eine ist die Musica'.

182 Luther, *Deutsche Bibel* (*German Bible*), WA DB 7: 235.

183 Luther, *Tischreden* (*Table Talk*), WA Tr 1: 490: 22–3; cf., above at n. 177.

184 Luther, *Randbemerkungen zu den Sentenzen des Petrus Lombardus* (*Marginalia and Comments on Peter Lombard's Sentences*), 1509–12, WA 9: 44, 4 'Habitus autem adhuc est spiritus sanctus'.

185 Luther, *Praefatio* (*Preface*), WA 50: 371, 10–11: 'The Spirit's gifts were instilled in the Prophets through music' (*Dona sua* [*Spiritus Sancti*] *per eam* [*musicam*] *Prophetis illabi*).

186 Luther, *Von den letzten Worten Davids* (*Of the Last Words of David*), 1543, LW 15: 274, WA 54: 34, 1 'Wo der hauffe mit singet'.

187 *Worte Davids* (*Words of David*), LW 15: 273, WA 54: 33, 18–22: 'Redet und prediget von solcher verheissung und gnade Gottes, das ander Leute auch dazu komen, und der teilhaftig werden [...] auch die menschen nützlich zu reitzen und zu leren'.

for much of Luther's pedagogical concept, just as the composition and singing of hymns are central to the communication of his Reformation message.[188]

Notwithstanding this appreciation and effective use of music as a practical instrument in spreading the theological insights of his Reformation, for Luther music remained an art: both a philosophical art as well as a practical art. It is his positioning of music at the nexus between the Reformation, on the one hand, and the late-medieval schools, theology and philosophy, the arts and the sciences, on the other, combined with his profound appreciation of music as a gift of God capable of inspiring a response of love for the Creator, which makes Luther's theory and practice of music so valuable and fascinating. There is no doubt that, among the reformers, Luther was indeed both 'the musician and erudite philosopher'.[189]

---

188 For Luther's educational use of hymns and music, see Chapter 2, and Brown, *Singing the Gospel*, pp. 54–76.

189 Crotus Rubeanus [Johannes Jäger] to Luther, October 1520, *Briefe 1520–22*, WA Br 2: 91, 141–2; cf., n. 3 above.

CHAPTER 2

# Hymns and Sacred Songs

The establishment of an enduring choral tradition is one of the hallmarks of the Lutheran Reformation.[1] One of the key motivators for the development of such a distinctive devotional tradition that placed music and singing at the centre of its worship and teaching was undoubtedly the personal affinity Martin Luther had for music. As we have seen in the previous chapter, he was not only a competent singer, hymn writer and composer but also strongly believed that music was an ideal means to come to know and proclaim the mystery of God.[2] Luther particularly valued the combination of music and message, the 'singing preaching and praising of God's grace and mercy' afforded by spiritual songs.[3] The deliberate promotion of music and music-making became a central part of his Reformation.

In the same way in which Lutheran compositions were able to convey insights into the being and nature of God, the performance of these works enabled communities to share in 'singing and preaching' the good news.[4] Communal music-making played an important part in bringing communities together and helped create the specifically 'Lutheran' identity associated with singing and music that prevails to date.[5] Luther's insight into the essential beauty of the combination of Scripture and music was so attractive, and his appreciation of music as a means of promoting his message so compelling, that it motivated composers, hymn writers, cantors, teachers and, above all, singers, to promote Scripture and the message of the Reformation by encouraging people to sing together in harmony, 'adorned by polyphony'.[6]

1 An earlier version of this chapter was published as Loewe, 'Why do Lutherans sing?', 69–89.

2 See, in particular, Luther, *Praefatio zu den Symphoniae Iucundae* (*Preface to the Symphoniae Iucundae*), *1538*, LW 53: 321–324, WA 50: 371, 38–39.

3 Luther, *Praefatio* (*Preface*), WA 50: 372, 19: 'Klingendem predigen vnd rhümen von Gottes güte vnd gnade'. LW only translates the Latin version of the *Preface*. See below, Appendix 1: Luther's Preface to the *Symphoniae Iucundae*, for the Latin and German versions, and an English translation by Dr Leofranc Holford-Strevens.

4 Luther, *Praefatio* (*Preface*), WA 50: 372, 4: 'Sonora praedicatione', LW 53: 323 has chosen to render this with the more generic 'proclaiming the Word of God through music'. As in the previous chapter, we will be using the translation included in Appendix 1.

5 Luther, *Praefatio* (*Preface*), WA 50: 372, 19: 'Klingendem predigen'.

6 Luther, *Praefatio* (*Preface*), WA 50: 372, 13–4: 'Mit viel stimmen geschmückt'.

 | DOI:10.1163/9789004527430_004

## 1 Singing, Preaching, and Praising God through Music

Spurred on by his insight that music was an ideal means to communicate theological truth, from an early point of his Reformation onwards Luther intentionally began to use popular song as a means to broadcast his message effectively to a large cross-section of society. His popular vernacular hymns were able to reach people swiftly, regardless of their ability to read, their social standing or their actual location, and effortlessly crossed national, cultural, and socioeconomic boundaries. They skilfully bridged the divide between the secular and sacred, the domestic and the public, the here-and-now and the eternal. While all his hymns served to underline the importance of the Reformation not all of them primarily spoke of the mystery of God.

Luther's first published hymn was, in fact, a *Zeitungslied* (newspaper song) in which he commented on current affairs as an editorial or opinion piece:[7] a ballad based on a popular *Volkslied* or *Meistersinger* tune, his *Eyn newes lyed wyr heben an* ('A New Song Here Shall Be Begun') strongly condemned the burning of two young Augustinian canons turned Protestant 'at Brussels in the Netherlands' in July 1523.[8] Luther commended their conversion to the Reformation, censured their condemnation by the Catholic authorities, and celebrated their gospel witness: 'for [God's] Word they life disdained, and have become his martyrs'.[9] Using their witness as an example, he encouraged the singers and listeners of his hymn to use their own voices to 'go gladly singing' about their deeds and doctrine, 'in every land / in tongues of every people'.[10]

In an age of significant illiteracy, singing the Reformation message to popular tunes was a powerful and effective means of disseminating Luther's views.[11]

7 For an extensive reflection on Luther's *Eyn newes lyed*, see Kai Bremer, 'Bekenntnis und Bekehrung. Überlegungen zu Text und Kontext von Luthers "Eyn newes lied"', in *Musik und Reformation—Politisierung, Medialisierung, Missionierung*, ed. by Christiane Wiesenfeldt and Stefan Menzel, Beiträge zur Geschichte der Kirchenmusik im Auftrag der Görres-Gesellschaft, 22 (Paderborn: Ferdinand Schoenigh, 2020), pp. 175–86.

8 Luther, *Lieder*, WA 35: 411, 8: 'Zu Brüssel in dem niederlandt'; for a detailed development history of the song, see WA 35: 91–97, for a consideration of the song and the genre of *Zeitungslieder* (newspaper songs), see Paul F. Casey, '"Start spreading the News": Martin Luther's first published song', in *In laudem Caroli: Renaissance and Reformation Studies for Charles Garfield Nauert*, ed. by James V. Mehl and others (Kirksville: Thomas Jefferson University Press, 1998), pp. 75–94.

9 Luther, *Eyn newes lyed wyr heben an* ('A New Song Here Shall Be Begun'), LW 53: 214, WA 35: 412, 8–9: 'Fur sein [God's] wordt sind gestorbenn/ Sein martrer sind sie worden'.

10 Luther, *Eyn newes lyed* ('A New Song'), LW 53: 216, WA 35: 415, 9: 'Gar frolich lassen singen', 7–8: 'An allem ort / mit aller stym und zungen'.

11 For Luther's early hymns, see *Luthers geistliche Lieder und Kirchengesänge*, ed. by Markus Jenny, AWA, 4 (Köln: Böhlau, 1985), pp. 12–13.

His combination of pithy, vernacular words with popular tunes not only provided a 'meeting point between the illiterate, the semi-literate and the literate' but enabled the rapid spread of Lutheran thought across national boundaries.[12] Communicated by word of mouth, letter and broadsheet, Luther's hymns were soon sung throughout Germany, even in Catholic regions where his writings were banned. At the turn of the seventeenth century, the Leipzig theologian Cornelius Becker reflected on how freely Luther's hymns had been able to spread to Catholic principalities that otherwise routinely intercepted Reformation writings at the border:[13]

> Since his sacred songs were carried to people in far-away places by letter, as well as in the souls and minds of pious Christians, it was not as easy to block their progress as [it was to intercept Luther's] books and writings.[14]

For most of his early hymns, Luther provided new vernacular words for existing popular sacred and secular tunes. He explained that he had derived this ingeniously simple method of word-setting from Virgil's *Menalcas*: 'If you sing the music, I will sing the text'.[15] In his word-setting as well as in his translation of Scripture, he closely imitated the way people spoke: 'both the text and notes, accent, melody and manner of rendering ought to grow out of the true mother tongue and its inflection'.[16] At the same time, he took great care in setting words to melodies that people knew well. For Luther, a popular plainchant melody was as useful as a *Volkslied* or *Meistersinger* tune; he was convinced

12 Scribner, *For the Sake of Simple Folk*, p. 5; for a critique of Scribner's methodology, see Brown, *Singing the Gospel*, pp. 4–5.

13 For Becker and his Lutheran Psalter, *Der Psalter Davids Gesangweis* (Leipzig: Apel Lantzenberger, 1602), see Friedrich Wilhelm Bautz, 'Cornelius Becker', in *BBKL* (Hamm: Traugott Bautz, 1990), II, 449–50.

14 Cornelius Becker, *Der Psalter Davids Gesangweis*, reproduced in Philipp Wackernagel, *Bibliographie zur Geschichte des deutschen Kirchenliedes im XVI. Jahrhundert* (Frankfurt a.M.: Heyder & Zimmer, 1855), No. 100, 679–689 (p. 680): 'Sinetmal diesen nicht so leicht, wie andern seinen Büchern vn Schrifften, der Weg hat verhawen warden, wenn die geistlichen Geseng in Brieffen, auch im sinn vnd gedechtnis frommer Christen fortgebracht, vnd den Leuten frembder örten mitgetheilet worden'.

15 Luther, *Tischreden* (*Table Talk*), WA Tr 1: 490, 20–21: 'Wie der [Menalcas] sagt beym Virgilio: Tu calamos inflare leves, ego dicere versus; Singe du die Noten, so will ich den Text singen'; WA Tr 4: 32, 21–22: 'Sing du die noten, so will ich den text singen'; see Virgil, *Bucolica: Eclogue 5, Daphnis*, 3–4.

16 Luther, *Wider die himmlischen Propheten* (*Against the Heavenly Prophets*), 1525, LW 40: 141, WA 18: 123, 22–23: 'Es mus beyde text und notten, accent, weise vnd geperde aus rechter mutter sprach und stymme kommen'.

that 'the notes make the text come to life'.[17] His vernacular hymns were therefore carefully attuned to his audience. It was not sufficient to set his German translations of Latin hymns to existing plainchant tunes, since in the end 'it doesn't sound polished or well done'.[18] Well crafted, sung to well-known tunes and with a familiar turn of phrase, they were popular, topical and quickly and widely disseminated.[19] At a time when vernacular hymns were rarely sung in church (although they were frequently used in Passion or Corpus Christi plays), their widespread use in Protestant worship was 'a mark of religious change as notable as the marriage of clergy or the distribution of the cup to the laity', and proved to be just as transformational.[20]

Luther's first published sacred hymns, a paraphrase of Psalm 130, *Aus tiefer Not schrei ich zu dir* ('From Trouble Deep I Cry To Thee'), and a paraphrase of Psalm 51, *Es woll uns Gott genädig sein* ('May God Have Mercy On Us All'), were both published in the first half of 1524.[21] Both are documented to have been important vehicles in furthering the Reformation. Travellers who had learnt them by heart took them beyond Wittenberg into areas where Luther's writings were banned.[22] The town chronicle of the Catholic archiepiscopal see Magdeburg records that in May 1524 *Aus tieffer Not* ('From Trouble Deep') and *Es woll uns Gott* ('May God Have Mercy') were taught to locals and that the hymns proved to be ready agents of conversion:

17 Luther, *Tischreden* (*Table Talk*), WA Tr 2: 518, 6–7, no. 2545b: 'Die nothen machen den text lebendig'.

18 Luther, *Wider die himmlischen Propheten* (*Against the Heavenly Prophets*), LW 40: 141, WA 18: 123, 22: 'Es laut nicht ertig noch rechtschaffen'.

19 For a discussion on the debate concerning whether Luther intentionally used popular tunes, see Leaver, *Luther's Liturgical Music*, pp. 12–18.

20 Brown, *Singing the Gospel*, p. 9. For the use of hymns and secular songs in late-medieval Passion and Easter dramas, and Lutheran teaching dramas, see Chapter 6 below.

21 For the hymn, *Aus tieffer not schrey ich zu dyr* ('From Trouble Deep I Cry To Thee'), see LW 53: 221–224, WA 35: 419, 11; for a detailed development history of the hymn, see WA 35: 97–109. For the hymn, *Es woll uns Gott genedig seyn* ('May God Have Mercy On Us All'), see LW 53: 232–234, WA 35: 418, 4–5; for its development history, see WA 35: 123–124 (AWA, 4, pp. 55–61 suggests a slightly different development history).

22 AWA, 4, pp. 19–23; see also R. W. Scribner, 'Flugblatt und Analphabetentum', in *Flugschriften als Massenmedium der Reformationszeit, Beiträge zum Tübinger Symposion 1980*, ed. by Hans-Joachim Köhler and others, Spätmittelalter und frühe Neuzeit, 13 (Stuttgart: Klett-Cotta, 1981), pp. 65–76 (pp. 69–70), and Christopher Brown, 'Devotional Life in Hymns, Liturgy, Music and Prayer', in *Lutheran Ecclesiastical Culture 1550–1675*, ed. by Robert Kolb and others, Brill Companion to the Christian Tradition, 11 (Leiden: Brill, 2008), pp. 205–58 (pp. 209–10).

> Husband and wife, young women and men, so many people learnt [Luther's hymns] that his German hymns and Psalms became so well known that they were sung by the people daily in all churches before the sermons commenced, publicly, over and over again.[23]

The recurrent massed singing of Lutheran hymns in Magdeburg before the beginning of Catholic services caused such a public disturbance that it led to the imprisonment of the distributor of the hymns, 'an itinerant peddler'.[24] The city chronicle records how in turn this arrest led to an 'uproar' in St John's Parish on 6 May 1524 that brought 'six to eight hundred people together to liberate the prisoner by force'.[25] When Luther came to Magdeburg to preach at St John's Church on 26 June 1524, therefore, his visit merely formalised the introduction of the Reformation in the city: his hymns had, in fact, already won over the majority of residents.[26]

When the first printed collection of Lutheran hymns was published in the second half of 1524, Luther commented in his introduction on why he wrote hymns: 'I have [...] compiled several hymns, so that the holy gospel which now by the grace of God has risen anew may be noised and spread abroad'.[27] So popular was this collection of hymns that they were sold in the streets: printers worked feverishly to meet demand and made effective use of advertising to keep up sales.[28] Indeed, Luther remarked that printers made their hymnal 'attractive to the people with all sorts of ornamentations' in order to sell more of them, and commended them for their contribution to spreading his

23 *Die Chroniken der niedersächsischen Städte: Magdeburg*, ed. by Gustav Hertel and others, Die Chroniken der deutschen Städte vom 14. bis 16. Jahrhundert, 27, 2 vols (Leipzig: Verlag von S. Hirtzel, 1869–99), II, 143, 8–10: 'Leret Mann und Weib, auch Jungfrawen und Gesellen, so viele, das die deutschen Lieder und Psalmen so gemeine worden, daß die von gemeinem Volcke dieselbigen dornach teglich in allen Kirchen, ehe man die Predigten angefangen, offentlich gesungen und noch singet'.

24 *Chroniken der niedersächsischen Städte*, II, 143, 5: 'Ein loser Bettler'.

25 *Chroniken der niedersächsischen Städte*, II, 143, 20: 'Aufruhr', 14–16: 'Kamen im nw uber sechß– oder acht hundert Menschen zusamen und brachten den gefangenen mit gewalt darauß'.

26 For Luther's influential Magdeburg sermon on true and false righteousness, see Oliver K. Olson, 'Theology of Revolution: Magdeburg, 1550–1551', *The Sixteenth Century Journal*, 3.1 (1972), 56–79 (pp. 63).

27 Luther, *Vorrede des Wittenberger Gesangbuches* (*Preface to the Wittenberg Hymnal*), 1524, LW 53: 316, WA 35: 474, 11–4: 'Hab ich auch [...] ettliche geystliche lieder zusamen bracht, das heylige Euangelion, so itzt von Gottes gnaden wider auff gangen ist, zu treyben und ynn schwanck zu bringen'.

28 *Chroniken der niedersächsischen Städte*, II, 143, 5–6; for the impact of the mass-distribution of Luther's hymns, see Brown, *Singing the Gospel*, pp. 5–7 (p. 2, Figure 1.1).

doctrine:[29] 'the printers do well if they publish a lot of good hymns [...] so that they may move [people] to joy in faith and to gladly sing'.[30] Once printed, just as in Magdeburg, vendors would teach Luther's hymns to the illiterate or semiliterate. Cornelius Becker's reflection on the progress of the Reformation message through Luther's hymns is not exaggerated:

> By God's blessing, Luther's hymns and other sacred songs swiftly furthered the progress of the Word of God from Saxony to other places throughout the German Nation, unfettered by the dreaded darkness and terrible tyranny of the papacy, and they have done well.[31]

Luther's contemporaries shared his success; indeed, the reformer's fear that there might be a dearth of suitable poets to promote Reformation doctrine through songs and hymns, first articulated in 1523, proved to be entirely unfounded.[32] In 1528, Luther reflected in his introduction to a second collection of hymns how the number of Reformation hymns and hymn writers had significantly increased: 'Now there are some who have given a good account of themselves and augmented the hymns so that they by far surpass me and are my masters indeed'.[33] Towards the end of his life, in 1545, Luther reflected once again on the success of his hymns: his spiritual songs had communicated the message of the liberty of the gospel with joy and had proved to be infectious. Luther explained:

---

29 Luther, *Die Vorrede zum Babstschen Gesangbuch* (*Preface to the Babst Hymnal*), 1545, LW 53: 333, WA 35: 477, 14: 'Mit allerley zierde den leuten angeneme machen'.

30 Luther, *Vorrede zum Babstschen Gesangbuch* (*Preface to the Babst Hymnal*), LW 53: 333, WA 35: 477, 13–5: 'Darumb thun die drucker sehr wol daran, das sie gute lieder vleissig drucken [...] damit sie [the people] zu solcher freude des glaubens gereitzt werden, und gerne singen'.

31 Wackernagel, *Bibliographie zur Geschichte*, p. 680: 'Das auch Gottes Wort, durch die grausame finsternis vnt schreckliche tyranny des Bapstthumbs vngehindert, schnellen lauffes, aus Sachsen an andere örter Deutscher Nation fort gerückt, vnd so wol gerathen, darzu haben für andern Lutheri Psalmen vnd andere Christliche Gesenge, durch Gottes segen treffliche beförderung gethan'.

32 Luther, *Formulae Missae* (*Order of Mass*), 1523, LW 53: 37, WA 12: 218, 31–2: 'I mention this to encourage any German poets to compose evangelical hymns for us' (*Si qui sunt poetae germanici, extimulentur et nobis poemata pietatis endant*). For Luther's liturgical reforms, see Leaver, *Luther's Liturgical Music*, pp. 227–73, and Joseph Herl, *Worship Wars in Early Lutheranism: Choir, Congregation and Three Centuries of Conflict* (New York: Oxford University Press, 2004), pp. 23–36.

33 Luther, *Ein newe Vorrede Martini Luthers* (*Preface to the Weiss Hymnal*), 1528, LW 53: 317, WA 35: 475, 13–4: 'Nu haben sich etliche wol beweiset und die lieder gemehrdt, also das sie mich weit ubertreffen und ynn dem wol meine meister sind'.

Those who believe this earnestly cannot be quiet about it. But they must gladly and willingly sing and speak about it so that others also may come and hear it.[34]

## 2 Lutherans, Music, and the Reformation

In the formative years of the Lutheran Reformation, Luther's understanding of music as an instrument to disseminate the biblical and Reformation message was promoted at all levels of society. The illiterate and semiliterate, reluctant and competent readers alike, clergy and laypeople, working people, clerks, teachers and children, all shared a common hymnody. Singing and music were central to proclaiming the teachings of the Reformation and helped to create a specifically Lutheran identity. Hymns served 'not only as a means of public instruction and of corporate worship, but also as the basis for the private pedagogy and devotions of individuals and households'.[35] From the outset of the Reformation, music was used as an instrument to improve literacy, unlock Scripture and promote evangelical learning, in particular among the young.[36] In Lutheran schools, students were 'taught to sing Psalms and spiritual songs', a dual process that enabled them both to recall Reformation teachings and fostered their reading skills.[37] Even if children could not be taught to write, then they should at least be taught to read, the 1543 Brunswick School Ordinances (*Schulordnungen*) stipulated, 'which they ought to be able to learn in a year or two'.[38] It is uncertain whether in Lutheran schools the alphabet was taught

---

34 Luther, *Vorrede zum Babstschen Gesangbuch* (*Preface to the Bapst Hymnal*), 1545, LW 53: 333, WA 35: 477, 8–9: 'Wer solchs mit ernst gleubet, der kans nicht lassen, er mus fröhlich und mit lust dauon singen und sagen, das es andere auch hören und herzu kommen'.

35 Brown, *Singing the Gospel*, p. 8.

36 Luther, *An die Ratsherren aller Städte deutschen Landes* (*Appeal to the Councillors of all Cities of the German Nation*), 1524, LW 45/2: 368, WA 15: 44, 25–33: 'This one consideration alone would be sufficient to justify the establishment everywhere of the very best schools for both boys and girls, namely, that in order to maintain its temporal estate outwardly the world must have good and capable men and women [...] Therefore, it is a matter of properly educating and training our boys and girls to that end' (*So were doch alleyn dise ursach gnugsam, die aller besten schulen beyde fur knaben und meydlin an allen ortten auff zu richten, das die wellt, auch yhren welltlichen stand eusserlich zu halten, doch bedarf seiner geschickter menner und frawen.* [...] *Darumb ists zu thun, das man kneblin und meydlin dazu recht lere und auff zihe*).

37 *Evangelische Schulordnungen, I: Die evangelischen Schulordnungen des Sechzehnten Jahrhunderts* [*ES*], ed. by Reinhold Vormbaum (Gütersloh: Bertelsmann, 1860), p. 50: 'Men schal en dar Psalme vnd Geistliche Gesänge singen leren'.

38 *ES*, p. 50: 'Welk se in einem edder twen Jahren lehren könen'.

by singing or, as suggested by Gawthrop and Strauss, that 'children learned to sound out words by intoning Luther's *Shorter Catechism*'.[39] However, there is no doubt that pupils learnt their Psalms by first singing and then reciting Psalm hymns as was the case in the Wittenberg Girls' School (*Junckfrawen Schuele*).[40] Psalm hymns used for teaching in Wittenberg schools included Luther's paraphrases of Psalm 12, *Ach Gott im Himmel sieh darein* ('Ah God, From Heaven Look Down') or Psalm 14, *Es spricht der Unweisen Mund* ('Although the Fools Say With Their Mouth').[41] Similarly, Brunswick students first leant the Catechism by singing Luther's Catechism hymns (*Katechismuslieder*), including *Wir gleuben all an einen Gott* ('In One True God We All Believe') and *Vater unser* ('Our Father').[42]

As a result, in Lutheran schools, students sang a lot, preferably in four-part harmony. In his preface to the 1524 Wittenberg Hymnal Luther had explained that the hymns had been 'arranged in four parts, for no other reason than that I should like the young to be trained in music and other fine arts; for that they should and ought to be'.[43] The ordinances of the Wittenberg Girls' School translated Luther's wishes into curriculum requirements, stipulating that the girls 'shall all learn to sing Psalms and other spiritual songs together' in four-part harmony.[44] Twice a week, on Wednesdays and Saturdays, they would spend a

---

39 Richard Gawthrop and Gerald Strauss, 'Protestantism and Literacy in Early Modern Germany', *Past and Present*, 104 (1984), 31–55 (pp. 48); see *August Hermann Francke: Schriften über Erziehung und Unterricht*, ed. by Karl Richter, Pädagogische Bibliothek: eine Sammlung der wichtigsten pädagogischen Schriften älterer und neuerer Zeit, 5 (Leipzig: Siegismund und Volkening, 1872), p. 400: 'In order that children may learn to sing and, over time, recite by heart the old hymns by Dr Luther and other spiritual writers' (*Daß die Kinder die alten Gesänge D. Lutheri und anderer Geist-reichen Männer singen lernen, auch sie mit der Zeit auswendig hersagen können*). 'Recitieren' and 'hersagen' suggests that children repeated rather than intoned the *Shorter Catechism*.

40 ES, p. 27.

41 For *Ach Gott im Himmel* ('Ah God, From Heaven'), see WA 35, 109–120 and LW 53: 221–228; for *Es spricht der Unweisen Mund* ('Although the Fools Say With Their Mouth'), see WA 35, 121–2 and LW 53: 229–31.

42 For a thorough analysis of Luther's *Katechismuslieder*, see Groote, 'Musikalische Katechismen', pp. 201–220 (pp. 204–13), and Leaver, *Luther's Liturgical Music*, pp. 107–72; for an analysis of *Wir gleuben all in einen Gott* ('In One True God We All Believe'), see WA 35, 172–77 and LW 53: 271–73, for an analysis of *Vater unser* ('Our Father'), see WA 35, 270–81 and LW 53: 295–298.

43 Luther, *Vorrede des Wittenberger Gesangbuches* (*Preface to the Wittenberg Hymnal*), 1524, LW 53: 316, WA 35: 474, 18–20: 'Und sind dazu auch ynn vier stymme bracht, nicht aus anderer ursach, denn das ich gerne wollte, die iugent, die doch sonst soll und mus ynn der Musica und andern rechten künsten erzogen werden'.

44 ES, p. 27: 'Sollen sie alle miteinander lernen singen psalmen vnd andere geistliche gesenge'.

morning learning 'to pray the Catechism and learn other useful [Bible] verses and short Psalms' by heart.[45] Girls who had mastered literacy learnt to sing in parts and to read music: 'they shall be shown musical notation, so that they can learn to read music', the Wittenberg School Ordinances stipulated.[46] The same held true in Brunswick: in order to promote both literacy and music, the Brunswick School ordinances provided for cantors to teach music notation:

> Parts and clefs and whatever else is required for such music, so that they may learn to sing confidently and in tune. [...] In this way all children and youths shall be taught to sing at school.[47]

In the second half of the sixteenth century, the pastor of St Thomas', superintendent of Leipzig, and prolific hymn writer, Nikolaus Selnecker, commended the method of learning by singing to all people—characteristically by writing a hymn, *Vmb erhaltung bey der Christlichen Lehre des heiligen Kinder-Catechismi* ('Maintenance of Christian Teaching through the Holy Catechism for Children').[48] At a time when Lutherans needed to be kept 'from false teachers', in his hymn he commended the singing of the Catechism as a way of learning and remembering orthodox teachings:

---

45 ES, p. 27: 'Beten zu lernen Catechismum vnd andere nutzliche spruche oder kurtz psalmen'. The same was true in Brunswick; ES, p. 50: 'And in the Small Catechism of Doctor Luther, learn first the blessed words of the Catechism, and then the meaning of the words in the same Catechism' (*Vnnd den kleinen Catechismum Doctoris Lutheri, ersten die hilligen Wörde des Catechismi, darna die korte Bedüdinge der Wörder, alse in dem Catechismo steyt*).

46 ES, p. 27: 'Es soll auch den jhenigen, so lesen konnen, die scola musicalus furgemalt werden, daß sie etlicher maß lernen solemnisiren'.

47 ES, p. 16: 'Voces, Claues, vnde wat mehr höret to sulker Musica, dat se leren vaste singen vnde renlick [...] Su scholen in der Schole alle kyndere vnde ungen singen lernen'.

48 For Selnecker, author of the *History of the Augsburg Confession* (1584) and one of the editors of the *Formula of Concord* (1580), see Werner Klän, 'Der "vierte Mann". Auf den Spuren von Nikolaus Selneckers (1530–92), Beitrag zu Entstehung und Verbreitung der Konkordienformel', *Lutherische Theologie und Kirche*, 17 (1993), 145–74, and Wolfdietrich von Kloeden, 'Selnecker, Nikolaus', in BBKL, IX, 1376–79. Philipp Wackernagel, *Das deutsche Kirchenlied von der ältesten zeit bis zu Anfang des 17. Jahrhunderts: mit Berücksichtigung der deutschen kirchlichen Lieddichtung im weiteren Sinne und der lateinischen von Hilarius bis Georg Fabricius und Wolfgang Ammonius*, 4 (Leipzig: Teubner, 1870), no. 382, 'Vmb erhaltung bey der Christlichen Lehre des heiligen Kinder-Catechismi', 282: 'At this time, by your grace / keep us from false teachers, Lord' (*Es thut jetzt not, durch deine güt / für falschen Lehrern vns behüt*).

By the learning of our youth keep us,
By the Catechism, dear Lord, keep us!
By your truth, sanctify us,
By your Word, master our own.[49]

## 3 Lutheran Music in the Second Half of the Sixteenth Century

The time between Luther's death in 1546 and the turn of the seventeenth century saw significant growth in music education in Lutheran schools. By the second half of the sixteenth century, music education for children from all social backgrounds was firmly established in Reformation Germany. The 1559 Württemberg School Ordinances reflect the policies of other Protestant principalities in stipulating that all children, 'even working children' were to learn:

> to read and write for their own benefit and the benefit of others, so that they may be better educated and brought up as Christians, and be taught the singing of Psalms at the same time.[50]

Because music had become so central in communicating the Reformation message, the 1530s and 40s had seen the deliberate fostering of music education and music-making in Lutheran schools and parishes. Not only were students themselves taught through the medium of music, but they also were encouraged to promote the Reformation message by what they sang and how they worshipped: as the first Lutheran generation of students was educated, both teachers and students modelled Lutheran music, doctrine and forms of worship to the wider community. In his 1539 rejection of Catholic councils, *Von den Konziliis und Kirchen* (*On the Councils and the Church*), Luther explained how a new generation of students had the potential to convert the nation by their 'living example':

> Everybody learns from students, without any trouble or effort. Therefore the masses will also learn from the students what, when and how to sing

49 Wackernagel, *Kirchenlied*, no. 383, p. 281: 'Erhalt uns bei der kinderlehr, / beim Katechismo, lieber Herr! / Heilig uns in der wahrheit dein, / dein wort laß unsern meister sein'.

50 *ES*, p. 71: 'Derselben arbeitenden Kinder'; 'Schreibens und lesens jren selbs vnd gemeines Nutzes wegen, deßgleichen mit Psalmen singen dester baß vnderricht, vnd Christenlich aufferzogen'.

> in church. They will learn what to sing at the bier and the grave. When the students kneel and fold their hands in prayer, or when the school master beats time with his baton during the singing of 'And was made man'—everybody will imitate them […] if they are so moved by living examples.[51]

Protestant school ordinances stipulated that musically able schoolmasters or cantors were to be appointed in schools to promote the Reformation message through music. School children, in turn, were to teach their parents. In this way, entire cities would be converted to the Reformation cause, Luther had foreseen.[52] Music was 'essential to schools', the reformer believed, not only as a way of learning about Scripture and doctrine but more so as a way of promoting reforms in church and community.[53] Indeed, as early as 1528, the Zahna visitation orders made clear that the schoolmaster was to educate not only the children in reading, understanding and performing music and the basic teachings of Luther's doctrine but also to encourage them actively to re-educate their parents:

> The schoolmaster […] ought to teach the children the regular hymns at communion and the hymns before and after the sermon, assiduously teach the children their Catechism, and to instruct them to teach their parents the usual grace at table, and a verse from Scripture, or another good authority, in Latin or German.[54]

---

51 Luther, *Von den Konziliis und Kirchen* (*On the Councils and the Church*), 1539, WA 50: 619, 8–16: 'Denn von den Schülern lernen es die anderen alle, on alle auffsetze und mühe. Also was, wenn und wie die schüler in den Kirchen singen oder beten, so lernts der hauffe hinach. Und was sie uber der leiche oder beim grabe singen, so lernen es die anderen auch. Wenn sie niderknien und die hende falten, so der Schulmeister mit dem stecken klopfft unter dem gesang: "Et homo factus est", so thuts der hauffe hinach […] als durch lebendige exempel bewegt'. The Latin words, 'and was made man', were sung to double note values in order to reflect on the mystery of the Incarnation (and, in Catholic liturgies, to allow clergy and people to genuflect), hence the need to direct the singers.

52 Luther, *Von den Konziliis und Kirchen* (*On the Councils and the Church*), WA 50: 619, 8–10.

53 Luther, *Tischreden* (*Table Talk*), WA Tr 5: 557, 19–20, no. 6248: 'Man muß musicam necessario in der schulen behalten'.

54 *Die Registraturen der Kirchenvisitationen im ehemals sächsischen Kurkreise*, I: *Die Ephorien Wittenberg, Kemberg und Zahna*, ed. by Karl Pallas (Halle: Otto Hendel, 1906), p. 367: 'Der schulmeister […] soll […] die geordneten gesenge der kirchen bei der messen, auch vor und nach ietzlicher predigt singen, und in sunderheit soll er vorflissen sein, die schuler im Catechism zu unterrichten, und das die den eltern die gewonliche segen zu ietzlicher malzeit fur dem tische, abends aber einen seuberlichen sententz oder spruch aus der heiligen schrift oder sunst einem guten lehrer lateinisch under deutsch aufsagen'.

In the second half of the sixteenth century, educators therefore were often musicians who had been recruited according to Luther's own stated preference for musically able candidates: 'A schoolmaster has to be able to sing: otherwise I shall not look at him'.[55] School cantors frequently fulfilled the dual role of church organists and choirmasters. This was the case not only in large cities with established choir schools such as Leipzig, where the cantor of St Thomas' had a significant teaching load at St Thomas' School,[56] or in Wittenberg where the cantor taught at the Latin School,[57] but also in smaller towns and villages such as Düben near Coswig, where the school's director and cantor shared in 'leading the school choir on Wednesdays, Fridays and Sundays at church'.[58]

The arrangements at Düben reflect the teaching practice in smaller Lutheran schools in late sixteenth-century Saxony as a whole: numerous other schools also employed schoolmasters who taught music or cantors who acted as teachers.[59] The Zerbst School Ordinances of 1557, for instance, stipulated that the 'choir be led by the director of the school, just as everywhere else'; the Schmiedeburg Ordinances of 1575 show that the cantor taught Latin as well as music, while the Hornburg Ordinances of 1589 specify that the task of teaching music was to be shared by the school's director and his deputy, the 'baccalaureus'.[60] By the last decade of the sixteenth century, most schoolmasters in Lutheran schools taught music theory and singing (and therefore were able to sing themselves or at least delegated the task of musical education to a cantor).[61] Their teaching of reading and understanding music went hand in

---

55 Luther, *Tischreden* (*Table Talk*), WA Tr 5: 557, 19–20, no. 6248: 'Ein schulmeister muß singen können, sonst sehe ich ihn nicht an'.

56 See, for instance, *Bach-Dokumente*, ed. by Werner Neumann and Hans-Joachim Schulze, 7 vols (Kassel: Bärenreiter, 1963–79), II (1969), no. 129.

57 Pallas, *Registraturen der Kirchenvisitationen*, p. 42 n. 1.

58 Landeshauptarchiv Sachsen-Anhalt Abteilung Merseburg, *Visitationsakten der Superintendatur Eilenburg 1574*, Rep. 47, Kap. II Nr. 43, BL 99: 'Mittwoch, Freitag und Sonntage in der Kirche den Chor zu regieren'; Pallas, *Registraturen der Kirchenvisitationen*, p. 45: 'Zugleich cantor'.

59 Georg Gottfried Müller, *Das kursächsische Schulwesen beim Erlaß der Schulordnung von 1580* (Dresden: Jahresbericht des Wettiner Gymnasiums zu Dresden, 1888), p. xiv.

60 Friedrich Sintenis, *Zur Geschichte des Zerbster Schulwesens: Einladungsschrift zur Feier des fünfzigjährigen Bestehens des Herzoglichen Francisceums zu Zerbst 18. und 19. Mai 1853* (Zerbst: Friedrich Römer, 1853), p. 15: 'Der Rector scholae regiere wie überall den Chor'; Pallas, *Registraturen der Kirchenvisitationen*, pp. 325–6.

61 At Annaberg, for instance, the task of music teaching was delegated to a cantor, as the 1579 School Ordinances make clear: Stadtbibliothek Leipzig, *Annaberger Schulordnung*, 179: 'The inspection and overall leadership of the choir of musicians lies particularly with the cantor' (*Cantoris specialia: suprema inspectio et gubernatio chori musici incumbat*).

hand with teaching students how to sing in harmony.[62] Schoolmasters who acted in this dual capacity had their work cut out: in addition to their teaching commitments of educating the young in the classics, philosophy, theology and 'the Catechism in Latin and German', teachers in the Wittenberg Latin elementary school also taught music theory and singing and were responsible for leading 'singing in church on four days per week'.[63] On Saturdays, they rehearsed the Sunday readings with their classes, interpreting the gospel text and declining its verbs before singing the gospel reading.[64] No wonder that in 1555 the schoolmasters in the birthplace of Luther's Reformation formally complained that they worked too hard for too little pay:

> In the Wittenberg Latin primary school the schoolmasters have to shoulder a lot of work—teaching singing, polyphony as well as reading to a large number of children, both locals and outsiders. For the amount of work they are paid very little.[65]

Like their Wittenberg colleagues, in 1575 the Schmiedeburg rector and cantor also complained that they were overworked:

> The two of them, on their own, had to teach so many students—80 of them, in three separate classes—to read, to learn lessons by heart etc., while the schoolmaster also has to play the organ and the cantor has to serve as verger.[66]

---

62 Contemporary textbooks on music theory, such as the *Compendium Musices* by the Lüneburg Cantor and later pastor of Halberstadt, Auctor Lampadius (Bern: Samuel Apiarius, 1554), sig. B i$^{r}$, shed more light on the dual functions of music as a theoretical method and performance art: 'What is music [theory]? It demonstrates the proper form of singing, in German: the art of singing' (*QUid* [*sic*] *est Musica? Est quae rectas cantandi formulas demonstrat teuto: ein singe kunst*). Luther himself carefully distinguished between the two, as shown in Chapter 1 above.

63 Pallas, *Registraturen der Kirchenvisitationen*, p. 14: 'Singen in der kirchen an diesen vier tagen in der wochen'; 'Catechismus [...] latine und deutsch'.

64 Ibid.: 'Des suntags evangelium exponirn [...] grammatice declariren, darnach soll man ubersingen'.

65 Ibid., p. 42 n. 1: 'Die schuldiener in der lateinischen kinderschul zu Wittenberg haben grosse arbeit mit singen, figurieren und lessen und eine grosse menig von burgerskindern und frembden zu versorgen und ihrer arbeit nach sehr geringe besoldung'.

66 Ibid., p. 316: 'Das sie beide allein ein solche menge schuler, der sich in die 80 und in drei classes unterschieden weren, mit lesen, repetieren und andern versorgen, und doneben der schulmeister die orgel, der cantor die custerei vorsehen musten'.

While the visitation approved the employment of a 'tertius' at Schmiedeburg to assist the two masters in their multiple tasks, the pay of the Wittenberg schoolmaster-cantors was not increased: after unsuccessfully petitioning the parish authorities for a pay rise, the visitation recommended that the cantors should play at more weddings and funerals to top up their meagre pay with additional fees.[67]

## 4 Lutheran 'Kantoreien' as Instruments of Reform

Luther's vision of singers as agents of liturgical and doctrinal reform was enthusiastically implemented in electoral Saxony. While work among school children was clearly a priority, Luther's doctrine was also disseminated through church and secular choirs, and in chamber music groups meeting in private homes.[68] Luther himself regularly assembled singers and instrumentalists at his home in order to make music and discuss theology. In his autobiography the reformer and pastor of Joachimsthal, Johannes Mathesius, reflected on the meetings of the 'honourable Musica and *Kantorei*' that met at Luther's house:[69]

> In this *Kantorei* folks sing and play with Christian folk, praise God, sing good Psalms just as David did on the harp, or sing a good Swiss Chorale or a Psalm by Josquin [de Prez], gently, quietly and harmoniously: both words [and music]. Even the instruments sing.[70]

In the certain expectation that Lutheran music would help reform the life of the wider community, private musical ensembles like the musicians meeting at Luther's home were complemented with larger, civic foundations.[71] Significant church funds were expended to establish civic choirs with the specific intention of reforming church worship and music. The 1555 visitation report of the

---

67 Ibid.: 'Einen tertium zu trachten, welchs sie gewilliget'. See above at n. 65.

68 Rautenstrauch, *KS*, p. 61.

69 *Herrn Magister Johannes Mathesii weyland berühmten und frommen Pfarrers im Joachimsthal Lebens-Beschreibung*, ed. by Johann Balthasar Mathesius (Dresden: Zimmermann, 1705), p. 32: 'Ehrliche Musica und Cantorey'; for Reformation music-making in Joachimsthal under Mathesius, see Brown, *Singing the Gospel*, pp. 26–42.

70 *Lebens-Beschreibung*, ed. by Mathesius, pp. 32–33: 'Eine ehrliche Musica und Cantorey, darinnen man von [mit] christlichen Leuten singet und klinget, Gott preiset, gute Psalmen singet, wie David in der Harffen, einen guten Schweitzerischen Choral oder Josquinischen Psalm singet, fein leise und gelinde, sammt den Text, auch in die Instrumenta singet'.

71 For Lutheran music-making in Joachimsthal homes, see Brown, *Singing the Gospel*, pp. 105–19.

parish of Döbeln, for instance, suggests that the parish spent a fourth of its income on the establishment and maintenance of a town choir (*Kantorei*):[72]

> In order to foster Christian worship and singing in church, and to teach the youth music and give them opportunity for practice, ten guilders of the forty guilders income shall be given to the civic choir for the edification of the burghers as a whole.[73]

*Kantoreien* intentionally provided for a mix of singers, pairing students at Lutheran schools with locals from a wide cross-section of society: burghers as well as crafts- or tradespeople.[74] The 1570 statutes of the Großenhain *Kantorei* made provision for students (*iuniores* or *Junioren*) as well as local citizens (*seniores* or *Senioren*), stressing that the *Kantorei* was established 'for the edification and building up of society as a whole'.[75] Since the Großenhain statutes provided the basis for many similar choral foundations in the region and served as a model for the statutes of the *Kantoreien* in Lützen (1570), Leisnig (1581), Grimma (1602) and Finsterwalde (1605), they give a representative insight into the make-up and membership of Lutheran *Kantoreien* in Saxony.[76] Other statutes, such as the 1607 *Leges Generales* of the Döbeln *Kantorei* also admit both 'apprentices of craftspeople and the children of burghers' and make provision for the democratic election of choir representatives to take care of the affairs of the *Kantorei*; a remarkable arrangement in an age where any form of social interaction was still strictly regulated.[77]

72 The parish church of St Nicolai also housed the famous *Mirakelmann* (Miracle-Man), a movable image of Christ as Man of Sorrows, which formed the subject of Luther's criticism of *Götzenbilder* (Idolatrous Images); see Chapter 4 below, p. 107.

73 Hauptstaatsarchiv Dresden, Loc. 1987, *Visitationsbericht des Meißnischen Kreises: Visitationsabschied für die Stadt Döbeln*, XVI, 656ff: 'Domit auch in der Kirchen mit den christlichen ampten vnd gesengen dest mehr fleißes angewendet und die jugent in der musica dest besser gelehret vnd geubet werde, so sollen von den vierzig gulden, wen sie erhalten, gemeiner cantorei zu geburlicher ergetzlichkeit zehn gulden gegeben werden'.

74 Ernest Livingston, 'The Place of Music in German Education around 1600', *Journal of Research in Music Education*, 19.2 (1971), 144–67 (p. 164): '*Kantorei* members represented all trades and professions'; see also Arno Weber, *Geschichte der Kantorei-Gesellschaften im Gebiete des ehemaligen Kurfürstentums Sachsen*, Publikationen der Internationalen Musikgesellschaft: Beihefte IX [*KG*] (Leipzig: Breitkopf und Härtel, 1902), p. 27.

75 *Satzungen der Großenhainer Kantorei 1570*, in Rautenstrauch, *KS*, pp. 450: 'Zur Erbauung vnd Zuerhaltung der gantzen gesellschaft'.

76 Rautenstrauch, *KS*, p. 139, notes that subsequent statutes cited the Großenhain statutes 'verbatim in a number of instances' (*wörtliche Übereinstimmung einzelner Punkte*); see also Weber, *KG*, p. 20.

77 *Leges Generales de Constitutione Corporis Musici*, in Weber, *KG*, p. 27: 'Handwerks-Gesellen, Bürgers Söhne'. The concept of social interaction through common music-making

Not only were *Kantoreien* reasonably democratic institutions where craftspeople and councillors, students and apprentices shared in music-making on an equal footing, they also served as centres of learning where adult singers were taught to read music and encouraged to reflect more deeply on the Lutheran message of their singing. The statutes of the Lützen *Kantorei* (1570) closely echo Luther's vision that choristers might set an example to their elders and so convert them by their practice: schoolteachers and students, church leaders and townspeople learn and sing together, a practice that was emulated in many other *Kantoreien*.[78] Not only was the Lützen choir made up of schoolchildren and *seniores*, explicit provision was also made for the local schoolmaster to meet all members of the choir for special classes before 'Christmas, Easter and Pentecost' in order to:[79]

> Foster the service of Almighty God in Church, to encourage the members of the choir to greater fervour, and to refresh them for their impending duties [...] by singing, at school, in the presence of the pastor and deacon.[80]

This arrangement not only enabled the parish clergy to 'be aware of what will be sung in church', but also provided important opportunities for schoolchildren and senior members of the *Kantorei* to sing and learn together under the leadership of a schoolmaster.[81] Certainly, by the time the Großenhain *Kantorei* statutes were drawn up in 1570, much of the leadership of the town's *Kantorei* lay in the hands of the schoolmaster: business meetings of the *Kantorei* took place in school, although regular rehearsals still took place in church and

modelled by Lutheran *Kantoreien* is reflected in the establishment of work-place choirs, see Christina Purcell and Carolyn Kagan, 'Joy at work: the impact of non-professional singing workshops on employee well-being', in *Report of the Joy at Work Singing Workshops included as part of the RIHSC Annual Conference, Manchester 2007* (Manchester: Research Institute for Health and Social Change Manchester Metropolitan University, 2008), pp. 2–15.

78 Livingston, 'Place of Music', pp. 165–6.

79 *Satzungen der Kantorei-Gesellschaft zu Lützen vom Jahre 1570*, in Weber, *KG*, p. 79, IV: 'Uff Weihnachten, Ostern und Pfingsten'.

80 *Satzungen der Kantorei-Gesellschaft zu Lützen*, in Weber, *KG*, p. 79, IV: 'Damit Gott dem Allmechtigen Inn der Kirchen desto vleissiger sein dinst geleistet, und die Jhenigen, so der Cantorei teglich beiwohnen Zu grösseren vleiß gereitzt werden, und vor Ihren geleisten dinst eine erquickung haben kondten. [...] Inn der Schulen [...] Zu übersingen [...] Inn gegenwart des Herrn Pfarrherrn und Diacony'.

81 *Satzungen der Kantorei-Gesellschaft zu Lützen*, in Weber, *KG*, p. 79, IV: 'Domit denen [the parish clergy], waß in der Kirchen gesungen werden soll, bewust sein möge'. The statutes specified the presence of the schoolboys (*knaben*) for this rehearsal (*tentamen*).

formal provision was made for the members of the *Kantorei* to meet and socialise with the town's superintendent and other clergy.[82]

The 1595 statutes of the Strehla *Kantorei* sum up well how Luther's vision of ordered worship in German, led by a choir that brought together town, school and church, had been developed forty years after the reformer's death. Both members of the *Kantorei* and congregation shared in the singing at worship in such a way that enabled choir members to show off their art while enabling ordinary worshippers to join in their singing as well, thereby 'not only praising God and adorning our worship, but also gladdening the hearts and building up the entire Christian congregation'.[83] Following Luther's insight that music 'ought to grow out of the true mother tongue and its inflection' to the letter, the schoolteachers leading the *Kantorei* were enjoined to use the vernacular whenever possible:[84]

> [Singing and music] is much better in our own common German mother tongue, rather than in a foreign, unknown language. Therefore, schoolteachers should use German motets as often as possible.[85]

Finally, there was to be a clear musical relationship between the new and the familiar, the artistic and the devotional. In worship, both congregation and *Kantorei* were to share in the singing and the choir's performance was to be carefully balanced by opportunities for congregational singing: 'when the choir sings polyphony, a German sacred hymn by Luther' should be sung as well, 'but only the first verse of the same to be sung by the choir in polyphony, the remaining verses to be sung by the people in plain unison'.[86] Members

---

82 *Satzungen der Großenhainer Kantorei*, in Rautenstrauch, *KS*, p. 449: 'Schulregenten ampt'; *KS*, p. 451: 'the meetings of the singers are to be held in school' (*die samlung der Cantorum sol auf der Schulenn geschehenn*), while the choir met in the 'in church [...] for rehearsals' (*kirchen* [...] *zum Tentiren*); see also *KS*, p. 452: 'Johannis Baptistae Jerliche Zeche belangend'.

83 *Satzungen der Strehlaer Kantorei 1595*, in Rautenstrauch, *KS*, p. 181: 'Nicht allein zum Lobe Gottes vndt zur Zierde der Gottesdiensten, Sondern auch zur auffmunterung der Hertzen vnd zur Erbauung der gantzen christlichen gemein'.

84 Luther, *Wider die himmlischen Propheten* (*Against the Heavenly Prophets*), *1525*, LW 40/2: 141, WA 18: 123, 22–23: 'Aus rechter mutter sprach und stymme kommen'.

85 *Strehlaer Satzungen*, in Rautenstrauch, *KS*, p. 181: 'Viel besser durch vnnsere bekannte Deutzsche Muttersprache, als durch eine fremde vnbekannte Sprache geschehen kann, so sollen sich die Schuldiener so viel möglich auff deutzsche Muteten befleißigen'.

86 Ibid.: 'Darann man figurieret [...] einen Deutzschen Kirchengesang Lutheri [...] vnd zwar nur den ersten Vers aus demselben zu Chore figuraliter, die anderen Versus aber mit dem

of the *Kantorei* and the congregation were to form one worshipping community, the choir making an offering of their skills and musical gifts to the wider community, as the 1588 statutes of the Colditz *Kantorei* explained. After all, the Colditz choir sang in order to 'edify this society and add to its welfare'.[87]

At the same time, a *Kantorei* was an instrument of order, reflecting in their ordered singing the order of church and magisterium. The Colditz statutes specifically state that the choir existed 'to please the servants of Church and state'.[88] While the maintenance of the church's discipline and earthly magisterium were good Lutheran reasons for establishing a *Kantorei*, the statutes cited three further theological reasons for their existence. Musical order and disciplined practice reflected the earthly magisterium; the beauty of their singing foreshadowed the heavenly realm; while their communal act of thanksgiving and their acknowledgement of graces and gifts already received affirmed the singers' hope of enjoying the bliss of heaven hereafter:

> Above all, [the *Kantorei*] exists to honour and serve God and to give thanks for his gifts of grace and skill, and out of a hearty desire for the heavenly *Kantorei* and in confident expectation of Christ, that we may join the angels there and sing *Te Deum laudamus* properly: it certainly will sound better there.[89]

A *Kantorei*, then, served as a model of Luther's two realms as much as an instrument to praise God through music and to enthuse others to join their praises.[90] Indeed, the Colditz statutes specify that those members of the

---

Volcke choraliter vollendts hinaussingen'. The evidence from Strehla suggests that Herl, *Worship Wars*, p. 129, is right in his assertion that 'an increase in polyphonic music competed with congregational singing', although the increase in polyphonic singing there certainly did not constitute a 'worship war'.

87 *Colditzer Kantoreiordnung*, in Rautenstrauch, KS, p. 188: 'Ergetzung in dieser gesellschaft oder wohlstandes wehen'.

88 Ibid.: 'Zu willen vnnd gefallen […] den Kirchendienern vnd der Obrigkeitt'.

89 Ibid.: 'Ergetzung in dieser gesellschaft oder wohlstandes wehen, […] zu willen vnnd gefallen […] den Kirchendienern vnd der Obrigkeitt, […] sondern darumb am allermeistenn, daß Gott dadurch geehret vndt gedienet wirdt vndt zur Dancksagung, daß Ihnen Gott solche gnadt vnnd geschicklichkeit vorliehen hatt, auch aus einem herzlichen Verlangen nach der himmlischen Cantorey vnd gewissen zuvorsicht in Christo, daß wir dort mit den Engeln einstimmen vnnd das Te Deum laudamus recht singen, do es denn besser klingen wird'.

90 For an introduction to Luther's understanding of the two realms, see William J. Wright, *Martin Luther's Understanding of God's Two Kingdoms: A Response to the Challenge of*

community who did not make use of their musical gifts and chose not to join the choir, or who had joined but did not take their practices seriously, rejected not only the town's order and the church's discipline but the Giver of grace himself. By their actions or inactions, those citizens publicly 'profess that they have no interest in order, obedience, peace and unity, yea even that God's Word means little to them', the Colditz statutes affirm.[91]

The statutes of Lutheran *Kantoreien* document well the progress of Luther's expectation that electoral Saxony would be converted through a ministry of music. As the sixteenth century came to its close, Lutheran *Kantoreien* had become institutions that fulfilled important educative, theological and social functions in ways similar to those of pre-Reformation religious confraternities.[92] They had become institutions in which Lutheran learning was fostered, where people gathered to sing and so created a sense of community through their art. Their regular involvement in public worship enabled the introduction of important liturgical reforms, such as the adoption of a fully vernacular liturgy, while their participation in important rites of passage including weddings and funerals enabled the shaping of a Lutheran society based on friendship and family ties. Finally, their secular foundation coupled with their distinctively Lutheran viewpoint made them important instruments of change in the decades immediately following the death of Martin Luther.

Towards the end of the first decade of the Reformation, Luther had made clear that music and other forms of artistic expression were useful and necessary instruments to further the Reformation message. In his 1526 *Deutsche Messe*, he linked the need to communicate the Word of God to 'simple folk and the young' with the work of education and the arts:[93]

> For the sake of simple folk and the young, who must be trained and educated in the Scripture and God's Word daily so that they may become familiar with the Bible, grounded, well versed, and skilled in it, ready to

---

*Skepticism*, Texts and Studies in Reformation and pre-Reformation Thought (Grand Rapids: Baker Academic, 2010).

91 *Colditzer Kantoreiordnung*, KS, p. 188: 'Der bezueget, das er zu ordnung, zu gehorsam, zu Friedt vnd zu einigkeit keine lust noch lieb hatt, ja daß ihn [*sic*] Gottes Wordt ein geringer Ernst ist'.

92 For pre-Reformation confraternities in Germany, see Bernd Moeller, *Religious Life in Germany on the Eve of the Reformation*, in *Pre-Reformation Germany*, ed. by Gerald Strauss (New York: Harper and Row, 1972), pp. 14–30 (pp. 24–30).

93 Luther, *Deutsche Messe und ordnung Gottis diensts* (*The German Mass and Order of Service*), *1526*, LW 53: 62, WA 19: 73, 18: 'Eynfeltigen und des jungen volcks'. LW renders 'eynfeltigen' as 'immature'.

> defend their faith and in due time to teach others and to increase the kingdom of Christ.[94]

In order to educate new generations to enthuse others for the Word of God, all forms of artistic endeavour, even bell ringing, were 'useful and necessary'.[95] Singing God's Word for Luther was as important as reading it, or preaching and writing it, he explained:

> The Word should be read, sung, preached, written and set in poetry. Wherever it may be helpful and beneficial, I should gladly have it rung out by all bells and played on all organ pipes and proclaimed by everything that makes a sound.[96]

By the turn of the seventeenth century, schools and civic *Kantoreien* had enthusiastically responded to Luther's challenge: the young were educated to teach their families and friends in the new doctrine; teachers, cantors and poets found ways of making the Word of God known through their skills; organists and town pipers found ways of accompanying singers in praising God and the success of the Reformation. By the end of the first century of the Reformation, the Word of God in the vernacular and Luther's doctrine were, indeed, 'played on all organ pipes and proclaimed by everything that makes a sound'.[97]

The establishment of a distinctive Lutheran musical tradition has been one of the most enduring features of Luther's Reformation. More than five hundred years after his Reformation, it still remains central to worship in the Protestant denominations that trace their cultural and doctrinal heritage back to Luther. Martin Luther's love of music, and his vision of music as an ideal means to convey a sense of the nature and being of God, continues to inspire composers and singers to use their art in the service of God and their communities. Why

---

94 Luther, *Deutsche Messe* (*German Mass*), LW 53: 62, WA 19: 73, 18–21: 'Umb der eynfeltigen und des jungen volcks willen, wilchs sol und mus teglich ynn der schrifft und Gottis wort geubt und erzogen warden, das sie der schrifft gewonet, geschickt, leufftig und kündig drynnen warden, yren glauben zuvertretten und anderer mit der zeyt zu leren und das reych Christi helffen mehren'.

95 Luther, *Deutsche Messe* (*German Mass*), LW 53: 62, WA 19: 73, 23: 'Hulfflich und fodderlich'.

96 Luther, *Deutsche Messe* (*German Mass*) LW 53: 62, WA 19: 73, 22–25: 'Umb solcher willen mus man lessen, singen, predigen, schreyben und tichten, und wo es hulfflich und fodderlich dazu were, wolt ich lassen mit allen glocken dazu leutten und mit allen orgeln pfeyffen und alles klingen lassen, was klingen kunde'.

97 Luther, *Deutsche Messe* (*German Mass*), LW 53: 62, WA 19: 73, 25: 'Mit allen orgeln pfeyffen und alles klingen lassen, was klingen kunde'.

do Lutherans sing? Because Luther's conviction that music would inspire and bring together many to sing God's praises still holds true:

> For God our loving Lord did music make
> to be a proper singer,
> she is master of composers:
> Day and night she sings and sounds his praise.
> Since nothing will tire her in praising him,
> my own song, too, shall honour him
> and give him thanks eternally.[98]

---

98 Luther, *Fraw Musica, 1538*, WA 35: 484, 33–40: 'Gott / Der sie [die Musica] also geschaffen hat, / Zu sein die rechte Sengerin, / Der Musicen ein Meisterin. / Dem singt und springt sie tag und nacht, / Seines lobs sie nichts müde macht, / Den ehrt und lobt auch mein gesang / Und sagt jm ein ewigen danck'; see also the discussion of the poem in WA 48: 293–297, and Leaver, *Luther's Liturgical Music*, pp. 73–76.

CHAPTER 3

# Martin Luther's 'Mighty Fortress'

Martin Luther wrote the hymn *Ein feste Burg ist unser Gott* ('A Stronghold Fortress Is Our God') in the late 1520s as 'a Psalm of comfort' (*ain trost Psalm*), inspired by Psalm 46, 'with its own newly composed tune'.[1,2] The hymn does not render the full biblical text into metrical form, but rather provides a paraphrase drawing on the major themes Luther identified in his commentaries on the Psalm: 'God is our confidence and strength' and 'the heathens (nations, *goyim*, גוים) must despair and the kingdoms fall'.[3] The hymn was written to encourage the faithful in the tumultuous and beleaguered first decade of the Reformation when believers were forfeiting their worldly goods and relationships. At the same time, it was intended as a propagandistic weapon in the spiritual and actual battles against the Reformation's many opponents.[4] It quickly became an international feature of the evangelical movement. In the four centuries since the words and music were first written, *Ein feste Burg* has often been appropriated as a hymn sung to reaffirm the earthly power and military prowess of Lutheran empires and German nationalists, particularly in the era centred around the Unification of the German Empire in 1871. The hymn has also been claimed as a Psalm of spiritual consolation, especially after the complete defeat of Nazi Germany in 1945.

This chapter tracks the hymn's reception from the 1520s to the present day. It offers a close reading of the German lyrics in the context of the Reformation and of Luther's other writings, which document that the hymn was intended for spiritual encouragement. A fresh translation into English is used here in the spirit of Luther's work in his translations of the Bible into the vernacular. In this way, we hope to contribute to the ongoing reassessment of the hymn, to understand *Ein feste Burg* as a spiritual and eternal refuge with God.

---

1 An earlier version of this chapter was published as Loewe and Firth, 'Martin Luther's "Mighty Fortress"', 125–45.

2 *Luthers geistliche Lieder und Kirchengesänge*, ed. by Jenny, AWA, 4, p. 249: 'In seiner aygnen weiß'.

3 Luther, *Der Psalter von 1524–28, 1531 und 1545*, WA DB 10: 250: 'Gott ist unsre Zuversicht und Stärke' and 'Die Heiden müssen verzagen und die Königreiche fallen'.

4 For the authors' previous work on propaganda, see Loewe, *Richard Smyth*; Katherine Firth, '"Bright flower breaks from charnel bough" The arts of peace and the 1953 Coronation', *The Finzi Journal* (March 2014), 90–118.

 | DOI:10.1163/9789004527430_005

## 1 Genesis and Dissemination

This section will trace the genesis and immediate dissemination and translation throughout the Protestant world of Luther's most popular hymn. The first generation of research on the hymn commenced with Johannes Line, *Wann wurde das Lutherlied Ein feste Burg ist unser Gott verfaßt* (1866), followed by Friedrich Spitta, *Ein feste Burg ist unser Gott* (1905), both drawing on the ground-breaking historical research on German hymnody by Philipp Wackernagel, *Das deutsche Kirchenlied* (1870).[5]

In 1923, Wilhelm Lucke compiled the first authoritative critical edition of Luther's hymns for the *Kritische Gesamtausgabe* of Luther's works (volume 35), followed in 1965 by its English counterpart.[6] Georg Wolfram's work on the genesis of the hymn (1936), and three brief reflections on the hymn in the *Deutsches Pfarrerblatt* by Karl Völker, concluded this first period of research two years before the outbreak of the Second World War.[7] Following the War, it was Konrad Ameln's brief note on the melodic origins of the hymn (1955), which marked the beginning of the second generation of German research. Conducted principally through the pages of the newly-established *Jahrbuch für Liturgik und Hymnologie*, studies included Markus Jenny's 1964 thorough analysis of the hymn, Ameln's and Karol Hławiczka's speculation on the origins of the tune, and Jenő Sólyom's analysis of the reception of Luther's hymn in German-speaking diaspora communities (1976).[8] Around the 500th anniversary of Luther's birth, Gerhard Hahn (1981) and Patrice Veit (1986) both

5 Johannes Line, *Wann wurde das Lutherlied Ein feste Burg ist unser Gott verfaßt? Historische kritische Untersuchung* (Leipzig: Rautenstrauch, 1886), followed by Friedrich Spitta, *Ein feste Burg ist unser Gott: Das Lied Luthers in ihrer Bedeutung für das evangelische Kirchenlied* (Göttingen: Vandenhoek und Ruprecht, 1905), both drawing on the ground-breaking historical research on German hymnody by Wackernagel, *Kirchenlied.*

6 *Luther's Works, Volume 53: Liturgy and Hymns*, ed. by Ulrich S. Leupold (Minneapolis: Fortress, 1965).

7 Georg Wolfram, *Ein feste Burg ist unser Gott: Die Entstehungszeit und der ursprüngliche Sinn des Lutherliedes* (Berlin und Leipzig: de Gruyter, 1936), Karl Völker, 'Die historischen Hintergründe von "Ein feste Burg"', *Deutsches Pfarrerblatt*, 40 (1936), 768–88.

8 Konrad Ameln, 'Die älteste Überlieferung der Weise "Ein feste Burg ist unser Gott"', *Jahrbuch für Liturgik und Hymnologie*, 1 (1955), 110–12, Markus Jenny, 'Neue Hypothesen zur Entstehung und Bedeutung von "Ein feste Burg"', *Jahrbuch für Liturgik und Hymnologie*, 9 (1964), 143–52, Konrad Ameln and Karol Hławiczka, 'Eine niederländische Psalm-Weise, Vorlage oder Nachbildung der Melodie von "Ein feste Burg"? Eine Diskussion', *Jahrbuch für Liturgik und Hymnologie*, 18 (1973), 189–95, Jenő Sólyom, '"Das Reich muß uns doch bleiben": Zur letzten Zeile des Liedes "Ein feste Burg"', *Jahrbuch für Liturgik und Hymnologie*, 20 (1976), 166–71.

contributed important monographs on Luther's hymnody.[9] Hellmut Thomke (1985) and Inge Mager (1986) further developed the understanding of Luther's famous hymn. Without a doubt, Martin Brecht's 'Zum Verständnis von Martin Luthers Lied "Ein feste Burg"' and Markus Jenny's critical edition, *Luthers geistliche Lieder und Kirchengesänge*, AWA, 4, remain the outstanding scholarly contributions of the period.[10] German-language scholarship on Luther's hymn in the 1990s included both Protestant and Catholic reflections on the hymn: Wichmann von Meding (1993) provides a thorough analysis of the Psalm sources of the hymn while Reinhart Staats (1998) and Frans Pieter van Stam (2002) both locate the hymn as an integral part of Luther's rebuttal of Zwinglian Eucharistic theology.[11] In the run-up to the quincentenary of the Reformation, Michael Fischer (2014) undertook an extensive cultural reception of the hymn during the Great War.[12] Finally, the proceedings of the congress 'Lutherstadt Wittenberg 2017', led to a good number of new publications on the creation, dissemination and reception of the hymn.[13] Foremost among

9 Gerhard Hahn, *Evangelium als literarische Anweisung. Zu Luthers Stellung in der Geschichte des deutschen kirchlichen Liedes*, Münchener Texte und Untersuchungen zur deutschen Literatur des Mittelalters, 73 (München and Zürich: Artemis, 1981), Patrice Veit, *Das Kirchenlied in der Reformation Martin Luthers*, Veröffentlichungen des Instituts für Europäische Geschichte Mainz (Stuttgart: F. Steiner, 1986).

10 Hellmut Thomke, 'Das Wort sie sollen lassen stahn! Überlegungen zur Sprache und zur poetischen Form von Luthers Liedern am Beispiel des Reformationsliedes "Ein feste Burg ist unser Gott"', *Jahrbuch für Liturgik und Hymnologie*, 29 (1985), 79–89; Inge Mager, 'Martin Luthers Lied "Ein feste Burg ist unser Gott" und Psalm 46', *Jahrbuch für Liturgik und Hymnologie*, 30 (1986), 87–96; Martin Brecht, 'Zum Verständnis von Martin Luthers Lied "Ein feste Burg"', *Archiv für Reformationsgeschichte*, 70 (1979), 106–21, cited in Martin Brecht, *Ausgewählte Aufsätze I: Reformation* (Stuttgart: Calver, 1995), pp. 105–8; *Luthers geistliche Lieder und Kirchengesänge*, ed. by Jenny, AWA, 4.

11 Reinhart Staats, '"Ein feste Burg ist unser Gott": Die Entstehung des Lutherliedes im Abendmahlsstreit 1527', *Theologische Literaturzeitschrift*, 123 (1998), 115–26; Frans Pieter van Stam, 'Luthers Lied "Ein feste Burg": Mitten aus dem Abendmahlsstreit mit Zwingli entstanden—1527', *Church History/NAKG*, 82.1 (2002), 35–60; Wichmann von Meding, 'Ein feste Burg ist unser Gott: Martin Luthers christliche Auslegung des Psalms 46', *Zeitschrift für Theologie und Kirche*, 90.1 (1993), 25–56.

12 Michael Fischer *Religion, Nation, Krieg: Der Lutherchoral Ein feste Burg ist unser Gott zwischen Befreiungskriegen und Erstem Weltkrieg*, Populäre Kultur und Musik, 11 (Münster: Waxmann, 2014).

13 Jürgen Heidrich, 'Zur Frühgeschichte des Liedes Ein feste Burg ist unser Gott im 16. Jahrhundert', in *Kulturelle Wirkungen der Reformation—Cultural Impact of the Reformation. Kongressdokumentation Lutherstadt Wittenberg August 2017*, ed. by Klaus Fitschen, Marianne Schröter, Christopher Spehr, and Ernst-Joachim Watschke, 1 (Leipzig: Evangelische Verlagsanstalt Leipzig, 2019), pp. 285–96; Thomas Schmidt, 'Ein feste Burg ist unser Gott? Der Choral in der Instrumentalmusik des 19. Jahrhunderts zwischen

them are Heidrich's early history of the hymn (2019), with its fascinating suggestion that *Ein feste Burg* might have been a response to a rival publication, Johannes Frosch's hymn, *Gott selbs ist vnser Schutz vund macht* ('God Himself Is Our Protection and Power'), which was published in Strassburg in 1529.[14]

For such a popular hymn, the genesis of *Ein feste Burg* is largely undocumented. No manuscripts or revisions exist, nor are there any extant reflections from Luther's hand on how the hymn came to be written. Nor is there any documentary evidence of a specific occasion or event, in spite of much speculation later. The hymn was apparently published as a broadsheet in Augsburg in about 1529 under the title, *Der .46. Ain trost Psalm. In seiner aygnen weiß* ('The 46th. A Psalm of Comfort. With Its Own Tune').[15] While numerous other such broadsheet publications survive, 'single sheets of paper printed on one side, and pamphlets, single gathering of leaves usually containing only one, two, or three hymns', the original single sheet publication of *Ein feste Burg* is no longer extant.[16]

Within that year, *Ein fest Burg* was incorporated into a collection of hymns published in Wittenberg by Joseph Klug (also no longer extant), and within two years it was translated into Low-German in an edition that is still extant.[17] The present chapter uses the text and spelling of the hymn as printed in the second 1533 edition of the Klug hymnal, the first High-German original still extant.[18] In 1535, *Ein feste Burg ist unser Gott* was published again, this time

Sakralem Andachtstopos und konfessionellen Statement', in *Kulturelle Wirkungen*, pp. 307–316; Stefan Menzel, '"Eine feste burgk ist unser got". Otto Kade, die "Inventio" des Luther-Codex und der deutsche Kulturprotestantismus', in *Kulturelle Wirkungen*, pp. 317–26; and Christine Roth, 'Das Lied Ein feste Burg im Schaffen des Michael Praetorius: Von der Aktualisierung musikalischer Traditionen', in *Kulturelle Wirkungen*, pp. 345–54.

14 Heidrich, 'Frühgeschichte', p. 291: 'a rival song that was launched practically at the same time as Luther's *Ein feste Burg*, and which apparently spread mainly in Upper Germany' (*ein praktisch zeitgleich mit Luthers Ein feste Burg lanciertes Konkurrenzlied, das offenbar vor allem im Oberdeutschen Gebiet Verbreitung fand*).

15 *Luthers geistliche Lieder und Kirchengesänge*, ed. by Jenny, AWA, 4, p. 249; Heidrich, 'Frühgeschichte', pp. 287–8.

16 Herl, *Worship Wars*, p. 88.

17 The first edition of the Klug hymnal has not been sighted since 1788 but was replicated in its entirety in a Low-German translation in the Rostock Hymnal; Joachim Slüter, *Geystlike leder vppt nye gebetert tho Wittenberch / dorch D. Martin Luther* (Rostock: Ludwig Ovetz, 1531). Heidrich, 'Frühgeschichte', p. 289, in assessing the hymn's source texts, affirms that while 'the Klug hymnal [...] of 1529—thus the current state of research—is lost; the evidence that it actually existed, however, is convincing' (*Das Klugsche Gesangbuch* [...] *von 1529—so der aktuelle Forschungsstand—ist verloren; die Indizien, dass es tatsächlich existiert hat, sind indes überzeugend*).

18 *Klug'sches Gesangbuch*, 2nd edn (Wittenberg: Klug, 1533); our analysis retains the spelling of this edition. In 1971, Konrad Ameln, 'Das Klugsche Gesangbuch, Wittenberg 1529:

under the title *Der xlvj. Psalm / Deus noster refugium et virtus / etc. Martinus Luther* ('The XLVJ. Psalm / God Is Our Refuge and Strength / etc. Martinus Luther').[19] The hymn thus retained its character as a 'Psalm' and is arranged among the metrical translations of the psalter the reformer created for his first two hymn collections (1524 and 1528).[20] Similarly, many contemporary hymnals, from the earliest publication in the Nürnberg *Achtliederbuch* and Erfurt *Enchiridion*, grouped *Ein feste Burg* among the Psalm hymns.

However, *Ein feste Burg* differs fundamentally from Luther's other Psalm hymns.[21] Where the others follow the biblical text in close metrical versions, *Ein feste Burg ist unser Gott* is a paraphrase that combines the Psalm, other biblical references (particularly portions of Jn. 16–18), and thematic reflection. Another comparison may be Luther's ballad *Eyn newes lied wir heben an* ('A New Song Here Shall Be Begun'), written soon after the burning of two Augustinian canons in Brussels in July 1523.[22] Luther's 'newspaper song' commending the 'two martyrs of Christ', significantly influenced the promotion of Luther's theological ideas, as we have shown above.[23] *Eyn newes lied* provided a theological

---

Versuche einer Rekonstruktion', *Jahrbuch für Liturgik und Hymnologie*, 16 (1971), 159–62 (p. 162) suggested that in spite of the likely close correlation between the two, 'the second edition [of the Klug] hymnal gives us a better understanding of the content of the first—especially as regards to the choice and order of hymns—than that of another hymnal altogether, which is a re-print of the Klug hymnal of 1529' (*Daß die zweite Auflage desselben GBs [Gesangbuches] uns eine bessere Vorstellung von dem Inhalt des ersten—vor allem von dem Liedervorrat und seiner Anordnung—vermittelt als irgend ein anderes GB, das ein Nachdruck des GB Klug von 1529 ist*).

19 *Klug'sches Gesangbuch*, sig. 46r: 'Der xlvj. Psalm / Deus noster refugium et virtus / etc. Martinus Luther'.

20 'Eyn vaste Borch ys vnse Godt', Slüter, *Geystlike leder*, sig. B viijr: 'De. Xlvj / Psalm / Deus noster refugium et virtus. Mart. Luth'.

21 *Etlich Cristlich lider / Lobgesang / vnd Psalm / dem rai- / nen wort Gottes gemeß / auf der / heyligen schrifft / durch mancher- / ley hochgelerter gemacht / in der Kirchen zum singen / wie es dann / zum ttayl berayt zu Wittenberg / in übung ist* (*A number of Christian songs / Songs of praise / and Psalms / according to the pure word of God- / from Holy Scripture / composed by a number of well-learned people / for singing in Churches / as is, in part, already practiced in Wittenberg*) ('Wittenberg' [Nürnberg: Jobst Gutknecht] 'M.D.X.iiij' [1524]), *Eyn Enchiridion oder Handbüchlein. / eynem ytzlichen Christen fast nutzlich bey sich zuhaben / zur stetter vbung vnd trachtung geystlicher gesenge vnd Psalmen / Rechtschaffen vnd kunstlich verteutscht* (*An Enchiridion or Small Handbook. / for each Christian very usefully to bear with them / for the constant practice and reflection on spiritual songs and Psalms / rendered skilfully and artfully into German*) (Erfurt: In der Permenter Gasse, zum Ferbefaß, 1524).

22 Luther, *Lieder*, WA 35: 411, 8: 'Zu Brüssel in dem niederlandt'.

23 Luther, *Lieder*, WA 35: 411, 8: 'zween Merterern Christi', see above in Chapter 2, p. 49. For the dissemination of Luther's thought through his hymns, see also Chapter 2 above, pp. 49–54.

commentary on the persecution of Luther's followers by the authorities in the Spanish Netherlands, similar to the purpose served in the next decade by *Ein feste Burg*.

It was from the early 1530s onwards that *Ein feste Burg* came to surpass the early Lutheran hymnals in popular use, through the combination of vernacular theological teaching and political commentary. It provided, in a single hymn, an expression of the confidence of Lutheran Christians in God and a reflection on the fragile political context in which believers found themselves at the beginning of the third decade of the sixteenth century. God alone, the hymn makes clear, would protect them from their enemies: whether they were human or supernatural foes. The four-stanza hymn speaks into the dichotomy of Christian living in a world of *Anfechtungen*: the challenges common to every Christian throughout the generations, as well as the particular challenges faced by the religious wars and conflicts of Luther's own generation. In times of struggle, God proves to be a safe refuge and fortress who provides shelter for believers, a place to weather the storms of the age. God is 'our lasting, blessed, and eternal comfort and joy against death, hell, devil, and every woe', Luther commented in the introduction to his 1542 collection of burial hymns: *Ein feste Burg* is a musical testament to that certainty.[24] Soon after its publication, this hymn of encouragement for the persecuted Lutheran community was widely disseminated and translated. The first translation of the hymn, *Eyn vaste Borch ys unse Godt*, was published by Joachim Slüter as part of the Low-German Rostock hymnal (1531).[25] A Swedish translation, most likely by Luther's former student in Wittenberg Olaus Petri, *War gud är oss een weldigh borg*, formed part of the 1536 *Swenske songer eller wisor nw på prentade / förökade* [...] *utsatte*.[26] In 1539, the hymn was translated into English by Miles Coverdale as 'Oure God is a Defence and Towre' and published in his *Goostly Psalmes and Spirituall Songes* in 1543.[27] By the time of Luther's death in 1545, the hymn was widely sung throughout Protestant Europe.

---

24 Luther, *Die Vorrede zu der Sammlung der Begräbnislieder* (*Preface to the Burial Hymns*), 1542, LW 53: 327, WA 35: 479, 17–8: 'Er ist unser endlicher, seliger, ewiger trost und freude wider den Tod, Helle, Teuffel und alle traurigkeit'.

25 Slüter, *Geystlike leder*, sig. B viij$^{r}$.

26 [Olaus Petri], *Swenske songer eller wisor nw på prentade / förökade* [...] *utsatte* (Stockholm: Kungliga Tryckeriet, 1536), sig. xii$^{r-v}$.

27 *Remains of Myles Coverdale, Bishop of Exeter*, ed. by George Pearson, Parker Society, 14 (Cambridge: Cambridge University Press, 1846), pp. 360–70. Intriguingly, Coverdale, himself a translator of the Psalter into English, retains Luther's metre, and augments Luther's texts by two verses to accommodate further literal references to the original Psalm.

In spite of its popularity, the exact occasion for the composition of the hymn remains unknown. Heinrich Heine's supposition that the hymn was a 'Reformation Marseillaise' sung by the reformer's party at their entry to the Diet of Worms (1521), while theatrical, is wholly implausible.[28] Three years later the people of then Catholic Magdeburg engaged in a massed marathon singing of Lutheran hymns to express their discontent with local Catholic authorities, but *Ein feste Burg* is not among the early Luther hymns sung in protest. Instead, local citizens are recorded as having sung Luther's *Aus tiefer Not* and *Es woll uns Gott genädig sein* for hours on end prior to the commencement of any Catholic worship.[29] An intriguing but equally unlikely theory is that the hymn was written in the run-up to the Marburg Colloquy (1529) in order to defend the doctrine of the real presence of the Lord's Supper against Zwingli, as put forward by Staats (1998) and van Stam (2002).[30] Their argument hinges on interpreting the 'single word' (*Wörtlein*) that would fell Satan (in verse three) as the *Verba* or words of institution: 'This Is My Body' (*Das Ist Mein Leib*), particularly the 'Is' (*Ist*) and 'My Body' (*Mein Leib*).[31] This is contradicted by Luther's own *Wochenpredigten über Johannes* (*Weekday Sermons on John's Gospel*), where he suggests the little words are in fact the 'I am he' that Jesus spoke at the moment of his betrayal when he was handed over to be crucified (Jn. 18.5), as will be shown below.[32] Moreover, there is little internal evidence that the hymn speaks to a specific sacramental debate. The Johannine character of the final two verses of the hymn, which depict a judgement of the prince of this world by the Saviour in judicial and combative terms, suggests that the Marburg theory is unpersuasive.

---

28 Heinrich Heine, 'Zur Geschichte der Religion und Philosophie in Deutschland, 1834' in *Der Salon: Zweiter Band* (Hamburg: Hoffmann und Campe, 1834), pp. 79–80: 'Ein Schlachtlied war jener trotzige Gesang, womit [Luther] und seine Begleiter in Worms einzogen. [...] Jenes Lied, die Marseiller Hymne der Reformazion [*sic*], hat bis auf unsere Tage seine begeisternde Kraft bewahrt'.

29 *Chroniken der niedersächsischen Städte*, II, 143, 8–10.

30 Klaus Burba, *Die Christologie in Luthers Liedern*, Schriften des Vereins für Reformationsgeschichte, 175 (Gütersloh: Bertelsmann, 1956), p. 12; Staats, '"Ein feste Burg ist unser Gott"', 115–26; van Stam, 'Luthers Lied "Ein feste Burg"', 35–60.

31 Staats, '"Ein feste Burg ist unser Gott"', no. 10: 'here it is first of all the *Wörtlein* in the words of Institution, "Is", and the "My Body", which have to remain' (*Hier sind es zunächst die 'Wörtlein' in den Einsetzungsworten 'Ist' und das 'Mein Leib', die stehen bleiben müssen*).

32 Luther, *Wochenpredigten über Johannes 16–20* (*Weekday Sermons on John's Gospel*), 1528–9, WA 28: 235, 25–30: 'Such an Almighty Person who with only five letters, "I am he" drives back and casts down both the soldiers and servants of the High Priest, as well as Judas the traitor' (*Solche Allmechtige Person, welche mit fünff Buchstaben 'Ich bins' zu rücke wirfft und auff den Erdboden stürtzt beide die Schar und der Hohenpriester Diener, Da zu auch Judam den Verrheter*).

Similarly far-fetched is the suggestion by Wolfram (1936), Völker (1936), and Merriman (2010) that the hymn was written in support of Protestant soldiers engaged in the siege of Vienna of 1528–1529, at the time Luther wrote and published *Vom Kriege wider die Türken* (*On the War against the Turks*).[33] The enemies at the time may have included Turks, but Luther's polemics were aimed more at Catholic opponents. Certainly, on hearing the hymn in May 1531, Catholic count Ernest II of Mansfeld-Vorderort identified the hymn as an attack on Catholic principles and, Luther's *Tischreden* (*Table Talk*) recounts, 'the dead tyrant Graf Ernst von Mansfeld, on hearing the hymn *Ein feste Burg ist vnser Gott etc.*, said, 'I will help destroy this fortress or prefer not to live'!'[34] The *Table Talk* laconically adds how 'three days later [on 9 May 1531] he died, without either confession or sacrament'.[35] Chronologically possible, but unfortunately equally undocumented, are the hypotheses that the hymn was written either for the Diet of Speyer (1529) or at the time of the Diet of Augsburg (1530) and sung at the presentation of the *Augsburg Confession*. The hymn was certainly in circulation at the time of both Diets, and may well have been sung at them, but again there is no documentary evidence as to such origins.

It is likely, then, that *Ein feste Burg* was not written as an occasional work to mark a specific event but rather as a general hymn of confidence in the saving works of the cross in times of great upheaval for the growing Protestant community. It may even have been written in response to Johannes Frosch's Strassburg hymn.[36] Drawing on theological principles deeply ingrained in the life of the reformer, and using Psalm 46 and parts of John 16–18 as its biblical base, the hymn encourages believers to sing about the realm that alone will remain when all other principalities fall: the kingdom of heaven where God himself is a stronghold and place of shelter for those who share this belief.

## 2 Reception from 1600 to 1945

Luther's most famous hymn began its life as a hymn of consolation. It soon became a triumph song in celebration of his Reformation and the later German

33 Wolfram, *Ein feste Burg ist unser Gott*, Völker, 'Die historischen Hintergründe', 768–88, and John Merriman, *A History of Modern Europe: From the Renaissance to the Age of Napoleon* (New York: W. W. Norton & Company, 2010), p. 101.

34 Luther, *Tischreden*, WA Tr: 2, 526, 25–527, 1, no. 2566b: 'Tyrannus mortuus Graff Ernst de Mansfelt. Is cum audireit canere Ein feste Burg ist vnser Gott etc. dixit: Ich will die Burg helffen zuschissen oder wil nicht leben!'

35 Luther, *Tischreden*, WA Tr: 2, 527, n. 1, no. 2566b: 'Et post triduum mortuus est sine confessione et sacramento'.

36 Heidrich, 'Frühgeschichte', pp. 292–94.

national movement that would claim Luther as its patriarch. At the turn of the seventeenth century, Michael Praetorius set the hymn for double choir in his influential *Musae Sioniae*, and produced multiple settings of the work, 'organ music, as choral music and as a vocal-instrumental figural composition'.[37] By the time of the centenary of the Reformation Luther's hymn in Praetorius' setting had become an anthem of Lutheranism, led by massed choirs and orchestras under the baton of Heinrich Schütz.[38] From the time of the first 'evangelical festival of exultation' in November 1617, marking the centenary of the Reformation, Martin Luther's hymn *Ein feste Burg ist unser Gott* began to develop into a hallmark of international Lutheranism.[39] As part of the three-day festival, Luther's hymn served as the centrepiece of celebrations on the second day of festivities at the then Lutheran Schlosskirche in Dresden. After the festival sermon by court preacher von Hoënegg on the subject of 'God's Word and Luther's teaching / now and never will decay',[40] five choirs joined the Hofkapelle to perform *Ein feste Burg* 'in a special arrangement with trumpets and military kettle drums' concluding the morning worship.[41] When Johann Sebastian Bach wrote his Reformation Cantata, *Ein feste Burg*, in about

---

37 Roth, 'Das Lied *Ein feste Burg* im Schaffen des Michael Praetorius', pp. 345–54 (p. 347): 'Als Orgelmusik, als Chormusik und als vocal-instrumentale figurale Komposition'.

38 Matthias Hoë von Hoënegg, *Chur Sächsische Evangelische Jubel Frewde: In der Churfürstlichen Sächsischen Schloß Kirchen zu Dreßden, theils vor, theils bey wehrendem, angestalten Jubelfest, neben andern Solenniteten, auch mit Christlichen Predigten* [...] *gehalten. Nach der Vorrede, findet der Christliche Leser, mit was für Solenniteten das Evangelische Jubelfest, in* [...] *Dreßden seye gehalten worden* (Leipzig: Lamberg und Kloseman, 1617), sig. b iij$^{v}$: 'The music set above has been performed solemnly and celebrated by the musicians appointed by the Elector of Saxony, our most gracious Sovereign, that is by 11 instrumentalists, 11 singers, 3 organists, 4 lutenists, 1 theorboist, 3 boys for the organ blower, 5 discant trebles, with manifold kinds of changes, by glorious instruments, with two organs, 2 portable organs, 3 clavicymbals, together with 18 trumpeters and two military kettle drums, under the direction of Heinrich Schütz of Weissenfels' (*Obgesetzte Music ist von des Churfürsten zu Sachsen / vnsers gnedigsten Herrn / bestekten Musicis, als Nemlichen: von 11. Instrumentisten / 11. Cantoribus. 3. Organisten / 4. Lautenisten / 1. Thiorbisten / 3. Organisten-Knaben / 5. Diskantisten / mit abwechselung allerley sorten / von herrlichen Instrumenten / mit zweyen Orgelwercken / 2. Regalen / 3. Clavicymbeln / nebenst 18. Tromptern / und zweyen Heerpaucken / Solenniter gehalten / vnd celebrieret worden. Sub Directorio Henrici Schützij Weissenfelsensis*); Roth, '*Ein feste Burg* im Schaffen des Michael Praetorius', p. 352.

39 *Chur Sächsische Evangelische Jubel Frewde*, sig. a ij$^{v}$: 'das Evangelische Jubelfest'.

40 *Chur Sächsische Evangelische Jubel Frewde*, 98: 'Gottes Wort vnd Luthers Lehr / Vergehet nun vnd nimmermehr'.

41 *Chur Sächsische Evangelische Jubel Frewde*, sig. b iij$^{r}$: 'Nach der Predigt / den Gesang Herrn Lutheri: Ein feste Burg / &c. auff besondere weise [...] mit 5. Chor [...] mit Trommetten vnd Heerpaucken'.

1723 it had become an essential part of the annual Reformation Day celebrations on 31 October.[42]

During the Thirty Years' War of Religion, the hymn is later said to have gained a secular dimension as the battle hymn of an international coalition of Swedish, German, Finnish, English and Scottish soldiers led by King Gustavus Adolphus. Although we have not been able to locate primary documentation between 1617 and 1814 for this use as a battle hymn, nineteenth-century poets and historians paint a vivid image of an army singing *Ein feste Burg* in defence of the Lutheran cause at the battle of Breitenfels (1631). In 1814, Karl Curths supposed that 'in profound solemn devotion the Swedish Army sang the two hymns *Ein feste Burg ist unser Gott* and *Es woll uns Gott genädig seyn*, accompanied by the sound of kettle drums and trumpets'.[43] Curth's retelling of the battle's beginning is contrasted by the contemporary eye-witness account of Scottish officer Robert Monro present at the battle of Breitenfeld, who does not recall any specific hymns sung in battle, but only a solemn act of dedication and their marching 'in order of Bataille, with Trumpets sounding, Drummes beating, and Colours advanced and flying, till we came within reach of Cannon of our enemies Armie'.[44] The Romantic realist poet, Theodor Fontane, intertwines both accounts in his ballad, 'The Sixth of November 1632: A Swedish Tale' (1868).[45] In the poem, a labourer on his way home to his farm in Sweden mysteriously overhears the sounds of the Battle of Lützen, at which King Gustavus Adolphus was killed and his armies gained a decisive victory:

> It is as if the battle throngs across,
> at times it sounds like a sacred song:
> I hear in the war horses' whinnying trot
> 'A mighty fortress is our God'.[46]

---

42 For Bach's Cantata, *Ein feste Burg* (BWV 80 and its 1735 version, BWV 80b), see Christoph Wolff, *Bach: Essays on His Life and Music* (Cambridge, MA: Harvard University Press, 1991), pp. 152–61.

43 Karl Curths, *Die Schlacht bei Breitenfeld unweit Leipzig am 7ten September 1631 und die Schlacht bei Lützen am 7ten November 1631* (Leipzig and Altenburg: Brockhaus, 1814), p. 66: 'In tiefer feierlicher Andacht sang das schwedische Heer unter Pauken- und Trompetenschall die beiden Lieder: Ein feste Burg ist unser Gott, und, Es woll' uns Gott genädig seyn'.

44 Robert Monro, *Monro His Expedition vvith the vvorthy Scots Regiment (called Mac-Keyes Regiment)* (London: William Jones, 1637), p. 65.

45 Theodor Fontane, 'Der 6. November 1632 (Schwedische Sage)'.

46 Fontane, 'Der 6. November 1632', lines 16–20: 'Es ist wie Schlacht, die herwärts dringt, / Wie Kirchenlied es dazwischen klingt, / Ich hör' in der Rosse wieherndem Trott: Eine feste Burg ist unser Gott!'

Three hundred years after Luther composed his hymn, Felix Mendelssohn immortalised the melody as a song of Lutheran triumph in the concluding movement (*allegro maestoso*) of his *Reformation Symphony* (1829).[47] By the time of the commemoration of the quadricentennial of Luther's birth in 1883, both the reformer and his hymn with its confident assertion about the 'Reich' remaining had been firmly recruited for the German nationalist cause. This literal, nationalist interpretation came to its crescendo in the Great War and the Nazi period. In the early stages of the First World War, the hymn served as a rallying song for enthusiastic soldiers and featured in slogans of encouragement chalked onto railway carriages transporting soldiers to the Western front.[48] A 1915 chalk inscription, written by soldiers on a Nürnberg troop carrier read:

> Germany sings the first verse:
> A stronghold fortress is our God
> a good defence and weapon.
> France sings the second verse:
> With our might nothing is done,
> we are completely, quickly lost.[49]

By the time of the four-hundredth anniversary of the Reformation, the *Lutherlied* ('Luther Hymn') had become the defiant anthem of imperialist Germany. For the 1917 *Recital-book for Reformation Celebrations*, the Naumburg teacher and playwright Ernst Heinrich Bethge provided a martial dramatic performance of the hymn as a victory song.[50] As the hymn was sung, a tableau of German soldiers was revealed, kneeling at the body of their fallen comrade on the battlefield. A German Lutheran pastor with 'New Testament in his raised hand,

47 Felix Mendelssohn, Symphony no. 5 in D major, op. 107, written in 1829 to mark the tercentenary of the presentation of the Augsburg Confession 1530.

48 Fischer, *Religion, Nation, Krieg*, p. 155: 'Deutschland singt den ersten Vers / Ein feste Burg ist unser Gott / ein gute Wehr und Waffen. / Frankreich singt den zweiten Vers: Mit unsrer Macht ist nichts getan / Wir sind gar bald verloren'. A year earlier, an Altenburg troop carrier had been inscribed with similar slogans: 'A German's prayer: "A stronghold fortress is our God"—A Frenchman's prayer: "With our might nothing is done"' (*Des Deutschen Gebet: 'Ein feste Burg ist unser Gott'—Des Franzosen Gebet: 'Mit unsrer Macht ist nichts getan'*).

49 Fischer, *Religion, Nation, Krieg*, p. 155.

50 Following the Great War, Bethge eschewed his erstwhile nationalist views. Following the 1944 attempt on Hitler's life, he was interned in Sachsenhausen concentration camp where he died later that year.

stands stage left. He sings together with the warriors, and then preaches to them'.[51] Against this dramatic backdrop, Bethge's verses were to be recited:

> The Luther hymn sounds across the battlefield,
> battle grey soldiers at prayer.
> The battle is over, the adversary shattered,
> the angels of God speak.
> Certainly came the adversary in greater might
> Certainly they gave us a hard fight
> God was wonderfully with us
> and helped subdue the adversary.[52]

Other German war poets and artists also used Luther's hymn to glorify the German cause and to entreat 'the Great Heavenly Ally' for success.[53] Even the defeat of imperial Germany did not rupture the close association of *Ein feste Burg* with German nationalism: the hymn remained part of the Nazi propaganda machine 'as a national battle hymn, a clarion call and rallying cry'.[54] Only after the complete collapse of Nazi Germany was the hymn again tentatively reclaimed, not as a song of triumph and self-confidence, but as a song of consolation in times of terror and great upheaval.

---

51 *Ein gute Wehr und Waffen: Vortragsbuch für Reformationsfeiern*, ed. by Ernst Heinrich Bethge and others (Leipzig: Strauch, [1917]), pp. 18–9: 'Ein Feldgeistlicher steht links, das Neue Testament in der erhobenen Hand. Er singt gleichsam mit den Kriegern, um dann zu ihnen zu sprechen'.

52 *Wehr und Waffen*, p. 19: 'Das Lutherlied klingt übers Feld / feldgraue Krieger beten. / Die Schlacht ist aus, der Feind zerschellt. / Die Engel Gottes reden. / Wohl kam der Feind in Übermacht, / wohl gab's ein hartes Ringen. / Doch Gott war mit uns wunderbar, / er half den Feind bezwingen'.

53 Michael Fischer, 'Zur lyrischen Rezeption des Lutherliedes "Ein feste Burg ist unser Gott" im Ersten Weltkrieg', in *Populäre Kriegslyrik im Ersten Weltkrieg*, ed. by Nicolas Detering, Michael Fischer, and Aibe-Marlene Gerdes, Populäre Kultur und Musik, 7 (Münster: Waxmann, 2013), pp. 67–97 (p. 68).

54 Karl Christian Thust, 'Luthers Lied "Ein feste Burg ist unser Gott". Nationalhymne des deutschen Protestantismus', *Deutsches Pfarrerblatt*, 112 (11/2012), 643–48 (p. 645): 'als nationales Kampflied, als so empfundener Posaunenschall und Schlachtruf'. Thust explains p. 645: 'In 1942 the melody had served as Nazi propaganda in the film "The Great King", "The empire must remain with us", at the helm of which Hitler stood as "the proper man", whom "God has firmly chosen"'. (*1942 musste die Melodie im Film 'Der große König' als Nazi-Propaganda herhalten, 'Das Reich muss uns doch bleiben', an dessen Spitze Hitler als 'der rechte Mann' stand, 'den Gott hat fest erkoren'*).

## 3 A Hymn of Confidence in God's Eternal Salvation

The language and themes Luther employs to create *Ein feste Burg* reflect recurrent themes in his letters, sermons, and writings. In English, the hymn is best known as 'A Mighty Fortress Is Our God', the first line of numerous singable translations used in Lutheran and other Protestant denominations across the English-speaking world since the nineteenth century. Yet, this translation obscures the meaning of the adjective '*feste*' for a safe or secure stronghold. The hymn was translated more accurately by John Christian Jacobi in 1722 as 'God Is Our Refuge In Distress, Our Strong Defence', and by Thomas Carlyle in 1831 as 'A Safe Stronghold Our God Is Still'.[55] For this chapter, we have used the term a 'stronghold fortress'—which we believe most closely matches the layers of meaning that '*feste*' would have suggested to Luther's contemporaries.

Luther articulated his understanding of the central themes of Psalm 46 in his three commentaries on the Psalms, as seen particularly in the Wittenberg group project known as *Nachbesserungen an der Deutschen Bibel: Psalter* (*Improvements on the German Bible: Psalter*), published only two years after *Ein feste Burg*. In multiple versions between 1524 and 1545, Luther reshapes his interpretation of the themes of the Psalter to address the conflicts faced by his contemporaries. 'God is our confidence and strength, a help in the greatest distress' (Ps. 46.1) is glossed to suggest that God will provide a joyful place of refuge from all evil in the eternal city: 'the city of God will be pleasant and cheerful [...] and be surrounded by joy'[56] The other theme of the Psalm demonstrates the significant development in Luther's understanding of the viciousness, and yet ultimate powerlessness, of the enemies of God. In verse 7, the 'heathens rage' (1524), 'must despair' (1531); 'the kingdoms bestir themselves' (1524), 'bend' (1528), 'must fall' (1531) 'the earth's empire melts' (1524), 'dies away' (1531). Both the early vision of a defeated violent upheaval and the later understanding of inevitable decline and despair for the enemies of the Lord of Hosts is expounded in *Ein feste Burg*. In the *Nachbesserungen* (*Improvements*), Luther glosses the verses 'the heathens (nations, *goyim*, גוים) must despair and the kingdoms must fall. [...] The LORD Sabaoth is with us, the God of Jacob is our defence' (Ps. 46.7–8) to mean that though we are in 'greatest distress', those

---

55 John [Johann] Christian Jacobi, *Psalmodia Germanica: Or, A Specimen of Divine Hymns, Translated from the High Dutch. Together with Their Proper Tunes and Thorough Bass* (London: J. Young in St Paul's Churchyard, 1722), pp. 83–4, and Thomas Carlyle, *Critical and Miscellaneous Essays in Five Volumes* (London: Chapman and Hall, 1899), II, 163–64.

56 Luther, *Nachbesserungen an der Deutschen Bibel: Psalter* (*Improvements on the German Bible: Psalter*), 1531, WA DB 3: 46, 14: 'Die stad Gottes fein lustig sein und [...] ynn freuden schweben'.

who have God's city as their place of confidence and strength will not fear any onslaught either of earthly or supernatural enemies.[57]

Luther there provides a list of examples of God's enemies, including both current Holy Roman Emperor Ferdinand, Duke George of Saxony and the Ottoman armies, as well as historic enemies of the people of God such as Xerxes.[58] These may rage, they even may attempt to scale God's city but, ultimately, they will fail. In his characteristic macaronic Latin and German: 'sollen die stad persequi, sed et ynn ein ander fallen et tamen zu schanden werden' (*Should they attempt to take the city, they will fall in ruin and thus come to shame*).[59] His commentary concludes with his confession of confidence in God's provident care, and the encouragement that 'we, too, should sing that verse'.[60] Thus the famous hymn Luther wrote at about the same time as he was writing the commentary may be understood as a practical contribution to enable his contemporaries 'to sing that verse'. Luther's hymn is the result of a deeply rooted spirituality in which the devil was as real and ever present as was the saving presence of Jesus Christ. In the same way in which Christ bestowed his goodness and grace in defence of his followers, the devil had held sway over the forces of evil. Certainly, since the Diet of Worms in spring 1521, Luther consistently spoke of his opponents as 'devils' (*Teufel*). In a letter dated 5 March 1522 to his patron, Elector Friedrich the Wise, Luther recollects that 'had I known that so many devils were targeting me as there were roof-tiles, I would nevertheless have jumped joyfully straight into their midst'.[61] A world populated with devils, as the third verse of his hymn states, was a natural consequence of human sinfulness. Even though the influence of evil for Luther is ever present, in the mid-1520s, the religious conflicts of his day did take a turn for the worse. The central theme in the first verse of Luther's hymn, 'The ancient evil enemy / With earnestness he now intends' (*der alt böse feind / mit ernst ers jtzt meint*), can be understood as a reflection in music on recent events:[62] in summer 1526 the Ottoman forces sacked Hungary, in 1527 the plague struck Wittenberg, and by the end of the decade Ottoman forces had begun their first siege of Vienna, threatening one of the administrative centres

57 *Deutsche Bibel* (*German Bible*), WA DB 3: 46, 20: 'Die heiden toben'.

58 *Deutsche Bibel* (*German Bible*), WA DB 3: 46, 20: 'ferdinandus, Dux Georgius', 27: 'Xerxen', 30: 'sic Turca'.

59 *Deutsche Bibel* (*German Bible*), WA DB 3: 46, 21–2.

60 Luther, *Deutsche Bibel* (*German Bible*), WA DB 3: 47, 2–3: 'Das versichen wollen wir auch singen'.

61 Luther, *Briefwechsel* (*Letters*), WA Br 2: 455, 52–54, no. 455: 'Wenn ich hätte gewußt, daß so viel Teufel auf mich gehalten hätten, als Ziegel auf den Dächern sind, wäre ich dennoch mitten unter sie gesprungen mit Freuden'.

62 Luther, *Geistliche lieder auffs new gebessert zu Wittemberg* (Wittenberg: Klug, 1535), sig. $45^{r-v}$.

of the Holy Roman Empire. The devil and his forces were always active, Luther knew, but evangelical Christianity was particularly under threat 'now' (*jtzt*).

In this time of spiritual uncertainty and faced with physical acts of persecution and threat, God alone will prove to be 'a stronghold fortress' (*ein feste Burg*) and 'a good defence and weapon' (*ein gute Wehr und Waffen*) for the believer. The political and theological circumstances in which the hymn writer and his followers find themselves closely resemble those described in the Psalm Luther loosely follows: 'The heathens must despair and the kingdoms must fall' (Ps. 46.7).[63] In times of turmoil, 'The LORD Sabaoth is with us, the God of Jacob is our defence' (Ps. 46.8).[64] For the reformer, his hymns served as a vehicle for disseminating this theological message.

While the second verse of the hymn will emphasise the utter dependency of the believer on this free act of grace, the first verse serves to illustrate the stark dichotomy between the apparently overpowering might of evil and the goodness and grace of God: the armies of evil (*der alt böse feind*), clad in the terrible armour of power and deception (*gros macht vnd viel list / sein grausam rüstung ist*), are gathering at this very time (*jtzt*). They are rallying, preying on believers and drawing them away from the teaching of God's goodness and grace. For Luther, the armies of evil are real forces. Just as 'the ancient evil adversary' (*der alt böse feind*) is a very real power, so Satan has control over all who oppose this teaching. Muslims, Jews, Catholics, and Zwinglians for Luther are all numbered, to a greater or lesser degree, among the forces of evil. Previous battles have been fought between the armies of Satan and those who have faith, but the war that 'jtzt' is brewing 'on earth is not his equal' (*auff erd ist nicht seins gleichen*).

Faced with this amassed opposing force Luther encourages the believer to rely on God's true champion, Christ. On their own, they are utterly powerless: 'with our might nothing is done' (*mit vnser macht ist nichts gethan*). Indeed, any who would attempt to challenge evil by force 'are very quickly lost' (*sind gar bald verloren*). The only way to face evil at all is by the believers' acknowledgement of their utter dependency on God. Luther here draws on an image from medieval courtly life and the battles of classical antiquity: for the war between good and evil to be won, two champions will need to enter into personal combat on behalf of their respective forces. The successful champion will hold the field for their followers. Where the individual believer alone is utterly vulnerable, the champion sent by God to save humankind is 'the proper man' (*der rechte man*) to deprive evil of its ultimate power. God himself has 'chosen' (*erkoren*)—the

---

63 Luther, *Der Psalter von 1524–28, 1531 und 1545*, WA DB 10: 250, 7: 'Die heyden toben vnd die konigreiche regen sich'.

64 Luther, *Psalter*, WA DB 10: 250, 8: 'Der HERR Zebaoth is mit vns, Der Gott Jacob ist vnser schutz'.

German used here echoes the ceremonial election of a prince or the crowning of a victor in a contest—the rightful champion to enter into the battle against evil. The interjection to the singer, 'you ask, who he is?' (*fragstu wer der ist?*) is rhetorical: only one person could attempt this epic struggle: 'Jhesus Christ'. Again, alluding to the Psalm that inspired the hymn, Luther identifies Christ as 'der Herr Zebaoth', the Lord Almighty, the King of glory (Ps. 46.8).[65] 'No other divinity' (*kein ander Gott*), not even the prince of darkness, could ever expect to win and hold the field of battle for his followers: 'das felt mus er behalten'. Luther's Trinitarian beliefs mean that he can see Jesus as both God's champion and part of the one God himself. The manner in which this champion maintains his stand on behalf of the believer is shown in the Psalm that inspired this hymn: 'he has ended the fray to the ends of the world, he has broken the bow and shattered the spear, and burnt the chariots with fire'.[66] Such works reveal the true champion in the Psalm: 'cease the fight, and recognise that I am God: I will be exalted among the heathen, I will be exalted throughout the earth'.[67]

Immediately juxtaposed with the identification of the champion on behalf of humankind as God Almighty is the human reality. Where the final two lines of the second verse seek to inspire believers to place their trust in 'no other God' (*kein ander Gott*) than the Almighty and confidently expect that in the end, God will remain victorious, the first two lines of the third verse depict the human reality until that final victory is accomplished. Luther paints a world filled with devils roaring to devour their prey. Even if 'if the world full of devils were' (*die welt vol Teufel wer*), the fact that Christ has entered the battle on their behalf means that believers need never be paralysed by fear. Ultimately, the battle can be won because evil has already been overcome: 'despite them we shall succeed' (*es sol vns doch gelingen*). The 'prince of this world' (*der Fürst dieser welt*) may rail and roar now, but he has been judged conclusively in the event of Calvary. Indeed, the 'single word' (*wörtlein*) that will so effectively slay the prince of this world was the self-revelatory 'I am he' Jesus spoke at the moment of his betrayal when he was handed over to be crucified (Jn. 18.5), Luther explains.[68] Just as the soldiers who have come to arrest Jesus fall back at the moment of Jesus' self-revelation, so also the 'prince of this world [...] is judged' (*Fürst dieser welt* [...] *ist gericht*) by the suffering and death of Christ.[69] In the same way in which his physical opponents are overthrown, Christ has

---

65 *Deutsche Bibel* (*German Bible*), WA DB 10: 250, 8.

66 *Deutsche Bibel* (*German Bible*), WA DB 10: 250, 10: 'Er hat die streyt auff gehaben bis an der welt ende, Er hat bogen zu brochen, spies zu schlagen, vnd wagen mit fewr verbrand'.

67 *Deutsche Bibel* (*German Bible*), WA DB 10: 250, 11: 'Lasst ab, vnd erkennet das ich Gott byn, Ich werd erhaben seyn vnter den heyden, Ich werd erhaben seyn auff erden'.

68 Luther, *Wochenpredigten* (*Weekday Sermons*), 1528–9, WA 28: 234, 31.

69 Luther, *Wochenpredigten* (*Weekday Sermons*), WA 28, 235, 25–30.

overcome all human suffering. The 'wörtlein' that slays evil also slays human reliance on self, so Luther elucidates in his *Wochenpredigten über Johannes* (*Weekday Sermons on John's Gospel*), preached a couple of years before his hymn:

> Under the Papacy these words ['I am he'] were forgotten. [...] Yet in the same way in which Christ casts to earth with a single word such a large company of the soldiers and temple servants, so his merit and suffering will drive back the merit and suffering of all humankind: so that his suffering alone grants us salvation before God.[70]

If only a few letters, 'I am he', can overthrow the agents of evil that have come to capture God's champion, how much more powerful is the Word of God in its entirety.[71] Luther's hymn places the appointment of the champion to combat the world and its many devils—Jesus Christ—at its heart. The final verse of the hymn is a natural development of the theme of the efficacy of both the incarnate Word in history and also the preached Word in its contemporary setting. Internally it juxtaposes the effective Word of Christ as a 'good defence and weapon' (*gute Wehr vnd Waffen*) against the 'earnestness' (*ernst* [...] *gross macht vnd viel list*), the 'inhumane armaments' (*grausam rüstung*) of the 'ancient evil adversary' (*alt böse feind*) in the first verse of the hymn. The only effective means of defeating evil is the Word of God: 'That word they should let stand' (*das wort sie sollen lassen stahn*). While Christians will experience suffering in this world, Luther draws confidence from the Johannine assurance that 'in this world you will have tribulation; but be comforted, I have overcome the world' (Jn. 16.33). In his *Wochenpredigten* (*Weekday Sermons*), Luther reflected: 'Christians are not left in peace, they do not leave them their honour. However, tyrants and Satan may let the heathen go, no one takes their goods, their honour'.[72] For the Christian, tribulations certainly will include the loss of honour and goods, families, and even life, Luther preached.

70 Luther, *Wochenpredigten* (*Weekday Sermons*), WA 28, 237, 27–238, 26: 'Im Babpstumb hat man dieser Wort gar vergessen [...] Und gleich wie Christus mit einem Wort so grossen Hauffen der Schar und der Diener zu Boden stösset, Also sol sein Verdienst und Leiden aller Menschen Verdienst und Leiden zurück treiben und zu boden stossen, Das sein Leiden allein gelte uns zur Seligkeit für Gott'.

71 Luther, *Wochenpredigten* (*Weekday Sermons*), WA 28, 235, 25–30: 'Such an Almighty Person who with only five letters, "I am he" drives back and casts down both the soldiers and servants of the High Priest, as well as Judas the betrayer' (*Solche Allmechtige Person, welche mit fünff Buchstaben 'Ich bins' zu rücke wirfft und auff den Erdboden stürtzt beide die Schar und der Hohenpriester Diener, Da zu auch Judam den Verrheter*).

72 Luther, *Wochenpredigten* (*Weekday Sermons*), WA 28, 67, 11–4: 'Christianum lest man nicht mit rue sitzen, man lest yhm sein ehr nicht. Si tyranni non, tamen Satan, die heyden lest man ghen [*sic*], nemo aufert bona, honorem'.

Luther makes the same claim in the last verse of his hymn, in the line which speaks of the loss of 'life / goods / honour / child and wife' (*leib / gut / ehr / kind vnd weib*). Life itself proved fragile by 1529: for Luther, it was clear that 'if Satan does not snatch away your body and goods, [...] you will carry Satan around your neck'.[73] The threat of losing earthly goods and relationships was not important, compared to the eternal reign of Christ: 'therefore I may be confident: let them take house and farm, etc., you may nevertheless not dethrone Christ, you will leave him firmly in place to reign'.[74] For Luther, Christ joined humankind on the eternal battlefield between good and evil, and the loss of all that earthly life provided, including life itself, was worth it in order to secure eternal salvation: 'let them be transported thither / they will have no winnings' (*las faren dahin / sie habens kein gewin*). Ultimately, it is the eternal reign of Christ, the kingship of one whose kingdom is not of this world that would endure, Luther preached:

> I feel that I am a sinner and will die, but I believe that Christ will justify me, and is alive. Therefore, there is no other victory—go away, world (*far hin welt*).[75]

At the end of this 'wondrous battle' (*wunderlich krieg*) stood the certainty that 'life upheld the victory / it has swallowed up death [...] the power of death has vanished' (*das leben behielt den sieg / es hat den tod verschlungen* [...] *der sunden macht ist vergangen*), as Luther had written in his 1524 Easter hymn, *Christ lag yn todes banden* ('Death Held Our Lord in Prison').[76] At the end of the believers' personal struggle of life stand two certainties: God fights alongside the believers, 'is with us certainly on the field of battle' (*ist bey vns wol auff dem plan*), to support them by his Spirit and gifts' (*seinem Geist und gaben*), and that whatever Satan and the forces of evil may exact in this life, the overall conflict is won, and any gains by the forces arrayed against us are futile: 'the kingdom must remain with us regardless' (*das Reich mus vns doch bleiben*).

---

73 Luther, *Wochenpredigten* (*Weekday Sermons*), WA 28: 67, 18–9: 'Si non aufert leib und gut [...], so mustu dennoch den teuffel am hals tragen'.

74 Luther, *Wochenpredigten* (*Weekday Sermons*), WA 28: 67, 38–68: 'Ergo so mus ich ein hertz fassen: las nemen haus, hoff &c. du wirst dennoch den nicht herunter stossen, du wirst yhn sitzen lassen und regiern'.

75 Luther, *Wochenpredigten* (*Weekday Sermons*), WA 28: 69, 22–8: 'Ich fule, das ich ein sunder bin, morior, sed credo, quod Christus sit iustificator et vivat. Ergo non alia victoria, far hin welt. Das ist die letzte und beschluß seiner lieblich predig [*sic*], quam habuit cum discipulis in cena. [...] Ut verbum sit efficax, quot praedicavit'.

76 *Enchiridion* (1524), sig. $32^{r-v}$.

That this empire or kingdom is not a physical nation state, but the realm where Christ rules, is evident from Luther's preaching, as it is in the hymn itself. As long as believers remain steadfast, they will not lose their share in the kingdom of God, even if they lose control over their nations and principalities. As Luther commented on John's Passion account: 'The Lord [...] is a King, but not an earthly king. The Gospel is his reign, which brings rebellion—not earthly but spiritual rebellion, by which hearts are divided about the faith'.[77] In Luther's commentary on the reign of Christ, as played out in Christ's interrogation before Pilate, he takes care in spelling out in detail how Christ's kingdom is 'not of this world':

> He would therefore say: 'I will tell you [Pilate] in one word, what kind of a king I am and what kind of a realm I have. I am not such a king, who storms in, harnessed with weapons, with earthly power and might. Nor is my royal office to ride great impressive war horses, and stallions, and to bear an earthly sword. But rather [it is] to preach the spoken Word and testify to the truth'.[78]

Therefore the 'reign' (*Reich*) that will remain as the permanent solace and fortress of the believer is clearly a spiritual haven and place of safety in times of danger.

*Ein feste Burg* was not written to glorify the Lutheran princedoms or to promote an idea of a transnational Protestant empire. Rather it is a hymn of spiritual confidence in the eternal reign of Christ. Its eschatological character enables the hymn writer to look back to the events of Calvary in order to sing of his assurance and trust in God's reign. The heavenly kingdom is made present in the office of preaching the gospel, as Luther suggested in his *Wochenpredigten* (*Weekday Sermons*) and the introduction to his first collection of hymns.[79] The 'Word' therefore

---

77 Luther, *Wochenpredigten* (*Weekday Sermons*), WA 28: 312, 17–21: 'Darumb bleibet der HErr dabey, das er saget, Er sey ein König, aber doch nicht ein weltlicher König. Das Euangelium ist sein Regiment, welches erreget Auffrhur [*sic*], nicht weltliche, sondern geistliche Auffrhur, dadurch die Hertzen sich spalten uber dem Glauben'.

78 Luther, *Wochenpredigten* (*Weekday Sermons*), WA 28: 314, 19–315, 7: 'ER wil also sagen: Ich wil dir mit einem Wort anzeigen, was für ein König Ich bin und was Ich für ein Reich hab. Ich bin nicht ein solcher König. Der geharnischt und gewapnet erein platzet mit Weltlicher Gewalt und Macht. Und mein Königlich Ampt ist nicht, auff grossen herrlichen Caballen und Rossen reiten und das Weltlich Schwert füren. Sondern das mündlich Wort predigen und die Warheit zeugen'.

79 Luther, *Vorrede des Wittenberger Gesangbuches von 1524* (*Preface to the Wittenberg Hymnal*), LW 53: 316, WA 35: 474, 8–10: 'So that God's Word and Christian teaching might be instilled and implanted in many ways' (*Auff das da durch Gottes wort und Christliche leere auff allerley weyse getrieben und geübt werden*).

will remain, even in times of extreme hardship, even as the powers of evil, through their earthly regiments, persecute those who promote the 'spoken Word and testify to the truth'.[80] Through the office of preaching, the faithful already share in the citizenship of the regiment of Christ, and therefore can confidently expect a lasting fortress and strength in the coming kingdom.

The hymn was always intended as a weapon in the battle against 'devils', who infected other Christian denominations, as well as people of other faiths, or of political entities who opposed the growing influence of the Lutheran reformers. Luther's Reformation hymn, like his prose writings, demonstrates a man who could believe in the absolute consolation and acceptance of God for all peoples while simultaneously consigning his enemies to eternal damnation. This confidence and martial language were sometimes used to turn the hymn into a battle song for Lutheran rulers and German nationalists who looked to Luther as one of their founding fathers. Luther's sophisticated theological and rhetorical underpinnings of the hymn were lost in both German and translated versions, leading artists, scholars, and ordinary people to appropriate the hymn as a tool of nationalism. Particularly in the nineteenth century, with the rise of the idea of a unified Germany among poets, playwrights, and composers, an imagined history of the hymn was popularised.[81] During World War I and World War II, the hymn was further co-opted as a militaristic and nationalistic anthem in support of the German Empire and the Third Reich. Only since the latter half of the twentieth century has the hymn begun to be reclaimed as a 'Psalm of comfort' (*ain trost Psalm*). *Ein feste Burg* was intended to be sung as a collective affirmation of faith in God's eternal kingdom in the face of loss of life, liberty, family, and nation; a Psalm of spiritual consolation and solace in the face of overwhelming violence and loss.

We have shown how Luther proclaimed doctrine through sound, to incite faithful belief and reject wrong thinking and action. Luther's classification of music connected all forms of expression to the Creator, and therefore Luther used music to promote his message of how human beings could connect directly to the Creator through redemption by faith. In the next section, Luther similarly sets out a classification of images under the *Ebenbild*, the image and complete likeness of God in the person of Jesus Christ, whose representation in images such as *Law and Grace* would help spread the story of the new reformed faith. At the same time, just as in hymns like *Ein feste Burg*, images depict the demons and enemies of the new faith, who must be resisted if the believer is to escape damnation.

80 Luther, *Wochenpredigten* (*Weekday Sermons*), WA 28: 315, 7.

81 Benedict Anderson, *Imagined Communities: Reflections on the Origin and Spread of Nationalism* (London: Verso, 2006).

CHAPTER 4

# Martin Luther on Images

## 1 Radical Reforms in Wittenberg

In March 1522, Martin Luther rushed back from hiding in the Wartburg, in order to intervene in the destruction of images in his parish church, St Mary's Wittenberg. Following the spread of the Reformation message in Saxony, theologians like Andreas Bodenstein von Karlstadt worked hard to advance the Reformation in Wittenberg. While Luther was in protective custody on the Wartburg, following his imperial ban in the wake of the Diet of Worms, a radical form of Reformation in Wittenberg began to take shape. Inspired by Karlstadt's teaching, this mainly student-led movement had disrupted worship, harassed clergy and town officials, and caused the Saxon elector on 10 October 1521 to instruct his chancellor Gregor Brück to hold urgent talks with the ecclesiastical and university authorities of Wittenberg to prevent 'division, sedition and any other troubles'.[1]

On 4 December, a group of university students, intent on preventing the custom of multiple private masses being said in the Franciscan Priory Church, committed the first destructive acts in Wittenberg. They tore down a wooden altarpiece and decapitated the statue of the monastery's patron, St Francis.[2] The following day, fearing escalation, the town council petitioned the elector to intervene, 'in order to prevent further insurrection as well as to protect the clergy among us'.[3] The elector responded by dispatching the magistrate (*Amtmann*) of Belzig, Christoph Groß and the magistrate of Gräfenheinichen Fabian von Bresen, to investigate the situation, and to instigate protective measures.[4] By Christmas Eve, however, the situation had escalated: worship in Wittenberg's churches was disrupted by 'chanted street songs in church and

---

1 Reproduced in Nikolaus Müller, *Die Wittenberger Bewegung 1521 und 1522* (Leipzig: Heinsius, 1911), 27, no. 8: 'Domit zcwispaldigkait, aufrur vnd ander beswerung verhut werden'.

2 As reported by Duke George of Saxony on Christmas Day 1521, in *Akten und Briefe zur Kirchenpolitik Herzog Georgs von Sachsen*, ed. by Felician Gess (Leipzig: Teubner, 1905), I, 237, 1–5: 'They took down the statue of St Francis and decapitated it, and threw stones at the image of the annunciation' (*St Francicus bilde gnomen und enthaubtet, des heiligen geists botschaft mit stein beworfen*).

3 Müller, *Wittenberger Bewegung*, 77, no. 36: 'wir vor weytherem auffroer zu sambt der Cleriseyn beyn vns vorhutten vnd vorsehen'.

4 Müller, *Wittenberger Bewegung*, 115, no. 53, and 120, no. 54.

 | DOI: 0.1163/9789004527430_006

howling in the church yard', clergy celebrating mass were threatened and the lamps of St Mary's Church smashed. At midnight mass at the Priory Church a mob interrupted the worship, shouting from the gallery, that 'all clergy were destined for pestilence and the fire of hell', the Priory Canons reported to the elector on 29 December 1521.[5]

Into this mêlée, Karlstadt introduced further sudden Reformation measures. Following the restless Christmas night at the Priory Church, hours later, on Christmas morning, Karlstadt led the first German celebration of the Eucharist there, where all participants received the sacrament as both bread and wine. The Prior, Justus Jonas, reported: 'On Christmas Day and the Feast of the Epiphany as well as on the Feast of the Circumcision nearly the entire city came here and the entire citizenry communicated in two kinds'.[6] On Boxing Day, Karlstadt actively promoted clerical marriage by his own marriage to the fifteen-year-old Anna von Mochau. He used the occasion of his marriage to encourage professed monks and nuns to leave their monasteries and persuaded Wittenberg's town council to secularise monastic property.

In Luther's absence, Karlstadt's radical and swift set of reforms encouraged the removal and destruction of images in the city's churches. On the Feast of the Epiphany, 6 January, the Chapter General of the German Augustinians met at the *Black Cloister* (*Schwarzes Kloster*) to discuss monastic vows. Following their meeting, on 10 January, the Augustinian monk Gabriel Zwilling and a number of his confrères determined to remove the furnishings from the Priory Church of the Holy Spirit: 'altars, crucifixes, images, statues of saints and other paraphernalia of the previous ritual observance were carried into the Cloister Yard and burnt; stone statues were decapitated'.[7] In the light of this unregulated removal of images from churches and their destruction, the city fathers, with advice from Karlstadt, Jonas, and Arnstadt, published a new church ordinance, in which they ruled that any further removal of images should occur in an orderly fashion. All images were to be removed, but under the authority of the council:

---

5 Ulrich Bubenheimer, 'Luthers Stellung zum Aufruhr in Wittenberg 1520–22 und die frühreformatorischen Wurzeln des landesherrlichen Kirchenregiments', *Zeitschrift der Savigny-Stiftung für Rechtsgeschichte—Kanonistische Abteilung*, 102 (1985), 147–214 (p. 169); Müller, *Wittenberger Bewegung*, 133, no. 61.

6 Müller, *Wittenberger Bewegung*, 165, no. 69: 'Die natalis et die Epiphaniae et Circumcisionis hic pene urbs et cuncta Ciuitas communicauit sub vtraque specie'.

7 Helmar Junghans, *Martin Luther und Wittenberg* (München: Koehler & Amelang, 1996), p. 94: 'Altäre, Kruzifixe, Bilder, Heiligenfiguren und sonstige Gegenstände des alten Kultus werden auf den Klosterhof getragen und verbrannt, steinernen Figuren die Köpfe abgeschlagen'.

> Images and altars in the church shall also be abolished, in order to avoid idolatry, since three altars, without images, are sufficient.[8]

The date of the promulgation of the new ordinance, 24 January 1522, was also to be the date on which images were to be removed from Luther's own church, St Mary's. For the next six weeks, throughout January and February 1522, statues of saints, crucifixes, carved altarpieces, and painted reredoses in Wittenberg's town churches were taken down and dismantled. Some images were destroyed altogether.

In order to prepare for the purge of Wittenberg's churches from images, in January 1522 Karlstadt had composed a sermon series. The radical reformer concentrated on two issues: the removal of images from churches, and the alleviation of poverty. If the funds expended on images were spent on the poor, Karlstadt argued in his *Von Abtuhung der Bilder und Das Keyn Bedtler undther den Christen seyn sollen* (*On the Abolition of Images and that there should no Beggars among Christians*), then two wrongs would be righted at once.[9] The same held true when images made from precious metals and stones were destroyed and the materials appropriated for the poor. Karlstadt's sermon series was published at the end of January 1522 and served as a theological and materialistic attack on the late-medieval image culture.

In the Decalogue and throughout the Hebrew Scriptures as a whole, the worship of images had been explicitly forbidden, Karlstadt rehearsed in his sermons. Images were an incitement to idolatry, the radical reformer argued, and as such were against the will of God. Even where images were not an object of worship in themselves, they were inherently wasteful. The funds used to

---

8 Emil Sehling, ed., *Die Evangelischen Kirchenordnungen des XVI. Jahrhunderts*: Sachsen und Thüringen, nebst anliegenden Gebieten (Leipzig: O. R. Reisland, 1902), p. 697: 'Item die Bild und altarien in der kirchen söllen auch abgethon werden, damit abgötterei zu vermeiden, dann drei altaria on Bild genug'. Volker Leppin, 'Kirchenausstattungen in territorialen Kirchenordnungen bis 1548', in *Ordnungen für die Kirche—Wirkungen auf die Welt: Evangelische Kirchenordnungen des 16. Jahrhunderts*, ed. by Sabine Arend, Gerald Dörner, and others (Tübingen: Mohr Siebeck, 2015), pp. 137–55 (p. 139), stresses that 'the singular "in the church" should be taken seriously because of the precarious legal situation' as referring only to the City Church (*Angesichts der prekären Rechtsverhältnisse ist hier wohl der Singular 'in der kirchen' ernst zu nehmen*). The council would have been precluded from interfering in the ordering of the Chapel Royal (*Schlosskirche*) or other Collegiate or monastic churches in Wittenberg, Leppin suggests.

9 Andreas Bodenstein von Karlstadt, *Von Abtuhung der Bilder und Das Keyn Bedtler undther den Christen seyn sollen* (*On the Abolition of Images and that there should be no Beggars among Christians*) (Wittenberg: [n. pub.], 1522).

create ecclesiastical furnishings and art would be much better used to provide financial support for the poor and needy. In the same way in which he had argued that monastic property should be used to create a common chest in support of Wittenberg's poor, he now argued that the city's churches should divest themselves of their artistic treasures. God was more pleased with the support of the weak and poor than by the commissioning of costly images of saints, Karlstadt maintained, and persuaded the town council of Wittenberg to commence with the removal of images, and their decommissioning, deconstruction, or destruction.

The zeal with which Karlstadt spearheaded this iconoclastic program led Luther to describe the radical reformer and his followers as 'enthusiasts'. The German term *Schwärmer* which Luther coined for Karlstadt has overtones both of a 'head in the clouds' loftiness, and a buzz of activity as if a swarm of bees or hornets had taken flight. The 'enthusiasts' were just as dangerous as a swarm of hornets when it came to the swift, and often disorderly, removal of images in Wittenberg, Luther implied. By the end of February, the situation in Wittenberg had deteriorated significantly. The Saxon elector had appealed in vain to the town authorities to return to the old order. The local Bishop, Johann von Schleinitz of Meissen, announced a visitation during Lent.

Moved by this local crisis, Luther ignored the elector's advice to remain within the safe precinct of the Wartburg and instead returned to Wittenberg. By the first Sunday in Lent (*Invokavit*), he was back in the pulpit, monastic tonsure freshly applied to provide a clear visual reminder that the old order was in the process of being reformed, and not destroyed or disbanded. He proceeded to preach a week-long series of sermons censuring the hasty reform measures in the city. No one, Luther argued, would be persuaded of the tenets of the Reformation by force: 'In short, I will preach it, teach it, write it, but I will constrain no one by force, for faith must come freely without compulsion'.[10]

His return from the Wartburg put an immediate halt to the brief flurry of iconoclast activity driven by Karlstadt. In Wittenberg, the removal and destruction of images ceased completely, Karlstadt and his followers were reprimanded, and the Wittenbergers were encouraged to stand up for themselves to challenge ungodly leadership. Luther placed the blame for the destruction of church property squarely on his parishioners: 'this trouble has been caused by you' and proceeded to lecture them on how they were each responsible

10 Luther, *Invokavit Predigten* (*Invocavit Sermons*), LW 51: 78, WA 10/3: 18, 10–12: 'Summa summarum predigen will ichs, sagen will ichs, schreuben wil ichs. Aber zwingen, dringen mit der gewalt will ich nyemants, dann der glaube will willig, ungenötigt angezogen werden'.

for resisting temptation and standing up for the truth.[11] Each individual was responsible for upholding good order. Their contention that they either simply followed orders, or were part of a larger mob, simply did not hold, Luther told them:

> It is not enough to say: this person or that person did it, I followed the crowd, according to the preaching of the Dean [of the Chapel Royal, Justus Jonas], Dr Karlstadt, or Gabriel [Zwilling], or [St] Michael [the archangel—Gabriel's 'twin', a pun to match Gabriel Zwilling]. Not so; everyone must stand on their own feet and be prepared to give battle to the devil.[12]

The leadership of Wittenberg reacted with great relief that Luther had returned to take charge. On 15 March 1522, jurist and one-time councillor Hieronymus Schürf wrote to the elector how 'the return of Doctor Martin among us has led to great joy and rejoicing among the learned and unlearned', particularly noting that his words to the people were full of common sense and were such 'reverend and mature sermons'.[13]

## 2 Luther's Understanding of Images

Luther never set down a structured theoretical approach to the image, unlike his *Praefatio zu den Symphoniae Iucundae* (*Preface to the Symphoniae Iucundae*) in which he dealt in some detail, and in one place, with his understanding of music as we have shown above.[14] The way in which he thought about images has to be gleaned from numerous sources, therefore. This does not mean that Luther did not have strong views about images and their use, but rather that he articulated his views solely in disputations and admonitions, commentaries and sermons, just as he occasionally set them out in conversation in his parlour, the so-called *Tischreden* (*Table Talk*). There has been slight engagement

---

11 Luther, *Invokavit Predigten* (*Invocavit Sermons*), LW 51: 86, WA 10/3: 35, 9: 'Das habt jr gemacht'.

12 Luther, *Invokavit Predigten* (*Invocavit Sermons*), LW 51: 79–80, WA 10/3: 21, 7–10: 'Es ist nicht genüg, das du sprechen wolltest: der und der hat es gethan, jch hab dem gemeynen haüffen gefolget, als unns hatt der Probst, Doctor Carlestatt, Gabriel oder Michael gepredigt. Neyn. Ein yetlicher müß vor sich stehen und gerüst seyn, mit dem theüffel zü streytten'.

13 Reproduced in *Invokavit Predigten* (*Invocavit Sermons*), critical introduction, WA 10/3: li.

14 See above, 'Chapter 1: Luther's Theory of Music'.

with Luther's artistic theory but, in the same way in which Luther's sources are fragmentary and spread across numerous publications, the engagement with his theory of the image has been patchy and incomplete.

A recent commentator on Luther's visual culture, Elke Anna Werner (2016), acknowledges the need for greater engagement with the reformer's theoretical framework. While scholars note that Luther approved of some images and opposed certain others, they do so without any further reference to Luther's theory of the image which underpinned the very judgement that determined which images were deemed 'didactically useful' (and therefore to be retained) and which were to be condemned and (therefore be destroyed or repurposed).[15] It is true that 'more recent art historical studies have attempted to decipher to what extent Luther's positive understanding of an inner, imaginary vision could have affected the artistic production of his time', but that work is very much in development.[16]

Werner does bring some of the elements of Luther's theory of the image to her work. But only the most obvious are present: *Merkbilder* (Images of Remembrance) and *Feindbilder* (Images of Enmity).[17] She also clearly recognises the limitations of these two broad categories: the Merkbild is 'a status [...] too commonly attributed in a sweeping way to Protestant images in general'.[18] Frustratingly, she does not dig more deeply into how these two generic terms might be broken down, and the development of Luther's theory of the image is placed firmly in the 'topics of further research'-basket.[19]

The present chapter attempts to address this gap by outlining the theory of the image developed by Luther across his work. As with his theory of music, we have examined his writings, sermons, and *Tischreden* (*Table Talk*) to establish Luther's understanding of images. In philosophical terms, Luther followed Augustine, who himself ultimately followed Plato (via Plotinus) and the Western Fathers, such as Hilary of Poitiers and Ambrose of Milan.[20] Luther's statements on images broadly distinguish between three types:

15 Werner, 'Pictorial Concepts of Law and Grace', p. 141.
16 Werner, 'Martin Luther and Visual Culture'.
17 Werner, 'Pictorial Concepts of Law and Grace', p. 141.
18 Ibid., p. 151.
19 Werner, 'Feindbild', I, pp. 301–305; Werner, 'Visual Culture'.
20 For Augustine's understanding of the image, see Gerald P. Boersma, *Augustine's Early Theology of Image: A Study in the Development of Pro-Nicene Theology* (Oxford: Oxford University Press, 2016), particularly Chapter 6: 'The Analogical and Embodied Imago Dei'. For Boersma's definition of 'pro-Nicean Theology', see Lewis Ayres, *Nicaea and Its Legacy* (Oxford: Oxford University Press, 2004).

1. the *Ebenbild* (True Image and Likeness)
2. the *Spiegelbild* (Reflection or Mirror Image), which includes
   a. the *Merkbild* (Image of Remembrance)
   b. the *Trostbild* (Image of Comfort)
3. the *Schandbild* (Image of Defamation)
4. the *Trugbild* (Image of Deception), which includes
   a. the *Götzenbild* (Idolatrous Image)
   b. the *Furchtbild* (Image of Fear)

Luther's writings and conversations show that he is very interested in the visual arts and their role in Christian devotion. He regularly comments on images displayed in churches both in Germany and beyond. He both comments on images he was able to view in person in places like Italy, as well as images of which he has heard but not seen, such as the image of our Lady of Walsingham in Norfolk. Luther had visited Rome in 1510–1511, travelling via Milan and Florence.[21] The fact that he describes a stunning contemporary fresco of the Last Judgement at San Marcello Paruzzaro in Piedmont suggests that he may have seen the work in situ on his journey to Rome.[22]

In Rome, Luther visited both classical and contemporary pilgrimage sites. He reflected on his viewing of the remains of the Diocletian thermae: 'ah, here are the world's treasure and riches; that is why the Romans took them'.[23] Because of this worldly wealth, Luther surmised, the Romans 'did whatever they pleased'. This moral and religious latitude found an expression in art, particularly in the display of idolatrous images (*Götzenbilder*), quite literally, in the case of his visit to the Pantheon. In his *Tischreden* (*Table Talk*), he reflected how

> High on the vault the heathen gods were displayed, Jupiter, Neptune, Mars, Venus and whatever more their names may have been. These gods all once agreed that they should entice and deceive the entire world.[24]

---

21 Brecht, *Martin Luther*, trans. by Schaaf, I: *His Road to Reformation 1483–1521* (1985), pp. 98–105.

22 Attributed to Sperindio Cagnoli (*fl.*1505–1530), For Luther's description of the work, see his *Wochenpredigten* (*Weekday Sermons*), 1530/33, LW 23: 57, WA 33: 83, 20–41. For Cagnoli and San Marcello, see Paola Manchinu OSB, 'Sperindio Cagnoli, una creatura di Gaudenzio Ferrari', in *Fermo Stella e Sperindio Cagnoli seguaci di Gaudenzio Ferrari: una bottega d'arte nel Cinquecento Padano*, ed. by Giovanni Romano, Quaderni del Museo Bernareggi, Museo Adriano Bernareggi Bergamo, X (Milano: Silvana, 2006), pp. 102ff.

23 Luther, *Tischreden* (*Table Talk*), WA Tr 3: 346, 36–37, no. 3479a: 'Ah, da sind der Welt Schätze und Reichthum gewest, drüm nahmen sie auch für und thaten, was sie gelüstete'.

24 Luther, *Tischreden* (*Table Talk*), WA Tr 1: 232, 25–27, no. 507: 'Oben am Gewölbe waren alle Götter der Heiden gemalet, Jupiter, Neptunus, Mars, Venus und wie sie mehr geheißen

Where Christ had once driven out the pagan gods, 'now the Popes have come and driven Christ out'; not least by their creation and toleration of images that Luther regarded as idolatrous and therefore *Images of Deception*.[25] In his own understanding of images, only true images, such as the *Ebenbild* (Image and Complete Likeness) and the *Spiegelbild* (Mirror Image) were worth holding onto.

### 2.1 Ebenbild (*Image and Complete Likeness*)

For Augustine, the 'imago Dei', on which Luther based his use of the word *Ebenbild*, was a complete likeness, both in nature and substance, of the person depicted. Augustine uses the term principally Christologically (as does Luther), in order to expound on the relationship between the incarnate Christ and Godhead. Augustine's *imago Dei* is a 'true image' because both substance and nature are fully and truly reflected in the image. In this way, Augustine goes beyond the Western Fathers in incorporating a Platonic understanding of the image—that is its capacity to be in union with its invisible archetype—into his theology. The image is a true image because it is in complete union with its source, its original. Reflecting on Augustine, Gerald Boersma explains:

> An image is true rather than deceptive when it is recognised to exist in a participatory union with its source—that is to say, when the temporal, material order is not absolutised, but is recognised to be a reflection of ultimate reality.[26]

Luther regarded the *Ebenbild* (Image and Complete Likeness) in much the same way. Only Christ may be said to be the *Ebenbild* of the invisible Godhead. Only he shares the same nature and substance as the Godhead and makes both visible to the beholder. Again, this understanding almost completely follows Augustine's theology of the image. For Luther as for Augustine, an *Ebenbild* was a complete reflection of an original. It was this complete reflection that made *Ebenbilder* true, rather than deceptive or false images. In the same way, identical twins for instance may be said to be an *Ebenbild* of one another, because each completely shares the other's substance and nature. They are a true image of one another.

---

haben. Diese Götter allzumal waren mit einander eins, auf daß sie nur die ganze Welt bethöreten und betrügen möchten'.

25 Luther, *Tischreden* (*Table Talk*), WA Tr 1: 232, 27–29, no. 507: 'Da Jesus Christus kömmet, den wollen sie nicht leiden; noch hat er sie ausgestäupert. Jtzt sind nu die Päpste kommen und haben ihn wieder vertrieben'.

26 Boersma, *Augustine's Early Theology of Image*, p. 13.

The Augustinian idea of a true image in which the depiction or object and its source or subject shared common substance and nature, made them useful illustrations for Luther. Indeed, in his *Exposition on the Creeds*, the reformer only resorts to a lengthy definition of a true image and complete likeness precisely because of its Christological value. Christ is the *Ebenbild* of the divine, he is the perfect image of the substance and nature of God, Luther argues, and thus is the 'inner natural image and likeness (*Ebenbild*) of God'.[27] In his 1543 *Von den letzten Worten Davids* (*Of the Last Words of David*), the reformer explains:

> Only the Son is like God, or only he is 'the image of the invisible God', as we read in Colossians 1.15, and the image of his divine essence, who 'bears the very stamp of God's nature', as Hebrews 1.3 tells us.[28]

It was not possible to represent such an *Ebenbild* artistically. Only a complete likeness in nature, such as the likeness of identical twins, was able to represent for humans the relationship between the divine *Urbild* and his living *Ebenbild*, Jesus Christ, Luther believed. An *Ebenbild* was a complete representation of both the substance and nature of its source, and therefore impossible to reproduce in art.

### 2.2 Spiegelbild (*Mirror Image*)

Depictions in art by necessity may only ever reflect or represent the nature of their source, Luther argued, they never share their substance. He termed such images *Spiegelbilder*, mirror images. Luther here once more followed Augustine. In his *De diversis quaestionibus octoginta tribus* (*On Eighty-Three Diverse Questions*), the Church Father had differentiated between 'true' and 'false' images by introducing a concept of 'equality' between images. True and complete images were also equal images, Augustine had proposed:

> Image and equality and likeness must be differentiated, because where there is an image there is necessarily a likeness but not necessarily equality; where there is equality there is necessarily a likeness but not

27 Luther, *Von den letzten Worten Davids* (*Of the Last Words of David*), LW 15: 339, WA 56: 88, 32: 'das inwendige natůrliche Gottes Ebenbilde sein, dem Son gleich, wie die Veter'.

28 Luther, *Von den letzten Worten Davids* (*Of the Last Words of David*), LW 15: 339, WA 56, 88, 25–27: 'Denn allein der Son ist gleich, oder "das Ebenbilde des unsichbarn Gottes", Col. 1. Und "das Ebenbilde seines Gốttlichen wesens", der dem Vater gleich ist in einer Gottheit, Ebre. 1'.

> necessarily an image; where there is a likeness there is not necessarily an image and not necessarily equality.[29]

Conversely, unequal images were defective images, Augustine had argued. Their 'defect' lay not in their lack of detail, but in the fact that they did not share the same substance as their object. Christ and the invisible Godhead shared substance, nature and equality, and therefore were a perfect image of one another. The fact that a mirror image did not share equality with its source was what made it 'defective', Augustine believed.[30]

Luther shared Augustine's differentiation between a 'true image' (*Ebenbild*) and a 'defective image' or 'mirror image' (*Spiegelbild*). For Luther, the mirror image was the most natural depiction of a person: 'the reflection of my face naturally appears in the water when I look into it', he remarked.[31] While the image reflected in a mirror might be the most natural form of depiction, it was not an *Ebenbild* that shared substance and nature with its subject. Rather, it remained an object that only ever reflected or represented a given subject.

However detailed and accurate a painted image was, the sitter (the subject) and their depiction (the object) could never share in the same substance. Nor could the image ever capture the sitter's being or nature. Both subject and object remained entirely separate from one another in substance, being and nature. In theological terms, this meant that the image in itself did not possess any life. Indeed, in his 1515–1516 *Diui Pauli apostoli ad Romanos epistola* (*Lectures on Romans*), Luther had explained how 'images that resemble' an original are in themselves 'a lifeless picture or portrait'.[32] In the same way in which the Romans had exchanged the glory of the living God for lifeless images (Rom. 1.23), the images humans created were also mere depictions.

In his 1538 *Die drei Symbola oder Bekenntnis des Glaubens Christi* (*The Three Symbols or Creeds of the Christian Faith*), Luther reflected at length on the nature of a painted or sculpted image or *Spiegelbild*. A picture 'is and is called an image of the person or an imitation of the person', Luther made clear: 'thus

---

29 Augustine, *De diversis quaestionibus octoginta tribus. De octo Dulcitii quaestionibus*, ed. by A. Mutzenbecher, Corpus Christianorum Series Latina [CCSL], 44A (Tournhout: Brepols, 1975), 74, 213–14: 'Imago et aequalitas et similitudo distinguenda sunt: quia ubi imago, continuo similitudo non continuo aequalitas; ubi aequalitas, continuo similitudo non continuo imago; ubi similitudo, non continuo imago non continuo aequalitas'.

30 Augustine, *Quaestiones*, 74, 214.

31 Luther, *Wider die himmlischen Propheten* (*Against the Heavenly Prophets*), LW 40/2: 99–100, WA 18: 83, 11–12: 'gleich als sich meyn andlitz naturlich entwirfft yns wasser, wenn ich dreyn sehe'.

32 Luther, *Diui Pauli apostoli ad Romanos epistola* (*Lectures on Romans*), 1515–16, LW 25: 11, WA 56: 13, 1: 'similitudinem imaginis', 14, 1: 'simulachro mortuo corruptibilis'.

it remains and must remain a fashioned image of the person out of a different substance or nature'.[33] He explained that it was the lack of a shared substance and nature that made images mere reflections of their subject: 'they do not have and are not composed of the same single substance or nature of that which is being depicted but are of another nature and substance'.[34]

The lifelikeness of the painted image lay not in its mode of depiction or the skill of the artist, Luther knew. Paintings or drawings in themselves could certainly be life-like and dynamic and painted by outstanding artists. Only because they did not share in the substance or nature of the person or object they showed, they had no life of their own, and thus were mere representations:

> When a painter, a carver, or a stonemason depicts a king or a prince on a canvas, in wood, or in stone with all the exact similarity that he can possibly produce, so that all who look upon the work of art must declare, 'See, it is this or that king, prince, or person', etc., then that is indeed an image or 'counterfeit', but it is not the substance or nature of the king, prince, or person, etc. It is a mere image.[35]

These 'mere images' were in fact 'natural similes' (*natürlich gleichnis*) of the object they portrayed, Luther explained in his 1528 *Vom Abendmahl Christi Bekenntnis* (*Confession concerning Christ's Supper*). They should be readily

33 Luther, *Die drei Symbola oder Bekenntnis des Glaubens Christi* 1538 (*The Three Symbols or Creeds of the Christian Faith*), LW 34: 221, WA 50: 277, 14–17: 'ist ein bilde des menschen oder dem menschen nachgemacht, so kans doch nicht sein ein Ebenbilde seines wesen oder natur, ist auch nicht seiner natur noch aus seiner natur entstanden oder worden. Also bleibts und mus bleiben ein gemacht Bilde des menschen aus einem andern wesen oder natur'.

34 Luther, *Die drei Symbola* (*The Three Symbols*), LW 34: 221, WA 50: 276, 39–277, 1: 'Das sich nicht haben noch sind dasselbe einig wesen oder natur des abgebildeten, sondern sind einer andern natur oder wesens'.

35 Luther, *Die drei Symbola* (*The Three Symbols*), LW 34: 221, WA 50: 277, 1–7: 'Als wenn ein Maler, Schnitzer oder Steinmetze einen König oder Fürsten bilder auff ein tuch, holtz oder stein, so eben und ehnlich als er jmer kan, das auch alle augen müssen sagen: Sihe, das ist der oder diser König, Fürst oder mensch &c, Solchs ist wol ein Ebenbild oder controfect. Aber es ist nicht das wesen oder natur des Königes, Fürsten oder menschen &c. Sondern ein schlecht Bilde, figur oder gestalt desselben, und hat ein ander wesen'. The 'counterfeit' (*controfect*) to which Luther refers denoted a particularly detailed representation of an object by the form of an image, rather than a forgery. Spinks, *Monstrous Births and Visual Culture in Sixteenth-Century Germany* (London: Pickering & Chatto, 2009), p. 67, explains that the term 'was used frequently in broadsheets to testify to the realism of their imagery'. However detailed or true to the original the depiction, it remained defective, since it did not share in substance with the subject.

perceived for what they represented, without much further explanation or interpretation by the artist. In such a

> natural simile [...] everyone naturally perceives the object of reference, without any instruction, as is the case with pictures. For anyone who knows what a rose is need not be told that a painted rose resembles a natural rose.[36]

In his defence of images, Luther reiterates the argument that *Spiegelbilder* are the most natural form of an image and therefore are not to be condemned. If people rejected mirror images or realistic natural depictions, 'we should not be allowed to have images on coins, or a maiden would be forbidden to have a mirror, with which a viewer may gaze on their countenance or form', he argued.[37]

### 2.3 Merkbild (*Image of Remembrance*)

*Spiegelbilder* were not restricted to living subjects or scenes. In his reflections on the Decalogue as part of his 1529 *Predigten über das 5. Buch Mose* (*Sermons on Deuteronomy*), Luther included factual depictions among the *Spiegelbilder*. An image that was shared in the telling of a story or history was more accurately termed 'Merckbild' (*Merkbild*, image of remembrance or recollection).[38] Because in this recollection it was akin to the spoken or preached word, Luther argued, such an image certainly was neither to be rejected nor to be destroyed:

> But we do not reject [...] images in which one may view events of the past or objects as in a mirror, for they are mirror images (*Spiegel Bilder*), which we do not reject, for they are not images of superstition.[39]

---

36 Luther, *Vom Abendmahl Christi Bekenntnis* (*Confession concerning Christ's Supper*), LW 37: 268, WA 26: 20: 'Denn das heist ein natürlich gleichnis, wenn ein iglicher von natur werckt on alles leren, was es zeige, wie die bilder zeigen, Denn wer eine rose kennet, dem darff niemand sagen, das eine gemalte rose einer natürlichen rose gleich ist'. In the same way, Luther argues, it cannot be said that the body of Christ is a mere simile, depicted in the Eucharistic bread.

37 Luther, *Predigten über das 5. Buch Mose* (*Sermons on Deuteronomy*), WA 28: 677, 34–36: 'Sonst duerfften wir auch kein Bilde auff der Muentze haben und es duerffte eine Jungfraw auch keinen Spiegel haben, darin man des Gestalt und Angesicht schawet, der hinein gucket'.

38 Luther, *Predigten über das 5. Buch Mose* (*Sermons on Deuteronomy*), WA 28: 677, 37: 'Penny images [i.e., pamphlets] are not worshipped either, nor do people place their trust in them, they are images to remember things by' (*Die Groschen Bilder betet man auch nicht an, man setzet kein vertrawen drauff, sondern es sind Merckbilde*).

39 Luther, *Predigten über das 5. Buch Mose* (*Sermons on Deuteronomy*), WA 28: 677, 31–34: 'Aber die andern Bilder, da man allein sich drinne ersihet vergangener Geschicht und

It was the *Merkbild* that was principally fostered by Lutheran artists such as Lucas Cranach for use in the cause of the Reformation: most of the visual art commissioned by Luther and his followers fell into the category of story-telling images. This wide-ranging field included woodcut pamphlets, alongside paintings and sculptures.

Luther explicitly included crucifixes, and those statues of the saints that were not objects of devotion, among the *Merkbilder*. Like drawn or painted depictions, such statues were 'images for memorial or witness'.[40] They enabled Christian congregations to internalise the story of salvation. In his *Wider die himmlischen Propheten* (*Against the Heavenly Prophets*), Luther asserted his views against Karlstadt and his disciples:

> we do not request more than that one permit us to regard a crucifix or a saint's image as a witness, for remembrance.[41]

## 2.4 Trostbild (*Image of Comfort*)

For Luther, painted or carved representations of the crucifixion were the most powerful of any image. Depictions of the crucifixion made it possible to 'know and regard our Lord as an enemy of death', and therefore were a symbol of comfort to believers, the reformer knew, which is why he referred to such images as a *Trostbild*.[42] Especially in adversity, or at the moment of death, the image of the crucified was a supreme source of comfort. For Luther, the term *Trostbild* was synonymous with *Gnadenbild* (image of grace) and *Himmlisches Bild* (heavenly image). Not only did such images give comfort (*Trost*) in affliction, but they also declared God's heavenly plan and showed forth his grace-filled action in the world. Crucifixes and depictions of the cross reflected the victory of heaven on earth, Luther believed. In his 1519 *Ein Sermon von der Bereitung zum Sterben* (*A Sermon on Preparing to Die*), he spoke of Christ as the 'heavenly image', who in defeating death and sin fully reflected the attributes and powers of the Father to humankind. He alone, therefore, is rightly said to be the 'living

---

Sachen halben als in einem Spiegel, Das sind Spiegel Bilde, die verwerffen wir nicht, denn es sind nicht Bilder des Aberglaubens'.

40 Luther, *Wider die himmlischen Propheten* (*Against the Heavenly Prophets*), LW 40/2: 92, WA 18: 74, 16: 'gedenck bilder odder zeugen bilder'.

41 Luther, *Wider die himmlischen Propheten* (*Against the Heavenly Prophets*), LW 40/2: 96, WA 18: 80, 6–7: 'Nü begeren wyr doch nicht mehr, den das man uns eyn crucifix odder heyligen bilde lasse zum ansehen, zum gedechtnis, zum zeychen'.

42 Luther, *Predigten des Jahres 1522* (*Sermons preached 1522*), LW 28: 132, 36: 'das wir unsern Herrn lernen ansehen und kennen als einen feind des todes'.

and immortal image against death' as well as the 'image of the grace of God against sin'.[43]

The image of comfort is an inherently 'lovely picture' (*lieblich bild*) because it shows death as it truly is: emptied of its power and utterly destroyed by Christ.[44] Whether the image of the crucified was evoked in the words of Scripture, as in the case of the Pauline epistles, or depicted as a painting, for Luther those who enabled the contemplation of the crucified Saviour were among the most expert of all artists. For this reason, Luther names St Paul a masterful artist, because in his description of the crucifixion in the first epistle to the Corinthians 'he portrays death as it must be portrayed'.[45] Therefore, Paul showed himself to be a 'true painter and carver' in words and should be praised as one of the masters.[46]

Ultimately the image of comfort showing 'Christ on the cross and of all his dear saints', Luther argued, was best kept not in a gallery or church but it needed to be enshrined in human hearts.[47] It was good to paint and display the crucifixion in altarpieces and images, or to describe it evocatively in sermons, books and hymns. But the most effective form of the image of comfort was when humans chose to 'look only on the image of grace, engraved the picture in themselves (*ynn sich bilden*) with all their power and kept it before their eyes'.[48] For Luther it was just as important to picture the image of comfort in oneself, as to read and believe the act of salvation wrought on the cross:

> Grace and mercy are there where Christ on the cross takes your sin from you, bears it for you, and destroys (*erwurget*) it. To believe this firmly, to keep it before your eyes and not to doubt it, means to view the image of grace (*gnaden Bild*) and to engrave it in yourself (*ynn sich bilden*).[49]

---

43 Luther, *Ein Sermon von der Bereitung zum Sterben* (*A Sermon on Preparing to Die*), LW 42: 107, WA 2: 691, 19: 'Er ist das hymelisch Bild', 15: 'Er ist das lebendig und unsterblich Bild widder den tod', 17: 'Er ist das Bild der gnaden gottis widder die sund'.

44 Luther, *Predigten des Jahres 1522* (*Sermons preached 1522*), LW 28: 132, WA 36: 579, 33.

45 Luther, *Predigten 1522* (*Sermons 1522*), LW 28: 132, WA 36: 579, 32–33: 'mallet den tod, wie man jn malen sol'.

46 Luther, *Predigten 1522* (*Sermons 1522*), LW 28: 131, WA 36: 579, 32–33: 'ein rechter maler und bildschnitzer'.

47 Luther, *Bereitung zum Sterben* (*On Preparing to Die*), LW 42: 104, WA 2: 689, 29: 'Christus am Creutz und alle seyne lieben heyligen'.

48 Luther, *Bereitung zum Sterben* (*On Preparing to Die*), LW 42: 104, WA 2: 689, 27–28: 'gnaden Bild ansehen, und dasselb Bild mit aller craft yn dich bilden und vor augen halten'.

49 Luther, *Bereitung zum Sterben* (*On Preparing to Die*), LW 42: 105, WA 2: 689, 30–33: 'das ist gnade und barmhertzigkeit, das Christus am Creutz deyne sund von dir nymmet, tregt sie

## 2.5 Schandbild (*Image of Defamation*)

Images of defamation fall among the *Spiegelbilder* (Mirror Images). They clearly are depictions of reality, but with deliberate polemical intent. They are sometimes called *Feindbilder* (Images of Enmity) and are of such importance to Luther's Reformation that they are discussed in detail in our next chapter; namely, 'Chapter 5: Teaching the Reformation to Read Images of Hate'.[50]

## 2.6 Trugbild (*Image of Deception*)

A final category of image for Luther is Images of Deception (*Trugbilder*). These kinds of images seek to imitate or falsify genuine natural images. The origin of such images for Luther lies with the devil. Satan both leads people to generate physical pictures with the intent to promote evil or idolatry (*Teufelsbilder*), and also creates mental images of evil and temptation such as nightmares, so-called 'devil's phantasms' (*Teufelsgespenster*). Because all *Trugbilder* are inherently false or evil, Luther also refers to them as *Lügenbilder*.

For Luther, the devil's ultimate aim had been to inhabit the image and likeness of God and usurp Christ's divine *Ebenbild*. Indeed, it had been the devil's attempt to become such an *Ebenbild* that led to his fall, the reformer contended in his 1543 *Von den letzten Worten Davids* (*Of the Last Words of David*):

> The devil himself had experienced this fall in heaven and with his angels had learned his lesson from his opposition to the same *Ebenbild*, the Son of God.[51]

As a result of the fall, the devil's image stood forever diametrically opposed to the *Ebenbild*. Where the *Ebenbild* was a true and complete reflection of the nature and substance of God and reflected God's goodness, grace, mercy and promise of eternal life, images conjured up by the devil were inherently false. While they pretended to reflect goodness, in reality, they showed forth evil, sin, temptation, condemnation and the certainty of death. They might appear to be good, but ultimately only ever showed forth the author of all evil.

---

fur dich und erwurget sie, und dasselb festiglich glauben und vor augen haben, nit drann zweyfellnn, das heyst das gnaden Bild ansehen und ynn sich bilden'.

50 For a more extensive reading of these *Schandbilder*, see R. W. Scribner, 'Demons, Defecation and Monsters: Luther's "Depiction of the Papacy" (1545)', in R. W. Scribner, *Popular Culture and Popular Movements in Reformation Germany* (London: Hambledon Press, 1987), pp. 277–99. For *Feindbilder*, see Werner, 'Feindbild', 1, pp. 301–305.

51 Luther, *Von den letzten Worten Davids* (*Of the Last Words of David*), LW 15: 339, WA 56: 88, 27–29: 'Der Teuffel hatte zuvor den selben fal im Himel gethan und gelernt mit seinen Engeln eben an dem selben Ebenbilde, dem Son Gottes'.

It was by imitating divine images that the devil generated his *Trugbilder*. In his 1539 *Von den Konziliis und Kirchen* (*On the Councils and the Church*), Luther describes well this process of satanic subversion of external things like images:

> This is how he did it: he noticed that God utilised outward things, like baptism, Word, sacrament, keys, etc., whereby he sanctified his church. And since the devil is always God's ape, trying to imitate all God's things and to improve on them, he also tried his luck with external things.[52]

In his 1531 *Glosse auf das vermeinte kaiserliche Edikt* (*Commentary on the Alleged Imperial Edict*), Luther again highlighted the devil's skill in creating his deceptions through the works of human agents. The devil 'subtly paints his own portrait', and imprints 'the seal of his art' on human work 'so that you cannot miss the fact that he has been at work here', the reformer knew.[53] In fact, Luther explained, any human work that leads away from God—whether images or written works—was the very reflection (*controfeyt*) of the devil: 'his likeness, image and unmistakable fruit'.[54] Luther's use of the technical term *controfeyt* only reinforced the understanding that any image created by the devil was, truly, the work of a 'liar and murderer' and therefore 'counterfeit'.[55]

Luther did include forgeries of original artworks or historic relics among the *Trugbilder*. In his *Table Talk*, he reflected on the 'true image', or *vera eikon* of Christ's face, taken by Veronica on the Way of the Cross. Luther saw the purported facial imprint of Christ on the sweat-cloth (*sudarium*) of Veronica at old St Peter's during his 1510–1511 visit to Rome. In conversation in July 1543, he argued that this relic was a clear example of a *Trugbild* (Image of Deception) because it had been purposefully created to 'coax people into believing with a made-up image'.[56] Luther explained how the image shown at old St Peter's was 'merely a black tablet, with nothing on it', which had 'covered with two cloths

---

52 Luther, *Von den Konziliis und Kirchen* (*On the Councils and the Church*), LW 41: 167–168, WA 50: 644, 15–16: 'Und thet jm also. Er sahe, das Gott eusserlich ding nam, als Tauffe, Wort, Sacrament, Schlüssel &c., dadurch er seine Kirche heiligte, Wie er den allezeit Gottes Affe ist und wil alle ding Gott nach thun und ein bessers machen, nam er auch eusserliche ding fur sich, die solten auch heiligen'.

53 Luther, *Glosse auf das vermeinte kaiserliche Edikt* (*Commentary on the Alleged Imperial Edict*), LW 34: 97, WA 30/3: 376, 31–32.

54 Luther, *Glosse auf das vermeinte kaiserliche Edikt* (*Commentary on the Alleged Imperial Edict*), LW 34: 97, WA 30/3: 376, 34–36: 'sein controfeyt, bilde und ehnliche frucht'.

55 Luther, *Glosse auf das vermeinte kaiserliche Edikt* (*Commentary on the Alleged Imperial Edict*), LW 34: 97, WA 30/3: 376, 33: 'ein lügner und mörder'. For the full range of meaning of the term *controfeyt*, see also above at n. 35.

56 Luther, *Tischreden* (*Table Talk*), WA Tr 4: 537, 25–26, no. 4829: 'Beredt also die Leute mit einem erdichten Bilde'.

of silk of which only ever one is removed' in order to maintain the deception of a true relic of Christ's face.[57] In this way, the 'image persuaded the imagination' that the reproduction was a true image, causing people to fall into disbelief.[58]

It was images of deception like these which were evidence of how 'by superstition and idolatry the Pope had deceived the entire world'.[59] The counterparts of such *Trugbilder* in Germany similarly were signs of the 'great power of the devil who is able to fascinate our eyes and senses, as he does with the seamless robe of Christ', a prized relic still housed in Trier Cathedral today.[60]

## 2.7 Götzenbild (*Idolatrous Image*)

The reason why images of deception had spread so readily across the globe was simple, Luther knew: 'the world wants to be deceived'.[61] This held true quite literally in the case of those images that Luther denoted as *Götzenbilder* (Idolatrous Images). For the reformer, any images that were venerated were idolatrous. Worse still were mechanised pilgrim images that suggested (*vorgaukeln*) an active response to a pilgrim's petition. Images that had been made movable to nod the head, for instance, or to shed tears, were none other than 'truly idolatrous images and the devil's hospice'.[62]

Luther had seen such images on his travels through Saxony. In his *Table Talk*, he recalled visiting the pilgrimage image of the Madonna and Child at the church St Maria beim Birnbaum (St Mary's Church by the Pear Tree). Located in Rötha near Leipzig, 'Birnbaum' was a relatively recently constructed pilgrimage place. The pilgrim church had only been built in 1520, to commemorate a threefold apparition of the Blessed Virgin Mary to a shepherd who had grazed his flocks under the eponymous pear tree (*Birnbaum*).[63] The church's pilgrimage image of the Madonna and Child had been mechanised, Luther suggested, in order

57 Luther, *Tischreden* (*Table Talk*), WA Tr 4: 537, 26–27, no. 4829: 'nur ein schwarz Täfelin, darauf nichts stehet', 24–25: 'mit zweien seidenen Tüchern, da man nur das eine wegnimmet'.

58 Luther, *Tischreden* (*Table Talk*), WA Tr 4: 537, 9, no. 4829: 'imaginem imaginatam persuadebant'.

59 Luther, *Tischreden* (*Table Talk*), WA Tr 4: 537, 16, no. 4829: 'wie der Papst mit seiner Superstition und Abgötterei die ganzte Welt bethöret hat'.

60 Luther, *Tischreden* (*Table Talk*), WA Tr 4: 582, 26–27, no. 4925: 'Magna est vis Diaboli, et potest fascinare nostros oculos et mentes, ut fecit cum tunica Christi'.

61 Luther, *Glosse auf das vermeinte kaiserliche Edikt* (*Commentary on the Alleged Imperial Edict*), WA 30/3: 511, 6: 'Die welt wil betrogen sein'.

62 Luther, *Wider die himmlischen Propheten* (*Against the Heavenly Prophets*), LW 40/2: 91, WA 18: 74, 21–75, 3.

63 Richard Steche, *Amtshauptmannschaft Borna*, Beschreibende Darstellung der älteren Bau- und Kunstdenkmäler des Königreichs Sachsen, 15 (Dresden: C. C. Meinhold & Söhne, 1891), pp. 103–06.

to solicit greater donations.[64] By use of an internal mechanism 'placed in the internal cavity, equipped with pulleys and strings', which was operated 'by a mischief maker who always pulled the strings', the Birnbaum Madonna and Child were able to turn towards (or away from) the faithful who had come to pray at the image.[65] The largesse of each offering determined the position of the image, Luther recalled in his *Table Talk*: 'if the pilgrims pledged an even greater donation [to the monastery] the child smiled on them, and with outstretched arm made the sign of the cross'.[66] If they did not, the image turned away from them.

Ultimately, images such as the Birnbaum Madonna and Child only ever 'deceived people and led them into error'.[67] Because they literally were images of deception, the reformer called for the destruction of this and similar 'devil's delusions' (*teuffels gespenst*):[68]

> The destruction and demolishing of images at Eichen, in Grimmetal, and Birnbaum [i.e., Rötha] or places to which pilgrimages are made for the adoration of images (for such are truly idolatrous images and the devil's hospices), is praiseworthy and good.[69]

The former pilgrimage church of Rötha survives to date. Its interior still displays many Marian images, including a magnificent carved Coronation of the Virgin at the centre of the 1525 altarpiece by the unknown Master of Rötha and, at the Chancel step, Stephan Hermsdorf's 1520s statue of the Virgin and Child on a Crescent Moon. The mechanised pilgrim image of the Madonna and Child, however, is no longer extant, which suggests that it was indeed destroyed as Luther commended.[70]

---

64 Luther, *Tischreden* (*Table Talk*), WA Tr 4: 582, n. 16, no. 4925: 'The sign of Birnbaum which spontaneously moved its hands' (*Signo von Birnbaum quod sua sponte movit manus*).

65 Luther, *Tischreden* (*Table Talk*), WA Tr 6: 232, 19–21, no. 6848: 'Es ist aber hohl gewest innwendig, und mit Schlossen un Schnüren also zugrericht. Dahinter ist allzeit ein Schalk gewest, der die Schnure hat gezogen'.

66 Luther, *Tischreden* (*Table Talk*), WA Tr 6: 232, 17–19, no. 6848: 'Hat er aber noch mehr verheißen, so hat sich das Kind freundlich erzeigt und mit ausgestrackten Arm ein Creuz uber ihn gemacht'.

67 Luther, *Tischreden* (*Table Talk*), WA Tr 6: 232, 21, no. 6848: 'Die Leute verirt und betrogen'.

68 Luther, *Vermahnung an die Geistlichen versammelt auf dem Reichstag zu Augsburg* (*Exhortation to All Clergy Assembled at Augsburg*), 1530, LW 34: 25, WA 30/2:297, 1.

69 Luther, *Wider die himmlischen Propheten* (*Against the Heavenly Prophets*), LW 40: 91–92, WA 18: 74, 21–75, 10: 'Also man die bilder zur Eychen, ym Grimmetal, zum Birnbaum, und wo solchs geleuffte mehr zu den bilden ist (wilchs denn rechte abgöttische bilder sind und des teuffels herberge) zu breche und zu störete, ist löblich und gut'.

70 Steche, *Amtshauptmannschaft Borna*, pp. 104–06.

While all mechanised images were deceptions, not all of them were *Götzenbilder* (Idolatrous Images). Where the reformer called for the destruction of the 'truly idolatrous' pilgrimage images of Mary at Rötha, Eichen, and Grimmetal, he tolerated the reframing of the mechanical 'Miracle-Man' (*Mirakelmann*) at Döbeln from movable image to static crucifix and its continued display in church.[71] At the turn of the sixteenth century, the Nicolaikirche Döbeln had acquired an image of Christ as the Man of Sorrows. Carved from limewood, this anatomically precise life-size statue was most likely modelled on a real corpse.[72] Like the image of Mary at Rötha it was partially mechanised, and able to 'move its head, legs, shoulders, and elbows by invisible cords and flexible joints masked by skin-imitating fabrics or leather'.[73]

The Döbeln 'Miracle-Man' was used extensively in realistic devotional re-enactments of the Passion and soon became an object of pilgrimage and devotion.[74] During Passion plays, the wound in the image's right-hand side would 'be covered in wax and pierced by a lance [...] to exude an effluvium of real blood emitted from a concealed container in the back of the wooden figure'.[75] Similar images were displayed in the Ducal residences of Meissen and Wittenberg: in 1513 Duke Georg and Duchess Barbara donated a mechanised crucifix to Meissen Cathedral. In 1517 Elector Johann commissioned a mechanical rood for his Chapel Royal, the *Schlosskirche* in Wittenberg.[76] In conversation Luther condemned the creators of such mechanised crucifixes as satanic (*sathanica*), 'those are not lies made by human error, but they are satanic. Those who know very well what they are doing give out those lies in ungodly fashion'.[77]

Unlike the mechanical *Götzenbilder* of the Madonna and Child, however, Luther recommended retaining repurposed mechanised crucifixes as reminders

71 Barbara Bechter, *St. Nicolaikirche Döbeln*, DKV-Kunstführer, Nr. 598/2 (München: Deutscher Kunstverlag, 2002).

72 Ibid. After the Reformation, the same parish spent a fourth of its income on establishing a *Kantorei*, as we discuss above in Chapter 2, p. 62.

73 Hans Henrik Lohfert Jørgensen, 'Live Matter and Living Images: Towards a Theory of Animation in Material Media', *Konsthistorisk tidskrift/Journal of Art History*, 86.3 (2017), 251–70 (p. 264).

74 For Döbeln and other pre-Reformation pilgrimage centres in Saxony, see Birgit Franke, 'Mittelalterliche Wallfahrt in Sachsen—ein Arbeitsbericht', *Arbeits- und Forschunsgberichte zur sächsischen Bodendenkmalspflege*, 44 (2002), 105–16 (p. 114).

75 Lohfert Jørgensen, 'Live Matter and Living Images', p. 264.

76 Luther, *Tischreden* (*Table Talk*), WA Tr 4: 582, 28, no. 4925: 'signo quod habet elector'.

77 Luther, *Tischreden* (*Table Talk*), LW 54: 111; WA Tr 4: 235, 13–14, no. 4355: 'Ach, es seind nicht humana mendacia ex errore, sed Sathanica, qui prudenter scientes illa impie effunderunt'.

of the 'satanic deception' that led to their creation. When commenting on the destruction of the mechanised crucifix of the Rood of Boxley, England, in his *Table Talk* in February 1538, Luther advocated that 'the image should have been retained as a memorial'.[78] Indeed, at Döbeln, the 'Miracle-Man' was displayed as a Lutheran crucifix for more than 450 years, until its restoration in 1998 and its subsequent relocation to a purpose-built display cabinet in the church.

### 2.8 Furchtbild (*Image of Fear*)

A subset of the *Trugbilder* (*Images of Deception*) is the *Furchtbild*, or image of fear. Such images can be real depictions of terror as well as visions and dreams of terrible events. Frightful nightmares and terrifying visions, 'apparitions and ghosts of the dead' were the work of the devil in 'deluding the world', the reformer held.[79] Luther was certain that the devil was able to 'take possession of and bewitch people's eyes and other senses to such a degree that they would swear that these are true signs'.[80] The images of deception of the mind—visions and apparitions, dreams of judgement and visions of terror—had genuine power to take hold of human imagination and senses, Luther explained in his *Table Talk*:

> All bad dreams are of the devil, who is served by everything that aids death and fear, murder and lies: all this is the devil's handiwork.[81]

In spite of their power, the images of fear that Satan was able to conjure up were nothing other than deceit (*betrug*).[82] Once again Satan used images of fear and other such 'buffoonery and delusion' in order to terrify humanity, Luther argued, because he 'delights in making hearts afraid, cowardly and dejected'.[83]

---

78 Luther, *Tischreden* (*Table Talk*), WA Tr 3: 678, 22–23, no. 3873: 'Das bildt solt man behalten haben in memoriam'.

79 Luther, *Wochenpredigten* (*Weekday Sermons*), 1530/33, LW 24: 369, WA 46: 64, 4: 'mit erscheinung und poltern der todten die welt betrogen hat'.

80 Luther, *Wochenpredigten* (*Weekday Sermons*), LW 24: 369, WA 46: 64, 9–10: 'Denn er kan der leute augen und synne also gefangen nemen und bezeubern, das sie darauf schweren müssen, es seinen rechte zeichen'.

81 Luther, *Tischreden* (*Table Talk*), WA Tr 1: 232, 37–233, 1–2, no. 508: 'Tristia somnia sunt Satanae, quia alles, was zum tod vnd schreken, zu mord vnd lugen dienet, das ist des Teuffels handwerck'.

82 Luther, *Wochenpredigten* (*Weekday Sermons*), LW 24: 369, WA 46: 64, 9.

83 Luther, *Wochenpredigten* (*Weekday Sermons*), LW 24: 13, WA 33: 472, 36–38: 'Das ist nichts den des Teuffels affenspiel und bethörung, der daran seine lust hat, das er die hertzen erschrocken, feig und verzagt mache'.

Satan made people afraid by using their souls as canvases for three particularly terrifying images, Luther explained: 'first, the terrifying image of death; second, the awesomely manifold image of sin; third, the unbearable and unavoidable image of hell and eternal damnation'.[84] Satan 'deeply impressed' (*tieff yn sich bildet*) these images on human minds, and 'presses humankind to look closely at the gruesome mien and image of death to add to their worry, timidity, and despair'.[85] From the fear of death flowed the fear of judgement which, Luther believed, showed the devil practising his 'ultimate, greatest and most cunning art and power':[86]

> The evil spirit prods the soul so that it burdens itself with all kinds of useless presumptions, especially with the most dangerous undertaking of delving into the mystery of God's will to ascertain whether one is 'chosen' or not.[87]

In the same way in which the devil manipulated human souls to picture sin, death, and judgement, he used artists to recreate the images of fear of the mind through wall paintings and other images in churches, Luther held.[88] One such image, a contemporary depiction of the Last Judgement located in a church in Northern Italy, features prominently in Luther's reflections on *Furchtbilder*. On his journey to Rome in 1510–1511, Luther very likely visited the Piedmontese church of San Marcello in Paruzzaro.[89] The village is located in close proximity

84 Luther, *Bereitung zum Sterben* (*On Preparing to Die*), 1519, LW 42: 101, WA 2: 686, 33–35: 'Das erschrockliche Bild des todts, die ander das graulich manichfeltig bilde der sund, die dritte das untreglich und unvormeydliche Bild der hellen und ewiges vordammnüß'.

85 Luther, *Bereitung zum Sterben* (*On Preparing to Die*), LW 42: 101, WA 2: 687, 2–4: 'Auff das der mensch das greßlich geperd und Bild des todts tieff betrachte, da durch bekummert, weych und zaghafft werd'.

86 Luther, *Bereitung zum Sterben* (*On Preparing to Die*), LW 42: 102, WA 2: 688, 6: 'Hie ubet der teuffell seyn letzte, groste, listigste kunst und vormugen'.

87 Luther, *Bereitung zum Sterben* (*On Preparing to Die*), LW 42: 102, WA 2: 688, 3–6: 'Da hin der boße geyst die seel treybet, das sie sich mit ubrigem unnutzen furwitz, Ja mit dem aller ferlichsten furnhemen beladet und forschen sol gottlichs radts heymlichkeit, ob sie vorsehn sey odder nit'.

88 Luther, *Bereitung zum Sterben* (*On Preparing to Die*), LW 42: 102, WA 2: 687, 31–33: 'Alßo vorkeret unß der boße geyst alle ding, am leben, da wir solten des todts, der sund, der helle Bild stetig voraugen [*sic*] haben'.

89 For an attempt at reconstructing Luther's travel route to Rome, see Hans Schneider, 'Luthers Romreise', in *Martin Luther in Rom: Die Ewige Stadt als kosmopolitisches Zentrum und ihre Wahrnehmung*, ed. by Michael Matheus, Arnold Nesselrath, Martin Wallraff, Bibliothek des historischen Instituts in Rom, 134 (Berlin: de Gruyter: 2017), pp. 3–32

to Lago Maggiore, on one of the likely travel routes from Northern Europe across the Alps to Rome.[90] The parish church boasted a recently-created fresco of the Last Judgement by local artist Sperindio Cagnoli, which Luther references in his *Weekday Sermons on John's Gospel* (*Wochenpredigten über Johannes*).[91] For the reformer, Cagnoli's large-scale fresco was 'shameful and blasphemous'.[92] It depicted God the Father seated on a double rainbow, judging the righteous and the wicked. The Father is vested as a priest, a sword raised in his right and a thunderbolt proceeding from his left. Christ kneels at his right, displaying his wounds and pleading his prevailing death. Saints, including St John the Baptist, with his decapitated head on a platter, share in Christ's intercession on behalf of the viewers. At the Father's left is Mary, presenting her breasts to her Son. In commenting on John 6, Luther described the fresco in some detail:

> We see the Son on his knees before the Father, showing him his wounds, and St John [the Baptist] and Mary interceding for us at the Last Judgment, the mother showing the Son the breasts he had sucked. This picture is based on St Bernard's writings, but these words, this picture, and this portrayal are not to St Bernard's credit.[93]

In his sermon, Luther argued that images like the fresco of the Last Judgement are images of fear. They had deliberately been created to frighten and discourage the faithful, he held: 'they have been used to frighten people's consciences

---

(pp. 12–21). For the various probable travel routes between Wittenberg and Rome, see Dietrich Denecke, 'Wege und Städte zwischen Wittenberg und Rom um 1500. Eine historisch-geographische Studie zur Romreise Martin Luthers', in *Genetische Ansätze in der Kulturlandschaftsforschung. Festschrift für Helmut Jäger*, ed. by Wolfgang Pinkwart, Würzburger geographische Arbeiten, 60 (Würzburg: Institut für Geographie der Julius-Maximilians-Universität, 1983), pp. 77–106.

90 Attributed to Sperindio Cagnoli (*fl.*1505–1530), For Luther's description of the work, see his *Wochenpredigten* (*Weekday Sermons*), 1530/33, LW 23: 57, WA 33: 83, 20–41.

91 Sperindio Cagnoli, *Last Judgment*, 1514–1524, fresco in the parish church of San Marcello in Paruzzaro, Northern Italy. Christ intercedes before God the Father, attended by St John the Baptist presenting his decapitated head, and the Virgin Mary presenting 'the breasts at which [Christ] nursed' (Lk. 11.27).

92 Luther, *Wochenpredigten* (*Weekday Sermons*), 1530/33, LW 23: 57, WA 33: 83, 29–30: 'schendlich und lesterlich bildt'.

93 Luther, *Wochenpredigten* (*Weekday Sermons*), LW 23: 57, WA 33: 83, 32–40: 'wie der Sohn fur dem vater niderfellet undt zeiget ihm seine wunden undt S. Ioannes undt Maria bitten Christum fur uns am Jungsten gerichte, und die mutter weiset dem Sohn ihre bruste, die her gesogen hat. Welches aus S. Bernhards buchern genommen ist undt ist nicht wohl geredet, gemahlet oder gemacht gewesen von S. Bernhardt'.

and to make them think that they must fear and flee from the dear Saviour, as though he wanted to drive us from him and avenge our sins'.[94] Human consciences, he argued, were already 'stricken with fear' making the average believer 'feel sufficiently repelled' from God.[95] Images of fear, such as the Paruzzaro fresco, hounded humans further: they were like a team of hunters that drove souls away from God. Luther condemned such images of fear and those who created them:

> I no longer need a hunter, a hound, a beater, or a painter to drive me from God. [...] Fear and terror prod and goad me away from him, so that I do not stay with him. Therefore such paintings should not be tolerated.[96]

The fresco of the Last Judgement he viewed was diabolical, Luther believed. Sowing the seeds of uncertainty in Christ's gift of salvation was a work of the devil, he reasserted in his *Wochenpredigten über Johannes* (*Weekday Sermons on John's Gospel*): 'the devil has no other dart with which to gain mastery over us than the picture of an unmerciful and angry God. If that shot hits the heart, no one is staunch enough to bear it'.[97] The only image able to withstand any *Furchtbild* (Image of Fear) was the *Trostbild* (Image of Comfort). Only with the image of Christ crucified enshrined in their hearts could believers withstand images of fear. In another sermon on St John's Gospel, Luther does exactly that. Returning once more to the fresco of the Last Judgement that terrified him, he sets the salvation wrought by Christ on the cross firmly against the fear of judgement:

> When Christ comes to you and says: 'I have shed my blood for you, my blood intercedes loudly for you', he brings with him the remission of our

94 Luther, *Wochenpredigten* (*Weekday Sermons*), LW 23: 57, WA 33: 83, 41–84, 4: 'Man hat damit den leuthen eingebildet, das sie sich fur dem lieben heilande furchten solten, leich als wolt ehr uns von ihm wegtreiben undt solte unsere Sunde straffen'.

95 Luther, *Wochenpredigten* (*Weekday Sermons*), LW 23: 57, WA 33: 84, 6–7: 'Dan wen sich mein gewissen furchtet, so ists gnug hinweg gestossen'.

96 Luther, *Wochenpredigten* (*Weekday Sermons*), LW 23: 57, WA 33: 84, 8–17: 'Ich bedarff dan keines Jegers, leitthundes oder Jagehundes, das ich von ihm gejagt wurde, [...] Die furch stört mich ab, das ich nicht bei ihm bleibe. Derhalben solte man solche gemelde nicht leiden'.

97 Luther, *Wochenpredigten* (*Weekday Sermons*), LW 24: 157, WA 33: 604, 26–28: 'Denn der Teuffel hat kein ander pfeil, damit er uns abgewinnen kann, den das er gott ungnedig und zornig furbildet, Wo er damit das hertz trifft, ist kein mensch so freidig, der es kan ertragen'.

> sins out of sheer and free grace and gives us the Holy Spirit, who is our Comforter and Advocate.[98]

It was the same attitude that Luther would employ in his campaign to reform images. He purposefully set the message of his Reformation, which for him was epitomised in the cross, against images of deception and fear. In some cases, images of fear were removed and destroyed. In others, as in the Döbeln 'Miracle-Man' images of fear were repurposed to serve the Reformation cause as a life-like reminder of 'Christ crucified in whom alone true theology and knowledge of God may be found'.[99]

## 3 Reading 'Law and Grace': A Composite 'Merkbild' (Image of Remembrance)

Having discussed Luther's attitude towards, and theory of the image, we now turn to his use of images to further the cause of the Reformation. Luther believed that images were how humans conceptualised the world 'since we have to visualise and picture that which is being told us in words, and cannot think or understand without such images'.[100] He believed that images had educational value and should be used to teach: 'And I am well pleased that in this manner one paints, plays, sings or tells the simple folk'.[101] Moreover, he was aware of the visceral power of images to connect ideas to feelings of disgust and horror: anti-clerical images are able to make a person feel 'sick whenever

---

98 Luther, *Wochenpredigten* (*Weekday Sermons*), LW 22: 146, WA 46: 664, 7–11: 'Wenn der [Christus] kömet und spricht: ich hab mein blut für dich vergossen, mein blut das schreiet für dich, der bringt die vergenung unser sünde aus lauter gnade und umbsonst, und gib tuns den h. Geist, der unser Tröster und Fürsprache ist'.

99 Luther, *Disputatio Heidelbergae habita* (*Heidelberg Disputation*), 1518, LW 31: 53, WA 1: 362, 18–19: 'Ergo in Christo crucifixo est vera Theologia et cognitio Dei'.

100 Luther, *Predigten des Jahres 1533* (*Sermons preached in 1533*), *'Auff den Ostertag'* (*'Upon Easter Day'*), WA 37: 63, 25–6: 'weil wir ja müssen gedancken und bilde fassen des, das uns jnn worten fürgetragen wird, und nichts on bilde dencken noch verstehen können'.

101 Luther, *Predigten des Jahres 1533* (*Sermons preached in 1533*), *'Auff den Ostertag'* (*'Upon Easter Day'*), WA 37: 63, 9–10: 'And I am well pleased that in this manner one paints, plays, sings or tells the simple folk' (*Und gefellet mir wol, das mans also den einfeltigen für malet, spielet, singet odder sagt*). In both of these concepts he draws on Bonaventure (1452), see R. W. Scribner, 'Das Visuelle in der Volksfrömmigkeit', in *Bilder and Bildertum in Spätmittelalter und in der frühen Neuzeit*, ed. by R. W. Scribner, Wolfenbütteler Forschungen, 46 (Wiesbaden: Otto Harrassowitz, 1990), pp. 9–20 (p. 10).

one sees or hears a cleric' (to use Bob Scribner's paraphrase).[102] Luther's categories of art-types, his own theory of visual art, can be used to interpret the artworks that he, and his collaborators, used to coach 'his followers to understand Scripture "correctly" so that they would arrive at its "true" meaning, that is, a reading consistent with his theology', and in this way, spread the Reformation message.[103]

Perhaps the most famous Lutheran image is the Cranachs' *Law and Grace* (*Gesetz und Gnade*), a work that has been widely reproduced—Verena Fleck has counted 338 individual reproductions of the work—and been considered in depth by countless scholars.[104] And rightly so: the whole story of creation and salvation is encapsulated in this image that retold the biblical narratives explained through the new Protestant understanding of direct salvation by belief in Jesus Christ. The image was created and recreated, in paintings and altarpieces rich with colour and fine details, but also in black and white woodcuts, and simplified to decorate the margins of title pages. *Law and Grace* was a collaboration between Luther and Lucas Cranach the Elder and Younger, and their workshops, over two decades beginning from about 1529.

*Law and Grace* didactically explains the entire story of human history through the lens of Christian salvation, in a composite image that depicts vignettes of Bible stories using traditional and new iconographies. The message is put across

---

102 Scribner, 'Demons, Defecation and Monsters', pp. 297–9.

103 Bonnie J. Noble, *Lucas Cranach the Elder: Art and Devotion of the German Reformation* (Lanham, MD: University Press of America, 2009), p. 32.

104 For a comprehensive overview of scholarly research on *Law and Grace*, see Ernst Badstübner, '"Gesetz und Gnade": Über einige Veröffentlichungen im vergangenen Jahrzehnt zur lutherischen Rechtfertigungslehre im Bild', in *Baugestalt und Bildfunktion. Texte zur Architektur- und Kunstgeschichte*, ed. by Tobias Kunz (Berlin: Lukas-Verlag, 2006), pp. 252–66. Important studies include, in German: Miriam Verena Fleck, *'Ein tröstlich gemelde'. Die Glaubensallegorie 'Gesetz und Gnade' in Europa zwischen Spätmittelalter und Früher Neuzeit*, Studien zur Kunstgeschichte des Mittelalters und der Frühen Neuzeit, 5 (Korb: Didymos-Verlag, 2010); *Das Bild des neuen Glaubens: das Cranach-Retabel in der Schneeberger St. Wolfgangkirche*, ed. by Thomas Pöpper, Susanne Wegmann, and others (Regensburg: Schnell & Steiner, 2011); Heimo Reinitzer, *Gesetz und Evangelium. Über ein reformatorisches Bildthema, seine Tradition, Funktion und Wirkungsgeschichte*, 2 vols (Hamburg: Christians, 2006), I, 312–13; and in English: Bonnie J. Noble, '"Law and Gospel" and the Strategies of Pictorial Rhetoric', in Bonnie J. Noble, *Lucas Cranach the Elder*, pp. 27–66 (first publ. as '*Law and Gospel*: Scripture, Truth, and Pictorial Rhetoric', *Southeastern College Art Conference Review*, 14.4 (2004), 314–32); Andrew Pettegree, '"The Law and the Gospel": The Evolution of an Evangelical Pictorial Theme in the Bibles of the Reformation', in *The Bible as Book: The Reformation*, ed. by Orlaith O'Sullivan and Ellen N. Herron (London: The British Library & Oak Knoll Press, 2000), pp. 123–36 (pp. 125–7).

by a carefully composed composite of image types. People burning in Hell (a *Furchtbild* or Image of Fear) is balanced by the crucifixion (a *Trostbild* or Image of Comfort). Mimetic, representational images of Luther's opponents, particularly the Pope, Catholic leaders, and Jews incorporate elements of *Spiegelbilder* (Mirror Images) and *Schandbild* (Image of Defamation). The image as a whole evokes, as its recurrent and most important theme, the *Ebenbild*, the complete likeness of God represented in Jesus Christ.

### 3.1 *Visual Literacy in the Medieval and Renaissance Period*

How would Luther's contemporaries have read a work such as the Cranachs' *Law and Grace*? The Medieval and Renaissance period were eras of sophisticated visual literacy among both elites and common people.[105] The visual culture of the period provided a rich array of image reading tools, which Luther, Cranach, and Melanchthon used to construct and deconstruct their images. However, Luther did not assume that every person already had that level of literacy, and new uses and new kinds of meanings needed to be taught, in order that the audience could tell the new story of the Reformation and identify its new enemies.

The *Merkbild* (Image of Remembrance) is an image that tells a story or history. It requires significant knowledge and skill to identify the stories and decipher their full meaning. All the images required sophisticated visual literacy techniques including identifying allegory, iconography, symbolism, and realism while recognising intertextual references, as well as understanding their theological, historical or cultural contexts. The images were sometimes accompanied by the written word, and the ability to read the captions or labels in German or Latin text also assumed some textual literacy. These images and their captions would have been read aloud for the benefit of the illiterate, according to Pettegree.[106]

Art historians have already set out a comprehensive account of how ordinary people were able to understand Lutheran images, with much of the foundational work being published in the 1980s. In his magisterial book on the art of the Renaissance, *Symbolic Images*, the art historian Ernst Gombrich sets out a theory of the function of the image in the Renaissance period, in which an image may simultaneously represent, symbolise and express objects, people, emotions and

---

105 For the best overview of this point in context, see Scribner, *For the Sake of Simple Folk*, p. 299, and Pettegree, *Reformation and the Culture of Persuasion*, pp. 102–126 (pp. 111–20).

106 Pettegree, *Reformation and the Culture of Persuasion*, p. 117.

ideas.[107] The representation is what Gombrich would call 'mimesis' in *Art and Illusion*, using realism or naturalism to depict recognisable images.[108] Symbolism was frequently conventional, but it could also be created 'by nature', or by revelation and interpretation, as Gombrich points out in his explanation of Luther and Melanchthon's didactic unpacking of the monstrous images of the *Papstesel* (*Pope Donkey*) and *Mönchskalb* (*Monk Calf*), which we will discuss at greater length in the next chapter.[109]

In his series of studies in *For the Sake of Simple Folk*, first published in 1981, Bob Scribner consistently shows how these images work as 'adversarial propaganda' that create, or rely on, 'stereotypes'.[110] They worked by reducing 'the intricacies of theology, politics and national grievance in a number of discrete and easily recognisable symbols'. The symbols were 'named figures presented in their own image and likeness', or realistic images using recognisable animals, clothing, actions and tools:[111]

> These images were drawn [...] from the popular culture of the time, and were readily recognisable by the ordinary reader. The creators of propaganda worked by taking such common images and reassembling them into new schemata, which could then be read by the unlettered.[112]

107 Ernst Hans Gombrich, *Symbolic Images: Studies in the Art of the Renaissance* (London: Phaidon, 1985), p. 124.

108 Ernst Hans Gombrich, *Art and Illusion: A Study in the Psychology of Pictorial Representation* (New York: Pantheon Books, 1961), pp. 116, 182, 330, for the Platonic concept of mimesis, see Alexander W. Byvanck, *De beeldende Kunst in den Tijd van Plato*, Mededelingen der Koniklijke Nederlandse Akademie van Wetenschappen, Afdeling Letterkunde, Nieuwe Reeks d. 18, no. 16 (Amsterdam: Noord-Hollandsche Uitgevers Maatschappij, 1955), pp. 429–75.

109 Ernst Hans Gombrich, 'Icones Symbolicae: The Visual Image in Neo-Platonic Thought', *Journal of the Warburg and Courtauld Institutes*, 11 (1948), 163–192 (pp. 180–81). Gombrich's consideration led to a wealth of scholarly attention on these two images from, *inter alia*, Lorenz Dittmann, 'Die Kunst der Reformationszeit', in *Martin Luther 1483–1983: Ringvorlesung der Philosophischen Fakultät Sommersemester 1983*, ed. by P. Erdmann (Saarbrücken: Universität des Saarlandes), 1983, pp. 141–72 (pp. 151–52); via Scribner, 'Demons, Defecation and Monsters', pp. 277–99 (pp. 151–52); to Tacke and Münch, 'Bildende Kunst und Reformation', pp. 131–44 (pp. 139–42).

110 Scribner, *For The Sake of Simple Folk*, p. xxii. In his 'Demons, Defecation and Monsters', pp. 277–99, Scribner offers an extended explanation of the visual purpose and context of the *Abbildung des Bapsttum* (*Depictions of the Papacy*), and explores the *Papstesel* and *Mönchskalb* in the context of the *Depictions* series, building on his iconographical and semiological analysis set out in *Simple Folk*.

111 Scribner, *For the Sake of Simple Folk*, p. 295.

112 Scribner, *For the Sake of Simple Folk*, pp. 295–99.

*Law and Grace* makes use of conventional symbols, natural images, and recognisable figures from popular culture, 'reassembling them into new schemata', in ways that could be decoded by the 'unlettered'. The image makes use of a visual language that would have been familiar to most people at the time. In 599–600, Pope Gregory had declared that church art was the 'Bible of the poor', and thus there was already a millennia-long history of visual images that even illiterate Christians were expected to be able to decode.[113] Church art images made use of both representational symbolism and rhetorical structures. The placement of images in relation to one another was purposeful, implying sequences, hierarchies, or contrasts. Biblical narratives might be set out through pictorial depictions of key scenes, and then arranged in chronological order, in windows, screens, sculptures, and frescoes. God's power over the world could be depicted by having God on high, and the lesser powers and creatures placed below. A contrast might be established between good and evil, usually the righteous to the right-hand and the unrighteous to the left, encouraging the viewers to choose virtue and shun vice. The images were sometimes consciously historicised, and sometimes styled the participants in contemporary clothing and hair. Emblems were also used to identify particular figures, whether saints bearing their attributes, nobles with their coats of arms, or church leaders with their distinctive vestments. The attributes of the images were explicitly intended to evoke emotions in the viewer and to lead to action or contemplation.

*Law and Grace* also makes use of textual elements, relevant in an era of increasing semi-literacy. The examples discussed in this section have textual glosses printed around the edges of the image in Latin or German, or were printed as the frontispiece of German-language books, such as the new translations of the Luther Bible or Melanchthon's *Loci Communes*. In these contexts, the images are explained by the accompanying text, but also help illustrate and summarise the text. The text was intended to help viewers understand the images better, and the images helped them to understand the text better. The images thus assume visual and textual literacies but also set out to explain and teach these literacies and the new theological understanding of human history.

---

113 See Scribner, 'Das Visuelle in der Volksfrömmigkeit', p. 10. For a more comprehensive overview of Pope Gregory's pronouncements, see Herbert Kessler, 'Pictorial Narrative and Church Mission in Sixth-Century Gaul', *Studies in the History of Art*, 16 (1985), 75–91.

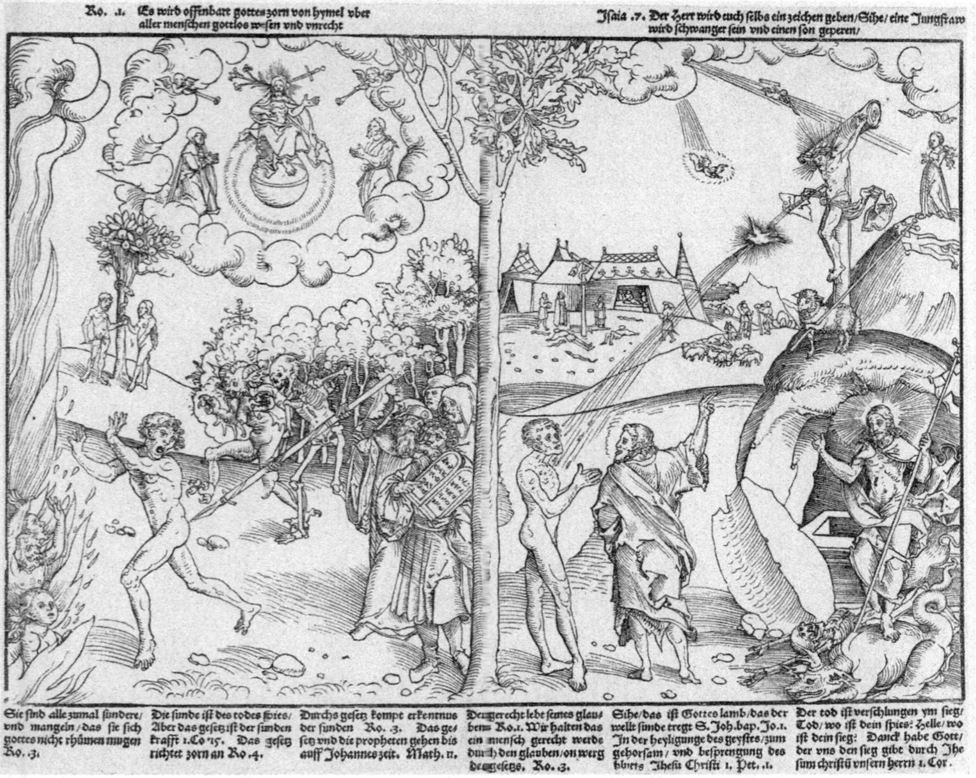


FIGURE 1 Lucas Cranach the Elder, *Law and Grace*, c.1530, woodcut and letterpress, 27 × 32 cm (KF no. 353)
PHOTOGRAPHY: THE BRITISH MUSEUM, LONDON

### 3.2 *'Law and Grace'*

The theological impact of *Law and Grace* on spreading the new Protestant message cannot be underestimated.[114] Cranach's masterful paintings in the 1520s were reproduced, and new versions were created as paintings, woodcuts

114 See, for instance, Bonnie J. Noble, '"A Work in Which the Angels Are Wont to Rejoice": Lucas Cranach's "Schneeberg Altarpiece"', *The Sixteenth Century Journal*, 34.4 (2003), 1011–37 (pp. 1018–25), and Noble, '"Law and Gospel" and the Strategies of Pictorial Rhetoric', pp. 27–66; Pettegree, '"The Law and the Gospel"', pp. 123–36, and Christiane Andersson, 'Religiöse Bilder Cranachs im Dienste der Reformation', in *Humanismus und Reformation in der deutschen Geschichte. Ein Tagungsbericht*, ed. by Lewis W. Spitz, Veröffentlichungen der historischen Kommission zu Berlin, 51 (Berlin: De Gruyter, 1981), pp. 43–79.

FIGURE 2 Lucas Cranach the Younger and Workshop, *Law and Grace*, 1550, woodcut, 30 × 20.8 cm, frontispiece from Martin Luther, *Die Propheten alle Deudsch* (Wittenberg: Hans Lufft, 1550) PHOTOGRAPHY: THE METROPOLITAN MUSEUM OF ART, NEW YORK

and engravings by both Cranach the Elder and Younger and their workshops.[115] A few versions existed in original or unique forms, like the Prague and Gotha paintings, or the Epitaph Altar of Elector Johann Friedrich I. in Weimar, where Cranach and Luther model the figures of John the Baptist and Adam beneath the cross. However, most people experienced the images through woodcuts that were distributed in widely available print runs.[116] The Cranachs' workshop and Lufft's printing press were central to the multiple forms of *Law and Grace*, and their wide distribution, as well as linking them directly to translated texts such as the Luther Bible. Yet the work was reused more broadly by reformers, for instance in the translation of Melanchthon's *Loci Communes* by Justus Jonas, printed by Rhau and his workshop.[117] A wide group of authors, translators, artists, and printers are all therefore active participants in establishing this practice of constructing and instructing the reading of these images of the new confession to the masses, through mass media and accessible material that the common person could understand and be encouraged to share.

*Law and Grace* is assembled as a composite of images drawn from across the Old and New Testaments, using conventional images that share the visual language of Medieval and Renaissance Western European art.[118] Thus Adam and Eve are depicted as two naked people, standing near a tree with a snake twirled

---

115 Fleck, '*Ein tröstlich gemelde*', gives a complete overview of the 338 extant versions of *Law and Grace*. In this section, we have selected a small cross sample of versions to explore in detail: Lucas Cranach the Elder, 1529, painting with textual gloss in German script, 82.2 cm × 118 cm, Herzogliches Museum Gotha (FR no. 221); Lucas Cranach the Elder, 1530, woodcut with textual gloss in German type, 27 cm × 32 cm, The British Museum, London (KF no. 353); The Cranach Workshop and Rhau, 1536, print frontispiece, from Melanchthon, *Loci Communes*, German translation by Justus Jonas (Kat. 53b); The Cranach Workshop and Rhau, 1541, print frontispiece, 30.1 cm × 20.9 cm, from *Die Propheten alle Deutsch* (*The Prophets in German*), volume 2 of Luther's *German Bible* (KF no. 279); Lucas Cranach the Younger, 1550, painting with textual gloss in Latin type, 19 cm × 25.5 cm, Brod Gallery, London (KF no. 355). For a full account of the versions, see KF nos. 401, 407, 505–10 and FR no. 114. Pettegree, '"The Law and the Gospel"', p. 126, believes 'that the Gotha type represents Cranach's original design'.

116 Lucas Cranach the Elder, *Law and Gospel*, tempera panel, 72 cm × 88.5 cm, Národní Galerie Praha (KF nos. 505–7). Norbert Michels, *Cranach in Anhalt: Vom Alten zum Neuen Glauben* (Petersberg: Michael Imhof Verlag, 2015), p. 48. See further Walter Benjamin, 'L'œuvre d'art à l'époque de sa reproduction méchanisée' ('The Work of Art in the Age of Mechanical Reproduction'), *Zeitschrift für Sozialforschung*, 5 (1936), 40–68.

117 Philipp Melanchthon, *Loci Communes, das ist die furnehmsten Artikel Christlicher lere Philippi Melanch[thonis] Aus dem Latin verdeudscht durch Justum Jonam* (Wittenberg: Rhaw, 1536).

118 For examples of these iconographic depictions across the Western art tradition, see James Hall, *Dictionary of Subject and Symbols in Art* (London: John Murray, 1979), 'Crucifixion', 'Adam and Eve', 'Annunciation', 'Lamb'; and *Encyclopedia of Comparative Iconography:*

around the trunk. Jesus being crucified is shown as a man, wearing a loincloth and a crown of thorns, arms outstretched on a cross with 'his cleansing and redeeming blood' spurting out of his side.[119] Three other common images in medieval art are also used repeatedly: people in flames depict the damned in hell; a lamb carrying a cross pennant depicts the *Agnus Dei* (Lamb of God, see Jn, 1.29, Rev. 5); and a man with a spear standing on a dragon, depicts Christ conquering death and sin.[120]

Primarily, *Law and Grace* is a *Merkbild*, an image of remembrance that tells a story or recounts history. Cranach's vignettes roughly follow the chronological order of their biblical source. In every version of *Law and Grace*, the reader should start at the top left corner and read down the left-hand column: 'unpacking the intentions that underlie the symmetry of Cranach's composition, we are thus led step by step through the Protestant theology of Justification'.[121] In some versions, the reader then returns to the top of the right-hand column and reads down, an 'ɪɪ-shaped' reading strategy. In other versions, the reader continues across the bottom of the image and then starts reading upwards, a 'U-shaped' reading strategy. In some versions, the reading strategy needs to navigate around other visual elements, for example, the frontispieces have to fit into the margins around a title block.

Visual and narrative clues lead the eye through the story. Internal clues help the viewer navigate to the next vignette. Sometimes those clues are chronological, sometimes the eye is directed by a pointed line to the next linked part of the story (a ray of light, a spray of blood, a spear, or literally a pointed finger). The parallels between the columns are shown opposite one another: so, for example, hell on the bottom far left is matched by Christ harrowing hell on the bottom far right; Eve in the upper mid-left is mirrored by Mary in the upper mid-right.

---

*Themes Depicted in Works of Art*, ed. by Helene E. Roberts, 2 vols (Chicago: Fitzroy Dearborn, 1998), 'Sin/Sinning', 'Damned Souls', 'Crucifixion'.

119 Maria Lucia Weigel, 'Bekenntnisbilder—Bekenntnisse im Bild', in *Bekennen und Bekenntnis im Kontext der Wittenberger Reformation*, ed. by Daniel Gehrt, Johannes Hund, Stefan Michel, and others (Göttingen: Vandenhoek & Ruprecht, 2019), pp. 259–78 (p. 272): 'reinigender und heiligender Blutstrahl'.

120 For other examples of images of people consigned to burn in hell, created in collaboration between Luther and Cranach, see their 1545 *Abbildung des Bapstum* (*Depictions of the Papacy*) II: *Regnum Satanae et Papae* (*Kingdom of Satan and the Pope*).

121 Koerner, *The Moment of Self-Portraiture*, p. 379. Interestingly, Koerner finds the end result of this visual journey of decoding the story of justification unsatisfying—for him, 'once interpreted, the image becomes as interesting as a solved crossword puzzle'—that is, it loses its appeal. We agree with Koerner that the visual images are sequential, in contrast to Roper, *Living I Was Your Plague*, p. 123, who sees them as non-linear.

The bottom third of *Law and Grace* always shows two ahistorical tableaux: Moses standing with other patriarchs of the Old Testament watching a demon and skeleton drive Adam into hell on the one side; on the other, Christ on the cross with the Lamb of God at his feet baptising Adam with his blood as John the Baptist looks on. In these tableaux, the chronological orders above are brought together into an eternal synthesis of the message of salvation, 'for as in Adam all die, even so in Christ shall all be made alive' (1 Cor. 15.22).

The vignettes are sometimes explained with a textual gloss, a short paraphrase, or a quotation from the Bible with a citation of the book and chapter. This gloss is interpretative rather than descriptive; for example, the Annunciation (Lk 1.26–38) is explained by a reference to the Prophecy of Isaiah foretelling the event (Isa. 7.14). Viewers are invited to use the glosses to understand better the theological meaning of the image within its visual narrative; to move from the iconographic to the theological.

However, *Law and Grace* is also arranged to make a rhetorical point. The image is bifurcated by a tree. The two sides portray a contrast between salvation on the right and damnation on the left, illustrating the argument in Paul's epistle to the Romans where the Jewish adherence to the Law is argued to be the basis for condemnation, and Christian belief in Christ the basis for salvation (Rom. 2–5). Paul summarises his position, focusing on the contrast between Adam and Christ:

> Therefore just as one man's trespass led to condemnation for all, so one man's act of righteousness leads to justification and life for all. For just as by the one man's disobedience the many were made sinners, so by the one man's obedience the many will be made righteous. But law came in, with the result that the trespass multiplied; but where sin increased, grace abounded all the more, so that, just as sin exercised dominion in death, so grace might also exercise dominion through justification leading to eternal life through Jesus Christ our Lord.
>
> Rom. 5.18–21

On the left side of *Law and Grace*, the tree's branches are entirely bare of leaves, and events from the Old Testament, including the fall of Adam and Eve in the Garden of Eden, are presented alongside a scene of fiery damnation. The right side shows branches with leaves and New Testament stories of the life of Christ, including his crucifixion. The Tree of the Knowledge of Good and Evil is shown on the left side, as this tree led to the fall of humankind. On the right side, the cross is shown, sometimes called a 'tree' (for example in 1 Pet. 2.24 and Acts 5.30), which leads to the salvation of humans.

Such a binary rhetorical structure would have been familiar to Reformation viewers: having a left side for the 'Law' and the right side for 'Grace' matches, for example, medieval images of Synagogue and Church from the ninth century onwards.[122] *Ecclesia* and *Synogoga* were a widely popular pair of images displayed at the entrances of cathedrals and churches in Germany and France; similar contrasting pairs of images include the *vita activa* and *vita contemplativa*, the wise and foolish virgins, or pairs of virtue and vice.[123] As Nina Rowe explains in her extensive study of the pair, the beautiful female personifications of the Church and the Synagogue were used to

> convey dichotomies that lay at the heart of the Christian understanding of history and Scripture: that the era of the law was a prelude to the era of grace; that the Hebrew Bible foretold both the life of Jesus and the principles of Christian belief; that the triumph of Christianity over Judaism was fundamental to the Lord's plan for humanity.[124]

The Lutheran image of *Law and Grace* however makes a significant change to the arrangement, and therefore to the argument set out. Rather than contrasting condemned Jewish figures with salvation through adherence to the Catholic Church, the Lutheran images group both Jewish and Catholic leaders together in the 'Law' column. The institutions of both 'Church' and 'Synagogue' are on the side of condemnation. On the right side of 'Grace' is the person of Christ alone, who thus offers the message of salvation directly to the believer

---

122 Luther also mobilises the common distinction of *Synogoga* in comparison with *Ecclesia* in his *Von den Juden und ihren Lügen* (*Of the Jews and their Lies*), WA 53: 522, 37–527, 31, '*Synagoga*' being equivalent to '*Equivocatio*' and '*Distinctio*' as suggested by Nina Rowe, 'Idealization and Subjection at The South Façade of Strasbourg Cathedral', in *Beyond the Yellow Badge: Anti-Judaism and Anti-Semitism in Medieval and Early Modern Visual Culture*, ed. by Mitchell B. Merback, Brill's Series in Jewish Studies, 37 (Leiden: Brill, 2007), pp. 179–202. Rowe develops this trope fully in her *The Jew, the Cathedral and the Medieval City: Synagoga and Ecclesia in the Thirteenth Century* (Cambridge: Cambridge University Press, 2011).

123 Rowe, *The Jew, the Cathedral*, pp. 1–4, 241; Tacke and Münch, 'Bildende Kunst und Reformation', p. 135, affirm the view that these antithetical juxtapositions 'have long been rooted in a common cultural understanding' (*daher im kulturellen Archiv lange verankert*). Sculptural examples in France and Germany include Worms, Erfurt, Minden, Magdeburg, Freiburg in Breisgau, Trier, Bamberg, Strasbourg, Reims, Chartres, Notre-Dame de Paris, all built between *c.*1220–1330.

124 Rowe, *The Jew, the Cathedral*, pp. 1–2, see also Wolfgang Seiferth, *Synagoge und Kirche im Mittelalter: Historische und theologische, literarische und kunstgeschichtliche Dokumentation zur Geschichte der Juden im Mittelalter* (München: Kösel Verlag, 1964).

from the cross. This choice places the emerging Protestant movement as the only true heir of both the Jewish faith and the Catholic Church.

Understanding the interplay of the biblical narrative, conventional iconography, and theological comparisons gives the reader flexibility to follow the intended messages, even when the vignettes are moved spatially within the larger construction. For example, in the Gotha painting (1529), a bronze serpent (Num. 21.6–9) is placed as a sign of God's judgement on the 'Law' side; but in a 1530 print, the bronze serpent is placed as a foreshadowing of the cross on the 'Grace' side.[125] In the frontispiece versions for Luther's translations of the Scriptures (1541 and 1544), two images are moved out of sequence, probably for pragmatic space reasons: the bronze serpent is slotted above the Garden of Eden on the Law side, and the Harrowing of Hell is slotted above Christ on the cross.[126] It is unlikely that this would have caused much confusion to viewers. Although *Law and Grace* was painted, repainted, printed and reprinted by multiple artists, over multiple decades, the story and its meaning remain consistent, and remained legible through consistent reading strategies.

Having learnt to 'read' Luther and Cranach's *Law and Grace*, viewers could re-read versions made by other artists. For example, Rhau's 1536 edition of Justus Jonas' translation of Melanchthon's *Loci Communes* uses a woodcut version of *Law and Grace* to illustrate the title page.[127] The image uses the same reading strategies but in a significantly different reading order.

Rhau's *Law and Grace* illustrates Melanchthon's typical systematisation of Luther's thought.[128] Melanchthon's systematic way of explaining concepts is demonstrated in the almost tabulated structure of the images.

---

125 Incidentally, twinned apothecary serpents are the device of the Wittenberg printer Hans Lufft, just as the crowned and winged serpent was Cranach's heraldic device; see Steven Ozment, *Serpent and the Lamb: How Lucas Cranach and Martin Luther Changed Their World and Ours* (New Haven, CT: Yale University Press, 2011), pp. 1–2, and Donald L. Ehresmann, 'The Brazen Serpent, a Reformation Motif in the Works of Lucas Cranach the Elder and His Workshop', *Marsyas*, 12 (1967), 32–47

126 This version was used twice, first for the cover of Luther's whole translated *German Bible* in 1541, and then in 1544 it was reused for volume II, *Die Propheten alle Deudsch* (*The Prophets all in German*), both published by Hans Lufft, with the artwork attributed to Cranach the Younger.

127 Melanchthon, *Loci Communes*. Peter Seitz's 1539 edition of Jonas' translation, *Loci Communes, das ist die furnehmsten Artikel Christlicher lere Philipp*[*i*]. *Melanch*[*thonis*] *Aus dem Latein verdeudscht durch Justum Jonam* (Wittenberg: Peter Seitz, 1539), uses a more traditional decorative frontispiece of curlicues and angels displaying the face of Christ and the instruments of the Passion, which the printer had previously used for his Latin edition, *Loci Commvnes Theologici Recens Collecti et Recogniti a Philippo Melanthone* [*sic*], *Vitebergae M.D.XXXVI* (Wittenberg: Peter Seitz, 1536).

128 See the following chapter for more extensive discussion of Melanchthon's systematisation.

TABLE 1 Reading the *Law and Grace* frontispiece on Melanchthon's *Loci Communes*

| **Left side** | | **Right side** | |
|---|---|---|---|
| **'Law' image** | **Law meaning** | **'Grace' image** | **Grace meaning** |
| Bare branches on the tree | Death | Leafy branches on the tree | Life |
| God in heaven presents the tablets of the law to Moses | The word of the Law is passed down from heaven | The dove of the Holy Spirit hovers over Mary and Joseph | The Word of Grace flies down from heaven to be made incarnate |
| The tree of Knowledge, with a serpent wrapped around the trunk and Adam and Eve eating the fruit | Tree of the fall: 'as in Adam all die' sin comes into the world | Christ on the cross with the Lamb of God at his feet | Cross, tree of salvation: 'so in Christ shall all be made alive' 'takes away the sins of the world' |
| Adam driven to hell | Humans are all damned | Christ harrowing hell | Humans can be saved |
| Demon and skeleton driving Adam | Death and demons have power | Christ stands on dragon and skeleton and spears dragon | Death and demons are defeated |
| Moses and another patriarch point to the tablets of the law | The word of the Law condemns us | John the Baptist points to Jesus, and an angel brings the good news to the Shepherd | The good news of the living Word will save us |

### 3.3 *Contemporary Representations*

There are three places in the Luther versions of *Law and Grace* where the artist goes beyond the biblical story and interpolates contemporary images: the depiction of the demon who drives Adam into hell, the depiction of the people in hell, and the depiction of the Old Testament Patriarchs gathered at the base of the *Law and Grace* tree. The contemporary images are recognisable mimetic (*Spiegelbild*) images, some with defamatory (*Schandbild*), characteristics that make recognisable humans into monsters and demons.

In all the versions of *Law and Grace*, the three motifs that use contemporary elements are clustered in the bottom left corner, the conclusion to the

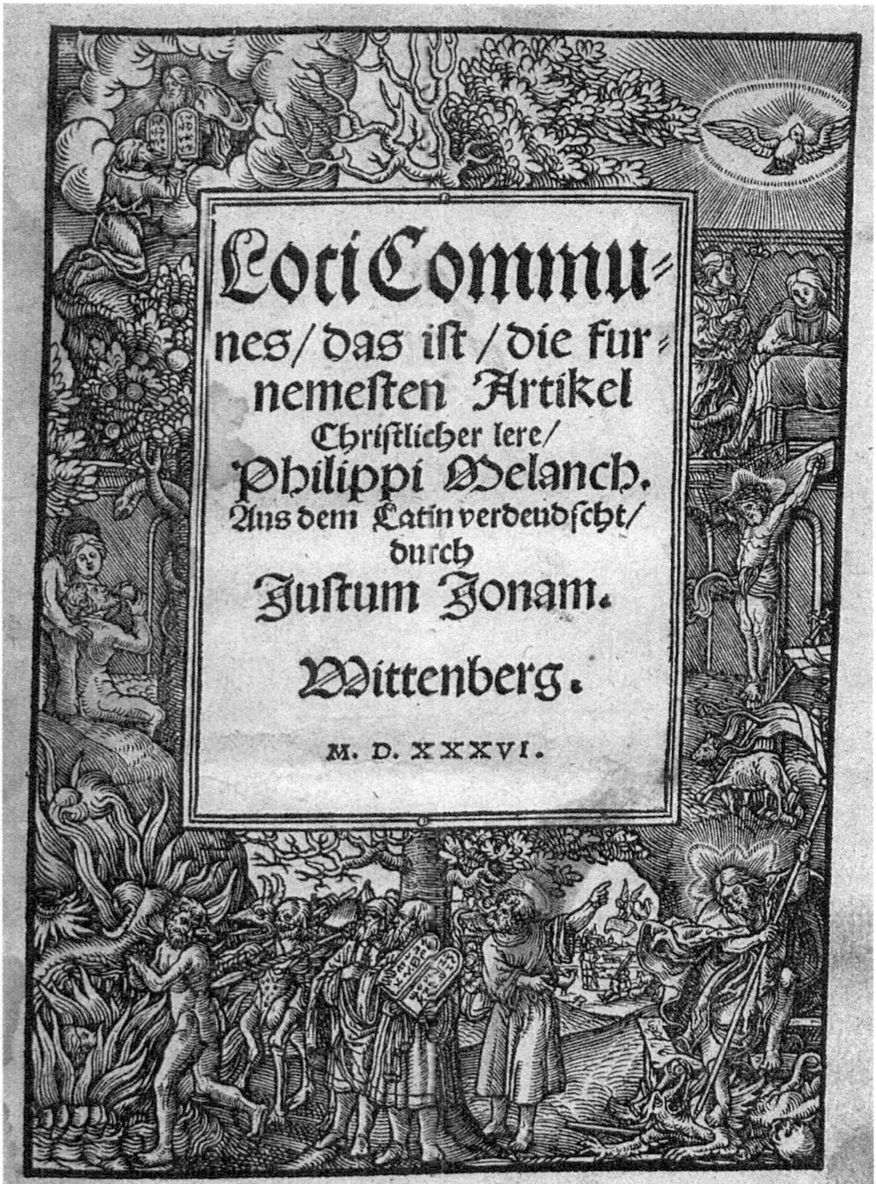


FIGURE 3 Cranach Workshop, *Law and Grace*, 1536, woodcut frontispiece, from Philipp Melanchthon, *Loci Communes*, German translation by Justus Jonas (Wittenberg: Georg Rhau, 1536), Sig. 4 Dogm. 387
PHOTOGRAPHY: BAYERISCHE STAATSBIBLIOTHEK MÜNCHEN

story of 'Law'. A tower of flames and smoke curls up the left edge, and three mostly naked torsos peer out from the flames. A naked or semi-naked man is driven towards the fires by a spear held by a skeleton and menaced by a bestial demon. Finally, a group of men dressed in robes gather at the right of the column next to the trunk of the tree of Law, looking onto the scenes of damnation, conferring, some with beards or hats, and one carrying the tablets of the law either wrapped or displaying the text.

The skeleton represents death. The demon, and torsos among the flames represent hell and eternal damnation. 'The evil spirit prods the soul', Luther wrote in his *Sermon von der Bereitung zu Sterben* (*A Sermon on Preparing to Die*), and in *Law and Grace*, the skeleton literally prods Adam toward the flames of hell with a highly detailed sharp spear.[129] The men holding the tablets of the law represent the judgement of sin.[130]

Who is in the hell flames? In the 1541 frontispiece, a head wearing a papal tiara, and a head with a tonsured haircut are depicted. Adam is driven towards the hell flames by a demon wearing a cardinal's hat. The anti-Papist imagery of this scene is unambiguous, portraying a demonic cardinal along with a monk and the Pope burning in hell. In the 1550 painting, Adam is chased towards hell by a man wearing a hood with bird legs ending in a claw instead of a foot—a human-animal hybrid that calls to mind the popular *Papstesel* (*Pope Donkey*) and *Mönchskalb* (*Monk Calf*) anti-Catholic images that had also been regularly republished by Luther, Melanchthon and the Cranachs from the 1520s into the 1550s.[131] The figures all turn away from Christ on the cross, thus turning away from salvation.[132]

A group of men with hats and beards are clustered at the tree trunk, one of them carrying the tablets of the law, designating Moses. The tablets of the law are drawn in a range of ways across the versions, sometimes with Hebrew-like lettering on the tablets, sometimes wrapped in cloth, or identifiable by the double tablet outline depicted on some medieval 'Yellow Badges'.[133] The other

129 Luther, *Ein Sermon von der Bereitung zum Sterben* (*A Sermon on Preparing to Die*), 1519, LW 42: 102, WA 2: 688, 3–6: 'da hin der boße geyst die seel treybet, das sie sich mit ubrigem unnutzen furwitz, Ja nit dem aller ferlichsten furnhemen beladet und forschen sol gottlichs radts heymlichkeit, ob sie vorsehn sey odder nit'.

130 Luther, *Bereitung zum Sterben* (*On Preparing to Die*), LW 42: 101, WA 2: 686, 33–35: 'Das erschrockliche Bild des todts, die ander das graulich manichfeltig bilde der sund, die dritte das untreglich und unvormeydliche Bild der hellen und ewiges vordammnüß'.

131 See the following chapter for a detailed reading of these two images.

132 Rowe, *The Jew, the Cathedral*, p. 244.

133 Sara Lipton, *Dark Mirror: The Medieval Origins of Anti-Jewish Iconography* (New York: Metropolitan, 2014), p. 7. For 'Hebrew-like script', see Ruth Mellinkoff, *Outcasts: Signs of Otherness in Northern European Art of the Late Middle Ages* (Berkeley: University of

bearded figures are less individually identifiable, representing Jewish patriarchs of the Old Testament, the 'all the law and the prophets' (Mt. 22.40).

The Cranachs' *Law and Grace* reinscribes what Luther had set out in *Daß Jesus Christ ein geborener Jude sei* (*That Jesus Christ was Born a Jew*), that the Old Testament was a necessary precursor to the New Testament. In the biblical glosses, the verses are primarily drawn from the New Testament (Mt. 2, Rom. 2–4, 1 Pet. 1, 1 Cor. 15, Jn. 1, Gal. 5, see Appendix 2, Table 4). There is only one Old Testament verse, 'A virgin will conceive and bear a son' (Isa. 7), which explains the Annunciation of the birth of Christ to the Virgin Mary. Jewish stories were thus given Christian interpretations, and New Testament events given Jewish prophetic foretelling. Versions of *Law and Grace* were printed both as the frontispiece of Lufft's 1544 *Die Propheten alle Deudsch* (*The Prophets all in German*) and, the following year, for the electoral Saxon authorised version of the entire Bible, Luther's *Biblia: das ist; Die gantze Heilige Schrifft: Deudsch Auffs new zugericht* (*Biblia: that is: The entire Holy Bible German newly translated*).[134] The Reformation canon incorporated Jewish Scriptures and reused them for Christian purposes, and this negotiation about the value and status of the Jewish Scriptures is replicated in the images.

The patriarchs are always depicted as well-dressed, elite, and passive. Sometimes the group of patriarchs stands in judgement, as in the 1530 print where Moses points to the tablets of the law and looks straight at Adam. Sometimes they stand by, powerless to save Adam. Like the elegant female depictions of *Synogoga* carved into cathedrals across Germany, passivity and powerlessness are applied to Jewish figures.[135] Nonetheless, the patriarchs participate in sending Adam to hell, even though they neither hold a spear nor do they push Adam into the flames. This image enacts the argument in Romans 3, for no human will be 'justified [...] by deeds prescribed by the law, for through the law comes the knowledge of sin' (Rom. 3.20).

---

California Press, 1993), I, 97–108, and Shalom Sabar, 'Between Calvinists and Jews: Hebrew Script in Rembrandt's Art', in *Beyond the Yellow Badge*, ed. by Merback, pp. 371–404. These versions suggest a familiarity with contemporary Jewish beliefs and practices. In 1541, a bearded face appears in the hell flames, directly above the papal figure. The bearded man in the hell flames may be intended to be understood as a Jew. See the next chapter for a fuller discussion of identifying Jews in the visual arts in the medieval and early modern periods.

134 Luther, *Die Propheten alle Deudsch. D. Mart*[*in*] *Lut*[*her*] *Gedruckt zu Wittemberg Durch Hans Lufft M.D.XLIII* (Wittenberg: Hans Lufft, 1544) and Luther, *Biblia: das ist; Die gantze Heilige Schrifft: Deudsch Auffs new zugericht D. Mart*[*in*]. *Luth*[*er*]. *Begnadet mit Kurfürstlicher zu Sachsen Freiheit. Gedruckt zu Wittemberg Durch Hans Lufft M.D.XLV* (Wittenberg: Hans Lufft, 1545).

135 Rowe, *The Jew, the Cathedral*, pp. 1–3.

Because the story being told is that Law leads to condemnation to death, and belief in Christ leads to salvation through Grace alone, all those identified with the Law are condemned. Luther upended traditional modes of how to read the story of salvation by placing both *Synogoga* and *Ecclesia* on the side of condemnation by the Law. Both Jews and Catholics are made identifiable through contemporary representational elements of dress or ritual. However, in *Law and Grace*, the stronger *Schandbild* elements of defamatory depictions are reserved for Catholic leaders who are depicted as monsters and demons.[136] These messages were congruent with the reformer's anti-Jewish and anti-papal polemical sermons and pamphlets, which we will discuss in Chapter 5 below.

By contrast, there are no representational images in the 'Grace' column. It is not the new Lutheran institution that offers salvation to the viewer, but only the person of Christ and the words of the Bible (Rom. 3.21–25). The believer is represented as Adam and the path to faith is represented as John the Baptist, and thus the new Protestant message positions itself as more faithful to the Scriptures and Jesus' own words and deeds.

### 3.4 *Towards Images of Salvation*

The hellfire section of the fresco in Paruzzaro that so disturbed Luther on his visit to Rome is now badly damaged. What is still visible, shows a writhing mass of naked bodies being consumed by a giant fiery red hellmouth. Unlike the individualised portraits of saints and apostles that surround it, Cagnoli here did not focus on one individual sinner but rather on a mass of the damned. The less damaged upper sections and apse frescoes are delicately coloured, detailed and distinct, so we can imagine the impact the lower section would have had on contemporary viewers. The images of the damned are located in the nave of the church, at the same height as the viewer, confronting the audience with the possibility and imminence of their own damnation.

It might seem that the depiction of hellfire in *Law and Grace* would also be a *Furchtbild* (Image of Fear). However, in contrast to the Paruzzaro fresco, the largest and most central figure in *Law and Grace* is Adam, who represents each of the viewers as a metonym for all of humankind: 'As in Adam all have died, so in Christ shall all be made alive' (1 Cor. 15.20). Rather than visually engulfing the crowds of viewers into the crowd of the damned, the fires of hell threaten a single representative of humankind, who is therefore somewhat distinct from the viewer.

---

136 See the next chapter for examples of *Schandbilder* applied to both Jewish and Catholic figures.

The hell flames of *Law and Grace* differ in one other significant way from the fresco in Paruzzaro, too. The mirroring images reassure the viewer that there is no need to question whether one is 'chosen' or not because any soul who seeks salvation is granted it at the foot of the cross. For Luther, depictions of the crucifixion made it possible to 'know and regard our Lord as an enemy of death'.[137] These comforting images, *Trostbilder*, were powerful counters to the terrors of death and hell.

In every version of *Law and Grace*, the most prominent depiction on the right-hand 'Grace' column is the image of Christ crucified, nailed to a cross, and crowned with a nimbus or circlet of thorns. John the Baptist, the prophet who reveals Christ's role in salvation, stands next to Adam and points at the cross. At the foot of the cross is a small lamb carrying a pennant flag with a cross emblem upon it, the medieval icon of the 'Lamb of God' or *Agnus Dei*. The biblical glosses in the 1530 and 1550 versions make this unambiguous, quoting John the Baptist, 'See, that is God's lamb, that bears the world's sins' (Jn. 1.29), as he explains the sacrifice that Christ will undertake to save the world. John the Baptist and Adam were both dead before the crucifixion, and at the foot of the cross instead were St John and Mary the mother of Jesus. Rather than depicting the characters in the biblical scene, *Law and Grace* depicts John the Baptist and the metaphor of his prophecy, and at the same time makes visible the theology set out by St Paul in 1 Corinthians 15.21–27; 45–56, that:

> For since death came through a man, the resurrection of the dead comes also through a man. For as in Adam all die, so in Christ all will be made alive.

The biblical glosses explain further that this means, 'death has been swallowed up in victory':

> Where, O death, is your victory?
> Where, O death, is your sting?
> The sting of death is sin, and the power of sin is the law. But thanks be to God! He gives us the victory through our Lord Jesus Christ.[138]

137 Luther, *Predigten des Jahres 1522* (*Sermons preached 1522*), LW 28: 132, 36: 'das wir unsern Herrn lernen ansehen und kennen als einen feind des todes'.

138 In his *Predigten 1522* (*Sermons 1522*), LW 28: 131, WA 36: 579, 32–33, Luther had described St Paul's description of the crucifixion in 1 Corinthians as a 'true painter and carver in words' (*ein rechter maler und bildschnitzer*) of death as it should be depicted.

Close by this vignette is a depiction of Christ harrowing hell. The repeated iconography shows Jesus in a cave. Wearing a cloak and half tunic, and carrying a spear or staff, Christ stands on a skeleton and a dragon, or sometimes the demonic beast from the Law column, representations of death (skeleton), hell (demon) or Satan (the dragon in Rev. 12).

In some of the images, the blood and water spurting from his side in an enormous arc, lands on Adam's chest, purifying his heart from sin, painting the image of Christ's salvation in his own human body.[139] The redeemed are cleansed by literally being 'washed in the blood of the lamb' (Rev. 7.14). In the Eucharistic words of institution (Mt. 26.26–28 and synoptic parallels), the 'blood' of the new covenant replaced the lamb's blood of the first covenant; that is Christ's own blood shed on the cross, but also the wine of the shared cup at the Last Supper. The images in the lower right of *Law and Grace* thus depict the three Lutheran sacraments that are the reminders of salvation: baptism, the forgiveness of sins, and the Lord's Supper.

Images of God the Father, Jesus Christ on his heavenly throne, or the Holy Spirit are depicted across the top of each version of the image; placing the whole narrative under heavenly authority and seen in the light of heavenly understanding of human history. Thus, the *Trostbilder* (Images of Comfort) are *Gnadenbilder*, images that depict God's grace towards human beings; and *Himmlische Bilder*, images that depicted reality from the viewpoint of heaven. These images declared God's heavenly plan and showed forth his grace-filled action in the world. By drawing together the images from the Passion narratives with texts and images that drew on theological interpretations from the Bible, Luther and the Cranachs encouraged the viewer to not only look at these images of grace but to interpret them and make them part of their own journey of faith.

Luther's message in *Law and Grace* was legible because viewers understood what was represented, what it symbolised, and what it meant.[140] The images were interpreted as typical Christian iconography, contemporary emblems, mimetic likenesses, and defamatory portrayals. The images were structured chronologically, theologically, and rhetorically. Pre-existing iconographies were repurposed to promote the new faith by identification of individuals and groups recognisable through icons, symbolism, or representation. Luther disrupted traditional accounts of the story of salvation by placing both *Synagoga* and *Ecclesia* on the side of condemnation by the Law. Instead, the believer is saved by Grace alone, directly granted the sacraments of communion, baptism, and absolution by Jesus himself.

---

139 1530, 1541, 1550, see Jn. 19.34.

140 Gombrich, *Symbolic Images*, p. 124.

By accompanying *Law and Grace* with newly translated text the reformers also challenged the assumption that simple folk must content themselves with pictures from the Bible, rather than access the Scriptures themselves. The Bible translated into German, *Loci Communes* translated into German, as well as churches where the liturgy was translated into German, are the context in which these images of *Law and Grace* were distributed and reproduced. German translations and paraphrases of Scripture were an integral part of some of the images themselves, expanding and explaining the meaning of the pictures.

*Law and Grace* demonstrates that Luther's categories of images could co-exist within a single composite artwork. *Law and Grace* evokes the *Ebenbild* of Christ as the one true image and complete likeness of God. The composition overall uses *Spiegelbild* mimetic, representational elements to identify figures and scenes from the Bible and contemporary life. The primary purpose of *Law and Grace* is to be a *Merkbild* (Image of Remembrance) that helped the faithful to remember and understand the story of salvation. It contained a *Trostbild* (Image of Comfort) of faith and salvation depicting Christ on the cross washing a believer in his blood, and Christ defeating death and hell. It also contained a *Furchtbild*, an image of damnation and terror. By placing recognisable Catholic figures in the *Furchtbild* as demons or the damned, the painting takes on elements of *Schandbild* (Image of Defamation).

Most of all, *Law and Grace* was an image designed to teach. Just as in his hymns and spiritual songs, by making use of a popular, widely accessible, and potentially transnational art-form, Luther and his collaborators used images to explain his new confession.

CHAPTER 5

# Teaching the Reformation to Read Images of Hate

In hymns and plays and sermons, Luther and his collaborators taught believers of every language, nation, class, and age to love God and sing his praises, as we have shown throughout this book. But it is also true that in sermons, letters, pamphlets and images, Luther and his collaborators taught Reformation believers to hate. Not only should believers hate evil and the devil, Luther's followers were taught, but also non-Lutherans, particularly Catholics and Jews.[1] In Chapter 2 we noted how, in his 1538 *Praefatio to the Symphoniae Iucundae*, Luther had spoken evocatively of the capacity of music to lift up people to the heights of God or take them down to the 'music of pigs' and, ultimately, the devil.[2] In this chapter, we show how Luther similarly uses the visual arts to consign his enemies to monstrousness, demonisation, or hell itself. These woodcuts have been extensively described and analysed; this chapter therefore focuses on the ways in which Luther's polemical pamphlets use images and rhetoric in similar ways to his popular music and drama: to educate, engage, persuade, and convert audiences to his Reformation message of salvation.[3]

Luther's *Kampfbilder* (Adversarial Images) were most commonly woodcuts that accompanied pamphlets and other ephemeral polemic publications. In these populist, disposable texts, Luther brings together polemical rhetoric with black and white images. The use of religious art through printed woodcuts, reproduced cheaply and in bulk, using satirical, allegorical, direct, indirect, and symbolic ways of telling visual stories readily enabled people to access the

1 On Luther and the devil, see Hans-Martin Barth, *Der Teufel und Jesus Christus in der Theologie Martin Luthers* (Göttingen: Vandenhoek und Ruprecht, 1967). Luther occasionally does have good things to say about his theological opponents, particularly when he sees them as potential Lutheran converts or as agents to further Lutheran aims. For example, in his *Daß Jesus Christus ein geborener Jude sei* (*That Jesus Christ was born a Jew*), Luther's tolerance of Jewish believers is predicated on their likelihood of imminent conversion. In this chapter, 'hate' is used in the technical sense of 'denoting hostile actions motivated by intense dislike or prejudice' (such as in 'hate speech').

2 See Appendix 1, 5.3: 'porcorum Musicam'; 6.4: 'certain that the devil seizes them against nature' (*quod Diabolus eos rapiat contra naturam*).

3 Hartmann Grisar and Franz Heege, *Luthers Kampfbilder*, 4 vols (Freiburg im Breisgau: Herder, 1921–1923), III: *Luthers Kampfbilder: Der Bilderkampf in den Schriften von 1523 bis 1554* (1923), and its companion volume, II: *Der Bilderkampf in der deutschen Bibel* (1922), are still seminal. Contemporary commentators include Noble, '"Law and Gospel" and the Strategies of Pictorial Rhetoric', pp. 27–66, and Werner, 'Feindbild', I, pp. 301–305.

 | DOI:10.1163/9789004527430_007

Reformation message. As Bridget Heal notes, Lutheran art 'is often categorised as primarily polemical or pedagogical'.[4] While the cartoons of the Reformation period broadly follow a populist and simple woodcut art style, they require a high level of visual literacy to understand them. As Scribner and others argued, they require a 'hybrid' literacy of 'reading' the image alongside the accompanying text of title, pamphlet, caption, speech bubble or label.[5] In the previous chapter, we discussed Luther's own categories for reading visual art. The present chapter, by contrast, draws more particularly on art history techniques, especially from scholars who are impacted by this hate speech, which offer more developed analytical tools. We employ here research from marginalised groups—including theorists, art historians and historians writing from feminist, Jewish, black, Indigenous and people of colour perspectives—in order to read three highly offensive Lutheran *Kampfbilder* (Adversarial Images): Lucas Cranach's 1523 woodcuts of the *Papstesel* (*Pope Ass*) and *Mönchskalb* (*Monk Calf*) and Luther's rhetorical illustration of the Wittenberg *Judensau*.

Lutheran polemical art uses the allegorical and iconographic visual language of the Early Modern period but also draws on the genres of the *Schandbild* (Image of Defamation) and *Furchtbild* (Image of Fear) in rendering Luther's opposition as diabolical or monstrous to instruct believers. Luther's most frequent collaborators were the Cranach family, who produced the majority of the woodcuts used in Luther's publications; the publisher Hans Lufft who printed many of Luther's works, including his *German Bible*; and Luther's fellow reformer and 'teacher of Germany', Philip Melanchthon. Luther and, following him, Melanchthon, provided explicit didactic advice on how to 'read' *Kampfbilder* (Adversarial Images).

We will be considering three *Kampfbilder* in detail. Significant for our analysis are two famous anti-Catholic woodcuts created by Lucas Cranach the Elder: the *Papstesel* (*Pope Ass*), to accompany the eponymous 1523 pamphlet by Philipp Melanchthon, and the *Mönchskalb* (*Monk Calf*), which Luther published as a companion piece. Also relevant is the anti-Semitic image of the *Judensau*, a pre-existing sculpture embedded in the external walls of Luther's own church, St Mary's Wittenberg. Although the image of the *Judensau* was not rendered as a woodcut until it was commissioned for a Latin anti-Semitic pamphlet by

4 Heal, *A Magnificent Faith*, p. 9, following Scribner, *For the Sake of Simple Folk*, p. 205. In the previous chapter, we explained how Pope Gregory famously had called church art the 'Bible of the poor'. The woodcuts of the Reformation take further the concept of religious images as the 'Scripture for the illiterate', and gives literate, illiterate, and semiliterate people ready and easy access to the theological debates of the time.

5 Scribner, *For the Sake of Simple Folk*, p. xiv.

the Wittenberg publisher Wolfgang Meissner in 1594,[6] in *The 'Judensau'*, Shachar points out that 'Luther constantly used anti-Jewish metaphors that were very similar to visual depictions', calling them 'verbal *Kampfbilder*' (Adversarial Images).[7] Luther's 1543 pamphlet *Vom Schem Hamphoras und vom Geschlecht Christi* (*Of the Ineffable Name and the Generations of Christ*) teaches his audience to 'read' the sculpture of the *Judensau* outside his parish church. We will show how Luther establishes a connection between local sculpture, a text and a multi-lingual pun that turns the unspeakable Name of God into 'here is dirt'. Luther's long history of teaching people how to read images meant that his method of reading the sculpture, and subsequent images of it, was understood by contemporary scholars as educational and was used well into the eighteenth century.[8]

## 1 Luther's Adversarial Images

Luther's adversarial images were intended to change the minds of confessional theological opponents; to satirically ridicule competing institutions; and to express abject disgust. We have seen how Luther wrote newspaper hymns, evangelistic appeals, and broadsides against his theological opponents—Catholics, Jews, 'Turks' (Muslims), Zwinglians, Calvinists and witches.[9] Lutheran *Kampfbilder* (Adversarial Images) were produced and reproduced as black and white line drawings, sometimes as frontispieces or illustrations in publications

---

6 *Effigies Monvmenti in Reproborvm Rebinorvm Iudæorvm Apostatrvm Confvsionem et Ignominiam. Ad VVitebergensis Templi oppidani murum, versus ortum antiquitus positi* (VVitebergæ: Excusa typis VVolffgangi Meissneri, M.D. XCVI).

7 Isaiah Shachar, *The 'Judensau': A Medieval Anti-Jewish Motif and its History*, Warburg Institute Surveys, 5 (London: Warburg Institute, 1974), p. 43.

8 Anti-Semitic scholarship that used Luther's form of reading the statue included the Wittenberg professor of Hebrew Laurentius Fabricius' *De Schemhamphorasch usu et abusu apud Iudaeos orationes duae* (Wittenberg: Johann Dörfler, 1596), and many more, including Swiss Reformed theologian Johannes Wolf (1600), Simon Maiolus (reprinted multiple times), Pierre de l'Ancre (1622), Herman Hermes (1663), and F. E. Brückmann (1739).

9 For Luther's *Zeitungslied*, see Chapter 2, nn. 7–8 above, and Bremer, 'Bekenntnis und Bekehrung', pp. 175–86. For Luther's polemic against witches, see Jörg Haustein, *Martin Luthers Stellung zum Zauber- und Hexenwesen*, Münchener kirchenhistorische Studien, 2 (Stuttgart: Verlag W. Kohlhammer, 1990). For his polemic against Turks, see Thomas Kaufmann, *'Türckenbüchlein', Zur christlichen Wahrnehmung 'türkischer Religion' in Spätmittelalter und Reformation*, Forschungen zur Kirchen- und Dogmengeschichte, 97 (Göttingen: Vandenhoek & Ruprecht, 2008), and Christopher Ocker, *Luther, Conflict, and Christendom: Reformation Europe and Christianity in the West* (Cambridge: Cambridge University Press, 2018), pp. 242–70.

and pamphlets; sometimes as satirical broadsheets; sometimes as individual images that believers might display in their homes or public buildings.

The images have been described as simple and crude, however, they required significant literacies to be able to understand them. While Joseph Koerner styled the images as therefore having a lower 'artistic value' than Cranach's oil paintings—'less visually seductive, less emotionally charged' and 'less semantically rich'—we suggest instead that Cranach's woodcuts are equally seductive, emotionally charged and semantically rich.[10] However, the seductions, emotions and semantics are of a different form entirely. As Scribner has argued, the 'visual message was far more complex' than the written text; the images 'often seemed to work on several levels at once [...] building up layers of allusion'.[11]

Luther's adversarial images were published alongside text, either as the illustration for a book, or with explanatory information such as passages from the Bible, captions, or even a booklet full of interpretative material. Luther did not create the images himself, though he likely had a hand in shaping some of them. However, he did personally contribute to the theory and rhetorical use of images. Through striking 'metaphors that were very similar to visual depictions', he created what Shachar has called 'verbal *Kampfbilder*'.[12] Luther's polemical pamphlets combining images and text were incredibly successful in this age of semi-literacy.[13] New uses and new kinds of meanings needed to be elucidated from the images to tell the new story of the Reformation and identify its new enemies. Thus, there are examples of Luther and his collaborators carefully instructing the reader on how to decode his adversarial messages, teaching people to 'read' the images.

Luther's polemical rhetoric is frequently crude, shocking, scatological, and violent. Like all polemical writing of the time, it makes use of argumentative tactics, including insults, *ad hominem* attacks, selecting tendentious examples, exaggeration, appeals to stereotypes and shock value.[14] Lutheran woodcuts are likewise intentional *Schandbilder* (Images of Defamation), depicting shocking and grotesque depictions of monstrous and titillating bodies, political cartoons, and contemporary events rendered, again in exaggerated and violent style using an appeal to stereotype. While Luther's style was cruder than that of many other polemicists, the sectarian and aggressive content was the same: calling

10 Joseph Koerner, *The Reformation of the Image* (Chicago: University of Chicago Press, 2003), p. 28, see also, pp. 226ff.

11 Scribner, *For the Sake of Simple Folk*, p. xiv.

12 Shachar, *The 'Judensau'*, p. 43.

13 Scribner, 'Flugblatt und Analphabetentum', pp. 65–76.

14 For examples of Reformation polemics across the denominational spectrum, see Loewe, *Richard Smyth*, pp. 7–17, 218–37.

for death, expulsion or damnation of enemies, and exhorting the faithful to reject heresy. The reformer typically distinguished between the rambunctious and aggressive rhetoric appropriate to a polemical dispute across confessional lines, the final judgement of God in the afterlife, and real-world judicial and political violence. Unlike, say, the Oxford Catholic theologian Richard Smyth whose polemical pamphlets called for the destruction of Protestants, and who actively participated in burning them at the stake,[15] Luther typically recommended a position of toleration—though not equality—for his religious opponents, leaving them to being ravaged by his pamphlets and the eternal fires of hell, but sparing them torture, fines, imprisonment or death in this life.[16] This is what Grayzel calls a 'Sicut' approach—named after the papal bulls 'Sicut Judaeis' and 'Turbato Corde' in which Christians were called to allow Jews to live among them (though not to convert, and with strict limitations).[17]

In his discussion of the *Judensau* carving Luther's viscerally disgusting imagery uses abject body horror. The same mode of iconographic 'reading' is used by Luther to unpack the only extended analysis of sculpture in his polemics. The *Judensau* discussed in *Vom Schem Hamphoras* is an anti-Semitic sculpture of Jewish men, identified by stereotypical conical hats, suckling from a sow's udder and raising her tail. While the actual physical image that Luther teaches his audience to 'read' is set high into the wall of the Wittenberg Church looking out onto the city square, across central Europe three dozen or so *Judensäue* survive, mainly on Christian places of worship.[18] The passage in which Luther uses the *Judensau* to deride his Jewish opponents is one of the most scatological in his works and was widely condemned at the time by fellow reformers, Catholics, Jews and civil authorities. While Jews were more concerned by the practical damaging recommendations to reduce their civil liberties in Luther's *Von den Juden und ihren Lügen* (*On the Jews and their Lies*), the Christian opposition was directed to the tone of the work, seen to be

15 Ibid., pp. 53–6.

16 This does not hold true in the case of witches, who Luther categorically commends should be killed in his 1525–1527 *Reihenpredigten über das zweite Buch Mose* (*Sermon Series on Exodus*), WA 16: 552, 22–23: 'They cause manifold harm, and therefore ought to be killed, not only because they cause harm, but because they have intercourse with Satan' (*Varie nocent, ergo occidantur, non solum qui nocent, sed etiam quia commercia habent cum Satana*).

17 *The Church and the Jews in the XIIIth Century: Volume II, 1254–1314*, ed. by Solomon Grayzel and Kenneth R. Snow (New York: The Jewish Theological Seminary Press, 1989), pp. 3–23.

18 For a comprehensive overview of the use of this image in central and northern Europe, see Isaiah Shachar, *The 'Judensau'*. Most of the images are embedded in the fabric of churches, though in Cadolzburg, Frankfurt, Kelheim, Salzburg, and Spalt the image was also displayed on civic buildings, and in Zerbst, even on a private homes.

disgusting, unfit for public discourse, and likely to cause riots or unrest among peasants.[19]

The norms of polemical discourse in the period allowed for opposition expressed in ridicule or offensive language addressed to ideas, beliefs, institutions or customs: *ad hominem* attacks, straw man arguments, satire, scatological references, caricatures, or *Schandbilder* (Images of Defamation). Polemical tropes that use cultural, personal and bodily tactics were widely recognised as a valid part of intellectual debate across European Reformation debates.[20] Their purpose was to effect a change of mind or behaviour, perhaps even a conversion, renouncing one confession and taking up another.[21] Bob Scribner explains how polemical Reformation images are fundamentally 'affective', and constitute a 'rhetorical appeal to the feelings of their readers'.[22] Luther regularly used such strategies in writing against Catholics, Muslims, Zwinglians, Jews and others with whose beliefs he disagreed. Such depictions did not generally receive the condemnation expressed against *Vom Schem Hamphoras*. This is likely because the sculpture and text mobilise not merely anti-Jewish polemic, but anti-Semitic disgust.[23]

In his discussions of the *Judensau*, Luther suggests that Jewish bodies are fundamentally marked as different, and monstrous.[24] From as early as the 1520s, Luther's works promoted the idea of a distinct Jewish body: the frontispiece to the 1522 imprint of Luther's *Sermon von dem Wucher* (*Sermon on Usury*), for instance, depicts a money-lender with a distinctive 'Jewish' nose

---

19 Luther, *Von den Juden und ihren Lügen* (*Of the Jews and their Lies*), WA 53: 522, 37–527.31; cf., 53: 536, 19–537, 28.

20 Loewe, *Richard Smyth*, pp. 10–11.

21 See, for example, Jaqueline E. Jung, 'The Passion, the Jews and the Crisis of the Individual', in *Beyond the Yellow Badge*, ed. by Merback, pp. 145–77 (pp. 148ff). See further Grayzel and Snow, *The Church and the Jews in the XIIIth Century*.

22 Scribner, *For the Sake of Simple Folk*, p. xxviii.

23 Bryan Cheyette, *Constructions of 'The Jew' in English Literature and Society: Racial Representations 1875–1945* (Cambridge: Cambridge University Press, 1993) was helpful here in differentiating and linking cultural thinking and race thinking, as was *Beyond the Yellow* Badge, ed. by Merback, and Christopher J. Probst, *Demonizing the Jews: Luther and the Protestant Church in Nazi Germany* (Bloomington: Indiana University Press, 2012). We offer an expanded commentary on this issue in Loewe and Firth, 'The Debate about Interpreting and Identifying anti-Judaism and anti-Semitism in Bach's *St John Passion*', forthcoming.

24 See especially *The Monstrous Middle Ages*, ed. by Bettina Bildhauer and Robert Miles (Toronto: University of Toronto Press, 2003), *Monster Theory*, ed. by Jeffrey Cohen (Minneapolis: University of Minnesota Press, 1996), and Jeffrey Cohen, 'The Use of Monsters and the Middle Ages', *SELIM: Journal of the Spanish Society for Medieval English Language and Literature*, 2 (1992): 48–71, as well as Spinks, *Monstrous Births and Visual Culture*, Chapter 3.

wearing an armband inscribed in faux-Hebrew letters (see below, Figure 4).[25] While the modern scientific idea of a 'race' was not yet formulated in early modern Europe, racial thinking was already present.[26] Medieval and early modern anti-Semitism relied on both confessional and bodily differences between Christians and Jews.

This polemical strategy does not use intellectual, rhetorical or philosophical techniques, but rather reaches directly for visceral disgust, something Luther does again and again in his anti-Semitic and anti-papal works: through racial anti-Semitism, misogyny, bestiality, animalism, anti-witchcraft, homophobia, faecal matter, fear of birth-defects, demonisation, and monsters.[27] Examples of these images are often an incoherent mass of multiple of these tropes: for example, the *Judensau* combines racial anti-Semitism, bestiality and misogyny in the image of Jewish men suckling at a sow's teats and thrusting their arm up her anus. Similarly, in Luther's *Wider das Papsttum zu Rom* (*Against the Papacy in Rome*), he combines homophobia and misogyny with demonisation by applying the epithets 'holy virgin St Paul III, Lady Pope' (*heiligen jungfrawen S. Paula tertius fraw Bepstin*), 'Sodomite Pope' (*Sodomiten Bapst*) and 'fart donkey' (*fartz Esel*, a crude wordplay on the Pope's family name, Farnese) to Pope Paul III.[28] Unlike the polemicism of persuasion, the opponent cannot change their thinking but is excluded from rational discussion and choice by being rejected as an abject, irrational, irreconcilable Other.[29]

---

25 Luther, *Eyn Sermon von dem Wucher Doct. Mar. Luther Augustiner zu Witte[n]bergk* (Wittenberg: Johann Rhau-Grunenbeg, 1520).

26 See Debra Higgs Strickland, *Saracens, Demons and Jews: Making Monsters in Medieval Art* (Princeton, NJ: Princeton University Press, 2003) and Geraldine Heng, *The Invention of Race in the European Middle Ages* (Cambridge: Cambridge University Press, 2018). For a historical overview of the emergence of aesthetic theories of race in Western Europe, see Sabrina Strings, *Fearing the Black Body: The Racial Origins of Fat Phobia* (New York: New York University Press, 2019); especially her analysis of the work of Albrecht Dürer, an earlier contemporary of Luther and the Cranachs, on African physical beauty.

27 On Luther and sexuality, see Helmut Puff, 'Martin Luther, the Sexual Reformation and Same-Sex Sexuality', in *Martin Luther: A Christian between Reforms and Modernity (1517–2017)*, ed. by Alberto Melloni, 3 vols (Berlin: De Gruyter, 2017), I, pp. 663–78. On Luther and witchcraft, see *Mit dem Schwert oder festem Glauben: Luther und die Hexen*, ed. by Markus Hirta, Katalog Mittelalterliches Kriminalmuseum Rothenburg (Darmstadt: Wissenschaftliche Buchgesellschaft/Theiss, 2017).

28 Luther, *Wider das Papsttum zu Rom. Vom Teufel gestiftet* (*Against the Papacy at Rome. Founded by the Devil*), WA 54: 214, 30; 227, 25; 222, 4. See also Mark Edwards, *Luther's Last Battles: Politics and Polemics 1531–46* (Leiden, Brill, 1983), p. 4. For Luther's insulting puns, see Roper, *Living I Was Your Plague*, pp. 94–98, 124–25.

29 We therefore disagree with scholars such as Egil Grislis, 'Martin Luther and the Jews', *Consensus*, 27.1 (2001), 63–84, who argues, at p. 4, that Luther's opposition to Jews was theological not racial: 'Of course, Luther was thinking theologically and not biologically'.

In her foundational study of the abject Other, *Powers of Horror*, Julia Kristeva defines the response to the abject as revulsion, 'directed against a threat that seems to emanate from an exorbitant outside or inside, ejected beyond the scope of the possible, the tolerable, the thinkable'.[30] The abject arouses not only disagreement or derision, but physical distress or bodily horror. In the chapter of the essay that directly discusses anti-Semitism, Kristeva identifies anti-Semitic tropes as demonstrating a fear of being 'reduced to the same abjection, a faecalised, feminised, passivated rot'.[31] Roper comments on this intentionally overwhelming effect of Luther's cumulative scatological insults: 'Luther's rhythmic writing assaults the senses—smell, sight, and sound—making it hard to think'.[32]

In the sexual and ingestive rhetoric in Luther's *Vom Schem Hamphoras* (*Of the Ineffable Name*), the monstrous bodies of the *Papstesel* (*Pope Ass*) and *Mönchskalb* (*Monk Calf*) in his *Deutung der czwo grewlichen Figuren* (*Interpretation of the two monstrous figures*), and the monstrous birth of the Papacy from the enlarged pudenda of fury in his *Abbildung des Bapstum* (*Depictions of the Papacy*), we see parallel fears being mobilised.[33] Like images, puns and other slippages in language allow someone to access the abject from the side—aslant—where they could not do so head-on.[34] It is notable, that the *Mönchskalb* (*Monk Calf*) is a pun for a *Mondkalb* (*Mooncalf*) and the disgusting expression of anti-Semitism in *Vom Schem Hamphoras* (*Of the Ineffable Name*) emerges slipping between a description of a sculpture and a multi-lingual pun.

As the abject is always obscene, the mode of such polemic is always condemned as crude, rude and inappropriate. It is not just the rough and tumble of Reformation debate but hate speech. This explains the criticism of Luther's

---

There is significant work on this third form of opposition in the scholarly literature on anti-Semitism in the Middle Ages, particularly Lipton, *Dark Mirror* and Strickland, *Saracens, Demons and Jews*.

30 Kristeva, *Powers of Horror*, p. 4. Mary Rambaran-Olm, M. Leake Breann, and Micah James Goodrich, 'Medieval studies: the stakes of the field', *postmedieval: a journal of medieval cultural studies*, 11 (2020), 356–70, point out that 'Julia Kristeva's paradigms of abjection that violently recapitulate rather than challenge the imperial and colonial projects that generate abject subjects', and point to the work of Imogen Tyler, *Revolting Subjects: Social Abjection and Resistance in Neoliberal Britain* (London: Bloomsbury [ZED Books], 2013) as a useful revision.

31 Kristeva, *Powers of Horror*, p. 185.

32 Roper, *Living I Was Your Plague*, pp. 97–98.

33 Luther, *Abbildung des Bapstum durch Mert[in] Luth[er] D. Wittemberg* (Wittenberg: [Hans Lufft], 1545).

34 Sigmund Freud, *Totem and Taboo: Resemblances between the Psychic Lives of Savages and Neurotics* (New York: Moffat, Yard and Co., 1919), p. viii, see further Kristeva, *Powers of Horror*, passim.

obscene revulsion about Jewish bodies expressed in *Vom Schem Hamphoras* by thinkers who would be broadly in agreement with his political and judicial position. That is, they did not disagree with the anti-Judaism, the anti-Jewishness, or even the anti-Semitism; it was the obscenity of the irrational being made explicit that revolted them.[35]

An assessment of Luther's visual collaborations offers a wealth of anti-Papist images, a small group of anti-Semitic images, a small collection of anti-Muslim images, and no anti-reformed images.[36] This is broadly consistent with Luther's written output. The majority of Luther's polemic work was focused on Catholics and the Papacy. There is comparatively less material in his written corpus on Jews, his various reformed opponents, or Muslims.[37]

Anti-Catholic images include works expressly commissioned to accompany Lutheran polemical texts. The artwork for the 1523 publication on *Papstesel* and *Mönchskalb*, and the 1545 anti-Papist cartoons *Abbildung des Bapstum* (*Depictions of the Papacy*) were distinctive and detailed illustrations that complemented the text and polemical intent of the publication. These are less common in the other oppositional images that are more likely to reuse existing material. A notable exception is the extremely racially anti-Semitic cartoon in the Rhau-Grunenberg 1520 edition of Luther's *Eyn Sermon von dem Wucher* (*A Sermon on Usury*).[38] There, a scowling man with a hooked nose, a Jewish hat and long pointed beard, a prominent knife and an armband with nonsense

35 In this chapter, we use the term 'anti-Semitic' to refer to works that reject Jewish bodies, as opposed to anti-Jewish works that reject Jewish beliefs. Both had negative consequences for individuals and communities of Jewish people. These levels are not sharply defined. There is slippage or overlap or intersection of the political and the theological, between the rational and irrational. Many aspects of the previous level are doubled by inclusion also in the space below. While in her *The Singular Beast: Jews, Christians and the Pig*, Fabre-Vassas chronicles a wide range of popular and legal abject practices and beliefs linking Jews and pigs; most scholars suggest that Jews and Christians are 'not entirely distinct categories', as Bildhauer points out. Claudine Fabre-Vassas, *The Singular Beast: Jews, Christians, and the Pig* (New York: Columbia University Press, 1997), p. 217. Bettina Bildhauer, 'Blood, Jews and Monsters in Medieval Culture', in *The Monstrous Middle Ages*, ed. by Bettina Bildhauer and Robert Miles (Toronto: University of Toronto Press, 2003), pp. 75–96 (p. 85).

36 Thomas Kaufmann, 'Das Judentum in der frühreformatorischen Flugschriftenpublizistik', *Theologie und Kirche*, 95.4 (1998), 429–61.

37 On Luther and Muslims, see Adam S. Francisco, *Martin Luther and Islam: A Study in Sixteenth-Century Polemics and Apologetics*, The History of Christian-Muslim Relations, 8 (Leiden: Brill, 2007).

38 Luther, *Eyn Sermon von dem Wucher Doct. Mar. Luther Augustiner zu Witte[n]bergk* (Wittenberg: Johann Rhau-Grunenberg, 1520), frontispiece. See Thomas Kaufmann, *Luther's Jews: A Journey into Anti-Semitism*, trans. by Lesley Sharpe and Jeremy Noakes (Oxford: Oxford University Press, 2017), pp. 48–9, for more on this early publication.

FIGURE 4 *Image of Usurer*, 1520, woodcut frontispiece in Martin Luther, *A Sermon on Usury* (Wittenberg: Johann Rhau-Grunenberg, 1520), Sig. Fl 289
PHOTOGRAPHY: UNIVERSITÄTS- UND LANDESBIBLIOTHEK SACHSEN-ANHALT HALLE AN DER SAALE

Hebrew-like characters,[39] points his finger at a caption, 'Pay or give me interest / as I desire profit' (*Bezal odder gib zinß / Dann* [*sic: denn*] *ich begere gewinß*).[40]

More commonly, pre-designed frontispieces and illuminated initial letter decorations were selected by printers because they could be interpreted as relevant to the text they illustrated. In his 1520 *Verklärung etlicher Artikel in dem Sermon von dem heyligen Sakrament* (*Explanation of numerous Articles in the Sermon on the Sacred Sacrament*), Luther states that he had 'truly not time [...] to take notice of what kind of pictures, lettering, ink or paper the printer uses' for the frontispieces of his pamphlets.[41] The frontispieces of polemical pamphlets were likely selected by the printer because they offered apposite elements to support the adversarial purpose of the text.[42] Images that generically suggest greed, gluttony or excess were deployed in pamphlets about moneylending and usury (stereotypically Jewish professions).[43] For example, in Hans Lufft's 1524 edition of Luther's *Von Kauffshandlung vnd wucher* (*On Trade and Usury*), figures celebrate in an exuberant scene of excess.[44] In Braubach's Frankfurt Latin edition of the work, *De usuris taxanda, ad pastores Ecclesiarum Commonefactio* (1554), naked voluptuous figures cavort around the initial 'S' on the first page of the treatise.[45] These images are not racially anti-Semitic, nor were they created to denigrate Jews, but they are deployed in ways that draw the viewers' attention to culturally anti-Semitic tropes.[46] In turn, the texts they illustrated would come to inform the readers' and viewers' understanding of the images, reinforcing the stereotypes.

---

39 Probably a version of the 'Yellow Badge'. For nonsense 'Hebrew', see Sabar, 'Between Calvinists and Jews', pp. 371–404, and Mellinkoff, *Outcasts*, I, 97–108.

40 For a complete list of iconographies for recognising a depiction of a Jew, see Lipton, *Dark Mirror*, p. 7. Lipton explains, at p. 172, how by 1340 the 'Jewish face' had emerged as a visual shorthand in European art, and so was well established by the time Luther's works were printed.

41 Luther, *Verklärung etlicher Artikel in dem Sermon von dem heyligen Sakrament* (*Explanation of numerous Articles in the Sermon on the Sacred Sacrament*), 1520, WA 6: 82, 20–2: 'Ich furwar die zeyt nit hab, das ich müge sehen, was der Drucker für Bild, buchstaben, tindten odder payr nympt, und ist mir vor nie geschehn, habs mich auch nicht fursehen, das man von solchs begerend wurd', trans. by Kaufmann, *Luther's Jews*, pp. 49–50 n. 26.

42 See Edwards, *Printing, Propaganda and Martin Luther*, 16.

43 Lipton, *Dark Mirror*, p. 7.

44 Luther, *Von Kauffshandlung vnd wucher* (Wittenberg: Hans Lufft, 1522), WA 15: 293–322.

45 Luther, *De usuris taxanda, ad pastores Ecclesiarum Commonefactio* (Frankfurt [a.M.]: Peter Br[a]ub[ach], 1554), 9 (sig. A 5ʳ). In stark contrast, there is no cavorting on the first letter 'G' of the dedicatory epistle, sig. A2ʳ.

46 Lipton, *Dark Mirror*, p. 7.

By contrast, Lufft's 1530 edition of Luther's *Libellus de Ritv et Moribvs Turcorum. Cum Praefatione Martini Lutheri* (*Preface to the Book on the Rites and Customs of the Turks*) has woodcut illuminated initial letters showing foliage for each section, not human depictions.[47] Nickel Schirlenz's 1529 edition of Luther's *Ein heer predigt wider den Türken* (*A Military Sermon against the Turk*), shows a frontispiece of the birth of Christ with Christian iconography, establishing its confessional opposition to the Muslim faith without visually denigrating Ottoman culture or peoples.[48] Georg Rhau's 1541 reprint uses an alternative title page, depicting a clean-shaven young David using a large pointed sword against a bearded Goliath lying flat on his back.[49] The giant has been knocked out by a stone from David's slingshot (1 Sam. 17), and the discarded slingshot and unneeded stones are depicted close by. In the background, a group of men with hats and beards are also visible brandishing weapons. Here, the armed conflict between the Ottoman Empire and the German princes is both literally and metaphorically depicted on the page, using biblical imagery to inscribe moral and aspirational implications: that the Ottomans will be defeated because God is not on their side.

It was possible to deploy the same image in different contexts and by implication a visual message that may be more neutral or more offensive. For example, the case of an architectural frontispiece with a bearded man in a hat playing a keyboard. The iconographic elements could have been initially intended as a generic representation of a contemporary German musician who frequently wore hats and beards in the period. This frontispiece, presumably created by Lucas Cranach the Elder's first son Hans, was reused at least three times by Lufft within a decade, each time illustrating radically different works.[50]

In Hans Lufft's 1536 edition of Ambrosius Moibanus' *Der XXIX. Psalm Davids* [...] *Mit einer vorrede D. Martini Luthers* (*The 29th* [*30th*] *Psalm of David, with a Preface by Martin Luther*), the image is used to denote a musician, likely a Psalmist, and probably King David.[51] In 1542, the same image is used as the frontispiece of *Verlegung des Alcoran Bruder Richardi* (*Translation of the Qur'an by Brother Richard*), Luther's translation of the repudiation of the Qur'an

47 Luther, *Libellus de Ritv et Moribvs Turcorum Ante LXX. Annos Aeditus VVittemberge apud Iohannem Lufft* (Wittenberg: Hans Lufft, 1530), WA 30.2: 205–08.

48 Luther, *Eine Heerpredigt widder den Tuercken* (Wittenberg: Nickel Schirlenz, 1529), frontispiece.

49 Luther, *Eine Heerpredigt Wider den Türcken Gedrückt zu Wittenberg durch Georgen Rhaw* (Wittenberg: Georg Rhau, 1541), frontispiece.

50 Lucas Cranach the Elder's oldest son, who died in his mid-twenties in 1537, KF no. 269.

51 Luther, *Der XXIX Psalm Davids* [...] *Mit einer vorrede D. Martini Luthers* (Wittenberg: Hans Lufft, 1536), WA 50: 42–44.

FIGURE 5 Frontispiece of Lufft's 1536 edition of *Der XXIX. Psalm Davids* (KF no. 269). Cranach Workshop, *Man playing a Clavichord*, 1536, woodcut, frontispiece from Ambrosius Moibanus, *Der XXIX. Psalm Davids*, foreword Martin Luther (Wittenberg: Hans Lufft, 1536) (Johannes Luther Tafel 39), Sig. Phys. Sp. 840 i, Res/Phys.sp. 840 i. The artwork was very likely created by Lucas Cranach the Elder's first son, Hans Cranach. Lufft later reused the same image of the horned keyboard player to illustrate Luther's anti-Muslim and anti-Jewish writings.

by Dominican friar Ricoldus de Monte Croce.[52] Here, the hat and beard are repurposed to perhaps suggest a generic Muslim figure.[53] The following year, the frontispiece is reused again: this time to illustrate the title page of one of Luther's most explicitly anti-Semitic pamphlets, *Von den Jüden und jren Lügen* (*Of the Jews and their Lies*).[54] The latter context leads Shachar to read the image here as a 'horned, full-bearded Moses in a fool's dress'.[55]

As Lipton has demonstrated elsewhere, publishers and readers are therefore expected to reinterpret the image to identify congruences between the generic stock picture and the polemical content.[56] Such interpretative strategies demonstrate a sophisticated ability of literate and semiliterate audiences to unpack the implications of Luther's adversarial writings and their accompanying images. In the case of the frontispieces, these strategies exploit the fluidity of iconography in Medieval and Renaissance art, where images could be reapplied and reinterpreted to new contexts as they were used to loosely illustrate different texts.

In other places, where the images carried a didactic moral message, the iconography had to be clearly established in order to confirm that the reader would not be led astray by incorrect interpretation. In their companion pamphlets on the *Papstesel* and *Mönchskalb*, Melanchthon and Luther set out their point-by-point interpretation (*Auslegung*) of satirical woodcuts to develop an allegorical lesson about the monstrousness of Catholic leaders. In Luther's sermon published as *Vom Schem Hamphoras*, he uses the anti-Semitic sculpture carved on the outside of the church building to parody Talmudic 'close literary and conceptual readings, and their far-reaching dialectical comparisons and resolutions', in order to teach his readers about their foolishness and ignorance in comparison to his reformed message.[57]

---

52 Luther, *Verlegung des Alcoran Bruder Richardi Prediger Ordens Anno 1300 verdeutscht durch D. Martin Luther* (Wittenberg: Hans Lufft, 1542), frontispiece, WA 53: 272–396.

53 See, for example, Strickland, *Saracens, Demons and Jews*, p. 238.

54 Luther, *Von den Jüden und jren Lügen D. M. Luther, Gedrückt zu Wittemberg Durch Hans Lufft* (Wittenberg: Hans Lufft, 1543), WA 53: 417–552.

55 Shachar, *The 'Judensau'*, p. 43. While the man shown in Lufft's frontispiece is not wearing a specifically Jewish hat from medieval iconography, nor is his beard the medieval goatee but, as Lipton, *Dark Mirror*, p. 5 has shown, iconography to represent Jews was often more fluid. It moreover is unclear whether the depicted hat has horns or not, and if it did whether the horns were intended to be a sign of cuckoldry (as with a jester's outfit) or a sign of Jewishness. Any ambiguity of the visual semiotic is, however, clarified by the text.

56 Lipton, *Dark Mirror*, p. 7.

57 Ephraim Kanarfogel, 'Ashkenazic Talmudic Interpretation and the Jewish-Christian Encounter', *Medieval Encounters*, 22 (2016), 72–94 (p. 72).

### 1.1 *Reading the 'Donkey Pope' and 'Monk Calf' (1523)*

For Renaissance audiences, 'it is not we who select and use symbols for communication, it is the Divine which expresses itself in the hieroglyph of sensible things' (that is the things we perceive with our senses), as Ernst Gombrich explains in the section of *Symbolic Images* on 'Apparitions and Portents'.[58] As his example, he considers the 'signs of the times', the monstrous births of the hybrid donkey human and the Mooncalf. 'Both Luther and Melanchthon applied the subtleties of allegorical or "hieroglyphic" interpretation to the individual features of these natural symbols', Gombrich makes clear.[59] Scholars often translate the names of these two monsters as *Pope Ass* or *Papal Ass* and *Mooncalf.* While the English homonym for donkey and anus is in keeping with the tone of the other *Abbildung des Bapstum* (*Depictions of the Papacy*) images, this pun does not work in German. A pun of the same kind is, however, to be made in German for *Mooncalf/Monk Calf, Mondkalb/Mönchskalb*. For this reason we use the terms 'Donkey Pope' and 'Monk Calf'. Luther and Melanchthon based their reading on anti-Papist and anti-clerical images that depict grotesque hybrid monsters, said truly to have appeared in the previous century, recreated in 1523 and attributed to Lucas Cranach the Elder or his workshop.[60]

The original image of the Pope Donkey was a copperplate created by Wenzel von Olmütz in January 1496, with labels locating the event in 'Rome, Capital of the World' (*Roma Caput Mundi*).[61] Depicted behind the donkey-human-fish-monster is the river Tiber, labelled 'Tevere', with two fortresses one on either side of the river. A circular fortress is labelled 'Castel SA', the papal fortress and residence, Castel Sant'Angelo; and the square fortress labelled 'Tore Dinona', is the Torre di Nona papal prison. As Scribner notes, the image was originally part of a 'campaign of vilification of Pope Alexander IV' soon after the papal states had been defeated by the French.[62]

Olmütz's drawing was adapted freely by Cranach and other artists who made multiple versions of this image to accompany texts by Luther and Melanchthon. Depicting the Pope as a donkey is a recurrent theme in Cranach's woodcuts. For his illustrations to Luther's *Abbildung des Bapsttums* (*Depictions of the Papacy*), he created an image of a donkey sitting beneath a canopy playing a bagpipe

58 Gombrich, *Symbolic Images*, p. 178; Gombrich, 'Icones Symbolicae', pp. 180–1.

59 Gombrich, *Symbolic Images*, p. 178; Gombrich, 'Icones Symbolicae', p. 180.

60 For a more extensive reading of both these images and those in the next section in their wider context, see Scribner, 'Demons, Defecation and Monsters', pp. 277–99, and Spinks, *Monstrous Births and Visual Culture*, pp. 62–72. For a full history of the versions of the *Papstesel* image, see KF, 361ff, and Margaret Meserve, 'A Roman Monster in the Humanist Imagination', in *Et Amicorum: Essays on Renaissance Humanism and Philosophy*, ed. by Margaret Meserve and Anthony Ossa-Richardson, Brill's Studies in Intellectual History, 273 (Leiden: Brill, 2018), pp. 118–43.

61 Wenzel von Olmütz, *Roma Caput Mundi*, British Museum, E, 1.15 (KF no. 203).

62 Scribner, *Popular Culture*, p. 285.

with Luther's caption: 'Only the Pope can interpret / the Scriptures and sweep out error. / Like only the donkey can play the pipes and finger the notes correctly' (*Der Bapst kan allein auslegen / Die schrifft: und jrthum auslegen / Wie der Esel allein pfeiffen kan: und die noten recht greiffen*).[63]

In the woodcut called *Der Bapstesel zu Rom* (*The Pope Donkey at Rome*), the full height of the oblong woodcut is taken up by a central figure facing to the left of the woodcut, depicted as the foreground. The figure used different proportions but reproduces the various monstrous parts of the figure's body first included by Olmütz. The figure has a donkey's head, a fish scale neck and a left arm ending in a human hand, while the right arm ends in a donkey's hoof. The figure has two human female breasts, a rounded stomach, and cleft female pudenda. Its backside has a Green Man's face surrounded by hair and a beard, and the protruding tail has its own face with a bird's beak and mammalian ears. The figure's legs are covered in fish scales. The left leg ends in a bird claw, and the right leg ends in a cow or ox's cloven hoof.

This is only one of the many reproductions of these images during the period. A simplified version is the frontispiece for a solo publication of Melanchthon's work titled *Deuttung der grewlichē figur des Bapstesels tzu Rom in der Tiber gfunden* (*Interpretation of the Monstrous Figure of the Pope Donkey found in the Tiber at Rome*). The two images are placed together in a joint printing of both pamphlets in 1523 (KF no. 246). The version created for Luther's and Cranach's 1545 *Abbildung des Bapstum* (*Depictions of the Papacy*), has more detail (KF no. 248). A version of the same image, delicately coloured by the Cranach Workshop, gives us green grass, a blue river, a red and gold pennant, grey fur, blue scales and a green and yellow tail and purple wattle.

The river and fortresses in the background are identified through *Spiegelbild* (representational) elements, which can be identified by comparing the depiction with what things look like in the real world. On the right-hand side of the image, a square tower with a crenelated roofline depicts the Torre di Nona; on the left-hand side of the image, a composite fortress with round and square towers and multiple levels, flying a large guidon-style flag with the papal crossed keys, depicts the Castel Sant'Angelo. Including these true-to-life elements added evidence to the story that a monster truly had washed up out of the river Tiber in Rome. The monster was a 'natural symbol', a message directly from God that the world had strayed from its proper path. Thus, the purpose of the image was greater than its description of a sign or wonder. Its meaning is to be found in interpreting what these hybrid monsters mean, what message the Divine was sending into the world of the human senses and sense-making, for the believer to decipher and understand.

---

63 Luther, *Abbildung des Papsttums*, WA 54: 367.

FIGURE 6 Lucas Cranach the Elder, *Papstesel*, 1523, woodcut, 17.5 × 24.5 cm, from Martin Luther and Philip Melanchthon, *Deuttung der z̄wo grewlichen Figuren Bapstesels zu Rom vnd Munchkalbs zu freyberg jn Meyssen funden* (1523), Sig. Faust 114, fol. ai$^{v}$. Photography: Bayerische Staatsbibliothek München. The woodcut of the monstrous figure of the *Papstesel* (KF no. 46), believed to have been found dead in the Tiber river, was used by Lutheran theologian Philipp Melanchthon to promote the destruction of the Roman Church.

In 'Die Auslegung Philippi', Melanchthon sets out his interpretation of the *Papstesel*. Melanchthon begins by referencing two passages of Scripture (Dan. 8 and Mt. 24). In Chapter 8 of the Book of Daniel, the prophet is in the city of Susa by the Ulai canal where he has a vision of a monstrous ram and a monstrous goat. This vision is explained to Daniel as meaning that a terrifying ruler will emerge. In Matthew 24, Jesus foretells the disasters that will befall in the end times. Jesus quotes from Daniel 9 when he prophesies the 'abomination that causes desolation' (Mt. 24.9). Melanchthon then recounts this historical story, that a monster was found dead in the city of Rome, in the Tiber, in 1496, less than a generation before the time Cranach's woodcut was published.[64]

Melanchthon brings these biblical and historical facts together and explains them as a sign of the Empire of the Romish Anti-Christ. While the 1496 image by Olmütz does show the papal flag flying over the Castel Sant'Angelo, the imagery is all classical—the Castel San Angelo and the Torre di Nona are Roman buildings, the inscriptions are in Latin, and a classical urn is placed in the middle ground—all seem to gesture towards a more distant period of wonders than the contemporary church.[65] In the Cranach version, the depiction of the papal cross-keys ties the city of Rome to the Papacy, but also creates a clear link to the reformers' polemic. In his *Wider das Papsttum zu Rom* (*Against the Papacy at Rome*), for example, Luther had commended that the papal arms 'should be spat upon and pelted with dirt', since

> the papal arms are a public lie and devil's phantom which people reverenced in vain, and placed their trust in them as if God had ordained it, though they are nothing but lies and blasphemy, a true arch-idolatry.[66]

Since 1522, Luther had consistently 'spoken of the grubs, scales […] and tails of the Papacy'. In combination with its 'provenance', therefore, the monstrous animal was a fitting *Kampfbild* (adversarial image) of the Papacy.[67]

---

64 Luther and Melanchthon, *Deuttung der czwo grewlichen Figuren, Babpstesles czu Rom vnd Munchskalbs zu Freijberg in Meisszen funden* (*Interpretation of the two Monstrous Figures, the Pope Donkey found in Rome and the Monk Calf found in Freiberg in Meissen*), WA 11: 375, 8: 'Und newlich diße grewlich figur, der Bapstesel, welche zu Rom in der Tyber todt funden ist jm M.CCC.xcvij [1496] jar'.

65 KF no. 361.

66 Luther, *Wider das Papsttum zu Rom. Vom Teufel gestiftet* (*Against the Papacy at Rome. Founded by the Devil*), WA 54: 242, 10: 'dran speien und mit dreck werffen sol'; 13: 'ist ein oeffentliche luegen und teufels gespenst, dafuer sich die Leute vergeblich gefurcht haben, und darauff vertrawet, als were es Gottes befehl, so es doch eitel luegen und Gottes lesterung, ein rechte ertzabgoetterey ist'.

67 Luther and Melanchthon, *Deuttung der czwo grewlichen Figuren* (*Interpretation of the two Monstrous Figures*), WA 11: 356: 'Von des Papstthums Larven, Schuppen […] und Schwänzen gesprochen hatte'.

Next, Melanchthon moves systematically through the body of the donkey, from the head down. Usefully, each section is indexed by text printed in the margin: *Der Eselskopff* (the donkey's head), *Die rechte hant* (the right hand), *Der Weibische bauch* (the effeminate belly), and so on. In this first pedagogical step, the viewer is taught to take the image apart and to look at each aspect separately. Each aspect is then read in a way very much akin to Gombrich's approach: what the visual image represents, what it symbolises and then what deep meaning is expressed. For example, the right hand according to Melanchthon is not a donkey's hoof but rather an elephant's foot.[68] This heavy large animal goes wherever it wishes, he says; it represents the spiritual regiment of the Pope, which similarly goes wherever it wants. Again, Melanchthon references the end times, quoting Daniel 8 and 2 Timothy 4, where the apostle Paul warns of a time when people will turn away from sound doctrine and listen to lies. The spiritual allegory explained, Melanchthon moves on to the inner meaning that is expressed in the image: 'the right hand signifies the inner meaning, pertaining to soul and conscience' (*denn die rechte hand bedeut das ynnerlich, das die seelen und gewissen betrifft*).[69] Scribner notes that Melanchthon's 'allegorical interpretation' was 'too elaborate to become a popular interpretation'; however, his pedagogical intent is much clearer and more structured than Luther's, elucidating the strategies implicit in Luther's own more striking interpretations.[70]

Luther would return to the image of the Pope Donkey in his writings multiple times in the next decades. In a letter written to Wenceslas Linck on 16 January 1523, planning for the first publication of the two *Kampfbilder* (Adversarial Images), Luther had already referred to the image of the *Papstesel* as the 'Figure of the Anti-Christ Pope and his Synagogue', an anti-Semitic title that was later adopted for a two-page quarto fly-leaf publication of Melanchthon's interpretation.[71] Gombrich points forward to Luther's caption for the *Donkey Pope* in the *Abbildung des Bapstum* (*Depictions of the Papacy*) in 1545, the famous series of woodcut cartoons parodying the Pope, produced by Cranach under direction from Luther and accompanied by satirical verses.[72] This series includes a recutting by Lucas Cranach the Younger of his father's image from 1523, with

---

68 Melanchthon is incorrect in his zoological identification; elephants' feet do not look anything like the hoof depicted by Cranach which, with its well-developed frog, is typical of a donkey's.

69 Luther and Melanchthon, *Deuttung der czwo grewlichen Figuren* (*Interpretation of the two Monstrous Figures*), WA 11: 376, 15–6.

70 Scribner, *Popular Culture*, p. 285.

71 Luther and Melanchthon, *Deuttung der czwo grewlichen Figuren* (*Interpretation of the two Monstrous Figures*), WA 11: 358: 'Figur des Antichristlichen Bapsts und seiner Synagog'. For the quarto fly-leaf of Melanchthon's interpretation, see WA 11: 363, *alpha*.

72 Gombrich, 'Icones Symbolicae', p. 181.

the caption: "What God himself believes of Popery / Is shown in this dreadful picture. / Everyone should shudder / as they take it to heart".[73] In the same year, Luther reused the Pope Donkey image in his polemical attack on the Papacy, *Wider das Papsttum zu Rom* (*Against the Papacy at Rome*). Here the image accompanies his misogynistic and homophobic slurs against the Pope: 'Holy Virgin S. Paula III, Lady Pope', 'Hellish Father Pope and his hermaphrodites', 'Sodomite Pope, fount of all sins and master of sin and damnation'.[74]

As Gombrich notes, 'there is no clear borderline' between the signals of the natural world and our understanding of their meanings. So Melanchthon moves directly from noting the 'female belly and breasts of the Pope's body' to explain that this symbolises 'Cardinals, bishops, priests, monks, students and other whoring folk and fattened hogs who live in carnal voluptuousness'.[75] In this misogynistic framing, the rounded female body symbolises not only the Pope but all people who are lovers of pleasure, rather than lovers of God (2 Tim. 3.4), and whose god is their stomach (Phil. 3.19).[76]

In the *Papstesel* (*Pope Donkey*), the woodcut and text create an entirely imaginary composite monster to attack Catholic opponents—by using anti-Catholic characterisations, such as the two monstrous but weak feet on which the Papacy stands—to argue for the destruction of the Catholic Church. As long as the elephant foot still 'tramples on all faint consciences and perverts the souls', and the ox's foot 'that upholds and carries the papacy in such a subjugation of souls, which are the papal teachers, preachers, priests and confessors, and particularly also the scholastic theologians' still plods on, the Catholic Church is doomed, Melanchthon claims.[77] Further, he argues that the fact that the Pope Donkey 'was found dead confirms that the end of the Papacy

73 KF no. 248. Martin Luther, *Abbildung des Bapsttum* (Wittenberg: Hans Lufft, 1545): 'Was Gott selbs von dem Bapstum helt / Zeigt dis schrecklich Bild hie gestellt. / Dafur jederman grawen solt / Wenn ers zu hertzen nemen wolt'.

74 Luther, *Wider das Papsttum zu Rom* (*Against the Papacy at Rome*), WA 54: 214, 30: 'der heiligen jungfrawen S. Paula tertius fraw Bepstin'; 213, 32: 'der Hellische Vater Bapst und seine Hermaphroditen'; 227, 25: 'der Sodomiten Bapst, aller Suenden Stiffter und Meister, Suende und verdamnis', see also Scribner, *Popular Culture*, p. 285.

75 Luther and Melanchthon, *Deuttung der zwo grewlichen Figuren* (*Interpretation of the two Monstrous Figures*), WA 11: 376, 22–24: 'Der weybisch leib und brust bedeut des Bapsts Corper, das seind Cardinal, Bischöff, pfaffen, monch, studenten unnd der Gleichen hurn volck und mastsew'.

76 Luther and Melanchthon, *Deuttung der zwo grewlichen Figuren* (*Interpretation of the two Monstrous Figures*), WA 11: 376, 25: 'voluntptatum amatores', 'animalia ventris'.

77 Luther and Melanchthon, *Deuttung der zwo grewlichen Figuren* (*Interpretation of the two Monstrous Figures*), WA 11: 376, 2–3: 'zutritt alle schwache gewissen, den er verderbt die seelen', 377, 9–12: 'die das Bapstum yn solchem unterdrucken der seelen erhalten und tragen: das sind die bepstliche lerer, prediger, pfarrer und beychtvetter, sonderlich aber die Theologi Scholastici'.

FIGURE 7 Cranach's woodcut of the *Mönchskalb* (KF no. 246). Lucas Cranach the Elder, *Mönchskalb*, 1523, woodcut, 17.5 × 24.5 cm, from Martin Luther and Philip Melanchthon, *Deuttung der z̆wo grewlichen Figuren Bapstesels zu Rom vnd Munchkalbs zu freyberg jn Meyssen funden* (1523), Sig. Faust 114, fol. aij^r
PHOTOGRAPHY: BAYERISCHE STAATSBIBLIOTHEK MÜNCHEN

is here', means that God himself had passed judgement, and 'himself will kill and destroy it'.[78]

The second monstrous image, *Das Munchkalb zu Freyberg* (*The Monk Calf at Freiberg*), was interpreted by Luther. The *Mönchskalb* (*Monk Calf*) depicts a deformed animal which Luther again describes as a part-by-part allegory of the misbegotten Catholic Church. In Cranach the Elder's 1523 woodcut (KF no. 201), the Monk Calf stands upright in the foreground, with blotches perhaps suggesting the multi-coloured markings on a cow's hide. Horizontal lines as shading may suggest contours or fur. The figure has human arms which end in cloven calf hooves. The belly, upper hips and thighs are more human, while the lower legs have a prominent tuber calcaneus at the knee and rear dewclaws at the ankle that are more like a cow, again with hooves rather than feet. The backside has a fleshy tail that ends in a point. The figure's chest is prominently curved forward. A fold or flap, possibly a wing, hangs from its shoulders. The neck is short with two rings or perhaps bulging skin. The ears are animalistic and point out from the head. The skull has two round objects on top. The figure's face is neither shaped like a human nor a cow, with a wide flat sloping forehead, wideset turned down eyes, a fleshy snout-like space between the eyes and the wide flat human nose, a wide mouth with a tongue protruding from it, and a very prominent wide rounded chin.

A *Mondkalb* (Mooncalf) was a monstrous birth, originally the malformed miscarried foetus of a cow, blamed on the influence of the moon. It could also be used to refer to a stupid or foolish person. This specific calf was said to have been born on 8 December 1522 near Kleinwaltersdorf, just a year before the pamphlet was published.[79] The location might be implied in the woodcut by a background of some rolling hills and a mountain with a fortress, perhaps denoting the Ore Mountains near Freiberg and the *Rittergut* of Kleinwaltersdorf. Luther makes a pun in German, in which a Mooncalf becomes a Monk Calf. The birth of the monstrous calf reflects the monstrosities of the many abuses of monasticism, 'this abominable, dangerous station in life'.[80] The monster is a divine admonition (*gottis vermanung*) to turn from abuse and 'become other monks or nuns, or to leave cloister and cowls behind and become again

78 Luther and Melanchthon, *Deuttung der czwo grewlichen Figuren* (*Interpretation of the two Monstrous Figures*), WA 11: 379, 16–17: 'Unnd das es todt funden ist, bestettiget das des Bapstums ende da sey und das es nicht mit schwerd noch menschen hende zurstort, sondern von jm [Gott] selb tod und zurnicht warden muß'.

79 Luther and Melanchthon, *Deuttung der czwo grewlichen Figuren* (*Interpretation of the two Monstrous Figures*), WA 11: 356.

80 Luther and Melanchthon, *Deuttung der czwo grewlichen Figuren* (*Interpretation of the two Monstrous Figures*), WA 11: 385, 22: 'grewlicen ferlichen stand'.

Christians before the time is too late'.[81] While Luther is less systematic than Melanchthon in his *Auslegung und Deuttung* (Reading and Interpretation) of the allegorical body of the monster, Gombrich notes that Luther isolates the ears of the *Mönchskalb* 'to denote the tyranny of aural confession'.[82]

Luther's propensity to use puns to interpret monstrous visual images of his enemies was not a singular event, but would also prove to be the central interpretive strategy for his teaching readers to understand the sculpture of the *Judensau* that is carved high up into a wall outside St Mary's Parish Church in Wittenberg.

### 1.2 *Reading the 'Judensau'*

Martin Luther's *Vom Schem Hamphoras* (*On the Ineffable Name*), was a late sermon augmented into a tract, part of a selection of pamphlets written at the behest of Graf Wolfgang von Schlick zu Falkenau.[83] Luther very likely wrote *Vom Schem Hamphoras* quite quickly. Since the work involves a good deal of multi-lingual rambling and punning, it might therefore have been disregarded as an incidental work.[84] However, although the work was probably rushed off, as Edwards notes, 'the vulgarity and violence was [*sic*] by choice'.[85]

The tract did not gain widespread popular appeal. Rather, it was widely considered too shocking and inappropriate in Luther's own time. Soon after its publication, the leader (*shtadlan*) of the Jewish community in the lands of the Holy Roman Empire of the German Nation, Josel of Rosheim, succeeded in having the pamphlet suppressed in Strasbourg.[86] Fellow reformers also expressed

---

81 Luther and Melanchthon, *Deuttung der czwo grewlichen Figuren* (*Interpretation of the two Monstrous Figures*), WA 11: 385, 17–18: 'Werdet ander munch und nonnen odder last kloster und kutten ligen und werdet widderumb Christen ehe euch die zeyt ubereylet'.

82 Gombrich, *Symbolic Images*, p. 178; Gombrich, 'Icones Symbolicae', p. 181.

83 Edwards, *Luther's Last Battles*, pp. 5, 20, 125–36. E. Gordon Rupp, *Martin Luther and the Jews: Robert Waley Cohen Memorial Lecture* (London: The Council for Christians and Jews, 1972), p. 17, calls its companion volume *Von den Juden und ihren Lügen* (*On the Jews and their Lies*) a 'worst-seller', though the Leipzig theologian and Luther biographer Nikolaus Selnecker instead suggests in his *Historica Oratio: Vom Leben und Wandel des Ehrwirdigen Herrn vnd thewren Mannes Gottes D. Martini Lutheri* (Leipzig: H. & V. Werdenstein, 1576), that both works were suppressed.

84 Certainly, Kaufmann, *Luther's Jews*, p. 106, suggests that *On the Jews* started to be printed before Luther had finished writing the pamphlet.

85 Edwards, *Luther's Last Battles*, p. 18.

86 Selma Stern, *Josel of Rosheim: Commander of Jewry in the Holy Roman Empire of the German Nation*, trans. by Gertrude Hirschler (Philadelphia: Jewish Publication Society of America, 1965), pp. 139–55, and *The Historical Writings of Joseph of Rosheim, Leader of Jewry in Early Modern Germany*, ed. by Chava Fraenkel-Goldschmidt, Studies in European Judaism, 12 (Leiden: Brill, 2006), p. 400.

their disgust at Luther's anti-Semitic polemic. The Nürnberg reformer Andreas Osiander disapproved of the work, as did his Zürich counterpart, Heinrich Bullinger.[87] On 8 December 1543, soon after the publication of *Vom Schem Hamphoras*, Bullinger had written to the reformer of Strasbourg, Martin Bucer, condemning the work.[88] In 1545 he again publicly condemned the work in his rejection of Luther's doctrine of the Last Supper, the *Wahrhaftes Bekenntnis der Diener der Kirchen zu Zürich* (*Zurich True Confession*):

> There is available Luther's pig-like *Schemhamphoras* which, if it were the work of a swineherd, not a famous herder of souls, might have some excuse, if only a modicum of an excuse.[89]

At the Diet of Worms in 1545 *Vom Schem Hamphoras* was also robustly rejected: Catholic delegates to the Diet argued that the pamphlet was 'hateful', 'incited the rabble to violence', and further reported 'that numerous Jews had become victims of Luther's hate'.[90] Such criticism from Jews, Catholics, and reformers alike rebuffs assumptions that Luther's scatological anti-Semitism was generally acceptable in his own time, even though many of the Catholic and reformed critics would have agreed with imposing limitations on Jewish liberty and belief.[91] The criticism of *Vom Schem Hamphoras* was typically focused on its affective language. This was designed to elicit shock and disgust, particularly among the common people, 'the rabble' (*Haufe*), who would carry out its polemical message of violently ejecting the Jews.[92]

---

87 Rupp, *Martin Luther and the Jews*, p. 5.

88 Solomon Hess, *Lebensgeschichte M. Heinrich Bullingers, Antistes der Kirche Zürich* (Zürich: Friedrich Schultheß, 1828), pp. 404–5: 'Who, I pray, bears or seriously consults the book on the Schem Hamphoras?' (*Quis, oro, ferat, aut beni consultat librum de Schem Hamphoras?*)

89 Heinrich Bullinger, *Warhaffte Bekanntnuß der dieneren der kirchen zu Zürych: was sy vß Gottes wort, mit der heyligen allgemeinen Christenlichen Kirchen glaubind vnd leerind, in sonderheit aber von dem Nachtmal vnsers herren Jesu Christi: mit gebürlicher Antwort vff das vnbegründt ergerlich schmähen, verdam[m]en vnd schelten D. Martin Luthers* (Zürich: Christoph Froschauer, 1545), sig. 10r: 'So ist vorhanden Luthers Schwyninskatigs Schemhamphoras / welches so es geschrieben wäre von einem Schwynhirte[n] / nit von einem verrümpte[n] Seelhirten / etwas doch auch wenig entschuldigu[n]g hette'. See also Edwards, *Luther's Last Battles*, pp. 134–5, 234 n. 48, and Stern, *Josel of Rosheim*, p. 307, n. 6.

90 Rupp, *Martin Luther and the Jews*, p. 5, Wolfram Kinzig and Cornelia Kück, *Judentum und Christentum zwischen Konfrontation und Faszination* (Stuttgart: Kohlhammer, 2002), p. 94: 'katholische Gesandte auf dem Reichstag zu Worms berichteten 1545, dass zahlreiche Juden Opfer von Luthers Hetze wurden'.

91 Rupp, *Martin Luther and the Jews*, p. 5.

92 Edwards, *Luther's Last Battles*, p. 135.

While the pamphlet was successfully kept from a wide audience, the text was used by scholars. The pamphlet's arguments also served as a theological excuse for legal decisions by local rulers, such as Elector Johann Friedrich I. of Saxony who, in 1543, banned Jews from travelling through his territories and Elector Johann Georg of Brandenburg, Chancellor of the Holy Roman Empire, who, in 1571, permitted pogroms against Jewish money-lenders in Berlin, including the destruction of the synagogue in the Berlin Jewish quarter, *Am kleinen Jüdenhof*.[93] Moreover, after its publication, the words 'Rabini Schem HaMphoras' ('the ineffable name of the Rabbis', drawing on the title of Luther's tract, *Vom Schem Hamphoras*) were added above the carved image of the *Judensau* facing the Wittenberg market square.[94]

In medieval Germany, churches and civic buildings often displayed carved cycles of the vices, which could include a device against gluttony of people suckling on a pigs' teats. Similarly, carved screens of the life of Jesus and the vice cycles might depict Jews, either neutrally as characters, via visual shorthand such as the distinctive conical hat, or via less-than-human stereotypes including grotesquely exaggerated features or comparison to animals.[95] Sometimes the carving was a sculpture, a relief, or an architectural finial. The pigs are typically depicted either as a pig in profile or as a highly sexualised female body.

In the *Judensau* image, Christians and Jews would both see the uncomfortably close physical engagement of the men and the pig; sexual or infantile or scatological. The fluid concepts of body, food, and action of the medieval period mean that it was implied to all viewers that drinking a sow's milk could turn you into a pig, or that lifting a pig's tail could associate you with its dung.[96] Jews, as Christians knew well, would be even more offended by the fact that

93 See also Kaufmann, *Luther's Jews*, pp. 121–23, Shachar, *The 'Judensau'*, p. 45, and Eugen Wolbe, *Geschichte der Juden in Berlin und in der Mark Brandenburg* (Berlin: Kedem, 1937), p. 79.

94 Shachar, *The 'Judensau'*, p. 31. In 1594, Wittenberg printer Wolfgang Meissner published a woodcut of the Wittenberg *Judensau* with the recently added inscription above it, and an explanatory poem in Latin.

95 See, for example, Jung, 'The Passion, the Jews and the Crisis of the Individual,' pp. 145–77; Debra Higgs Strickland, 'The Jews, Leviticus, and the Unclean in Medieval Bestiaries', in *Beyond the Yellow Badge*, ed. by Merback, pp. 203–32.

96 Claudine Fabre-Vassas recounts how, in some myths, drinking pigs' milk turns a person into a pig, *The Singular Beast*, p. 99; and anti-Semitic myths frequently involve Jewish people being transformed into pigs, see Kathryn A. Smith *Art, Identity and Devotion in Fourteenth-Century England: Three Women and their Books of Hours*, The British Library Studies in Medieval Culture (Toronto, University of Toronto Press, 2003), pp. 275–78.

FIGURE 8 The medieval carving of the *Judensau* on the external walls of Wittenberg's parish church, with its Reformation inscription *Rabini Schem HaMphoras—The ineffable name of the Rabbis. Judensau, c.*1305, bas-relief with Reformation inscription, Wittenberg Parish Church
PHOTOGRAPHY: DR AVISHAI TEICHER

it was a pig—an animal that was notably forbidden by Jewish dietary laws.[97] Debra Higgs Strickland has shown that the uncleanliness of pigs was polemically

97 One of the most widely recognised distinguishing cultural differences between Jews and non-Jews in Europe, particularly in areas where the two groups lived side by side and had few other distinguishing characteristics was that Jewish food-laws forbade eating pork, which was a staple meat for their Christian neighbours. Roper, *Living I was Your Plague*, p. ix, notes that it was blasphemous to write out the Ineffable Name of God and even more so to do so by using a taboo food.

used in the middle ages to paint Jews as heretics. In her assessment she refers back to MS Bodley 764 where 'swine signifying sinners and unclean persons or heretics' are explicitly linked to Jews:

> Swine's flesh belongs to polluted things, which, among other precepts of the Old Testament, are prescribed as unclean. They have, moreover, passed on the remains of their sins to their children when they cried out, 'His blood be on us and on our children' (Mt. 27.25).[98]

At the turn of the thirteenth century, a *Judensau* was carved on the wall of St Mary's Church Wittenberg, in a prominent position facing the city and market square. This is one of the first times the device was used not as part of a cycle of carvings to exhort the faithful Christian inside the church, but as a direct visual attack on Jews in a place where the Jewish community would see it.[99] Like the Wittenberg sow, Luther's anti-Jewish tracts were addressed to Christian and Jewish audiences alike. Jews, converted Jews, and Catholics, as well as his Reformation audience all read Luther's texts. The arguments in *Vom Schem Hamphoras* (*Of the Ineffable Name*) are mostly aimed at Christians: both the Lutheran faithful who must remain true to Lutheran beliefs; and non-Lutheran Christian opponents, most likely to refute their arguments that Protestantism was derived from Judaism.[100]

However, in his foundational study on the subject, Shachar argues that the image of the *Judensau* itself was not used polemically until the Reformation. Under the influence of Luther, it became part of the *Schandbilder* (Images of Defamation) and *Kampfbilder* (Antagonistic Images) traditions, using 'aggressive obscenity', particularly 'oral and anal obscenity'.[101] The tropes which Luther elucidates in his explanatory pamphlet *Vom Schem Hamphoras* (*Of the Ineffable Name*)—which include bestiality and faecal matter—are thus typical.

98 Strickland, 'The Jews, Leviticus, and the Unclean in Medieval Bestiaries', pp. 203–32 (p. 226).

99 Shachar, *The 'Judensau'*, p. 31. Jews had been expelled from Wittenberg in 1304, the year before the image was crafted, but were allowed to resettle with a Jewish community existing in direct proximity to St Mary's church by 1339. Jews were again expelled from the city in 1440, and there was most likely no resident Jewish community in the city during Luther's lifetime (and certainly not after 1543 and the publication of his *Von den Juden und ihren Lügen*), see *Geschichte jüdischer Gemeinden in Sachsen-Anhalt: Versuch einer Erinnerung*, ed. by Landesverband Jüdischer Gemeinden Sachsen-Anhalt, Magdeburg (Wernigerode: Oemler-Verlag 1997), pp. 270–73.

100 The accusation that Lutheranism was derived from Judaism was founded on the fact that the reformer translated the Hebrew Scriptures from the original language.

101 Shachar, *The 'Judensau'*, p. 2.

The tropes of associating religious opponents with pigs and ordure were also used in the anti-papal polemical images contained in the *Abbildung des Bapstum* (*Depictions of the Papacy*), for instance in the woodcut, *Papa dat Concilivm* (*The Pope grants a Council*) by Cranach the Younger. In the cartoon, an older man with a beard, wearing ecclesiastical robes, including a cope and papal tiara, sits on the back of a female pig, her teats just visible. One hand is held in a two-fingered gesture of blessing. In the other is a neatly curled pile of faeces, the top of the pile blowing out an extravagantly curled burst of wind.[102] For Luther, as we have shown, pigs and excrement regularly went together as a polemical trope: in his preface to the *Symphoniae Iucundae*, for instance, he warned his readers to avoid 'some shit-poet or the music of pigs' (*aliquem Merdipoetam interim audiant vel porcorum Musicam*).[103] The cartoon was considered disgusting and inappropriate by contemporaries, as documented by Johannes Sleidanus: 'Many people did not consider Luther's ridicule as good, and felt that such did not befit a man like Luther, it being too crude'.[104]

A large part of *Vom Schem Hamphoras* (*Of the Ineffable Name*) is a crude and vivid deconstruction of a polemical work that, it is claimed, was written by Jews in order to convert Christians to Judaism. At about the same time the *Judensau* sculpture was carved into the walls of St Mary's Wittenberg, the Carthusian monk Salvaticus Porchetus compiled a Latin translation of this work. In 1520, Porchetus' work was first printed under the title *Victoria Porcheti*

102 The visualisation of the smell of shit, or flatulence, by extravagant curls or clouds is a recurrent theme in Cranach the Younger's *Abbildung des Bapstum* cartoons. The third image, *Hic Oscvla Pedibvs Pape Figvntvr* (*Here the Kissing of the Pope's Feet is shown*), depicts the tiaraed Pope seated on a throne and attended by two cardinals. In his hand he holds a fiery indulgence. Two barefooted men stick out their tongues and bare their bottoms in derision of the Pope and his authority. Opulent clouds of flatulence issue like clouds of incense from their bottoms. For the development of the genre as a whole, see also David Kunzle, *The Early Comic Strip, Narrative Strips and Picture Stories in the European Broadsheet from c. 1450 to 1825* (Berkeley: University of California Press, 1973), pp. 212, 242.

103 See Appendix 1, 5.3.

104 Johannes Sleidanus, *Warhafftige Beschreibunge allerley fürnemer Hendel, so sich in Glaubens vnnd anderen Weltlichen sachen, bey Regierung des Großmechtigsten Keyser Carls des Fünfften, mehrerntheyls in Teutscher Nation zugetragen* (Frankfurt a.M.: [Sigmund Feyerabend], 1565), sig. N n iij$^v$: 'Solch des Luthers gespött hielten viel Leuthe nicht für gut / vnd maineten es stünde einem solchen Man[n] nit wol an / darzu were es zu grob'. Sleidanus himself, however, believed the cartoon prophetic. Sleidanus, *Warhafftige Beschreibung*, sig. N n iij$^v$: 'But he [Luther] has had his reasons why he has published [this cartoon], and one thought that he was more far-sighted than others' (*Aber er hatte seine vrsachen / warumb ers that / vnd man hielte es darfür / daß er etwas weiter denn ein ander hette gesehen*).

FIGURE 9 Lucas Cranach the Younger, *Papa Dat Concilivm in Germania* (*The Pope grants a Council in Germany*), 1545, from Martin Luther, *Abbildung des Bapstum* (Wittenberg: [Hans Lufft], 1545), Sig. Lynar S 527
PHOTOGRAPHY: STAATSBIBLIOTHEK ZU BERLIN—PREUSSISCHER KULTURBESITZ

*aduersus impios Hebraeos* (*Porchetus' Victory against the Impious Hebrews*).[105] The alleged original asserted that Jesus was a sorcerer, that he gained his powers

105 Salvaticus Porchetus, *Victoria Porcheti aduersus impios, in quia ex sacris literis, tum ex dictis Talmud, ac Caballistarum, et aliorum omnium authorum, quos Hebraei recipient, monstratur veritas catholicae fidei* (Paris: François Regnault, 1520).

by theft and trickery, that he was wrestled down from heaven by Judas Iscariot (who also had the magic powers) and that he was hanged in the Temple. In his retelling of Porchetus' account, Luther mocks the Jewish Temple's ritual and bronze statues. He variously describes Jews as 'children of the devil' (*Teuffels kinder*), 'full of lies' (*voller lügen*), 'like a monkey' (*wie ein Affe*), 'bewitched' (*bezaubert*), full of 'vain blindness, mad, and senseless' (*eitel blindheit, rasend, wansinnig*) among other more extended slurs.[106]

Luther's pamphlet does not respond to the profane violations that are fictionally imparted to Jesus' body in Porchetus' account—cutting it open, wrestling it, hanging it by the neck—by imparting similar violations to Jewish bodies. This is unlike the anti-Semitic stories of ritual murder, poisoned well or violated hosts which roused mob violence against Jews across Europe in the period and would, for instance, later form a theological justification for the Spanish Inquisition.[107] However, *Vom Schem Hamphoras* did advocate for the legal oppression of Jews. Luther argues that toleration of Jews living among Christians must end, and reiterates that they should be again expelled.[108] Moreover, while we agree with Roper that technically Luther does not call for riots or violence against Jews, it would require the most careful reading of *Vom Schem Hamphoras* to avoid that implication:[109]

> Even if they were punished in the most gruesome manner that the streets rang with their blood, their dead would not be counted, not in the hundred thousands but in the millions, as happened under Vespasian in Jerusalem and at Betar under Hadrian, still they must insist on being right.[110]

---

106 Luther, *Vom Schem Hamphoras* (*Of the Ineffable Name*), WA 53: 580, 6; 593, 36; 594, 4; 602, 38; 645, 5; translations from: Gerhard Falk, *The Jew in Christian Theology: Martin Luther's Anti-Jewish Vom Schem Hamphoras, Previously Unpublished in English, and Other Milestones in Church Doctrine Concerning Judaism* (Jefferson, NC: McFarland & Co., 1992), pp. 167, 184, 190.

107 See Smith, *Art, Identity and Devotion in Fourteenth-Century England*, pp. 275–80, for the development of this 'radical anti-Jewish ideology'.

108 See, for example, Luther, *Von den Juden und ihren Lügen* (*Of the Jews and their Lies*), WA 53: 541, 25–27.

109 Roper, *Living I Was Your Plague*, p. 144.

110 Luther, *Vom Schem Hamphoras* (*Of the Ineffable Name*), WA 53: 579, 25–29: 'Wenn sie auch so greulich gestrafft würden, das die gassen vol bluts rönnen, das man jre todten nicht mit hundert tausent, Sone mit zehen hundert tausent rechen und zelen müste, wie zu Jerusalem unter Vespasiano und zu Bittor unter Adrinao eschehen ist. Dennoch müssen sie recht haben', trans. by Falk, *The Jew in Christian Theology*, p. 167. Inexplicably, Falk's translation renders Luther's 'Bittor' as 'for evil'. However, Luther clearly refers to the Betar Fortress, the site of the Jewish last stand against the Romans in the bar Kochba revolt, see

The detailed description encourages the reader to vividly recall to mind these historic massacres and, from imagining, perhaps imagine carrying them out in the present day and time, although the grammatic formulation, 'even if they were', equivocates the call to violence. This threat was identified by Jewish, Catholic and reformed critics of the pamphlet, and did in fact lead to pogroms in Berlin in 1571.

Luther further dismantles the logic of Jews in Porchetus' account through multi-lingual arguments and wordplays in German, Hebrew, and Latin. Luther's two-paragraph reflection on the *Judensau* is part of a much longer diatribe against the idea of the Ineffable Name of God. Jewish believers refrain from saying God's name to avoid taking the Lord's Name in vain (Deut. 5.11). *Shem ha-Mephoras* (שם המפורש) is a kabbalistic term that means 'Hidden Name' or 'explicit name'. Maimonides believed that the *Shem ha-Mephoras* was only used for the Tetragrammaton, the four letters *YHWH* (יהוה) that denote the Holy Name of God.[111] By the thirteenth century, German Jewish kabbalists like Eleazar of Worms believed that the Ineffable Name might also be applied to the 'seventy-two-fold name'. Eleazar's *Sefer Razie'l* was readily taken up by early modern cosmologists and alchemists.[112]

In his discussion of the Tetragrammaton and the 'seventy-two-fold name', Luther extensively ridicules kabbalistic and Jewish mystical beliefs which imputed magical powers to any of the Names of God.[113] Using the numerical values of the Latin letters, M, C, D, L, X, V, and I, he sets out his own nonsense numerological argument:

---

*Von den Juden und ihren Lügen* (*Of the Jews and their Lies*): WA 53: 546, 33: 'Of Adrian the Emperor, who conducted the other and final battle against the Jews, defeated Kochba and fully and completely drove the Jews from their country' (*Adriani des Keisers, der die ander und letzte schlacht ubet an den Jüden, den Kochab schlug und die Jüden aus jrem Lande gentzlich vnd rein vertrieb*).

111 Moses Maimonides, *The Guide of the Perplexed*, ed. by Shlomo Pines, 3 vols (Chicago: University of Chicago Press, 1963), I, 62.

112 The thoughts of 'Rabi Eliezer' on the Ineffable Name are excerpted by Pforzheim professor of Hebrew, Johann Reuchlin, *De Arte Cabbalistica Libri Tres* (Hagenau: Thomas Anshelmus, 1517), sig. X^r^, and converted Jew, Anton Margarita, *Der gantz Jüdisch glaub, sampt ainer gründtlichen und warhafften anzaygunge aller Satzungen, Ceremonien, Gebethen, haymliche und offentlichen Gebreuch deren sich dye Juden halten, durch das gantz Jar. Mit schönen und gegründten Argumenten wyder jren Glauben* (Augsburg: Heinrich Steiner, 1530).

113 For a comprehensive introduction to the theology of the Ineffable Name, see Samuel S. Cohon, 'The Name of God, A Study in Rabbinic Theology', *Hebrew Union College Annual*, 23.1 (1950–51), 579–604.

TABLE 2 Luther's kabbalistic 'nonsense' table from *Vom Schem Hamphoras* (*Of the Ineffable Name*), WA 53: 597

| | | | | | | | | | | | |
|---|---|---|---|---|---|---|---|---|---|---|---|
| L | V | C | I | M | I | L | X | D | I | C | V |
| L | V | X | L | I | C | V | M | D | V | M | I |
| I | V | D | I | C | V | D | I | C | L | I | I |

Luther then proceeds to explain how, by alternating the first letter from the first column, the last from the second, and the first from the third, and proceeding by moving inwards, he was able to generate seventy-two three-letter words, each with their own different numerical value—but without any meaning. The same was true for the kabbalistic power of the seventy-two-fold name. Only when the first, second and third columns are read from left to right, the following German nonsense rhyme is revealed:

> Lucy milks the cow,
> Luxli, you come to me,
> Jew, chew the swill.[114]

In the same way in which Luther's seventy-two numerical combinations revealed no special powers so 'Moses' own text stands only in its natural meaning, in the way in which it is intended to be read', the reformer concluded.[115]

Having dismantled the Jewish thought that number combinations of the Ineffable Name carry specific meaning, ten paragraphs later Luther set up a rhetorical question of how Jews discovered the power of the Holy Name, to which he provides the following response: 'Well now, I don't know in detail where they got it from, but I can guess approximately'.[116] What follows is therefore imaginative, an opportunity for Luther to demonstrate his polemical skills:

114 Luther, *Vom Schem Hamphoras* (*Of the Ineffable Name*), WA 53: 597, 4–6: 'Luci milcks die Ku, / Luxle kum du zu mir, / Jüde kawe du die klyen', trans. by Falk, *The Jew in Christian Theology*, p. 179.

115 *Vom Schem Hamphoras* (*Of the Ineffable Name*), WA 53: 596, 36–7: 'In des stehet der Text Mosi fur sich selbs in seiner natürlichen deutung, wie er gelesen wird'.

116 *Vom Schem Hamphoras* (*Of the Ineffable Name*), WA 53: 600, 23–25: 'Wolan ich weis nicht sonderlich, wo sie es her haben, Aber nahe hinzu will ich wol raten', Falk, *The Jew in Christian Theology*, p. 182. Further on, WA 53: 636,33–637,3, Luther postulated that, 'when Judas Iscariot had hanged himself, his guts burst open, as happens to those who hang themselves. Maybe the Jews had had their servants with them, with gold pitchers and silver bowls, to catch this Judas piss (as it is called), along with all the other sacred objects.

> It is here [that they got it from], in Wittenberg on our parish church, a sow carved in stone, there lie young piglets and Jews underneath suckling her; at the sow's behind stands a Rabbi, who lifts up the right leg, and with his left hand drags the tail over himself,[117] bends and looks with great zeal under the tail into the Talmud inside, as if he wanted to read and perceive something difficult and exceptional. [...] Where had he read that? In the sow's (to put it crudely) butt.[118]

If it was so crudely put that even Luther felt he needed to acknowledge it, it was certainly expected to offend his readers, both Jewish and Christian.[119]

Next, Luther extrapolates from the sculpture into a multi-lingual pun, from *Shem ha-Mephoras* ('the Hidden Name') to *Sham ha-Peresh* ('here is dirt').[120]

---

Then they gorged and guzzled the shit themselves, which is what gave their eyes such sharp sight' (*Da Judas Scharioth sich erhenckt hatte, das jhm die Darme zurissen und, wie den erhenckten geschicht, die Blase geborsten, Da haben die Jueden vielleicht jre Diener mit gůlden kannen und silbern schůsseln dabey gehabt, die Judas pisse* (*wie mans nennet*) *sampt dem andern Heiligthumb auffgefangen, darnach unternander die merde gefressen und gesoffen, davon sie so scharffsichtige augen kriegt*); see also Roper, *Living I Was Your Plague*, p. 156.

117 We have translated 'zeucht er den pirzel uber sich' as 'to drag the tail over himself'; 'zeucht' is the obsolete version of 'ziehen'. Falk, *The Jew in Christian Theology*, p. 182, translates it as 'raises the behind of the sow'.

118 Luther, *Vom Schem Hamphoras* (*Of the Ineffable Name*), WA 53: 600, 26–601, 5: 'Es ist hie zu Wittemberg an unser Pfarrkirchen eine Saw jnn stein gehawen, da ligen junge Ferckel und Jüden unterm die saugen, Hinder der Saw stehet ein Rabin, der hebt der Saw das rechte bein empor, und mit seiner lincken hand zeucht er den pirtzel uber sich, bückt und kuckt mit grossem vleis der Saw unter dem pirtzel jnn den Thalmud hinein, als wolt er etwas scharffes und sonderlichs lesen und ersehen. Daher haben sie gewislich jr Schem Hamphoras. [...] Denn also redet man bey den Deudschen von einem, der grosse klugheit on grund furgibt: Wo hat ers gelesen? Der Saw im (grob heraus) hindern'. Our translation is amended from Falk, *The Jew in Christian Theology*, p. 239. Generally, Falk's translation is technically excellent, however, while the pun on 'behind' (*hinder/Hintern*) as both a preposition and a noun for hindquarters that Luther mobilises also works in English—the term in English is quite polite and the term in German is so rude that Luther himself acknowledges it is 'crudely expressed' (*grob heraus*). Luther is not notably coy about using graphic language, but this required an interpolation. Indeed, an online search for the terms 'Sau im Hintern' (with safe search turned off) indexes primarily pornographic videos.

119 For the theological implications of bestiality and homophobic elements of this imagery; see, for example, Erik Wade, 'The Beast with Two Backs: Bestiality, Sex Between Men, and Byzantine Theology in the Paenitentiale Theodori', *Journal of Medieval Worlds*, 2.1–2 (2020), 11–26.

120 Luther, *Vom Schem Hamphoras* (*Of the Ineffable Name*), WA 53: 601, 6: 'Hie zu möcht man leicht das wort Schem Hamphoras zihen und leren, nemlich "Peres Schama", oder wie sie es thun, künstlich meistern und machen "Schama Peres", so lautets nahe zu samen'.

This offensive play on words is achieved by two rhetorical moves. The first is misprision, the act of misreading or mishearing:[121]

> It is rather as if a German while listening or reading understood fooling (*narren*) instead of feeding (*nähren*), or 'he has improved (*gebessert*) my property', rather than 'he has watered (*gewässert*) my property'.[122]

In this case, Luther argues that the misprision is part of the 'devil's evil plan' (*leidige böse Geist*) to mislead the Jews into believing they are saying the Holy Name of God and that it has power for good; but what they are actually saying is 'Here is filth' or 'There is dirt'.[123] The word Luther uses here, *Dreck*, can mean filth, dirt, muck or dung. Luther's second move is to clarify that this *Dreck* is, in this case, faecal:

> However, he means *Sham ha-Peresh*, that is to say: 'Here is filth' [*Dreck*], not that lies in the alleyways, rather than comes out of the stomach, *sham* means: here or there, *peresh* that what is the intestines of the sow and all animals, as Moses requires in Leviticus, where he required the sin offering to be burned, with skin and hair, and with its 'Peres'.[124]

This time, Luther translates פֶּרֶשׁ (*peresh*) as 'mist, etc'. The German *Mist* is less generally filth, and more specifically 'dung, manure, droppings', animal faeces. Schramm translates it as 'there is the crap/dung/shit'.[125] Luther here references his own translation of Lev. 4.11, describing the practice of the Levitical sin offering:

> Aber das fell des farren mit allem fleysch samt dem kopff und schenckeln, und das eyngeweyde und den mist.[126]

---

121 Harold Bloom, *The Anxiety of Influence* (New York: Oxford University Press, 1997), p. 6, and Harold Bloom, *A Map of Misreading* (New York: Oxford University Press, 1976).

122 Luther, *Vom Schem Hamphoras* (*Of the Ineffable Name*), WA 53: 601, 8–10: 'Gleich, als wenn ein Deudscher im hören oder lesen verstünde Nerren fur Neeren, Item, Er hat mir mein gütlein fein gebessert, ja gewessert', Falk, *The Jew in Christian Theology*, p. 239.

123 Brooks Schramm, 'Luther's Schem Hamphoras', *Dialog: A Journal of Theology*, 56.2 (2017), 151–55 (p. 154).

124 Luther, *Vom Schem Hamphoras* (*Of the Ineffable Name*), WA 53: 601, 12–17: 'Er aber meinet "Scham Haperes" das heisst: Hie dreck, der nicht auf der Gassen ligt, sondern aus dem bauch kompt, "Scham" heisst: hie oder da, "Peres" das ist der Saw und allen Thieren jnn den Dermen ist, wie Moses des in Levit. breucht, da er gebeut, das Sündopffer zu verbrennen, mit haut und haar, und mit seinem "Peres", mist etc'.

125 Schramm, 'Luther's Schem Hamphoras', p. 154.

126 Luther, *Deutsche Bibel*, WA DB 8, 338: 'But the hide [skin] of the young steer with all flesh [meat], together with head and legs and the entrails and the dung'. Many English

Luther is thus reminding his audience of his fluency in Hebrew and his familiarity with texts which the majority of his readers would only know in translation (whether Latin or in Luther's own translation into German). This identification with Jewish scholarship, even as he plays with images of violent disgust, has been seen as 'puzzling' to some scholars, but it was central to medieval replacement theology.[127] Luther's text sets out both to out-perform kabbalists and out-exegete rabbinical interpreters, while at the same time reducing their sacred texts and spiritual practices to excrement. Luther concludes this section of *Vom Schem Hamphoras* (*On the Ineffable Name*) with a prayer for conversion by God's grace, and a promotion for his next pamphlet on a supersessionist, Trinitarian reading of the Hebrew Scriptures. However, the impact of the tract would not fade out so swiftly, as we will show in the following section.

## 2 Later Reception of Luther's Anti-Semitic Polemic

We have already noted the reception, both approving and disapproving, of Luther's anti-Semitic polemic in his own time. Luther produced anti-Jewish and anti-Semitic sermons and writings throughout his life. In his early sermons on the Psalms and Romans, he combined injunctions to reduce Jewish people's civil and religious liberties with invective against their beliefs. In *Wider die Sabbather* (*Against the Sabbatarians* 1538), Luther expressed his formal support of the 1536 strictures against Jews in Saxony.[128] In the generally more tolerant, *Daß Jesus Christ ein geborener Jude war* (*That Jesus Christ was born a Jew*), Luther nonetheless, demonstrated his continued opposition to Jewish religious practices, calling for Jews to convert to Christianity following Jesus' example.[129] His late pamphlets, *Von den Juden und ihren Lügen* (*On the Jews and their Lies*) and *Vom Schem Hamphoras* (*Of the Ineffable Name*) and his final letter and sermons from Eisleben, revile Jews for ignorance and stupidity in failing to convert.

---

translations also render פֶּרֶשׁ (*peresh*) as 'dung', notably the *Wycliffe Bible* (1382–1395), the *Geneva Bible* (1560), and the *King James Bible* (1604), though more modern translations choose to translate פֶּרֶשׁ (*peresh*) as 'offal'.

127 Roper, *Living I Was Your Plague*, p. 164.

128 Luther, *Wider die Sabbather* (*Against the Sabbatarians*), WA 50: 312–37.

129 Luther, *Von den Juden und ihren Lügen* (*On the Jews and their Lies*), WA 53: 412–552; *Vom Schem Hamphoras* (*Of the Ineffable Name*), WA 53: 573–648; *Daß Jesus Christus ein geborener Jude sei* (*That Jesus Christ was born a Jew*), WA 11: 307–36.

Not all of these texts have been readily available to English-speaking readers, but they have been extensively discussed and documented in the German literature.[130] They were collected in early editions of Luther's works, such as the mid-eighteenth-century Walch edition, and his writings against the Jews are included fully in the Weimar edition.[131]

From the nineteenth century onwards, therefore, Luther's works were easily accessible to thinkers looking for support for rising German anti-Semitism. In 1879, an anonymously published tract, by 'Islebensis' ('Eisleben-citizen'), *Dr Martin Luther und das Judenthum* extensively extracts Luther's late anti-Semitic writings, in order to, as Kaufmann notes

> reclaim Luther as the 'first anti-Semite', a man engaged in a struggle against a 'race not equal to that of the Aryans' and a 'Christian role model' fighting against 'the debauched vampire Judaism'.[132]

From the 1880s, Luther's late anti-Semitic writings were extensively used by German anti-Semites. Where Luther was not sufficiently anti-Semitic, the compilers created or attributed other sixteenth-century anti-Semitic invectives to the reformer, such as the one used on the title of 'Islebensis' work: 'The Jew is not a German, but a deceiver; not a foreigner, but an imposter; not a citizen, but a strangler!'[133] Frequently published under pseudonyms or anonymously, the resulting compilations of genuine and attributed Luther sayings against the Jews were both profitable and popular. In 1887, 'Thomas Frey' published an *Antisemiten-Katechismus* (*Catcheism for Anti-Semites*) which only six years

130 Thomas Kaufmann, *Luthers 'Judenschriften': Ein Beitrag zu ihrer historischen Kontextualisierung* (Tübingen: Mohr Siebeck, 2011); Thomas Kaufmann, *Luthers Juden* (Stuttgart: Reclam Verlag, 2014); Dietz Bering, *War Luther Antisemit? Das deutsch-jüdische Verhältnis als Tragödie der Nähe* (Berlin: Berlin University Press, 2014).

131 Luther, *Schriften 1543–46*, WA 54; Luther, *D. Martin Luthers sowol in Deutscher als Lateinischer Sprache verfertigte und aus der letztern in die erstere übersetzte Sämtliche Schriften: Zwanzigster Theil Welcher die Schriften wider die Sacramentirer, Fanaticos, Juden und Türken enthält, nebst einer historischen Einleitung in selbige; herausgegeben von Johann Georg Walch* (Halle: Johann Justinus Gebauer, 1747), W¹ 20: 2230–2630.

132 'Islebensis', *Dr Martin Luther und das Judenthum* (Berlin: O. Lorenz, 1879); Thomas Kaufmann, 'Luther and the Jews', *Antisemitism Studies*, 3.1 (2019), 46–65 (p. 56) (first publ. in *Jews, Judaism, and the Reformation in Sixteenth-Century Germany*, ed. by Dean Phillip Bell and Stephen G. Burnett, Studies in Central European Studies (Leiden: Brill, 2006), pp. 69–104).

133 'Islebensis', *Luther und das Judenthum*, translated by Kaufmann, 'Luther and the Jews', p. 56: 'Der Jude ist nicht ein Teutscher, sondern ein Täuscher; nicht ein Welscher, sondern ein Fälscher, nicht ein Bürger, sondern ein Würger'.

later was in its twenty-fifth edition, having sold in excess of 35,000 copies.[134] Now publishing under his own name, Theodor Fritsch, the author drew on 'Islebensis' work for his *Antisemiten-Katechismus*, which he augmented with further Luther 'attributions'.[135] Fritsch retained the genuine and attributed Luther quotes in his anti-Semitic polemical work, *Handbuch der Judenfrage* (*Handbook of the Jewish Question*); a book that, alongside his *Der falsche Gott. Beweis-Material gegen Jahwe* (*The False God. Material evidence against Yahweh*) was instrumental in claiming 'the German Luther' for the *völkische* cause.[136] The *Handbuch* was even more profitable than the *Antisemiten-Katechismus*: by the end of the Second World War, it was in its final—forty-ninth edition—and had sold in excess of 300,000 copies.[137]

Other influential works, such as *Luther und die Juden*—a 1921 *völkische* publication by Alfred Falb—set out to document how Luther's opinions on the Jews change profoundly, 'from pronounced friend of the Jews to their sharpest enemy', and to promote the claim that, had Luther had the benefit of modern anti-Semitic 'scholarship' he, too, would have appreciated that Jesus was in fact, not born a Jew, but an Aryan Galilean.[138]

National Socialist publications continued to highlight Luther's anti-Semitism. Indeed, the Nazis posited themselves as 'an extension of Martin Luther's efforts; and that Christianity repudiates Judaism'.[139] Relevant publications included Georg Buchwald's edition of Luther's *Von den Juden und ihren Lügen* (*Of the Jews and their Lies*, 1931) and Walther Linden's *Luthers Kampfschriften*

134 'Thomas Frey' [pseudonym for Theodor Fritsch], *Antisemiten-Katechismus. Eine Zusammenstellung des wichtigsten Materials zum Verständniß der Judenfrage* (Leipzig: Verlag von Theodor Fritsch, 1887), 'Frey, Thomas', *Antisemiten-Katechismus. Eine Zusammenstellung des wichtigsten Materials zum Verständniß der Judenfrage von Theodor Fritsch (Thomas Frey). Fünfundzwanzigste vermehrte Auflage (26–35tes Tausend)* (Lepizig: Verlag von Hermann Beyer, 1893).

135 Kaufmann, 'Luther and the Jews', p. 57.

136 Theodor Fritsch, *Der falsche Gott. Beweis-Material gegen Jahwe* (Leipzig: Hammer-Verlag, 1933), p. 190.

137 Theodor Fritsch, *Handbuch der Judenfrage. Die wichtigsten Tatsachen zur Beurteilung des jüdischen Volkes* (Leipzig: Hammer-Verlag, 1931); for Fritsch, and an analysis of the *Handbuch*, see Martin Kitchen, 'The Antisemite's *Vade Mecum*: Theodor Fritsch's *Handbuch der Judenfrage*', *Antisemitism Studies*, 2.2 (2018), 199–234.

138 Alfred Falb, *Luther und die Juden* (Munich: Boepple, 1921), see Christian Wiese, 'Luther's Shadow: Jewish and Protestant Interpretations of the Reformer's Writings on the Jews, 1917–33', in *Jews and Protestants: From the Reformation to the Present*, ed. by Irene Aue-Ben-David, Aya Elyada, Moshe Sluhovsky, Christian Wiese, and others (Berlin: de Gruyter, 2020), pp. 161–88 (p. 175), and Susannah Heschel, *The Aryan Jesus: Christian Theologians and the Bible in Nazi Germany* (Princeton, NJ: Princeton University Press, 2010).

139 Heschel, *The Aryan Jesus*, p. 81.

*gegen das Judentum* (1936).[140] After the *Reichskristallnacht* (*Night of the Broken Glass Pogroms*), Luther's works were disseminated internationally to provide a theological justification for Nazi pogroms against Jews, their properties, and their places of worship.[141] Luther's anti-Semitic writings were compiled into a highly popular volume, *Martin Luther über die Juden: Weg mit ihnen!* (*Martin Luther on the Jews: Away with them!*), by the Eisenach German-Christian Bishop, Martin Sasse.[142] Published first in German in November 1938, it was immediately translated and circulated to other Protestant nations, with a Dutch edition published the same year, and an English in January 1939.[143] Indeed, Kaufmann judges that 'Martin Luther's influence and antisemitism enabled all other German anti-Semites to act with a clear conscience and made Lutheran Christians susceptible to this evil ideology'.[144]

Post-war German secondary literature addressed Luther's writings on the Jews, Luther's Jewish contemporaries, and the implications of Luther's anti-Semitism in the light of the Shoah. Notable works include Heinrich Bornkamm, *Luther und das Alte Testament* (*Luther and the Old Testament*, 1948), Wilhelm Maurer, *Kirche und Synagoge: Motive und Formen der Auseinandersetzung der Kirche mit dem Judentum* (*Church and Synagogue: Motifs and Forms of the Engagement of the Church with Judaism*, 1953), Selma Stern, *Josel von Rosheim: Befehlshaber der Judenschaft im Heiligen römischen Reich deutscher Nation* (*Josel of Rosheim: Commander of Jewry in the Holy Roman Empire of the German Nation*, 1959), and Bienert's *Martin Luther und die Juden: Ein Quellenbuch mit zeitgenössischen Illustrationen* (*Martin Luther and the Jews: A Sourcebook with contemporary Illustrations*, 1982).[145] More recent work includes Heiko A. Oberman,

140 Martin Luther, *Von den Juden und ihren Lügen. Im Auszuge mitgeteilt von D. Georg Buchwald*, Luthers Flugschriften für unsere Zeit, 3 (Dresden: Verlag Landesverein für Innere Mission, [1931]), Walter Linden, *Luthers Kampfschriften gegen das Judentum* (Berlin: Klinckhardt und Biermann, 1936).

141 Kaufmann, 'Luther and the Jews', p. 60, argues that 'The wide circulation of *On the Jews and their Lies* makes the connection between the list of measures that Luther articulated in it and the events of *Reichskristallnacht* irrefutable'.

142 Martin Sasse, *Martin Luther über die Juden: Weg mit ihnen!* (Freiburg im Breisgau: Sturmhut Verlag, 1938).

143 Martin Sasse, *Martin Luther over de Joden!* (Eisenach: [n. pub.], 1938), and Martin Sasse, *Martin Luther on the Jews* (Freiburg im Breisgau: Bar & Bartosch, 1939).

144 Kaufmann, 'Luther and the Jews', pp. 60–61.

145 Heinrich Bornkamm, *Luther und das Alte* Testament (Tübingen: Mohr, 1948), Heinrich Bornkamm, trans. by Eric and Ruth Gritsch, *Luther and the Old Testament* (Philadelphia: Fortress, 1969), Wilhelm Maurer, *Kirche und Synagoge: Motive und Formen der Auseinandersetzung der Kirche mit dem Judentum* (Stuttgart: Kohlhammer, 1953), Selma Stern, *Josel von Rosheim: Befehlshaber der Judenschaft im Heiligen römischen Reich deutscher Nation* (Stuttgart: Deutsche Verlagsanstalt, 1959), Stern, *Josel of Rosheim.*

*Wurzeln des Antisemitismus. Christenangst und Judenplage im Zeitalter von Humanismus und Reformation* (*The Roots of Anti-Semitism in the Age of Renaissance and Reformation*, 1981), and Thomas Kaufmann, *Luthers Juden* (*Luther's Jews*, 2014).[146]

Notwithstanding this wealth of German-language scholarship, many of Luther's anti-Semitic writings have not been readily accessible to English-speaking scholars. The English critical editions have either not yet translated, or only recently translated, Luther's anti-Semitic texts. Some, in fact, have edited out anti-Semitic sections and softened the translations. In the standard English-language edition of Luther's writings, *Luther's Works*, for example, the anti-Semitism of Luther's final sermon delivered in Eisleben in February 1546 is heavily redacted.[147] A subsequent volume of sermons, published more than 51 years later in 2010, finally rectifies this.[148] The only academic translation into English of Luther's *Vom Schem Hamphoras* by Gerhard Falk, in his academic monograph *The Jew in Christian Theology*, was published as late as 1992.[149]

The field of English-language studies of Lutheran anti-Semitism was first opened by Gordon Rupp in 1972, and a slim pamphlet of his lecture was published the same year, on *Martin Luther and the Jews*.[150] For some time most of the contributions in English were limited to public lectures and conference presentations.[151] Significant work by English-speaking scholars has been carried out since the 1980s, including Mark U. Edwards Jr, *Luther's Last Battles* (1983) and Christopher J. Probst, *Demonizing the Jews: Luther and the Protestant Church in Nazi Germany* (2012).[152] Dean Bell's and Stephen Burnett's *Jews, Judaism, and the Reformation* (2006) includes important contributions by Thomas Kaufmann on 'Luther and the Jews', and by Timothy Wengert on 'Philipp Melanchthon and the Jews', both of which are pertinent to our work.[153] Schramm and Stjerna, *Martin Luther, the Bible, and the Jewish People: A Reader*

146 Heiko A. Oberman, *Wurzeln des Antisemitismus. Christenangst und Judenplage im Zeitalter von Humanismus und Reformation* (Berlin: Severin und Siedler, 1981), Heiko A. Oberman, *The Roots of Anti-Semitism in the Age of Renaissance and Reformation*, trans. by James Porter (Philadelphia: Fortress, 1984), and Kaufmann, *Luthers Juden*, Kaufmann, *Luther's Jews*.

147 Luther, *Sermons I*, LW 51: 383 considerably softens the original contained in WA 51: 194–96.

148 Luther, *Selected Sermons V*, LW 58: 458–9.

149 See Falk, *The Jew in Christian Theology*, pp. 163–224.

150 Rupp, *Martin Luther and the Jews*.

151 Rupp, *Martin Luther and the Jews*, is an extended version of the eighteenth Sir Robert Waley Cohen Memorial Lecture delivered in 1972.

152 Edwards, *Luther's Last Battles*, Probst, *Demonizing the Jews*.

153 *Jews, Judaism, and the Reformation in Sixteenth-Century Germany*, ed. by Bell and Burnett, including Thomas Kaufmann, 'Luther and the Jews', pp. 69–104, and Timothy J. Wengert, 'Philip Melanchthon and the Jews: A Reappraisal', pp. 105–135.

(2012) provides a much-needed teaching work on the subject.[154] In 2017, Bell followed up on his own work with a brief contextualisation piece, 'Martin Luther and the Jews: Context and Content' while Kaufmann also extended his own work in Bell's *Jews, Judaism, and the Reformation*, in his 2019 'Luther and the Jews'.[155]

Significant contributions are still being made at symposia and conferences: the 2000 *The Holocaust in an Age of Genocide* conference held at Oxford University, for instance, included a reassessment of the German Lutheran Church's and the Evangelical Lutheran Church in America's response to Luther's anti-Semitism.[156] A comprehensive assessment of anti-Semitism in the Reformation and its influence on Germany thereafter was made at a 2017 Reformation Conference held at the Leo Baeck Institute in Jerusalem, which led to the publication of the seminal work, *Jews and Protestants* (2020).[157] Similarly, the 2020 Luther Legacy Conference, held at Wilfrid Laurier University, published insights by faculty and students of Martin Luther University College on Luther's anti-Semitism and contemporary responses to it, in a special edition of *Consensus*.[158] The present chapter was partly developed in conversations around Lyndal Roper's public lecture at the University of Melbourne on 'Luther, the anti-Semite' (2018), developed and recently published in *Living I Was Your Plague* (2021), and our participation in the 2019 conference 'Media of Hate: Representations of Religious Persecution and Repression in Early Modern Europe'.[159] We hope this section provides some valuable contribution to the ongoing work of understanding and resisting the hate speech elements of Luther's polemical writing and engagement with the arts.

154 Brook Schramm and Kirsi I. Stjerna, *Martin Luther, the Bible, and the Jewish People: A Reader* (Minneapolis: Fortress, 2012).

155 Dean Phillip Bell, 'Martin Luther and the Jews: Context and Content', *Theology Today*, 74.3 (2017), 215–24, Kaufmann, 'Luther and the Jews', 46–65.

156 Rochelle L. Millen, 'On the Jews and the Lutherans: the ELCA Confronts History', in *Remembering for the Future: The Holocaust in an Age of Genocide*, ed. by J. K. Roth, E. Maxwell, M. Levy, and W. Whitworth (London: Palgrave Macmillan, 2001), pp. 587–602.

157 *Jews and Protestants*, ed. by Aue-Ben-David, Elyada, Sluhovsky, Wiese, and others (Berlin: de Gruyter, 2020).

158 *Martin Luther and Antisemitism*, ed. by Daniel Maoz (= Consensus, 41.2 (2020)).

159 Lyndal Roper's 'Luther, the anti-Semite', University of Melbourne, 15 October 2018—based on the Belfast Wiles Lectures (2015), the Princeton Lawrence Stone Lectures (2016)—and all of which shaped *Living I Was Your Plague*, which, though unpublished at the time of writing the first draft of this book, significantly influenced the outset of our thinking process. The proceedings of the conference 'Media of Hate: Representations of Religious Persecution and Repression in Early Modern Europe', University of Cambridge, CRASSH, 3–4 October 2019, have not been published yet. Daniel Trocmé-Latter's yet unpublished paper 'A common enemy?: Anti-Semitic singing during the Reformation' was similarly pertinent to our work.

In the polemical writings discussed in this chapter, Luther again draws on a pre-existing image and iconography and teaches his viewers to re-read it in the light of his new faith. Like Cranach's *Law and Grace*, Luther's consideration of the *Judensau* in *Vom Schem Hamphoras* (*On the Ineffable Name*) drew on established church symbolism and an iconography familiar to his audience but placed these alongside newly translated biblical passages. In reusing existing iconography of spiritual stories—such as the opposition of *Synogoga* and *Ecclesia* in *Law and Grace*, the church art of the *Judensau* in *Vom Schem Hamphoras* (*Of the Ineffable Name*), or the satirical print of the papal fish-donkey in the *Papstesel*—Luther repurposed pre-existing images of hate to promote his Reformation message. He achieved this in particular by rendering his opposition demonic, damned, monstrous, or animalistic through the iconography, representation or caricature he reused to promote his own polemic.

Some of these images may already have been hate images, as in the case of the *Judensau* or the *Papstesel*. Some may have been more neutral images of a figure or a religious scene, such as David slaying Goliath or the keyboard player on the frontispieces of various Luther works. However, when juxtaposed with their accompanying polemical text they are intended to be read as images of hate, derision, or disgust.

The hate images targeting Catholics and Jews frequently rely on other forms of hatred, including misogyny, homophobia towards gay, transgender, and intersex people, and disablism. They connect to the wider movements of anti-Semitism and anti-Catholicism and contribute to them. They make use of exclusionary models, creating monstrous Others as well as the in-group of the Lutheran faithful. As Bildhauer and Mills have argued:

> The monstrous is constitutive, producing the contours of both bodies that matter (humans, Christians, saints, historical figures, gendered subjects, and Christ) and, ostensibly, bodies that do not (animals, non-Christians, demons, fantastical creatures and portentous freaks).[160]

Catholics, Jews and Muslims were all religious opponents of Lutheranism who were literally depicted to exist at the edges of humanity, or in danger of damnation, in the hate images of Luther's Reformation.

160 Bettina Bildhauer and Robert Mills, 'Conceptualizing the Monstrous', in *The Monstrous Middle Ages*, ed. by Bettina Bildhauer and Robert Miles (Cardiff: University of Wales Press, 2003), pp. 1–27 (p. 2).

At the same time, these works establish newly Lutheran modes of reading or interpreting images, in which the newly translated Bible and vernacular explanatory texts are the primary means to understand and explain visual images. The Bible in German, and published sermons and pamphlets in German, are the context in which these images are distributed and reproduced. While images like the *Law and Grace* altarpiece, or the *Judensau* carved into the exterior wall in Wittenberg, existed in original or unique forms, for most people, they were experiencing the images through woodcuts and printed texts that existed in multiple print runs, incidental but essential to religious or polemical texts. These images and their interpretations were developed to spread the message of the new confession to the masses, through mass media and accessible material that the common person could understand and be encouraged to share. In the cases of educational drama, as discussed in the next chapter, this could have long-term beneficial impacts. In the case of the interpretation of the *Judensau,* those long-term impacts would lead to unimaginable cruelty and harm.

The focus on learning to read and understand images and the message of salvation has previously been explored in Luther's own university education in the seven liberal arts, and his participation in the establishment of *Kantoreien* and choir schools. In the next section, we focus on Luther's work with educators like Joachim Greff, who established Lutheran popular drama as part of Reformation school curricula. Learning about salvation could take place in churches, in town squares, in the home, on the battlefield, at Carnival or in schools. Learning to read, for Luther's project, occurred at many levels: from teaching children basic literacy, to developing the understanding of the illiterate and semiliterate, to making the Scriptures available to those who could read German but not Latin, to developing the ability to decode allegorical and metaphorical iconographies. At each level, however, the purpose was the same, to give individuals more direct access to the *Ebenbild*, the one true image and likeness of the Creator in Jesus Christ, the path of grace to salvation.

CHAPTER 6

# Luther and Drama

German historians of drama have long suggested that the creation of a distinctively Lutheran genre of school and community theatre was the result of the discontinuation of late-medieval ecclesiastical spectacle.[1] The nineteenth-century historian Heinrich Alt (1846) was one of the first to suggest that Lutheran drama was a replacement for the rich panoply of open-air religious ceremonies that had been abolished by Luther's Reformation. The community's hunger for spectacle, Alt argues, was 'stilled by Protestant dramas' which, in Lutheran Germany, compensated for the lack of the 'many processions, images, priestly ceremonies and masquerades'.[2] This chapter argues that Martin Luther was profoundly aware of the power of theatrical performances in furthering the cause of his Reformation. While the reformer undoubtedly caused the abolition of folk drama that he deemed harmful, such as Corpus Christi Day Play Processions, the active promotion of plays that promoted his message, such as biblical dramas, was not an act of compensation to replace lost ceremonies. Rather, it will be shown that Luther actively led a Reformation of religious community drama in order to further his message.

The paradigmatic view that Luther single-handedly put an end to popular religious drama in Germany remains hard to shift. From the middle of the nineteenth century to the middle of the twentieth century, both Reformation historians and historians of drama maintained the view that Martin Luther abolished popular Lenten traditions such as Carnival plays and dramatisations of the Passion in Reformation Germany. The seminal work of late nineteenth and early twentieth-century German scholars of Reformation and Renaissance drama, in particular Hugo Holstein (1886), Wilhelm Creizenach (1903), and Reinhard Buchwald (1907) provided the first comprehensive assessment of the Reformation perceptions of plays and religious traditions surrounding the celebrations of Carnival, Corpus Christi and Passiontide and the views held by Luther and his fellow reformers on popular drama.[3] Creizenach asserted that

1 An earlier version of this chapter was published as Loewe, 'Proclaiming the Passion', 235–82.

2 Heinrich Alt, *Theater und Kirche in ihrem gegenseitigen Verhältniß historisch dargestellt* (Berlin: Verlag der Plahnschen Buchhandlung, 1846), p. 471: 'Da man dem protestantischen Volke so viel Processionen, Bildwerke, Priesterceremonien und Maskeraden genommen hatte, so schien es um so billiger, die Schaulust durch dergleichen Schauspiele zu befriedigen'.

3 Hugo Holstein, *Die Reformation im Spiegelbilde der dramatischen Literatur des 16. Jahrhunderts*, Schriften des Vereins für Reformationsgeschichte, 14/15 (Halle: Verein für Reformationsgeschichte, 1886); Wilhelm Creizenach, *Geschichte des neueren Dramas: Renaissance und*

 | DOI:10.1163/9789004527430_008

the reformers 'had an aversion to dramatisations of the Passion', while Holstein suggested that Luther both 'excluded the Passion play' and single-handedly put an end to Passion drama in Protestant Germany.[4] Their contemporaries, in particular the prolific American philologist Joseph Gillet, frequently based their argument on the works of Holstein and Creizenach, and took up and disseminated their opinions.[5]

The theory that Luther sought to prohibit the performance of Passion plays in Reformation Germany formulated at the turn of the twentieth century remained unchallenged for more than a century. It certainly is maintained in important studies on Luther's theological views on drama, such as Thomas Bacon's *Luther and the Drama* (1976), and also finds expression in more general works on Renaissance and Reformation drama, such as Wolfgang Michael's *Das deutsche Drama der Reformationszeit* (1984) and James Parente's *Religious Drama and the Humanist Tradition* (1987).[6] While Glenn Ehrstine's comprehensive examination of religious drama, *Theater, Culture, and Community in Reformation Bern, 1523–55* (2001) introduced a first note of caution, the view that 'Luther disparaged Passion plays' remains alive and well today.[7]

Notwithstanding current expressions of the nineteenth-century paradigm, Ehrstine's observation that 'Protestants did not censure the staging of the

---

*Reformation*, 3/2 (Halle: Max Niemeyer, 1903); Reinhard Buchwald, *Joachim Greff: Untersuchungen über die Anfänge des Renaissancedramas in Sachsen*, Probefahrten: Erstlingsarbeiten aus dem deutschen Seminar in Leipzig, 11 (Leipzig: R. Voigtländers Verlag, 1907).

4 Creizenach, *Geschichte des neueren Dramas*, p. 401: 'Abneigung gegen Darstellungen der Passion'; Holstein, *Reformation im Spiegelbilde*, p. 25: 'Das Passionsspiel schloss Luther aus'; 'Luther's influence put an end to Passion plays in those regions [of Germany] where the Reformation was introduced' (*Luthers Einfluss [bewirkte], daß die Passionsspiele in den Gegenden, in welchen die Reformation Eingang fand, aufhörten*).

5 Joseph Eugene Gillet, 'Das Ziel des Dramas in Deutschland vor Gottsched', *Modern Philology* 12.8 (1915), 481–487; Joseph Eugene Gillet, 'Über den Zweck des Dramas in Deutschland im 16. und 17. Jahrhundert', *Publications of the Modern Languages Association* [PLMA], 32.3 (1917), 430–67; Joseph Eugene Gillet, 'Über den Zweck des Schuldramas in Deutschland im 16. und 17. Jahrhundert', *The Journal of English and Germanic Philology*, 17.1 (1918), 69–78; Joseph Eugene Gillet, 'The German Dramatist of the Sixteenth Century and his Bible', PLMA 34.3 (1919), 465–93 (p. 493): while adhering to the overall paradigm, Gillet nevertheless acknowledged that the Protestant Passion play adapted 'to changed standards of religion' and so survived.

6 Thomas Bacon, *Martin Luther and the Drama*, Amsterdamer Publikationen zur Sprache und Literatur, 25 (Amsterdam: Rodopi, 1976), pp. 42–45; Wolfgang Friedrich Michael, *Das deutsche Drama der Reformationszeit* (Bern: Peter Lang, 1984), p. 51; James A. Parente, Jr, *Religious Drama and the Humanist Tradition*, Studies in the History of Christian Traditions, 39 (Leiden: Brill, 1987), p. 77 n. 59: 'Luther's pronouncements on drama were generally confined to a defence of Terence and to the prohibition of Passion Plays'.

7 Philip Haberkern, '"After me there will come braver men": Jan Hus and Reformation Polemics in the 1530s', *German History*, 27.2 (2009), 177–95 (p. 188).

Passion per se, but rather the manner of its portrayal' encourages a thorough re-examination of Lutheran views on the performance of popular drama.[8] However, since Ehrstine's study chiefly concentrates on Swiss Reformation drama, it is timely and necessary to provide a reassessment of the views of Lutheran theologians on drama from a specifically German perspective.

In an age of semi-literacy, the power of the spoken and performed word was a highly significant tool in spreading Luther's message.[9] The reformer certainly encouraged the commissioning and performance of biblical dramas, both historical dramas bringing to the stage the stories of Jacob and his brothers or Susanna and the Elders, and dramatisations of gospel stories, such as the healing of the man born mute and blind.[10] By the middle of the sixteenth century, a school of Lutheran drama had developed that included a wide range of plays written to educate viewers and to promote the Reformation message both in Latin and in German. These included Latin plays written by schoolteachers for performance by their pupils as part of the reformed Lutheran curriculum, and community plays in German written by pastors and hymn writers for their local towns and villages. Schoolmasters and pastors repurposed Lent and Easter plays for the Reformation.[11] Master wordsmiths, such as Hans Sachs and the *Meistersinger* school, reformed Carnival and Passion Plays, and contributed to countless biblical dramas.[12]

Hans Sachs took to verse to describe the task at hand. In his epitaph on the death of Martin Luther in 1546, he imagined theology personified commending the reformer's 'lengthy efforts and hard labour / often risking [his] life' to purge

---

8 Glenn Ehrstine, *Theater, Culture, and Community in Reformation Bern, 1523–55*, Studies in Medieval and Reformation Thought, 85 (Leiden: Brill, 2001), p. 3.

9 Pettegree, *Reformation and the Culture of Persuasion*, pp. 81–88.

10 For instance, Joachim Greff, *Ein lieblich vnd nutzbarlich spil von dem Patriarchen jacob und seinen zwelff Sönen. Aus dem Ersten Buch Mosi gezogen, und zu Magdeburg auf dem Schützenhoff ym 1534. jar gehalten* (Magdeburg: Michael Lotter, 1534); Paul Rebhun, *Ein Geistlich Spiel von der Gotfurchtigen und keuschen Frauen Susannen, gantz lustig und fruchtbarlich zu lesen* (Zwickau: Meyerpeck, 1536); Cypriacus Spangenberg, *Comoedia: Ein geistlich Spiel vom Euangelio am Sontage Oculi, von dem besessenen, tauben vnd stummen Menschen, Lucä am XI.* (Schmalkalden: Michel Schmück, 1590).

11 Alt, *Theater und Kirche*, p. 476, notes that Rebhun's *Susanne*, for instance, was deliberately scheduled for performance on the first Sunday of Lent, as a 'Christian teaching festival at the time of Carnival' (*ein christliches Schulfest zur Zeit des Carnevals*).

12 For Hans Sachs and the Nürnberg *Meistersinger*, see Wolfgang Spiewok, *Das deutsche Fastnachtspiel: Ursprung, Funktionen, Aufführungspraxis* (Greifswald: Reineke, 1997); Brigitte Stuplich, *Zur Dramentechnik des Hans Sachs* (Stuttgart-Bad Cannstatt: Frommann-Holzboog, 1998) and *Hans Sachs and Folk Theatre in The Late Middle Ages: Studies in The History of Popular Culture*, ed. by Robert Aylett and Peter N. Skrine (Lampeter: Edwin Mellen Press, 1995).

faith of 'the teachings of deranged and godless folk'.[13] Where under the Papacy theology had been sullied and obscured, Luther had 'fought like a knight / with God's Word, to quell [theology's] enemy':[14]

> The people scarcely knew me,
> I was counted as absolutely nothing by them
> Until I was completed through you,
> You, dearer hero
> of God's grace.
> There you washed me and bathed me
> And made me my cleanest again
> From their lies and faeces.
> You also healed and anointed me
> That I would stay healthy all over,
> Completely clear and pure like in the beginning.[15]

Sachs' elaborate wordplay on purifying—'washing' (*waschen*), 'bathing' (*badn*), 'cleansing' (*reynigst*), 'healing' (*heylen*), 'anointing' (*salben*)—no doubt reflects the various ways of disseminating the Reformation message. Not only 'disputations / writings and sermons' were instrumental in liberating faith from its 'Babylonian captivity'.[16] Hymns and, of course, Sachs' own verses, would ensure the enduring success of Luther's reforms.[17] At the conclusion of his poem, Sachs addresses theology, vowing that he, and the *Meistersinger*, would 'never forsake you / and keep you clean / as you now are [...] against that helps no power or guile'. Indeed, 'the portals of hell will not overwhelm / nor fell' the purified faith.[18]

---

13 Hans Sachs, *Ein Epitaphium / oder klagred ob der leich / D. Martini Luthers* (Nürnberg: Georg Wächter, 1546), sig. A iii$^{r}$: 'schwerer arbeyt hart geplagt / Dein leben offt darob gewagt', 'jr gotlose menschen leer'.

14 Sachs, *Epitaphium*, sig. A ij$^{v}$: 'ritterlich zu kempffn / Mit Gottes wort mein feind zu dempffn'.

15 Sachs, *Epitaphium*, sig. A iij$^{r}$: 'Das man mich kaum kundt kennen mer / Ich galt endtlich gar nichts bey jn / Bis jch durch dich erledigt bin / Du thewrer held / auß Gottes gnadn / Da du mich waschen thest vnd badn / Vnd mir wider reynigst mein war / Von jren lügen und vnflat / Mich thestu auch heylen vnd salben / Das ich gesund steh allenthalben / Gantz hell vnd rein wie im anfang'.

16 Sachs, *Epitaphium*, sig. A ij$^{v}$: 'Disputirn / schreibn vnd predigen', 'Babylonischen gfencknus'.

17 Sachs, *Epitaphium*, sig. A iij$^{v}$: 'werden dich nicht verlassen / dich reyn behalten [...] wie du yetz bist / Darwider hillft kein gwalt noch list'.

18 Sachs, *Epitaphium*, sig. A iij$^{v}$: 'Dich sollen die pforten der hellen / nicht vberweltigen noch fellen'.

Sachs' confidence that after Luther's death his message would continue to be spread through the efforts of playwrights was not in vain. Towards the end of the first century of Luther's Reformation, the theologian, hymn writer and playwright Cyriacus Spangenberg attested to the success of the Reformation of religious drama. Lutheran plays, combined with Lutheran hymns were an ideal means to share the joy of the good news:[19]

> Sacred plays and comedies or tragedies, drawn from sacred godly Scripture and its beautiful stories, set in rhyme no differently from Psalms and sacred songs (though according to their own style), and adorned with various interpolated choruses and hymns, are principally intended to achieve nothing less than the propagation of God's glory and praise, and should be used thus.[20]

Indeed, 'there is no use disputing the benefit of such sacred and Christian plays. Experience proves it, as does the judgement of true, godly folk'.[21] There would be 'no better labour than to put the gospels, as set for the entire year, into such short Christian plays'.[22]

## 1 Martin Luther and Popular Pre-Reformation Drama

For Luther, reforming popular religious plays and the creation of a distinctively Lutheran genre of drama was a lengthy struggle. His famous admonition to the assembled clergy at the Diet of Augsburg in 1530 marked the endpoint of a long campaign against the dramatic excesses of popular celebrations of the Christian year. Luther believed that many religious folk traditions had

19 Spangenberg, *Comoedia*, sig. A iijr: 'geistlicher Gewissensfrewde'.

20 Spangenberg, *Comoedia*, sig. A iij$^{r-v}$: 'Die geistlichen Spiel vnd Comedien oder Tragödien, aus heiliger göttlicher Schrifft und derer schönen Historien gezogen, welche nichts wenigers als die Psalmen vnd geistlichen Lieder (doch nach jrer art) in Reymen gefast / vnd mit vnterschiedenen eingemischen Choren vnd Gesängen gezieret / vnd auch fürnemlich zu anders nicht / denn zu ausbreitung göttlicher ehre vnd lobes gerichtet sind / vnd auch dazu gebrauchet warden sollen'.

21 Cyriacus Spangenberg, *Eine Christliche Comoedia Von dem Cananeischen Weiblein, Matthei am 15. Capittel* (Schmalkalden: [n. pub.], 1589), sig. A vii$^{v}$: 'Des nutzes halben / so solche geistliche vnd Christliche Spiel mit sich bringen / darffs keines disputiren / die erfahrung zeigets / vnd wahrer gottseliger Leut iudicia bestetigens'.

22 Spangenberg, *Christliche Comoedia*, sig. A viii$^{r}$: 'kein besser arbeit thun köndte / denn wenn ich alle Euangelia durchs ganzte Jar in solche kurtze Spiele fassete'.

become more important than the festivals they marked.[23] He was incensed that, despite being 'child's play and fool's play', many expressions of popular piety such as the dramatic re-enactment of Christ's deposition from the cross on Good Friday and the raising of the cross from the tomb at Easter, or the St Mark's-tide and Corpus Christi processions, had been retained.[24] In raising these traditions to 'articles of faith', their very essence had been perverted, and it was time for them to be reformed or abolished.[25]

There were some ceremonies that might safely be retained, Luther admitted. There was no harm, for instance, in a donkey leading a church procession on Palm Sunday: 'they would not confuse any consciences'.[26] However,

> That we old fools march around in bishops' hats [at Nicholas-tide] and with clerical pageantry take it seriously, yes, not only seriously but as an article of faith, so that it must be a sin and must torment the conscience of anyone who does not venerate such child's play—that is the devil himself![27]

Most popular ceremonies, therefore, 'seriously storm against and corrupt the Christian faith and the proper celebration of the feasts', Luther concluded.[28] He exhorted the assembled clerical members of the Diet to set things right, or to suffer dire consequences: 'Your blood be upon your own head! We are and want to be innocent of your blood and damnation'.[29]

---

23 Luther, *An die gantze geistlickeit zu Augsburg versamlet auff den Reichstag* (*Exhortation to All Clergy Assembled at Augsburg*), 1530, LW 34: 59. WA 30/2: 353a, 29: 'practiced more often and more seriously than the really important things' (*noch ernstlicher getrieben und noch denn eben die rechten heubstück*).

24 Luther, *An die gantze geistlickeit* (*Exhortation to All Clergy*), LW 34: 54–57, WA 30/2: 351a, has a full list of ceremonies.

25 Luther, *An die gantze geistlickeit* (*Exhortation to All Clergy*), LW 34: 59. WA 30/2: 355a, 21: 'artikel des glaubens'.

26 Luther, *An die gantze geistlickeit* (*Exhortation to All Clergy*), LW 34: 59. WA 30/2: 353a, 20: 'da were kein gewissen mit verwirret'.

27 Luther, *An die gantze geistlickeit* (*Exhortation to All Clergy*), LW 34: 59. WA 30/2: 353a, 20–24: 'Aber das wir alte narren jnn Bisschoffs hüten und geistlichem geprenge daher gehen und machen ernst draus, Ja nicht allein ernst, sondern artikel des glaubens, das es sünde mus sein, und die gewissen martern, wer solch kinderspiel nicht anbetet, das ist der teuffel selbs'.

28 Luther, *An die gantze geistlickeit* (*Exhortation to All Clergy*), LW 34: 59. WA 30/2: 353a, 24–26: 'Daraus folget denn, das alle obgenante stücke, wie kindisch und lecherlich sie sind, dennoch mit ernst den Christlichen glauben und die rechten nötigen stück, so ob angezeigt, stürmen und verderben'.

29 Luther, *An die gantze geistlickeit* (*Exhortation to All Clergy*), LW 34: 60. WA 30/2: 355b, 29–30: 'Ewr blut sey auff ewrem kopff, Wir sind und wöllen unschüldig sein an ewrem blut und verdamnis'.

## 2 Luther's Objections to Popular Drama and Ceremonies

From the outset of his reforms, Luther had strongly objected to the folk tradition of marking the seasons of the church's year by popular drama, rejecting such plays on moral and doctrinal grounds. Performances linked to celebrations such as Carnival (*Fastnacht*) or dedication festival (*Kirchweih* or *Kermis*) raised a number of important moral questions for the reformer: they afforded easy opportunities for drunkenness, gambling and promiscuity (or at least the dramatic presentation of adultery), showed a blatant disrespect of authority and public order and, consequently, ought to be discontinued.[30] Moreover, dedication festival fairs also provided an opportunity for the ready sale of indulgences, which made them not only morally but theologically corrupt.[31] In his 1560 Carnival play, *Die fünff Elenden wandrer*, Hans Sachs portrays a priest who has fallen on hard times due to Luther's abolition of dedication festival fairs and other reforms:

> In previous years, things were even better for me,
> Dedication festivals and indulgences did well for me,
> Crusades and pilgrimages plugged me full,
> The peasants gave many presents.
> Then I ate chickens, birds and geese
> Boiled, baked and roasted fish,
> Drank wine and beer at my table.
>
> Now I eat mush / must swig water,
> Luther and his crowd did that,
> I hope he gets Saint Urban's[32] blight.[33]

---

30 Luther, *Tischreden* (*Table Talk*), WA Tr 3: 561, 2–3, no. 3719: 'They are celebrated for many weeks; and they cause all sorts of misfortune in their disguises' (*celebrantur multis hebdomadibus; do richten sie alles vnglück vnter der mummery an*); *Von der Beicht, ob die der Papst Macht habe zu gebieten* (*On Confession, Whether The Pope Has Any Authority*), 1521, WA 8: 167, 3–4: 'If it were vain carnival, and every day there was dancing and drunkenness' (*eyttel Fastnacht were und alle tag getantzt und getruncken wurd*); WA 12: 655, 3–4; WA Tr 4: 378, 3, no. 4558.

31 In his extended Reformation poem, *Die Wittembergisch Nachtigall, die man yetz höret uberall* (Bamberg: Georg Erlinger, 1523), B ij$^{r}$, *Meistersinger* Hans Sachs explains that clergy found dedication festivals a lucrative source of income: 'All dedication festival long they lust for cash / Setting up a fair with sanctuary / where they sell their bulls of indulgence' (*All kirchwey sy nach gelt auch tichtten / Ein jarmack mit heyltum auff richten / Darbey sy ablas bullen haben*).

32 *St Urbans Blag*: gout. In German folk piety, Pope Urban I. (*d.* 230) may be invoked against gout; see Hans Sachs, *Hans Sachs: Fastnachtsspiele und Gedichte. Mit einem Nachwort von Rudolf Mirbt*, ed. by Reinhard Barth (München: Christian Kaiser Verlag, 1988), p. 531.

33 Hans Sachs, *Ein Faßnacht Spil / Die fünff Elenden wandrer / mit sechs personen/ kůrtz-weylig zu hǒren* (Nürnberg: George Merkel, 1560), sig. A ij$^{v}$: 'Vor Jaren het ichs better noch /

At the same time, Luther objected to traditional late-medieval plays that retold the story of salvation, such as Passion or Corpus Christi plays, on doctrinal grounds.[34] While they may once have been a help to understand Scripture in an age of significant illiteracy, they had become so far removed from their biblical origins that they were now at best, a hindrance to belief and at worst, a perversion of faith. It was high time that such plays were either abolished (*begraben*) or reformed, Luther held.[35]

### 2.1 *Carnival Plays*

Among the most popular public performances of the church's year were undoubtedly the Carnival revels. Taking place from the weekend of the Sunday next before Lent (*Estomihi*) and culminating on Shrove Tuesday, these included a combination of public plays, processions with floats, dances, and tableaux vivants.[36] The celebrations that took place in Zwickau in the presence of Duke Johann of Saxony on Shrove Tuesday, 16 February 1518, illustrate some of the more salubrious Carnival traditions: elaborate masked processions, Morris dances and outdoor plays, among the

> sword and ring dances, 'Catching the Fox' and 'Stomping the Cow' [...] as well as comedies: how seven wives fought for a man, and seven farmers sought a bride.[37]

---

Kirchwey und Ablaß thet mir wol / Creutzfahrt vnd Walfart steckt mich vol / Die Bawren gaben viel Presens / Da aß ich Hüner / Vögl vnd Gens / Gesotten bachen vnd bratfisch / Dranck Wein vnd Bier an meinem Tisch // Jetzt iß ich Brey / muß wasser sauffen / Das macht der Luther vnd sein hauffen / Ich wolt er het Sant Urbans blag'.

34 In particular, in Luther's *Predigt am Fronleichnamstage* (*Sermon on the Feast of Corpus Christi*), 1523, WA 11: 125 and his *Predigt am Tag des heiligen Warleichnachs Christi* (*Sermon on the Day of the Blessed and True Body of Christ*), 1527, WA 17/2: 435–441, and in his *Tischreden* (*Table Talk*), WA Tr 3: 192, 39–193, 2, no. 3147.

35 Luther, *Predigt am Fronleichnamstage* (*Sermon on the Feast of Corpus Christi*), 1523, WA 11: 125, 14: 'but we shall bury it without any ceremony' (*sed wir wollens bescharren und begraben*); *Predigt am Tag des heiligen Warleichnachs Christi* (*Sermon on the Day of the Blessed and True Body of Christ*), 1527, WA 17/2: 438, 10–14.

36 For the socio-political impact of *Fastnacht* drama, see Werner Röcke, 'Literarische Gegenwelten: Fastnachtspiele und karnevaleske Festkultur', in *Die Literatur im Übergang vom Mittelalter und früher Neuzeit*, ed. by Werner Röcke and others, Hansers Sozialgeschichte der deutschen Literatur, 1 (München and Wien: Hanser Verlag, 2004), pp. 420–45; Volker Mertens, 'Das Fastnachtspiel zwischen Subversion und Affirmation', in *Topographies of the Early Modern City*, ed. by Arthur Groos and others, Transatlantic Studies on Medieval and Early Modern Literature and Culture, 3 (Göttingen: Vandenhoek and Ruprecht, 2008), pp. 43–60.

37 *Die Bistümer der Kirchenprovinz Magdeburg, Bistum Naumburg: Die Diözese*, ed. by Heinz Wiessner, Max-Planck-Institut für Geschichte: Germania Sacra Neue Folge, 35, 1/1 (Berlin: De Gruyter, 1996), p. 475: 'Schwert- und Reiftänze, das Fuchsprellen und Kuhhautschupfen. [...] Possen: wie sieben Weiber um einen Mann gezankt, und wie sieben Bauernknechte

The first surviving Carnival play scripts date back to the mid-fourteenth century. Satirical plays in German are written to make the audience laugh. They broadly fell into two categories: those that were characterised by sexual innuendo and coarse or sometimes obscene language, and those that explicitly challenged the established social order, portraying a 'topsy-turvy world' (*verkehrte Welt*).[38] Costumed characters mimed sexual acts or promiscuous behaviour; parodied civic and religious ceremonies by impersonating and ridiculing local councillors and clergy; and made use of their masked anonymity to deliver stinging critiques in the form of rhymed speeches and bawdy songs, while the audience watched and laughed at them, and with them at those they presented on stage.[39]

In the early years of the Reformation, Martin Luther and his fellow reformers had actively supported evangelical revellers mocking the hierarchy and promoting anti-papal polemics during Carnival.[40] In 1521 for instance, as part of the Wittenberg Carnival procession Lutheran students acted out an 'attack on the Pope, the attempt to overthrow him, which ended in the flight, in utter confusion, of Pope, courtiers and servants'.[41] In a letter to Spalatin on 17 February 1521, Luther wrote that their 'mockery was deserved by the enemies of Christ'.[42] The following year, in 1522, the reformer Andreas Osiander used the Nürnberg Carnival procession to ridicule anti-Lutheran practices

---

um eine Magd gefreit [haben]'; Ernst Fabian, 'Fürstenbesuche und Volksbelustigungen in Zwickau im 16. Jahrhundert', *Mitteilungen des Altertumsvereins für Zwickau*, 10 (1910), 119–28.

38 Mertens, 'Das Fastnachtspiel', pp. 45, 51. For the idea of a 'topsy-turvy world', see in particular Hedda Ragotzky, 'Der Bauer in der Narrenrolle: zur Funktion "Verkehrter Welt" im frühen Nürnberger Fastnachtsspiel', in *Typus und Individuät im Mittelalter*, ed. by Horst Wenzel and others, Forschungen zur Geschichte der älteren deutschen Literatur, 4 (München: Wilhelm Fink Verlag, 1983), pp. 77–101 (p. 95).

39 Mertens, 'Das Fastnachtspiel', p. 48: 'parodied festivities' (*Parodie-Festlichkeiten*), pp. 58–59: 'plays critical of the nobility and knighthood' (*adels- und ritterkritische Repräsentationen*); in 1523, Nürnberg councillors even imposed a short prison sentence on locals who 'paraded through the streets with pipes and drums, dressed up as priests and nuns' (*in pfaffen vnd nunnen dayder auf die gassen mit pfeiffen vnd trummen gangen*), see Eckehard Simon, 'Staging the Reformation in the Nuremberg Carnival', in *Topographies of the Early Modern City*, ed. by Groos, pp. 61–96 (p. 77).

40 Simon, 'Staging the Reformation', p. 65: At the 1522 Nürnberg Carnival, actors attempt to stage 'a play satirizing the Pope [...] a year before Niklaus Manuel dared to put on his anti-papal Carnival plays in the Bern marketplace'.

41 Luther, *Schriften und Predigten* (*Writings and Sermons*), 1509/21, WA 9: 687: 'mit einem Angriff auf ihn [den Papst], dem Versuch ihn herabzustürzen, und mit wilder Flucht des Papstes, seines Hofstaates und Gesindes endete'.

42 Luther, *Schriften und Predigten* (*Writings and Sermons*), 1509/21, WA 9: 687: 'Dignus hostis Christi hoc ludibrio'.

such as the selling of indulgences and votive masses for the dead.[43] Indeed, it was at Nürnberg that the harnessing of Carnival plays to proclaim the message of the Reformation took place. For more than four decades, between 1517–1561, the *Meistersinger* Hans Sachs wrote and produced dozens of reformed Carnival plays.[44]

Just as Sachs lent support to Carnival mockery of the Catholic hierarchy and contested spiritual practices, such as the sale of indulgences, Luther also made good use of the image of St Paul's 'fool for Christ's sake' to promote his message.[45] Like Erasmus almost ten years earlier, Luther deliberately employed rhetorical tropes valued in Carnival humour, such as satire or irony, in his Reformation preaching.[46] In a sermon preached at the beginning of Lent 1518, for instance, Luther likened himself to a fool (*Narr*), and appealed to his congregation to join him in his 'foolishness' for the sake of the gospel:[47]

> You well know, dear friends of Christ, that I do not understand much about preaching and therefore I shall preach a foolish sermon; for I am

43 Simon, 'Staging the Reformation', pp. 70–71, 81; R. W. Scribner, 'Reformation, Karneval und die "verkehrte Welt"', in *Volkskultur: Zur Wiederentdeckung des vergessenen Alltags*, ed. by Richard van Dülmen and others (Frankfurt a.M.: Fischer, 1984), pp. 117–52.

44 A selection of Sachs' Carnival plays is reproduced in *Fastnachtsspiele des 15. und 16. Jahrhunderts*, ed. by Dieter Wuttke (Stuttgart: Reclam, 2006), pp. 131–261. See, for example, the frontispiece of Sachs' Reformation poem, *Die Wittembergisch Nachtigall, die man yetz höret uberall*. The book's subtitle references Luke's account of Christ's triumphant entry into Jerusalem (Lk. 19.40). When the Pharisees admonished Jesus' followers to keep silent, he replied: 'I tell you, if these are silent, the very stones would cry out' (*Ich sage ewch / wo dise sweygen / so werden die stein schreyen. luce. xix*). In like manner, Sachs and his *Meistersinger* would continue to promote the Reformation message with their spectacular plays and poems.

45 1 Corinthians 1.18–31.

46 Nevertheless, Luther frequently condemned Erasmus' teaching, for instance, in *Tischreden* (*Table Talk*), WA Tr 1: 195, 25–36, no. 446. In Erasmus' *Moriae encomium* (*1509*) [*The Praise of Folly*], trans. by Clarence Miller (New Haven, CT: Yale University Press, 2003), Erasmus used the same literary tropes to deliver a stinging critique of superstitious religious practices and popular piety. Indeed, Barbara Könneker, *Wesen und Wandlung der Narrenidee im Zeitalter des Humanismus: Brant-Murner-Erasmus* (Wiesbaden: Steiner, 1966), p. 258, argues that Erasmus' ideas were deliberately adopted by the German reformers to suit a 'specifically religious' context (*entschiedene Wendung ins religiöse*).

47 For Luther's use of the idea of the 'fool for Christ's sake' (*Narr in Christo*), see Danielle Laforge, 'Wechselbeziehungen zwischen Narrheit und Weisheit: Abgrenzung des Narrenbegriffs und epochale Bewertung', in *Der Narr in der deutschen Literatur im Mittelalter und in der frühen Neuzeit*, ed. by Jean Schillinger and others, Jahrbuch für internationale Germanistik, Reihe A, 96 (Bern: Peter Lang, 2009), pp. 310–11.

> a fool and I thank God for it. Therefore I must also have foolish pupils; anybody who doesn't want to be a fool can close his ears.[48]

Similarly, in an undated parable Luther told the story of a fool as an example of someone who had heard and understood his theology of the cross and shunned the immorality of Carnival:

> In Würzburg—where exactly I don't know—there lived a fool who, during carnival, dressed sombrely and was sad, yet in Holy Week was cheerful and full of spirit. When asked why he did so, he answered: 'During carnival folks commit so many sins that it is right and proper to be sad. In Holy Week they preach that Christ died for poor sinners, therefore we should rejoice'. That was a fine speech for a fool, wasn't it?[49]

Notwithstanding his views on the potential usefulness of humour, foolishness, or indeed polemical Carnival processions, Luther nevertheless strongly condemned Carnival festivities themselves.[50] He objected to the bawdiness of the 'Bacchanalian festival', bemoaning that 'for many weeks [people] celebrate unsuitableness and happenstance, and so cause much harm by their masquerade'.[51] He objected to the fact that there was 'dancing and drinking all day' and denounced Carnival plays as 'too coarse'.[52] Carnival drama was not only subversive and potentially socially volatile, but inherently blasphemous, Luther concluded: 'a fine carnival play it would be that did not blaspheme the name of God'.[53]

---

48 Luther, *Predigt vom Blindgeborenen* (*Sermon On The Man Born Blind*), 17 March 1518, LW 51: 35, WA 1: 267, 5–9: 'Ir wisest wol, lieben Freunde Christi, das ich nicht viel predigens kan, und der halben werde ich ein Nerrisch predigt thun, denn ich bin ein Narr, das ich Gott dancke. Darumb mus ich auch Nerrisch schüler haben. Und wer kein Narr sein wil, der mag die Ohren zustopffen'.

49 Luther, *Nachträge zu Schriften, Predigten und Tischreden* (*Supplements: Writings, Sermons and Table Talk*), WA 48: 683, 3–8: 'Es ist ein Narr gewest—ich weis nicht, ob er zu Wurtzen ader wo er gewest ist—der hat sich jn der fastnacht vbel gekleidet, ist trawrigk gewest. Econtra jn der marterwoche hilari fuit vultu et animo. Interrogatus, cur id faceret, respondit: "Jn der fastnacht, tum sunt multa peccata, so sal man trawrigk sein. Jn der marterwochen predigt man, das Christus vor die armen sunder gestorben sey. Darumb sol man frolich sein". Das ist ein feine rede gewest von einem narren'.

50 Bacon, *Luther and the Drama*, pp. 19–21, 62–64, 75.

51 Luther, *Tischreden* (*Table Talk*), WA Tr 3: 561, 2–3, no. 3718: 'Festa Bacchanalia mira importunitate et temeritate celebrantur multis hebdomadibus; do richten sie alles vnglück vnter der mummery an'.

52 Luther, *Tischreden* (*Table Talk*), WA Tr 4: 378, 3, no. 4558: 'zu grob'.

53 Luther, *Von der Beicht, ob die der Papst Macht habe zu gebieten* (*On Confession, Whether The Pope Has Any Authority*), 1521, WA 8: 167, 3: 'alle tag getantzt und getruncken wurd';

By the mid-sixteenth century, Carnival plays in Lutheran principalities and imperial free cities had been reformed in line with Luther's stipulations. *Meistersinger* Hans Sachs, in his 1553 Carnival poem *Das Narrenbad* ('The Fools' Bath'), extends his earlier analogy of Luther cleansing faith in Germany to cleansing and reforming the attitude and behaviours of individual believers by dunking all 'fools' who remained opposed to Luther's reforms in the *Narrenbad* for cleansing:

> Now everyone might like to consider
> That what was lacking in the German lands
> Was such a spa for fools:[54]
> We would sit fellows in it
> When they didn't want to pay attention to wisdom.[55]

In his Carnival play, *Das Narrenschneiden* (*The Foolectomy*), Sachs likewise imagined the surgical removal of 'foolery'. In the same way that Luther removed the 'cancer of the Papacy' in Germany, a surgeon and his assistant forcibly proceed to remove 'folly' from their patient, ultimately eradicating the source of all folly, the 'fools' nest', deep in the heart of the patient. Sachs' Carnival play makes clear that the healing Luther brought to the soul of the German nation by excising the corruptions of the late-medieval church is available to every individual believer. The play concludes with the surgeon and his assistant succeeding in 'healing [the patient] from the addiction to folly by the promotion of their art'.[56] The art of healing ultimately is simple, Sachs makes clear. It is disciplined, godly living, according to the 'teachings and counsel of wise people', such as those of the reformer Luther, which overcomes folly:

*Predigten* (*Sermons*), 1523, WA 12: 655, 3–4; see also *Geist aus Luther's Schriften*, ed. by Friedrich Wilhelm Lomler and others (Darmstadt: Verlag Karl Wilhelm Leske, 1830), III, 1006: 'es wäre ein fein Spiel in die Fastnacht, ohne daß der göttliche Name unter Schein gelästert wird'.

54 Sachs uses the term '*Narrenbad*' or 'Fools' Bath', with the sense of a healing bath or spa, multiple times across his work.

55 Hans Sachs, *Der Narrenfresser. Mehr das Narren Bad* (Nürnberg: Georg Merckel, 1553), sig. B ij^r: 'Ein jeder mag betrachten hie / Das es wer Teudtschem land an schad / Wann es het auch ein Narren Bad / Das man darein setzt die gesellen / Die keiner weißheyt achten wȏllen'.

56 Hans Sachs, 'Ein lustig Faßnachtsspiel / mit drey Personen / Das Narrenschneiden', in Hans Sachs, *Das erste Buch, Sehr herrliche schöne & warhaffte Gedicht. Sehr Herrliche, Schöne vnd Warhaffte Gedicht Geistlich vnd Weltlich allerley art, als ernstliche Tragödien, liebliche Comödien* (Augsburg: Hans Kruger, 1612), pp. 938–946 (p. 946): 'mit vnser kunst mittheiln / Vnd an der narrensucht jhn heyln'.

To warn against such sickness
I lastly leave a good recipe,
A proper one, for as long as he lives
Let him be a reasonable master,
and ride himself with his own bridle
And look back at himself diligently.
[...]
Right be his thinking, word and deed,
According to the teachings and counsel of wise people.[57]

### 2.2 *Corpus Christi Processions and Passion Plays*

During the course of the Christian year, Carnival celebrations were undoubtedly the most elaborate expression of popular festivals. Despite Luther's misgivings, Carnival plays and processions continued to flourish and remained a nationwide phenomenon.[58] Other large-scale celebrations included annual fairs (*Jahrmärkte*) to mark the dedication festival of a parish church (*Kirchweih* or *Kermis*). Among 'the most popular peasant festival in fifteenth- and sixteenth-century Germany', they were local, often rural, festivals rather than national celebrations.[59] Luther objected to *Kirchweih* celebrations on moral grounds. Like Carnival revels, they merely promoted drunkenness and gambling, the reformer believed:

> We ought to abolish Dedication festivals outright, since they have become nothing but taverns, fairs and gambling places.[60]

Two other national festivals were marked by widespread dramatic performances: Passiontide and Corpus Christi.[61] Because of their association with the suffering

---

57 Sachs, 'Ein lustig Faßnachtsspiel', p. 946: 'Vor solcher kranckheit zu bewarn / Laß ich zu letzt ein gut recept / Ein ieglicher dieweil er lebt / Laß er sein vernunfft meister sein / Vnd reyt sich selb im zaum allein / Vnd thu sich fleissiglich vmbschauen / [...] Richt sein gedancken wort vnd that / Nach weyser leute lehr vnd rath'.

58 For the Lutheran development of Carnival drama by *Meistersinger* Hans Sachs, see Richard Erich Schade, *Studies in Early German Comedy 1500–1650*, Studies in German Literature, Linguistics and Culture, 24 (Columbia, SC: Camden House, 1988), pp. 73–96.

59 Alison Stewart, 'Paper Festivals and Popular Entertainment: The Kermis Woodcuts of Sebald Beham in Reformation Nuremberg', *The Sixteenth Century Journal*, 24.2 (1993), 301–50 (p. 307).

60 Luther, *An den Christlichen Adel deutscher Nation* (*To the Christian Nobility of the German Nation*), 1519, LW 44: 183. WA 6: 446, 19: 'Man [sollte] die kirchweye gantz austilgen, seyntemal sie nit anders sein dan rechte tabernn, Jarmarckt und spiel hoffe worden'.

61 In the Western Church, Passiontide traditionally commences on the Sunday before Holy Week and ends on Good Friday, while Corpus Christi is celebrated on the Thursday after Trinity Sunday.

of Christ they afforded fewer opportunities for revels. Nevertheless, there was a long-established tradition of performing Passion dramas in the run-up to Easter and Corpus Christi (*Fronleichnam*).[62] So popular was the Corpus Christi Passion play that the planning for certain parts of the procession was shared among each of the trade guilds (*Zünfte*).[63] Indeed, from the late fourteenth century onwards a number of German cities had specific Corpus Christi confraternities (*Confraternitates Corporis Christi* or *Prozessionsspiel-Bruderschaften*) that planned and staged Corpus Christi plays and processions.[64]

Both Passion and Corpus Christi-tide ceremonies commemorated the broken body of Christ. Both festivals, therefore, were marked by plays that told the story of salvation in the vernacular. Many began with the story of the creation and the fall; all concluded with a dramatisation of the events of Calvary and Easter. Where in a Passion play an actor would take on the role of Christ, in Corpus Christi plays the person of Christ was not only acted out by a player but was believed to be physically present in the form of the Eucharistic bread. Contained in a monstrance carried by the clergy, the consecrated host led the solemn procession through the city and fields, invoking both the presence and the blessing of God on their community and their crops.[65] At various points, the procession would stop to allow for a performance of scenes presenting 'the bitter suffering and Passion that God endured for us, and the whole human race [...] and to praise and honour the sufferings of Our Lord Jesus Christ' in

62 The earliest processions in Germany took place in Köln (1278), Aachen (1334), and Munich (1360); see Detlef Altenburg, 'Die Musik in der Fronleichnamsprozession des 14. und 15. Jahrhunderts', *Musica Disciplina*, 38 (1984), 5–24 (pp. 6, 8); the earliest German Corpus Christi play script to survive is the Innsbruck or Neustift play (1391); see Hans Moser, 'Die Innsbrucker Spielhandschrift in der geistlichen Spieltradition Tirols', in *Tiroler Volksschauspiel: Beiträge zur Theatergeschichte des Alpenraumes*, ed. by Egon Kühebacher and others, Schriftenreihe des Südtiroler Kulturinstituts, 3 (Bozen: Athesia, 1976), pp. 178–89 (p. 178).

63 Wilhelm Breuer, 'Zur Aufführungspraxis vorreformatorischer Fronleichnamsspiele in Deutschland', *Zeitschrift für deutsche Philologie*, 94 (Sonderheft 1975), 50–71 (p. 68): 'the painters' guild for instance generally took care of staging the scene in Paradise, the carpenters the scene on the Mount of Olives, the butchers' guild the [crucifixion scene with the] two thieves, etc'. (*Die Maler übernahmen beispielsweise in der Regel die Ausgestaltung der Paradiesszene, die Zimmerleute die Ölbergsszene, die Metzger bildeten die Gruppe der Schächer, usw.*) Their proximity to the Blessed Sacrament reflected their social standing; Altenburg, 'Die Musik in der Fronleichnamsprozession', p. 12.

64 Friedberg and Fulda in Hessen, for instance, had specific Corpus Christi guilds; see Freise, *Spiele und Spielinitiativen*, p. 131. For contemporary illustrations of the procession, see Debra Taylor Cashion, 'The Art of Nikolaus Glockendon: Imitation and Originality in the Art of Renaissance Germany', *Journal of Historians of Netherlandish Art*, 2.1–2 (2010) <https://dx.doi.org/10.5092/jhna.2010.2.1.2>.

65 Many German Corpus Christi processions superseded earlier Rogationtide processions (*Flurumgänge*).

order 'to incite the hearts of the faithful to greater devotion'.[66] Each scenic performance was an integral part of the Corpus Christi procession; procession and performance were, in fact, a procession-play (*Spielprozession*) in which both players and viewers together bore witness to the story of their salvation:

> Only during the [scenic] performances themselves were there two separate groups, actors and audience; following the performances the two groups merged once more to form one congregation taking part in the same procession.[67]

From the time of Pope Martin V and the granting of a generous indulgence for the participants of Corpus Christi processions in 1429, procession-plays had involved the greater part of the local population.[68] Since they celebrated the doctrine of transubstantiation by a combination of drama and worship, it was proper that processions commenced at the conclusion of mass with the singing of the *Agnus Dei* (thereby creating a further link between the Eucharistic bread and the person of Christ, 'the Lamb of God who takes away the sin of the world').[69]

Ultimately, the Corpus Christi procession-play was intended to represent the 'pathway to the [eternal] home in heaven'.[70] In the symbolic presence of the Saviour, in the form of the consecrated Eucharistic bread enshrined in a costly monstrance under a white damask or gilt canopy, surrounded by adult players

---

66 *Die Fuldaer Stadtpfarrei, II: Urkunden der Fuldaer Stadtpfarrei*, ed. by Ludwig Pralle and Gregor Richter, Veröffentlichungen des Fuldaer Geschichtsvereins, 32 (Fulda: Parzeller, 1952), pp. 39–42: 'deme bittern liden und martel, die god vor uns und alle menschlich geschlecht geliden hat [...] zu lobe und czu ern deme liden unsers hern Jesu Christi', 'ad excitandum devotionem in fidelium cordibus'.

67 Freise, *Spiele und Spielinitiativen*, p. 228: 'Nur während der [szenischen Darstellungen] standen sich Zuschauer und Darsteller als zwei voneinander getrennte Gruppen gegenüber; im Anschluß daran wurden sie wieder zu gemeinsam handelnden Prozessionsteilnehmern'.

68 Altenburg, 'Die Musik in der Fronleichnamsprozession', p. 7: the procession 'was a matter [...] for all townspeople' (*war* [...] *Angelegenheit aller Bürger einer Stadt*); see also Miri Rubin, *Corpus Christi: The Eucharist in Late Medieval Culture* (Cambridge: Cambridge University Press, 1991), p. 211.

69 John 1.29; the Fourth Lateran Council defined the real presence of Christ in the Eucharistic elements *sub specie accidentalis*, under the 'accidents' of bread and wine. The understanding that the Eucharist 'made present' Christ and his sacrificial death was later refined by Thomas Aquinas, *Summa Theologiae*, ed. by Thomas Gilby, 60 vols (London: Blackfriars, 1963–66), 3a, q. 79, a. 1, etc.

70 Guillaume Durand, *Rationale divinorum officium* I–IV, ed. by Anselme Davril OSB and Timothy M. Thibodeau, CCCM, 140 (Turnhout: Brepols, 1995), sig. 38r: 'ipsa vero processio est via ad celestem patriam'.

representing biblical characters who told the story of salvation, and a treble choir representing the heavenly choir, the celebrations were intended to give the congregation a foretaste on earth of the splendour and hierarchy of the kingdom of heaven.[71]

The scenes presented during the procession-play generally fell into three parts, the first centred on the creation and fall (Gen. 1–2) and the high-priestly sacrifice of bread and wine by King Melchizedek of Salem (Gen. 14.18), the second centred on scenes from the life, death, and resurrection of Christ, depicting particularly the Passion of Christ (Mt. 26–27 and synoptic parallels), while a third part would show the Last Judgement.[72] During the procession, Latin plainchant hymns were sung.[73] Over time, vernacular hymns and polyphonic anthems in Latin such as, for example, Josquin Desprez' setting of *Pange lingua*, were added to the musical repertoire.[74]

In his *Vom Mißbrauch der Messen* (*The Misuse of the Mass*), Luther commented disparagingly on the selection of these scenes and the hymns that accompanied them. The music sung at the feast of Corpus Christi was 'patched together from many passages of Scripture, [...] that God's worst enemy must have composed it, either that or it is the dream of a poor senseless idiot'.[75] The procession's scenic displays were equally mistaken:

> Here Melchizedek is remembered who offered bread and wine [Gen. 14.18]; then the lamb comes into it which the people sacrificed of old [Exod. 12.5–6], and the cake of Elijah [1 Kgs. 19.6], the manna of the fathers [Exod. 16.15], and Isaac, who was to be sacrificed [Gen. 22.2], and I don't know what has not been thought of. All these have had to serve as figures of the sacrament. It is a wonder that he did not include Balaam's ass [Num. 22.21] and David's

71 For the development and use of monstrances for Eucharistic processions, see Holger Guster, 'Die Hostienmonstranzen des 13. und 14. Jahrhunderts in Europa' (unpublished doctoral dissertation, University of Heidelberg, 2009), pp. 83–87, 154–68; for the splendour of the procession itself, see Machtelt Israëls, 'Altars on the Street: The Wool Guild, the Carmelites and the Feast of Corpus Domini in Siena (1356–1456)', *Renaissance Studies*, 20.2 (2006), 180–200 (pp. 193–94).

72 Altenburg, 'Die Musik in der Fronleichnamsprozession', p. 11.

73 Including Thomas Aquinas' sequence for the feast, *Ecce panis angelorum*, and his sequence *Verbum supernum prodiens* (in particular the verse *O salutaris hostia*).

74 Johannes Janota, *Studien zu Funktion und Typus des deutschen geistlichen Liedes im Mittelalter*, Münchner Texte und Untersuchungen zur deutschen Literatur des Mittelalters, 23 (München, Beck: 1968), pp. 211f.

75 Luther, *Vom Mißbrauch der Messen* (*The Misuse of the Mass*), 1521, LW 38: 181–182. WA 8: 523, 12–24: 'auß vill orttern der schrifft ist tzusamen geflickt, [...] das es auch der ergeste feynd gots muß gemacht haben; es weren den rewme eyns armen unsinnigen menschen'.

> mule [1 Kgs. 1.38]; they could have had no less significance to the stupid ass than these other stories and figures.[76]

Luther had begun to question the doctrine of transubstantiation from 1519 onwards. While he retained a high theology of the real presence of Christ in the Eucharist throughout his life, famously defending the doctrine against Zwingli at the 1529 Marburg Colloquy, he strongly objected to the theatrical nature that characterised early sixteenth-century processions of the Blessed Sacrament. Although he himself maintained a personal devotion to the Eucharistic elements by kneeling or genuflecting and did not abolish the elevation of the consecrated bread until 1542, he strongly held that 'the sacrament is no cultic object. While I will kneel, I do so out of proper reverence'.[77] In his *Table Talk*, Luther elaborated his discomfort at the theatrical spectacle of processing a monstrance through the community:

> Among all festivals Corpus Christi has the greatest and brightest splendour, yet despite all its paint and fake devotion it challenges and strives against the order and institution of Christ; for he did not command that the sacrament be carried about in this manner. Therefore, beware of such worship.[78]

In Wittenberg, the Corpus Christi Day play-procession had been stopped in 1522, although the festival continued to be marked with a Eucharist.[79] Preaching the following year at Corpus Christi, Luther condemned the practice of Eucharistic

---

76 Luther, *Vom Mißbrauch der Messen* (*The Misuse of the Mass*), 1521, LW 38: 181–182. WA 8: 523, 16–24: 'Do wirt Melchisedech gedacht, welcher brot und weyn geopffert hatt, do kumpt erfür das lemleyn, welchs das volck frwe geopffert hatt, das brott Helie, das hymmelbrott der vetter, Isaac, der do sollt geopffert warden, und weyß nit, weß nit gedacht wirt: diße alle haben müssen des sacraments figurn seyn. Und ist es wol eyn wunder, das er nicht auch den esell Balaam und den maulesell David hatt hynneyn gesatzt, welche nicht weniger hetten bedeutten konnen, daenn das dem groben esell die vorigen geschichte und figurn bedeutet haben'.

77 Luther, *Tischreden* (*Table Talk*), WA Tr 1: 139, 15–16: 'Man sol keinen cultus mit dem sacrament anrichten. Ich knie wol nider, sed propter revertiam', if the Word of God was accorded similar honour', *Vom Anbeten des Sakraments des heiligen Leichnams Christi* (*On the Worship of the Sacrament of the Blessed Body of Christ*), 1523, WA 11: 432, 31–434, 2.

78 Luther, *Tischreden* (*Table Talk*), WA Tr 3: 192, 39–193, 2, no. 3147: 'Das Fest Frohnleichs hat unter allen den größten und schönsten Schein, strebet und streitet mit seiner Schmink und erdichten Heiligkeit wider Christus Ordnung und Einsetzung; denn er es nicht befohlen hat also umher zu tragen. Darüm hütet Euch für solchen Gottesdiensten'.

79 Luther, *Predigt am Fronleichnamstage* (*Sermon on the Feast of Corpus Christi*), 1523, WA 12: 579.

processions because they 'abused and much disgraced the sacrament'.[80] Since it was impossible to separate Corpus Christi plays from processions, Luther believed that the entire festival—play, procession and ceremonies—ought to be discontinued. Rather than preach about the festival, Luther suggested, it was time to abolish the observance of Corpus Christi altogether.[81] In a sermon preached on the feast in 1525, he reiterated this belief:

> I advise that we abolish this [feast] now, for it is the most damaging in the church's calendar. Indeed, there is no feast day on which God and his Christ are more blasphemed than on this day, and particularly by the procession which of all things ought to be discontinued at once.[82]

Even had it been possible to separate Corpus Christi plays from the Eucharistic procession, Luther would have objected to their performance. They turned Christ's Passion into a spectacle and therefore should be discontinued. Since the same was true of traditional Passion plays, Luther objected to their performance on the same grounds. In a sermon preached on Good Friday 1518, Luther first suggested that external acts of contemplating the Passion, such as their re-presentation in worship or through art, had few spiritual benefits: depictions in drama and art merely further confused the essence of faith with external devotion.[83] Instead, he advocated a personal contemplation of the Passion that would lead to individual conversion:

> That is a proper contemplation of Christ's passion, and such are its fruits. And those who exercise themselves in that way do better than listen to

---

80 Luther, *Predigt am Fronleichnamstage* (*Sermon on the Feast of Corpus Christi*), 1523, WA 11: 125, 13: 'quod sacramentum wirt boslich behandelt et ignominia magna datur'.

81 Luther, *Predigt am Fronleichnamstage* (*Sermon on the Feast of Corpus Christi*), 1523, WA 12: 579., WA 11: 125, 14: 'Nor shall I preach on it, but we shall bury it without ceremony' (*Neque praedicassem, sed wir wollens bescharren und begraben*).

82 Luther, *Predigt am Tag des heiligen Warleichnachs Christi* (*Sermon on the Day of the Blessed and True Body of Christ*), 1527, WA 17/2: 438, 10–14: 'Doch wil ich geradten haben, man wölle diß fest gantz und gar abethun, dann es ist daß aller schedlichst fest, als es durch daß gantze jar ist. An kainem fest wird got und sein Christus serer gelestert dann an disem tag, und sonderlichen mit der Procession, die man vor allen dingen sol abstellen'.

83 Luther, *Eyn Sermon von der Betrachtung des heyligen leydens Christi* (*A Meditation on Christ's Passion*), 1519, WA 2: 142, 6–8: 'We have transformed the essence into semblance and painted our meditations on Christ's passion on walls and made them into letters' (*Wir haben das weßen yn eynen scheyn vorwandelt und das leyden Christi bedencken alleyn auff die brieff und an die wend gemalet*).

> every story of Christ's passion, or to read all the masses. (This is not to say that masses are of no value, but they do not help us in such meditation and exercise).[84]

The Passion neither ought to be objectified nor domesticated. It was certainly not a matter of light-hearted entertainment, in which children were dressed up as ministering angels or actors playing devils sought to intimidate the audience or raise laughs, as was the case in many contemporary Corpus Christi or Passion plays.[85] It was time to reclaim the real significance of Christ's act of redemption, Luther explained, referencing Bernard of Clairvaux:

> God's only Son had compassion upon me and offered to bear this sentence for me. Alas, if the situation is that serious, I should not make light of it or feel secure.[86]

Rather than watch facile dramatisations, therefore, believers ought to imitate Christ and so learn empathy. In order to do justice to the story of the cross, they should 'hear, meditate upon, and read the Passion in order to learn compassion, and thus suffer alongside Christ'.[87]

It was clear that a completely new form of religious drama, purged from popular comedic excesses and extravagant ceremonies, was required to communicate Luther's theology of the cross and the doctrine of justification by faith:

---

84 Luther, *Eyn Sermon von der Betrachtung des heyligen leydens Christi* (*A Meditation on Christ's Passion*), 1519, LW 42: 14. WA 2: 141, 30–34: 'Und das ist recht Christus leyden bedacht, das seynd die frucht seyns leydens, und wer alßo sich darynnen ubet, der thut besser dan das er alle passion hoeret adder alle messe leße, Nit das die messen nit gut seyn, sundern das sie an solche bedencken und ubung nichts helffen'.

85 Bacon, *Luther and the Drama*, pp. 12–13. Eichstätt Cathedral School provided their pupils with special costumes, including angels' wings, for the Corpus Christi procession-play: Theodor Klein, *Die Prozessionsgesänge der Mainzer Kirche aus dem 14. bis 18. Jahrhundert*, Quellen und Abhandlungen zur mittelrheinischen Kirchengeschichte, 7 (Speyer: Verlag der Jaegerschen Buckdruckerei, 1962), p. 35.

86 Luther, *Eyn Sermon von der Betrachtung des heyligen leydens Christi* (*Meditation on Christ's Passion*), 1519, LW 42: 9. WA 2: 138, 1–4: 'Ich sach, das der eynige gottis sun sich meyn erbarmet, erfurtritt unnd yn das selb urteyll sich für mich ergibt. Awe, es ist myr nit mer zu spielen [...] wann eyn solcher Ernst dahynden ist'.

87 Luther, *Duo sermones de passione Christi* (*Two Sermons on the Passion of Christ*), 1518, WA 1: 336, 26–28: 'Ideo qui vult fructuose passionem Christi audire meditari, legere, opertet eum induere affectum talis compassionis, ac si societatus Christo in passione'.

> We can do nothing at all through our own strength, other than open our eyes and behold the Saviour Christ, hanging on the cross, so that our own deaths may be overcome.[88]

It would take until 1538 for the first Lutheran drama on the Passion to be published in Wittenberg, and five more years for such a play to be performed.[89] In the meantime, many traditional forms of popular drama that had traditionally been performed to mark ecclesiastical festivals were discontinued or reformed as Martin Luther and his associate Philipp Melanchthon set out to foster and develop performances of German biblical plays in schools and churches.

## 3 Lutheran Biblical Drama

For Luther, the step from bringing to life the stories of the Bible by reading and preaching, to performing them in schools and churches was a small one. The reformer was convinced that the performance of biblical dramas was of great educational and evangelical benefit. On 2 April 1530, in response to a now no longer extant memorandum (*memoriale*) by the Zwickau superintendent minister (*episcopus*) Nikolaus Hausmann, Luther considered the subject of school plays:

> I would not at all be displeased to see the works of Christ performed in boys' schools as plays, or rather comedies, in Latin and German, if they are written decently and satisfactorily.[90]

Enacting biblical stories in school would enable students 'to remember and present the biblical stories themselves', Luther felt.[91] This would not only

88 Luther, *Die Passio oder das leiden unsers herren Jhesu Christi* (*The Passion, or the Suffering of our Lord Jesus Christ*), 1522, WA 10/3: 75, 11–13: 'das wir do nit werden auff yrgent aim ding beston mögen, sonder die augen bloß zû thûn, und auff den uberwinder sehen Christum, an den frey hangen, so wirdt der todt in uns verschlunden'.

89 Joachim Greff, *Das Leiden vnd Aufferstehung vnsers Herrn Jhesu Christi, aus den vier Euangelisten durch D. Johan Bugenhagen Pomern vleissig zusamen gebracht, vnd nachmals durch Joachimum Greff vo[n] Zwickau jnn Deutsch Reim verfasset, seliglich vnd tröstlich zu lessen* (Wittenberg: Nickel Schirlentz, 1538).

90 Luther, *Briefwechsel* (*Letters*), WA Br 5: 272, no. 1543: 'Name & ego non illibenter viderem gesta Christi in scholis puerorum luis sue comoediis latine & germanice, rite & pure compositis'.

91 Luther, *Briefwechsel* (*Letters*), WA Br 5: 272, no. 1543: 'repraesentari propter rei memoriam'.

'create a greater impression on younger students', but further the proclamation of Scripture among those who saw their performance.[92]

In his letter to Hausmann, Luther did not specify whether preference should be given to any particular part of the biblical canon for the choice of dramatic material. However, in his *German Bible* (1534), he singled out the stories of Judith and Tobit as particularly suitable for adaptation to the stage. Luther described them as dramatic poems: 'it may even be that in those days they dramatised literature like this, just as among us the Passion and other sacred stories are performed'.[93] In the *Introduction to the Book Tobit*, he likened the narrative to a proto-play and hinted at a direct link between the Hebrew writings of the Intertestamental period and Greek drama:

> It may even be that the Greeks picked up from the Jews their art of presenting comedies and tragedies [...] For *Judith* presents a good, serious, heroic tragedy, and *Tobit* presents a fine, delightful, devout comedy.[94]

Luther surmised that there were many more apocryphal stories that had been performed dramatically as part of the communal observance of Jewish holy days:

> It may even be assumed that beautiful compositions and plays like this were common among the Jews. On their festivals and sabbaths they steeped themselves in them; and through them, especially in times of peace and good government, they liked to instil God's Word and work into their young people.[95]

Stories like Judith and Tobit not only possessed the requisite educational character Luther valued so highly but, precisely because he regarded them as 'not held equal to the Scriptures but are useful and good to read', they were

---

92 Luther, *Briefwechsel* (*Letters*), WA Br 5: 272, no. 1543: 'affectum runioribus augendum'.

93 Luther, *Deutsche Bibel: Vorrhede auffs Buch Judith* (*Preface to the Book of Judith*), 1534, LW 35: 339. WA DB 12: 6, 21: 'Und mag sein, das sie [die Juden] solch geticht gespielet haben, wie man bey uns die Passio spielet, und ander heiligen geschicht'.

94 Luther, *Deutsche Bibel: Vorrhede auffs Buch Tobia* (*Preface to the Book of Tobit*), 1534, LW 35: 355. WA DB 12: 108, 9–13: 'Die Griechen [haben] jre weise, Comedien und Tragedien zu spielen von den Jüden genomen [...] Denn *Judith* gibt eine gute, ernste, dappfere Tragedien, So gibt *Tobias* eine feine liebliche, Gottselige Comedien'.

95 Luther, *Deutsche Bibel: Vorrhede Tobia* (*Preface Tobit*), LW 35: 355. WA DB 12: 108, 6–7: 'darinn sie [die Jüden] sich auff ire Feste und Sabbath geübt, vnd der jugent also mit lust, Gottes wort vnd werk eingebildet haben'.

outstanding tools to present the good news.[96] Their didactic value and potential to impress the value of Scripture on the young commended apocryphal works not only to be read but also to be performed in public. Through the medium of biblical drama, Luther believed, 'In a communal presentation or play they conceivably wanted to teach their people and youth to trust God, to be righteous, and to hope in God'.[97]

## 4 Joachim Greff and Popular Drama

Among the first theologians to take up Luther's suggestion that biblical drama was an outstanding medium to communicate Reformation teaching to a wide cross-section of society was the clergyman and schoolmaster Joachim Greff.[98] Greff shared Luther's theological views on the centrality of Scripture and his evangelistic zeal and turned out to be as prolific a playwright as the *Meistersinger* Hans Sachs. His plays were highly accessible, and his productions involved large parts of the community (*Volksdrama*):[99] the biblical landscape in his plays strongly resembled contemporary Saxony and was inhabited by numerous locals who joined the production as actors, members of the chorus or in mass scenes (*Massenszenen*).[100] Above all, as a formal investigation into his orthodoxy confirmed in 1543, his plays were thoroughly Lutheran.

The son of an organist, from an early age Greff had been exposed to the powerful combination of popular song and drama as a means to reach large audiences of different ages and educational backgrounds.[101] Music was not only 'a

---

96 Luther, *Deutsche Bibel*, WA DB 12: 3, 1–4, LW 35: 337n: 'Apocrypha: das sind Bücher so der heiligen Schrifft nicht gleich gehalten / vnd doch nützlich vnd gut zu lesen sind'.

97 Luther, *Vorrhede Judith* (*Preface Judith*), LW 35: 339. WA DB 12: 6, 22–23: 'Damit sie jr volck und die jugent lereten, als jnn einem gemeinem bilde odder spiel, Gott [zu] vertrawen'.

98 For Joachim Greff (*c.*1510–1552), see Buchwald, *Joachim Greff*; Andrea Seidel, 'Joachim Greff und das protestantische Schauspiel' (unpublished doctoral dissertation, Martin-Luther-Universität Halle, 1994); Andrea Seidel, 'Joachim Greff: Dramatiker im Dienste der Reformation', in *Mitteldeutsche Lebensbilder, Menschen im Zeitalter der Reformation*, ed. by Werner Freitag (Köln, Weimar, Wien: Böhlau Verlag, 2004), pp. 11–31.

99 Buchwald, *Joachim Greff*, pp. 49–51.

100 Ibid., p. 53.

101 Joachim's father Paul Greff was 'cantor of the [Zwickau Grammar] School' (*Cantor in der Schul*), Emil Herzog, *Geschichte des Zwickauer Gymnasium: Eine Gedenkschrift zur Einweihungsfeier des neuen Gymnasialgebäudes* (Zwickau: Richtersche Buchhandlung, 1869), p. 92; Scribner, *For the Sake of Simple Folk*, pp. 5–6, observed that such hybrid forms of communication created a 'meeting point between the illiterate, the semi-literate and the literate'.

sacred art' and the 'highest form of praising God', Greff wrote in the epilogue to his translation of *Lazarus Raised on the Fourth Day From the Dead* (1545).[102] Like music, drama was highly portable, readily 'available, and could be performed anywhere'.[103] At a time when probably ninety per cent of the population were illiterate or semiliterate, in his plays, Greff deliberately combined a variety of media in order to communicate Luther's Reformation message.[104] His belief that the gospel was not restricted to churches or schools, but could be equally well proclaimed by the performing and creative arts, is expressed well in the prologue to *The Tragedy of the Book of Judith in German Rhyme* (1536).[105] Greff cited Luther's views that the gospel message should be communicated through a multiplicity of media almost verbatim:[106]

> [God's Word] is written, read, and sung to us,
> it's painted on our neighbours' doors,
> it's heard in sermons everywhere,
> and often is performed for us:
> that we delight therein may gain.[107]

The prologue of *Judith* not only set out Greff's beliefs that the combination of drama and music afforded a new way of proclaiming the Reformation message but also gives an insight into his method of making that message more accessible. Greff believed that everyone—the literate, the illiterate, even the

102 Joachim Greff, *Lazarus: Vom Tode durch Christum am vierden tage erwecket* (Wittenberg: [n.p., most likely Rhau or Frischmut], 1545), a German translation of Johannes Sapidus, *Anabion sive Lazarus redivdus* (Köln: Gymnich, 1539).

103 Greff, *Lazarus*, Epilogus: 'sintemal ja diese heilige kunst der Music / zu Gottes lob vnd preis furnemlich vnd am allermeisten / in vnserm lieben Gott / darmit zu ehren erfunden vnd offenbart ist', 'wol vberal bekommen vnd anrichten'.

104 Pettegree, *Reformation and the Culture of Persuasion*, pp. 81–88 (p. 86).

105 Joachim Greff, *Tragoedia des Buchs Iudith jnn Deudsche Reim verfasset durch Joachim Greff von Zwickaw nützlich zu lesen* (Wittenberg: Georg Rhaw, 1536); later Lutheran playwrights shared Greff's reading of Luther: for instance, Matthäus Seydel, in his own gospel-play *Evangelia auffs einfeltigste in gemeine Teutsche reime gebracht* (Nürnberg: Christoff Heußler, 1565), cited Greff's prologue almost verbatim.

106 In a sermon preached at Torgau at Easter 1533, WA 37: 63, 9–10, Luther had affirmed: 'I am well pleased that people present the story of the resurrection to the simple through paintings, plays, music or preaching; and that should certainly remain so' (*Und gefellet mir wol, das mans also den einfeltigen für malet, spielet, singet odder sagt, Und sols auch da bey bleiben lassen*).

107 Greff, *Judith*, Prologus, sig. A $7^r$, 21–26: 'Man schreibts / man lists / man singt vns fur / Man sihts gemalt an jdermans thür / Es wird gepredigt vberall / Man spilts vns auch fur zum offtermal / Das wir solten lust darzu / Gewinnen'.

blind—should be given an opportunity to engage with Luther's Bible and Lutheran teaching. The provision of a familiar setting, frequent explanations of the events and homiletic reflections, musical accompaniment, and communal singing, all served the purpose of making the Reformation message as widely available as possible.[108] At the end of the prologue to *Judith*, the author emphasised once more the fact that the Word should not only be preached but should also be sung and dramatised:

> [God's Word] is read, it's sung, it's dramatised
> so that a blind man too may grasp
> that God will work the best for us.[109]

## 5 Dramatising the Bible

Greff began writing biblical dramas in 1534, the same year that saw the publication of Luther's complete *German Bible*. Then a teacher at the Magdeburg Latin School, he adapted the Genesis story of the patriarch Jacob and his twelve sons for the stage in an artistic collaboration with his school principal, the reformer Georg Major.[110] Greff not only wrote parts of *Jacob and his Twelve Sons*, but directed and introduced the play's first performance at the 'contest of marksmen in Magdeburg […] on the Thursday after St Laurence', 13 August 1534.[111] The experience both kindled Greff's passion for Protestant drama and fostered a lifelong friendship between the two men. When Greff's orthodoxy was formally scrutinised in 1543, it was Major who wrote in defence of his friend's

---

108 Bernd Moeller, 'Stadt und Buch: Bemerkungen zur Struktur der reformatorischen Bewegungen in Deutschland', in *Stadtbürgertum und Adel in der Reformation*, ed. by Wolfgang J. Mommsen and others, Studien zur Sozialgeschichte der Reformation in England und Deutschland, 5 (Stuttgart: Klett-Cotta, 1979), pp. 29–39; Scribner, *Popular Culture*, pp. 49–50.

109 Greff, *Judith*, Prologus, sig. A 7v, 18–21: 'Man lists / man singts / man spielts vns fur / Es möchts ein blinder greiffen schir / Das Gott solchs vns zum besten thut / Traun nem wirs an so ist es gut'.

110 Greff, *Ein lieblich vnd nutzbarlich spil von dem Patriarchen jacob und seinen zwelff Sönen*; although Barbara Könneker, '"Wold ihrs den nicht schir gleuben do?" Joachim Greffs protestantisches Osterspiel', *Daphnis* 23 (1994), 309–44 (p. 318), suggests that Greff was the sole author of the work, Buchwald, *Joachim Greff*, pp. 13–14, provides cogent arguments in support of the established view that the work was, in fact, an artistic collaboration.

111 Greff, *Jacob und seine zwelff Söne*: 'auff dem Schützenhoff […] Donnerstag nach Laurenti'; Buchwald, *Joachim Greff*, pp. 12–13.

beliefs that Lutheran teaching could and should without a doubt be communicated through the creative arts as well as by more conventional means.[112]

During the course of the next twelve years, Greff produced twelve German plays, most of them adaptations of Scripture. While the works composed in the second half of the 1530s were mainly based on stories from the Hebrew Bible, those written between 1538 and 1545 increasingly centred on the doctrine of the resurrection.

### 5.1 *Judith in Saxony*

Greff was one of the first German playwrights to take up Luther's suggestion that the Intertestamental apocryphal books were, in fact, proto-plays and therefore would lend themselves particularly well to adoption for the stage. Almost immediately after the publication of Luther's translation of the apocrypha, he set out to compose a verse drama based on the story of Judith and Holofernes. Greff's play is a faithful rendition of the biblical text in free rhyming couplets (*Knittelvers*), though somewhat augmented to relate the events to his local setting.[113] *Judith* was more than an opportunity to celebrate and promote the fact that Luther had made Scripture accessible in the vernacular. It gave voice to Luther's belief that in times of great upheaval nations and individuals could 'remain pure and holy in the Word of God and in the true faith'.[114] At a time of significant religious and political uncertainty, the play's enactment of one of the greatest crises in the history of God and his people staged Luther's belief that God would remain faithful to his people if the people remained faithful to the teaching of his Reformation.

In order to deliver this message, Greff explicitly linked the events of the Intertestamental period and his own times, providing the play with an unmistakably contemporary, local setting. The battles for the Holy Land in *Judith* mirrored the religious conflicts between supporters of Catholicism and Lutheranism, even within the ruling house, in Saxony. In the same year that saw Heinrich of Saxony's conversion to Lutheranism and the resultant increasing persecution of Lutherans by his Catholic brother Georg of Saxony, *Judith* provided a thinly

---

112 For Major, see Irene Dingel, Günther Wartenberg, and Michael Beyer, *Georg Major (1502–74): Ein Theologe der Wittenberger Reformation* (Leipzig: Evangelische Verlagsanstalt, 2005); and Robert Kolb, 'Georg Major as Controversialist: Polemics in the Late Reformation', *Church History*, 45.4 (1976), 455–68.

113 Greff's *Judith* is considered in detail in Henrike Lähnemann, *Hystoria Judith: Deutsche Judithdichtungen vom 12. bis zum 16. Jahrhundert*, Scrinium Friburgense, 20 (Berlin: Walter de Gruyter, 2006), pp. 371–90.

114 Luther, *Vorrhede auffs Buch Judith* (*Preface to the Book of Judith*), 1534, LW 35: 338. WA DB 12: 6, 13–14: 'vnd bleibt rein vnd heilig im wort Gottes, vnd rechten glauben'.

veiled commentary on current affairs: the faithful Israelite remnant represented the Lutheran cause, the Assyrian overlord the enemies of Lutheranism. As they went into battle at the beginning of Act II, the actors dressed in modern uniforms and carried rifles, High Priest Joachim resembling a Lutheran prince, leading his people into a modern battle, and commanding them: 'Let's fire our guns'.[115]

In the same way in which he set the biblical story among current conflicts between Protestants and Catholics in Saxony, the author also reframed the story in terms of conversion to Reformation beliefs. During their battle with the Assyrians, Nathan, an Israelite gunner, shoots an Assyrian soldier, Osias. Osias falls but survives and begs High Priest Joachim to set him free from his 'fetters of unbelief'.[116] Again, Greff leaves no doubt that God is on the side of the Lutherans. Though still dressed in the uniform of the oppressors, in his heart Osias has already converted to a living faith. The language of the Assyrian reflects his conversion. His song of praise for his deliverance might have come straight out of a Lutheran hymnal:

> Thanks and praise to God most high,
> Who has slain me by your might:
> By your hand he's set me free,
> Praise to him at all times be.[117]

## 5.2 *Transforming Audiences into Lutheran Congregations*

Greff not only gave his plays a setting that matched the socio-political and religious contexts of his audience but also adopted a lively interactive style to ensure that his Lutheran message would be heard and understood by all, regardless of age or education. Throughout the play, the characters elucidate the plot with brief homiletic reflections or explanations. They interrupt their lines to turn to the audience and ask, 'do you understand me?' (*verstet jr mich*) or 'do you understand this?' (*verstet jr das*), before proceeding to offer an explanation or interpretation of the events. The actors challenge their audience to put their trust in the message of the Reformation, and frequently profess their own Lutheran faith: 'believe me' (*gleub mir*), 'have no doubt' (*bin ich zweiffels an*).[118] Just as important as understanding and believing the message of the Lutheran

115 Greff, *Judith*, Act II, Scene 1, sig. B 8$^{r}$, 23: 'Last vns schiessn vnser püchssn ab'.
116 Greff, *Judith*, Act II, Scene 1, sig. C 1$^{r}$, 16: 'Erlöset mich from diesem band'.
117 Greff, *Judith*, Act II, Scene 1, sig. C 1$^{r}$, 25–27: 'Lob vnd danck sey dem höchsten Gott / Der mich durch euch erledigt hat / der mich durch euch hat ledig gmacht / Dem sey ehr vnd preis zu tag vnd nacht'.
118 For instance, Greff, *Judith*, sig. C 1$^{r}$, 31; C 1$^{v}$, 3; Lähnemann, *Hystoria Judith*, p. 382.

Reformation, however, was to listen attentively to that message. Greff's characters frequently encourage the audience to be 'silent, silent, all of you / and listen attentively' before communicating a central belief.[119]

Having heard and seen the biblical story acted out before them, the audience was invited to respond to the events on stage in the same way a Greek chorus would.[120] Following the heroine's triumphant soliloquy and the company's song of triumph, as *Judith* came to an end, both audience and players joined in singing the German Easter chorale *Christ ist erstanden* ('Christ the Lord Is Risen Again').[121] Greff frequently used hymn-like choruses in his dramas: some choruses reflect on the biblical events or, as in the Assyrian's very 'Lutheran-sounding' song of praise in *Judith*, reflect on religious allegiance and the experience of conversion.[122] Other choruses served the explicit purpose of ensuring 'that the people would continue to listen attentively'.[123] However, the communal singing of a popular Lutheran chorale at the end of an act or a play served an altogether different purpose than Greff's poetic reflections. It enabled the playwright to turn a passive audience of listeners into an active group of singers, sought to elicit an active response of faith, and therefore marked the transition from stage to church and the transformation of secular audiences into Lutheran congregations.

Once he had established his threefold dramatic pattern of biblical narrative combined with homiletic explanations and musical reflections in *Judith*, Greff continued to employ the same dramatic tools in his later plays. Regular interjections and explanatory asides complemented the retelling in verse of the biblical narrative in order to ensure that the audience heard and understood the theological message of his play. The actors' song-like lines at the beginning

---

119 Greff, *Judith*, Act IV, Scene 8, sig. E 8r: 'Schweigt schweigt alle nu / Vnd höret mir mit vleis zu'.

120 For instance, the chorale-like lines of Osias at the beginning of Greff, *Judith*, Act V, sig. F 2r: 'O Lord, O Lord, God most high / From our need deliver us / Stay close by us, forsake us not / O Lord, our God, that we do pray' (*O herr herr almechtiger Gott / Erret vns jtzt aus dieser not / Steh vns bey vnd verlas vns nicht / Herr vnser Gott das bit wir dich*).

121 Eberhard Möller, 'Joachim Greff und die musikalische Gestaltung des Schuldramas in Mitteldeutschland', *Musikgeschichte in Mittel- und Osteuropa*, 6 (2000), 201–20 (p. 203).

122 Other Lutheran playwrights followed Greff's example and also used music to illustrate religious allegiance. Sixt Birck, for instance, employed Latin plainchant melodies, such as Aquinas' *Pange lingua* to present the arrival of the priests of Baal in his play *Beel: Ain Herrliche Tragedi wider die Abgötterey auß dem Propheten Daniel* (Ausgburg: Philipp Ulhart the Elder, 1539), and German folk melodies to present Lutheran doctrine, as shown by Rochus von Liliencron, 'Die Chorgesänge des lateinisch-deutschen Schuldramas im XVI. Jahrhundert', *Vierteljahrsschrift für Musikwissenschaft*, 6 (1890), 309–87 (p. 323).

123 Greff, *Lazarus*, Epilogus, sig. T 1v: 'das volck ein wenig munterer vnd lustiger wird / weiter zu zu hören'.

or end of each act both provided the chorus of the classical theatrical tradition he sought to emulate and ensured that his audience remained attentive and receptive, while also giving the author an opportunity to compose poetic doctrinal reflections on the biblical narrative. Finally, the Lutheran chorales sung by players and viewers together at the conclusion of an act enabled the audience to participate in the performance itself by inviting the viewers to respond to the events on stage by their own sung confession of faith.[124] The resulting performances differed radically from the traditional Carnival, Passion or Corpus Christi plays that Luther had decried in 1530. Though still large-scale productions like their popular late-medieval predecessors, Greff's dramas were distinctively Lutheran and, if not acts of worship themselves, then certainly acts of Protestant proclamation.[125]

## 6 Towards a Protestant Dramatisation of the Passion

Because Luther's objection to the performances of traditional Passion and Corpus Christi plays was widely known, and dramatisations of the Passion in their late-medieval form had ceased in Lutheran Germany by the mid-1530s, it should not surprise that when Joachim Greff presented a Lutheran play on the Passion and resurrection in Dessau on Palm Sunday 1543, there was significant ecclesiastical opposition to the performance.

Greff had long intended to write a play on the Passion, 'including some of the miracles and the life of Christ'.[126] He had published his *Sacred New Play for Easter* in 1542, a year before its momentous performance.[127] Developed from his 1538 poetic adaptation of a popular gospel synopsis of the Passion narrative (*Evangelienharmonie*) by Hamburg reformer Johannes Bugenhagen, the play was dedicated to the council (*Rat*) of Freiberg in Saxony.[128] Until the

---

124 Liliencron, 'Die Chorgesänge', p. 344: 'Greff's *Lazarus*, 1545 and Narhamer's *Job*, 1546 are particular examples of audience participation in the action by the singing of spiritual songs and hymns, just as if they were a congregation at worship' (*Beispiele, daß auch die Zuschauer, fast wie die Gemeinde im Gottesdienst, mit eingreifen, indem sie geistliche Lieder singen, bieten Greff's Lazarus* (*1545*) *und Narhamer's Job* (*1546*).)

125 Buchwald, *Joachim Greff*, pp. 49–51, 53.

126 Greff, *Das Leiden vnd Aufferstehung*, Vorrede [Prologue]: 'samt etlichen mirakeln vnd dem leben Christi'.

127 Greff, *Ein Geistliches schönes newes spil auff das heilige Osterfest gestellet* (Magdeburg: Michael Lotter, 1542); see also Könneker, '"Wold ihrs den nicht schir gleuben do?"', 309–44.

128 Greff, *Das Leiden vnd Aufferstehung*; based on Johannes Bugenhagen, *Die Historia des leydens vnd der Aufferstehung vnsers Herrn Jhesu Christi aus den vier Evangelien, durch Johannem Bugenhagen Pomer vleyssig zusammen bracht* (Wittenberg: Hans Weiß, 1526).

introduction of the Reformation there in 1526, Freiberg had been the centre of a popular four-day Passion play. Performed every seven years, in 1509 the playwright had witnessed one of the play cycles as 'a child and young lad'.[129] Greff's dedication was pointed in its Protestant polemic: whereas the city's Passion play had previously 'honoured the Antichrist', his was a Lutheran play, devoid of all myth and superstition:[130] 'formerly people have added to the Passion and wove in far more than occurred or was mentioned by the evangelists in their gospels'.[131] His own work, on the other hand, was entirely Scriptural, and Greff therefore confidently commended the work to the city fathers in the hope that it might replace their former play cycle, and come to be performed in Freiberg on a regular basis.

The dedication to his *Sacred New Play for Easter* details the elaborate precautions the author had taken before going to press. Because of the delicate subject matter, in 1537 Greff had consulted Nikolaus Hausmann on how the subject of the Passion and resurrection should best be addressed; in 1541 he consulted Martin Luther. Both reformers were avid supporters of Reformation drama and Greff's works. Furthermore, Hausmann was the personal chaplain of the Princes of Anhalt in Dessau, where Greff was rector of the Latin School.[132] Equally importantly, he was a close friend of Luther and had previously corresponded with the Wittenberg reformer on the subject of biblical drama in schools.[133] Both cautiously encouraged Greff's project provided that Christ's death and resurrection were merely presented, not dramatised, lest the play turn into 'a spectacle' or 'cause people to laughter rather than worshipful reflection', as Luther made clear.[134]

129 Greff, *Osterfest*, Dedicatio, sig. A 5$^{v}$: 'als ein kindt vnd iunger knab'; for the Freiberg Passion play performed at Pentecost, see Creizenach, *Geschichte des neueren Dramas*, pp. 225–26.

130 Greff, *Osterfest*, Dedicatio, sig. A 5$^{v}$: 'dem Antichrist hofierten'; while Greff rigorously followed the biblical text, for instance by presenting Mary as a non-speaking part, he maintained certain aspects of the traditional play, such as the traditional four guards or the four angels at the tomb.

131 Greff, *Osterfest*, Dedicatio, sig. A 4$^{r}$: 'das man furzeite zu der passion vil mehr gethan und geflickt hiernan dan die Euangelisten in ihren Euangelien melden […] so möcht geschehen sein'.

132 In June 1532, Hausmann had been appointed personal chaplain of the Princes of Anhalt in Dessau, a post he held until his appointment as pastor of his native Freiberg in Saxony six years later, where he tragically died of a stroke as he delivered his first sermon, see Friedrich Wilhelm Bautz, 'Hausmann, Nikolaus', in *BBKL*, II, 607–10; Greff probably took up his Dessau appointment in 1536 or early 1537, Wolfgang Stammler, 'Greff, Joachim', in *Neue Deutsche Biographie* (Berlin: Duncker & Humblott, 1966), VII, 18–19 (p. 18).

133 Luther, *Briefwechsel* (*Letters*), WA Br 5: 272, no. 1543.

134 Greff, *Osterfest*, Dedicatio, sig. A 3$^{v}$: 'ein lecherey', 'das volck mehr zum lachen gereitzt dann zu andacht bewegt'.

Hausmann echoed Luther's views: 'this blessed story demands great sobriety', he insisted, cautioning that in the past Passion plays had been performed 'very badly and shamefully, and occasionally had even incited people to murder' (or at least to petty crime, as Melanchthon recounted elsewhere), and therefore required careful presentation.[135] Neither reformer, however, 'objected to the presentation of Christ's triumph over death', which encouraged the playwright to proceed with the composition of his Passion and Easter play.[136]

Greff followed the reformers' recommendation to the letter and avoided the dramatisation of Passion and resurrection. Instead, he introduced a reflection by the grief-stricken disciples to present the events of the cross and chose to herald the resurrection by an actor. As in the gospel narratives, the act of rising from the dead itself remained a mystery and an act of faith:

> Though in words clear and bold
> his rising is not shown, but told
> by the four evangelists,
> how we present it here today
> matters not: for we know well
> what by Christ accomplished was.
> Then, certain that he rose in glory,
> without sadness, let's hear the story.[137]

## 7 Performing the Passion and Resurrection

Although Greff had succeeded in publishing the first reformed Passion and Easter play with the full approval of Martin Luther, nevertheless the work's actual performance in Dessau a year later caused much offence.[138] The premiere of his Passiontide drama was planned to take place on Palm Sunday 1543. Like *Judith* (1536), it was to be accompanied by a combination of Greff's poetry set to music and the congregational singing of Lutheran chorales. During the

135 Greff, *Osterfest*, Dedicatio: 'aus Ursach, daß diese selige Histori einen großen Ernst fordere', 'sehr übel und schimpflich, auch nicht ohne Mord'; Melanchthon, CR 20: 576.

136 Creizenach, *Geschichte des neueren Dramas*, pp. 401–2: 'Gegen die Darstellung von Christi Triumph über den Tod fanden jedoch die Reformatoren nichts einzuwenden'.

137 Greff, *Osterfest*, sig. G 3ʳ: 'Ob es mit worten hel und klar / Gleich nicht ist ausgedruckt so gar / In den vier Euangelisten ebn / Wie wirs dan hie an den tag gebn / Da lest nicht an / Das wissen wir / Das von Christo sey geschehen hier / In seiner aufferstehung gwis / Lasts vns hören on verdries'.

138 Luther, *Briefwechsel* (*Letters*), WA Br 10: 236, 6: 'Zedel'.

play's rehearsals in spring 1543, the Dessau pastor Severinus Star and deacon Johannes Brusch objected to the production and sought to prevent its performance.[139] They considered the representation of the Passion and resurrection story 'histrionic like popish plays', and decried Greff's hymn-like reflections on the biblical narrative as 'lewd verses' (*Lotter reyme*).[140]

Star and Brusch were not successful in preventing the performance on Palm Sunday 1543. Consequently, following the performance of the play, they lodged an official complaint with the Chancellor of Anhalt, Georg Helt, leading to a formal investigation of the complaints. Suddenly the question of Lutheran performances of the Passion and resurrection stories had ceased to be a local matter and Greff's play became a test case about 'whether it was permissible to perform and attend dramatisations of Biblical stories [...] in both sacred and secular venues'.[141] Faced with significant local opposition and an official investigation on his hands, Greff travelled to Wittenberg in order to appeal directly to Luther and Melanchthon, and to lobby other influential Lutheran playwrights, poets, and schoolmasters, including his friend and former Magdeburg colleague, Georg Major, now professor of poetry at Wittenberg, the professor of Latin and later general superintendent minister of Kursachsen, Paul Eber, and Greff's former Zwickau schoolmaster, Hieronymus Nopus.[142] Greff's Wittenberg supporters coordinated their responses to the Anhalt authorities.[143] Two weeks after the performance of the Passion and Easter play, over the course of three days in Low Week 1543, Melanchthon, Major, Eber, and Nopus wrote in Latin to Chancellor

139 Buchwald, *Joachim Greff*, pp. 26.

140 Wilhelm Martin Leberecht de Wette, *Dr Martin Luthers Briefe, Sendschreiben und Bedenken* (Berlin: Reimer, 1828), 6 vols (Berlin: Reimer, 1828), v, 554: 'histrionicis, ut olim erant in papatu'; Luther, *Briefwechsel* (*Letters*), WA Br 10: 286, 8.

141 Luther, *Briefwechsel* (*Letters*), WA Br 10: 285: 'Quaerit Ioachimus Greff, an sacras historias carmine redditas [...] quovis in loco sacro vel prophano audiendas et spectandas liceat proponere'.

142 For Paul Eber, see Martin Riegel, 'Paul Eber (1511–69)', *Fränkische Lebensbilder*, 21 (2006), 103–117, and Martin Rößler, '"Helft mir Gotts Güte preise": Der Wittenberger Liederdichter Paul Eber', in *Dona Melanchthoniana: Festgabe für Heinz Scheible zum 70. Geburtstag*, ed. by Johanna Loehr and others (Stuttgart-Bad Cannstatt: Frommann-Holzboog, 2001), pp. 339–80.

143 Their correspondence with Chancellor Held, including a summary of the case, survives in Ratsschulbibliothek Zwickau, Codex XXXVI, and is reproduced in Bernd Neumann, *Geistliches Schauspiel im Zeugnis der Zeit: Zur Aufführung mittelalterlicher religiöser Dramen im deutschen Sprachgebiet*, Münchner Texte und Untersuchungen zur deutschen Literatur des Mittelalters, 84/85 (München: Artemis Verlag, 1987), II, 900–92, and Georg Buchwald, *Theologische Studien und Kritiken*, 59 (1886), 563–72; see also *Georg Helts Buchwechsel*, ed. by Otto Clemen, Archiv für Reformationsgeschichte Ergänzungsband, 2 (Leipzig: Verlag von M. Heinsius Nachfolger, 1907), pp. 132–3.

Held, while Luther addressed himself in German directly to the head of church and state, Prince Georg III of Anhalt.[144]

## 8 In Defence of Passion Drama

On 5 April, Georg Major wrote to the Chancellor of Anhalt in defence of the Palm Sunday performance. Major rejected the accusation that the performance had been 'histrionic as they used to be under the Papacy', and informed Helt that he believed the play to be thoroughly Lutheran and a powerful agent for conversion.[145] In those areas of Catholic Germany where Protestant preaching was forbidden, Lutheran plays like Greff's had won over many who had converted precisely because they had attended Protestant dramas, such as, for example, plays or 'presentations on the Law and Gospel'.[146] Rather than perpetuate a papist tradition, as was insinuated by the Dessau clergy, Greff's play presented a 'well measured and serious' tool to promote Lutheran teaching.[147]

Since both the Palm Sunday play, as well as its music, were under investigation, Major further affirmed that all aspects of the creative arts could beneficially be employed to promote the gospel. Greff should not be reprimanded for using his poetic and musical gifts in the service of the gospel, the later German poet laureate emphasised:[148]

> All people are charged to make known the Word of God the Father, in whatever way they are able to do so: not only by preaching (*voce*), but also

144 In his letter of 6 April, Eber suggests that Greff personally delivered the letters written in his support; Buchwald, *Joachim Greff*, p. 572.

145 De Wette, *Luthers Briefe*, V, 554: 'histrionicis, ut olim erant in papatu'.

146 De Wette, *Luthers Briefe*, V, 554: 'in inferiore Germania, ubi publica Evangelii prohibita est ex actionibus de lege et evangelio multos conversos et amplexos sincerorem doctrinam'; for a detailed examination of the dramatisation of Luther's theology on law and gospel, see Almut Agnes Meyer, *Heilsgewissheit und Endzeiterwartung im deutschen Drama des 16. Jahrhunderts: Untersuchungen über die Beziehungen zwischen geistlichem Spiel, bildender Kunst und den Wandlungen des Zeitgeistes im lutherischen Raum*, Heidelberger Forschungen, 18 (Heidelberg: Carl Winter Universitätsverlag, 1976), especially pp. 32–39 and her schematic representation at p. 53.

147 De Wette, *Luthers Briefe*, V, 554: 'gravibus tamen et moderate'.

148 In 1558, Major was made German poet laureate and a palatine count (*comes palatinus*) by the—Catholic—emperor Ferdinand I: see Manfred P. Fleischer, 'Melanchthon as Praeceptor of Late-Humanist Poetry', *The Sixteenth Century Journal*, 20.4 (1989), 559–580 (pp. 574, 576).

> by writing, through pictures and sculptures, as well as by Psalms, songs and instrumental music.[149]

Like Major, Eber and Nopus also addressed the place of drama in proclaiming the gospel: public performances, if soberly and well-conducted, were excellent tools to communicate the Word of God and dispel superstition.[150] Nopus went further and compared plays to sacraments. Signs of a greater truth, they helped to imprint the gospel more firmly in people's minds:[151]

> Plays and comedies are none other than talking ceremonies and speaking representations of past events. These, then, impress more on the hearts of the young than a straightforward retelling [of the story].[152]

Where such performances took place was irrelevant. What did matter was the intention of the play. Performances in private homes, in town squares or churches; before a small audience or, as had been the case in Dessau, an entire town, should all be commended if they set out to promote the Reformation cause. Greff's play, his friends robustly asserted, fulfilled this aim admirably: it was thoroughly Lutheran and evangelistic, reaching out to those who might otherwise not have heard about or understood Luther's theology of the cross.

## 9 A Matter of Church Polity

Where Greff's friends addressed aspects of the performance itself, in their correspondence Melanchthon and Luther did not enter into a debate about the play and the benefits of the creative arts at all. Instead, they addressed the manner in which the complaint had been made by the Dessau clergy. On the same day that Major wrote to Helt, Melanchthon also wrote to his friend the Chancellor,

149 De Wette, *Luthers Briefe*, V, 554: 'Mandatum est omnibus hominibus, verbum Dei Patris provenant at propagent, quibuscunque fieri potest rationibus, non tantum voce, sed scriptis, pictura, sculptura, psalmis, cantionibus, instrumentis musicis'.

150 Buchwald, *Joachim Greff*, p. 572.

151 Neumann, *Geistliches Schauspiel*, II, 910, no. 3754: 'Christ sought to imprint the Gospel of our salvation on our minds not by the Word alone, but all the more firmly through the performance-like nature of the sacraments' (*Christus Evangelium salutis nostrae non verbo tantum, sed et sacramentum quasi spectaculis quibusdam altius infingere mentibus nostris voluit*).

152 Neumann, *Geistliches Schauspiel*, II, 910: 'Et actiones istae comicae quid aliud sunt quam loquentes Ceremoniae et vocalis rerum gestarum repraesentatio, quae altius puerorum pectoribus res consuevit infigere quam simplex narratio'.

censoring the local clergy for instigating such an elaborate investigation in the first place:

> It is unfortunate that at a time of civil war in Germany, when, as I said before, the enemies of God are as vast and prodigious as Gog and Magog, some idle souls quarrel about unnecessary things and thereby upset the peace of the church.[153]

Like Luther, Melanchthon had long been an advocate of drama as a means to further humanist learning and the Reformation message.[154] He had not only edited and published numerous classical comedies for use in schools but, in the 1528 Saxon School Ordinances (*Kursächsische Schulordnung*), had wholeheartedly commended the performances of plays in schools.[155] In his letter to Helt, he reiterated his opinion that performing plays benefited the young. Biblical drama, even the dramatisation of the Passion or resurrection, was no different:

> Performances of the resurrection story and other similar true stories are useful exercises for the young. Those who decry such performances, when really they ought to seek the peace of the church, especially in these turbulent times, should be silenced.[156]

In his missive to Prince Georg, also written on 5 April, Luther was even more forthright. He was incensed that the Dessau clergy had acted without due respect for the proper governance of the church. By breaking the peace of the church in Anhalt, the complainants had acted against the mind and will of the church at large, Luther maintained.[157]

---

153 Melanchthon, *Epistolarum Liber IX*, 1543, CR 5: 86: 'dolendum est, in tanta publica moestitia cum Germania civilibus bellis dilaceratur, et hostis Dei adducit copias ingentes sicut de Gog et Magog praedictum est, ita adhuc otiosis animis aliquos rixari de rebus non necessariis'.

154 For a detailed consideration of Melanchthon's views on classical drama, see Parente, *Religious Drama*, pp. 20–27.

155 Melanchthon had in fact published a critical edition of the comedies of Terence, *Enarratio comoediarum Terentii* (1516), CR 19; *ES*, p. 6.

156 Melanchthon, CR 5: 86: 'de recitatione historiae resurrectionis et similium verarum historiarum sentio utiliter exerceri ea recitatione adolescentiam, et compescendos esse eos, qui hoc exercitium vituperant, qui rectius facerent, si hoc tristi tempore sua modestia tuerentur tranquillitatem ecclesiae'.

157 Luther, *Briefwechsel* (*Letters*), WA Br 10: 236, 1–23, especially 10–16.

In his letter to Prince Georg of Anhalt, Luther reiterated how the church arrived at a common mind. The will of the church was discerned 'by the heads of churches and their clergy, duly and with considered advice, and not unilaterally by one person alone, or in a piecemeal fashion'.[158] In his capacity as head of the church the Prince should determine whether the Anhalt church ought indeed to make a formal statement against the dramatisation of biblical stories in general, and Greff's Passion and resurrection story in particular. If he felt that there were sufficient grounds, he should convene a synod of Lutheran clergy and other heads of churches (*andere Oberherrn*) to re-consider the matter of Passion plays.[159]

However, until there was a considered and formally agreed statement against biblical or Passion drama, the mind of the church at large was that Passion plays were not central to the doctrine of the Lutheran church. Greff's play was to be considered one of the *neutralia* (or *adiaphora*) and, as such, ought not to be condemned publicly, that is made out to be among the *damnabilia*:[160]

> The schoolmaster of Dessau has asked me [...] what I thought about this furore (as he termed it) and the fact that both incumbent and preacher called the hymns and anthems of the Palm Sunday play the work of fools and lewd verses, and thereby both upset and stirred up the people. I did not like to hear that, because I fear that here is a small mind seeking to do its own thing: *neutralia* like these, especially because they do no harm and are an innocent custom, should be permitted.[161]

In bringing their complaint forward, the Dessau clergy had not only exceeded their authority and acted against the consensus of the church at large but also

158 Luther, *Briefwechsel* (*Letters*), WA Br 10: 286, 12–13: 'das nicht einer allein furneme im hauffen, sondern alle andere oberherrn vnd pfarrher solchs mit bedechtem Rat theten'.

159 Luther, *Briefwechsel* (*Letters*), WA Br 10: 286, 13.

160 Luther, *Briefwechsel* (*Letters*), WA Br 10: 286, 10, 15–16; see *The Arts and the Cultural Heritage of Martin Luther: Special Issue of Transfiguration: Nordic Journal for Christianity and the Arts*, ed. by Nils Holger Petersen and others (Copenhagen: Museum Tusculanum Press, 2002), p. 16: 'as long as such devotions were not (ab)used in a way that would make people believe that participation in them automatically granted spiritual advantages, he was not opposed to them'.

161 Luther, *Briefwechsel* (*Letters*), WA Br 10: 286, 5–11: 'Es hat der Schulmeister zu Dessen von mir begert [...] diese Zedel (wie ers nennet), was ich dauon hielte, Das der pharrher vnd prediger die leute bewegten vnd vnrugig machten, da sie lieder vnd gesenge des palmentags vnd ander mehr Narren werck vnd Lotter reymen schelten. Solchs hore ich nicht gern, Vnd sorge, Es kücke ein geistlin heraus, der raüm sucht, ettwas sonderlichs zu machen. Solche neutralia, weil sie ynn unschedlichen brauch vnd nicht ergerlich, Solt man lassen gehen'.

broken the peace among the Anhalt churches. Consequently, Luther requested that Prince Georg, in his capacity as their archdeacon, duly discipline the two complainants:[162]

> Your Princely Highness should neither have to suffer the tempers of these hotheads nor their desire to turn *neutralia* into *damnabilia*. They neither have authority nor sufficient learning to make such judgements. If they are read a lesson now, then they will, in future, learn to bite the bit and follow the bridle. [...] Your Princely Highness will know only too well what to do: thus, be commended to God. Amen.[163]

Faced with such overwhelming support for Joachim Greff's play, the Anhalt authorities naturally decided in favour of the playwright. The two clergymen were duly censured, while the author was encouraged to continue writing, producing, and directing biblical dramas.[164] As a sign of his gratitude, two years later Greff dedicated his *Lazarus Rising* to his many supporters at home and in Wittenberg.[165]

The Anhalt test case confirmed that there was no reason why biblical dramas should not be used to further Lutheran teaching. Furthermore, the Wittenberg reformers acknowledged that, in presenting his new Passion and Easter play, Greff had successfully reformed one of the mainstays of Catholic popular piety. From now on, representations of the Passion would be permissible subject matters for Lutheran poets and playwrights, provided they were depicted reverently. Even large-scale productions and outdoor performances were allowed, as long as they promoted Lutheran teaching and did not turn the

162 Luther, *Briefwechsel* (*Letters*), WA Br 10: 286, 14: 'nicht allein oberherr, sondern auch Archidiaconus'.

163 Luther, *Briefwechsel* (*Letters*), WA Br 10: 286, 14–19: 'sollen sie nicht leiden, das ein toller kopff aus ihm selber erfur fure vnd die Neutralia damnabilia schelte. Es ist ihm nicht befolhen, auch noch viel zu vngelert dazu. Lesst man yhm das Leplin, so wird er fort an lernen, das ledder fressen, da mus man zu sehen. Weiter werden E. f. g. [Eure fürstliche Gnaden] wol sich wissen hierin zuhalten. Hie mit Gott befolhen, Amen'.

164 The working relationship between Greff and his colleagues, however, remained strained in October 1543, the clergy again complained to Prince Georg that Greff spent too much time on his writing and producing and too little time on his teaching: a letter to the Prince by one of the later complainants, the Dessau pastor Egidius Faber, lodged in Landeshauptarchiv Sachsen-Anhalt, Dessau, and reproduced by Hermann Suhle, *Beiträge zur Geschichte der fürstlichen Schule zu Dessau, I: 1536–1628*, Sechster Jahresbericht des Herzoglichen Friedrichs-Realgymnasiums (Dessau: C. Dünnhaupt, 1888), p. 3, indicates that this time both clergy and playwright were read a stern lesson 'in the hope that they would comply' (*des verhoffens, sy warden denselbingen folge thuen*), but to no avail.

165 Greff, *Lazarus*, sig. B 2v: 'to our good supporters here in Dessau, as well as to my dear friends' (*vnsern alhie zu Dessaw / meinen zum teil lieben befreundeten auch guten günnern*).

drama of the Passion into a spectacle. As Greff's erstwhile artistic collaborator, Georg Major, had suggested, plays like Greff's had and would continue to lead to the conversion of people in those areas of Germany where Protestants were still forbidden to preach, and therefore were worthy of church support.

The support given for Greff's Passiontide play suggests that the well-rehearsed nineteenth-century paradigm that Martin Luther objected to all forms of Passion plays needs to be qualified. While there is no doubt that Luther rejected traditional late-medieval Passion and Corpus Christi plays on the basis of their doctrinal content, he certainly did not object to contemporary Lutheran dramatisations of the biblical story. Equally misleading is the claim that, when he sanctioned dramatisation of the life of Christ, Luther was 'referring to events in the life of Jesus other than the Passion'.[166] Greff's case makes clear that dramatisations of the Passion were permissible as long as they adhered to Luther's guidelines outlined above: plays ought not to turn into 'a spectacle' or 'cause people to laughter rather than worshipful reflection'.[167] Rather, the Passion was to be dramatised and performed in a Lutheran way: with the necessary 'sobriety this blessed story demands'.[168]

Similarly, the view that Luther actively 'used his influence to put an end to Passion plays in those regions where the Reformation was introduced' also needs to be reconsidered.[169] There is sufficient evidence to suggest that the tradition of Passion plays continued without interruption even in the heartlands of Lutheranism. In the direct vicinity of Zwickau, that 'noble ornament of the Saxon church' as Melanchthon affectionately called the city, Passion plays were certainly performed until the nineteenth century; they merely were turned into Lutheran plays.[170] Likewise, the performance of the Friedberg Passion play continued in a reformed format until 1821, even the original 'costumes were preserved in the sacristy of the town-centre church'.[171] Similarly problematic

166 Bacon, *Luther and the Drama*, p. 42.

167 Greff, *Osterfest*, Dedicatio, sig. A 3$^v$: 'ein lecherey', 'das volck mehr zum lachen gereitzt dann zu andacht bewegt'.

168 Greff, *Osterfest*, Dedicatio, sig. A 3$^v$: 'diese selige Histori einen großen Ernst fordere'.

169 Holstein, *Reformation im Spiegelbilde*, p. 25: 'so bewirkte Luthers Einfluß, daß die Passionsspiele in den Gegenden, in welchen die Reformatiom Eingang fand, aufhörten'.

170 Buchwald, *Joachim Greff*, p. 8: at Heinrichsort, near Zwickau, a Passion play was regularly performed until 1821; ibid., p. 12: 'nobile ornamentum ecclesiae saxoniae'.

171 Abraham Saur, *Theatrum Urbium: Warhafftige Contrafeytung und Summarische Beschreibung vast aller Vornehmen und namhafftigen Stätten, Schlössern und Klöster* (Frankfurt a.M.: Nicolaus Bassaeus, 1595), p. 309; *Deutsche Dichter des sechzehnten Jahrhunderts: Schauspiele aus dem sechzehnten Jahrhundert*, ed. by Karl Goedecke and Julius Tittmann (Leipzig: Brockhaus, 1868), p. xi: 'nebst den für dasselbe [Passionsspiel] bestimmten

is the widely held opinion that performances of Lutheran Passions plays took place only 'after Luther's death'. The evidence of Passion and Easter play performances in Lutheran Wernigerode in 1539 suggests that such performances certainly did take place during Luther's lifetime, and merely increased after his death.[172]

By the middle of the sixteenth century, the Reformation of popular drama and church customs that Luther had demanded of the clergy at the 1530 Augsburg Diet had, on the whole, been accomplished. Pioneering theologians such as Greff and accomplished *Meistersinger* such as Hans Sachs had transformed Carnival and biblical plays into a Protestant art-form. It is clear that their new, Protestant, form of dramatising biblical and traditional subject matters was enthusiastically received, mainly by dramatists and players' guilds in imperial free cities in Germany, but also further afield in Switzerland.[173] A request in 1553 by the Nördlingen *Meistersinger* guild to stage a performance of a Lutheran Passion play each Sunday and Monday in Lent, for example, was supported by the guild's assertion that this was in line with 'the well-established custom in other towns with *Meistersinger* guilds such as Nürnberg, Augsburg, Ulm and Esslingen'.[174] Indeed, five years later in 1558, Hans Sachs composed and produced a Passion play for performance by the Nürnberg *Meistersinger* guild.[175] Likewise, in 1566 the Augsburg *Meistersinger* Sebastian Wild wrote and produced his own influential Passion play which, until the nineteenth century, formed the basis not only for a number of Lutheran but, intriguingly, also for three Catholic dramatisations of the Passion, including the celebrated

---

Gewändern in einer Sakristei der Stadtkirche aufbewahrt'; for the late-medieval Friedberg Passion play, and the suggestion that the play may not have continued as was maintained by Saur, see Freise, *Spiele und Spielinitiativen*, pp. 207–256 (pp. 254–255).

172 Holstein, *Reformation im Spiegelbilde*, pp. 133–4; for the Wernigerode play, see Eduard Jacobs, 'Bemerkungen zur Geschichte des Schauspiels und der Sitten am Harz im 16. und 17. Jahrhundert', *Zeitschrift des Harz-Vereins für Geschichte und Altertumskunde*, 1 (1868), pp. 77–117, especially the section 'Über verschiedene, meist dem Mittelalter entstammende öffentliche Darstellungen, Aufführungen (Comödien) und Gebräuche in der Grafschaft Werningerode', pp. 99–117, 104–105, 111–113.

173 For performances of Lutheran Passions in Marburg (1561) and Schmalkalden (1564), see Creizenach, *Geschichte des neueren Dramas*, p. 401. For the development of Reformation drama in Switzerland, see Ehrstine, *Theater, Culture, and Community in Reformation Bern, 1523–55*, pp. 6–31, 67–79.

174 Creizenach, *Geschichte des neueren Dramas*, p. 413: 'daß die Meistersingeraufführungen in anderen Städten, wie Nürnberg, Augsburg, Ulm und Esslingen eine ständige Gewohnheit seien'.

175 Hans Sachs, 'Die ganz Passio', in Hans Sachs, *Sehr herrliche schöne und warhaffte Gedicht geistlich unnd weltlich allerley Art* (Nürnberg: Christoff Heußler, 1558).

Oberammergau Passion play.[176] By the end of the sixteenth century, Lutheran Passion and resurrection dramas were well established and continued to serve as a tool to make known the teachings of the Reformation and the theology of the cross that lay at the heart of Luther's reforms.[177]

176 Sebastian Wild, *Die Passion und Aufferstehung Christi*, in Sebastian Wild, *Schöner Comedien und Tragedien zwölff: Auß heiliger Göttlicher schrift und auch auß etlichen Historien gezogen* (Augsburg: Matthäus Franck, 1566). Until their revision by Joseph Daisenberger and Dom Othmar Weis in 1811, Wild's Lutheran play formed the basis for three Catholic Passion play cycles: Oberammergau, Waal, and Erl; for Wild's Lutheran plays, see Meyer, *Heilsgewissheit*, pp. 150–60, especially pp. 153–57, and at p. 204.

177 Among them in particular Bartholomäus Krüger, *Historia unseres Herrn und Heilandes Jesu Christi* (Augsburg: Matthäus Franck, 1580) which, as Holstein, *Reformation im Spiegelbilde*, p. 78 explained, dramatises 'the resurrection, Christ's harrowing of hell, sending of the disciples, the corruption of the church by the papacy and the beginning of the Reformation' (*Christi Auferstehung, seinen Sieg über die Hölle und die Aussendung der Jünger, die Verderbnis der Kirche unter der Herrschaft des Papstes, den Eintritt der Reformation*).

# Conclusion

In this volume, we attempt to consider a comprehensive cross-section of all of Luther's significant artistic endeavours, and collaborations: through hymns, song, poetry, painting, woodcuts and engravings, sculpture, drama, and rhetoric. We explored church, civil, political, and educational settings. This cross-disciplinary survey aims to be one of the most comprehensive studies to date of Luther's theoretical, practical, and theological engagement with different forms of art in ways that will be useful to both established scholars and researchers new to the fields.

As we have shown in our own earlier work on Luther and music or drama, and the many previous studies of Luther and the arts, scholars have usually concentrated on one art-form or artistic discipline alone. Both early contributions to the field considering 'Luther and the Arts'—such as Leslie Spelman (1951)—and more recent surveys—such as Johannes Schilling (2017)—also tend to centre only on a smaller range of artistic expression: Lutheran poetry, chorales, and church architecture in the case of Spelman; and music, poetry, and hymns in Schilling's.[1]

Recent German research has opened up the field of Luther's engagement in material culture and architecture, and includes fascinating archaeological discoveries from the Luthers' Wittenberg home that give a much better understanding of some of the domestic objects commissioned by or enjoyed and treasured by the Luthers.[2] These were judged to be outside the scope of this volume but would be a fruitful direction for future research to further develop our analyses connecting Luther's visual and performance theories to public and domestic buildings.

We have demonstrated that Luther developed theories about the arts and their uses. Even where there is no extended single work, as there was for his theory of music in *Praefatio zu den Symphoniae Iucundae* (*Preface to the Symphoniae Iucundae*), we have shown in our consideration of Luther's theory of the image that it is possible to reconstruct theoretical approaches across Luther's writings, sermons, *Table Talk*, letters and pamphlets. Luther created music, poems, rhetoric and captions for paintings and woodcuts. He also produced art

1 Leslie Spelman, 'Luther and the Arts', *The Journal of Aesthetics and Art Criticism*, 10.2 (1951), 166–75; Johannes Schilling, 'Martin Luther and the Arts: Music, Poetry, and Hymns', in *Oxford Research Encyclopedia of Religion* <https://doi.org/10.1093/acrefore/9780199340378.013.293>.

2 For instance, Gutjahr, 'Wie protestantisch ist Luthers Müll', pp. 43–5, and Nebelsick and Emmerling, '"Finding Luther"', p. 1186.

 | DOI:10.1163/9789004527430_009

criticism of sculptures, frescoes, popular music, and dramas. Through commissions and collaboration, he encouraged others to create musical, visual and dramatic works. Luther worked closely with other artists, craftspeople, teachers, and theologians to create and disseminate the new works, As we noted in our Introduction, he collaborated with princes, burghers and ordinary people, with women and men and children, across Germany and further afield.

We have shown that Luther was well-versed in the study of the seven liberal arts, and of existing popular and high-art traditions of music, images, and drama. He repurposed existing tunes, stories, iconographies, and analytical techniques. At the same time, Luther and his fellow reformers used innovative ways to develop new modes of making and understanding arts, to reach wider audiences, or to reflect the novel ways of thinking required by the insight that salvation could be granted directly from God and his gifts of the Scriptures and his Son, rather than through the institutions of the Catholic Church.

While Luther's uses of art-forms were affective and may have had sentimental uses for the reformer himself, we focus on the late-medieval philosophical theory that underpinned Luther's use of music, images, and polemic. Luther's theories of music and art were intentionally developed from these scholastic foundations and similarly constructed using logical processes of classification and hierarchy: namely, the processes of differentiating between the form, content, and purpose of art-forms and identifying some as superior according to the logic of the seven liberal arts.

In the case of Luther's anti-Semitic polemic, while we propose that his use of abject techniques may have kept the theoretical development in his Unconscious, Luther nonetheless drew heavily on late-medieval religious, legal, and racial theories to construct even his most scatological tracts. The logical continuity of Luther's reforming messages with earlier forms of anti-Semitism, Islamophobia, racism, and sectarian exclusion, as well as earlier forms of oppositional rhetoric, mean that such violent exclusions continued to be justified aspects of German national identity through the Enlightenment, and the German Nationalist movements of the nineteenth and twentieth centuries, including the systematic annihilation of Jewish communities in Nazi Germany some four-hundred years later.

It is notable that, throughout Luther's oeuvre, his works simultaneously attempt to include more people in accessing his teaching on salvation and to exclude any who threaten his Reformation project. In a single work, Luther and his collaborators might make choices to include the poor or illiterate, while excoriating the Catholic Church; to include women while dismissing Anabaptists; to include believers who spoke other languages while ridiculing the sacred texts, rituals, and languages of people of other faiths.

Ultimately, Luther's theories and practices of the arts were always subservient to his primary aim: to carry his new message of salvation to as many people as possible. Using Latin and German, images, drama and tunes, church art, sermons, lectures, books, and pamphlets, he reached out to the elites and the common people, the literate, semiliterate and illiterate. Luther and his Reformation collaborators used emotive as well as logical means, aversive as well as attractive strategies, and artistic as well as theological tools. We have shown that Luther targeted every aspect of human experience in his attempt to persuade people to turn to Jesus Christ and, by following his Reformation teaching, be saved. For Luther, this was an urgent task, since he believed those who refused his message would be damned. This meant that the arts could be used to invite new believers into the Lutheran fold and inspire the faithful, but also to encourage people to turn away from evil. It is this very real danger of error leading to eternal damnation that led Luther also to use his art-forms to vilify his opponents.

Luther's significance in theology and language translates into an ongoing significance in culture and the arts. His ideas and practices in the arts influenced religion, legal, political, and social movements in his own time to the present day, in Germany and globally. Even incidental and little-known treatises were used to justify, for example, pogroms in Luther's own time and the Holocaust in the twentieth century. Complete works editions from the eighteenth century onwards ensured that all of Luther's writings were easily accessible to German-speaking audiences. In order to represent this broad availability, we have included many previously unpublished primary sources in German, provided new complete translations, and have extensively drawn on secondary literature in German. In this way, we hope to make both established and new scholarship available to scholars for whom a lack of German (or Hebrew, Greek, or Latin) might have been a barrier, as well as to scholars who approach Luther's artistic endeavours from an interdisciplinary, and not a traditional church historical, perspective.

We believe that this book will enable readers to trace the sources, developments, and impact of Luther's engagement with the arts. We hope it will further the scholarly conversation about Luther's influence on high art and mass culture, from the Reformation to the present day, in Europe and globally.

# *Appendices*

APPENDIX 1

# Luther's Prefaces to the 'Symphoniae Iucundae'

TABLE 3 Luther's Preface to the *Symphoniae Iucundae* in Latin, English and German, English translation by Dr Leofranc Holford-Strevens[a]

| **Martinvs Lvther mvsicae stvdiosis** | **Martin Luther to students of music** |
| --- | --- |
| 1. [1]Salutem in Christo. [2]Vellem certe ex animo laudatum et omnibus commendatum esse donum illud diuinum et excellentissimum Musicam, [3]Sed ita obruor multitudine et magnitudine virtutis et bonitatis eius, vt neque initium neque finem neque modum orationis inuenire queam, et cogar in summa copia laudum ieiunus et inops esse laudator. [4]Quis enim omnia complectatur? [5]Atque si velis omnia complecti, nihil complexus videare. [6]Primum, si rem ipsam spectes, inuenies Musicam esse ab initio mundi inditam seu concretam creaturis vniuersis, singulis et omnibus. [7]Nihil enim est sine sono, seu numero sonoro, ita vt et aer ipse per sese inuisibilis et inpalpabilis, omnibusque sensibus inperceptibilis, minimeque omnium musicus, sed plane mutus et nihil reputatus, tamen motus sit sonorus et audibilis, tunc etiam palpabilis, mirabilia in hoc significante spiritu | 1. [1]Greetings in Christ. [2]I should heartily wish that divine and most excellent gift of music to be praised and commended to all. [3]But I am so much overwhelmed by the abundance and magnitude of its virtue and goodness that I cannot discover how to begin or end or limit my words, and am compelled, amidst such a multitude of things to praise, to be faint and inadequate in my praises. [4]For who could cover everything? [5]And if you wished to cover everything, you would seem to have covered nothing. [6]First of all, if you examine the thing itself, you will find that music was impressed on or created with every single creature, one and all. [7]For nothing is without sound, or sounding number, so that the very air, which on itself is invisible and impalpable, and imperceptible to all the senses, and least musical of all things, but utterly mute and of no account, yet in motion sounds and can be heard and even touched; in this the Spirit signifies |

a Commissioned by the editors of *Music and Letters*, as part of Andreas Loewe, '"Musica est optimum": Martin Luther's Theory of Music', *Music and Letters* 94.4 (2013), 573–605. Reproduced by permission.

**Vorrede des Heiligen Tewren man Gottes, Doctoris Martini Lutheri, von der Himlischen Kunst Musica, vormals nie Deudsch im Druck ausgangen**

1. [1]Allen Liebhabern der freien Kunst Musica wündsch Ich, Doctor Martinus Luther, Gnad vnd Fried von Gott dem Vater vnd vnserm HERrn Jhesu Christ.
[2]ICH wolt von hertzen gerne diese schöne vnd köstliche Gabe Gottes, die freie Kunst der Musica, hoch loben vnd preisen, [3]So befinde ich, das dieselbige also viel vnd grosse nutze hat, vnd also ein herrliche vnd edle Kunst ist, das ich nicht weis, wo ich dieselbe zu loben anfahen oder auffhören sol, oder auff was weise vnd form ich sie also loben möge, wie ich sie billich zu loben vnd von jederman tewr vnd werd zu achten ist, vnd werde also mit der reichen fülle des lobs dieser Kunst vberschüttet, das ich sie nicht gnugsam erheben vnd loben kan. [4]Denn wer kan alles sagen vnd anzeigen, was hieruon möchte geschreiben vnd gesagt werden? [5]Und wenn schon einer alles gern sagen vnd anzeigen wolte, so würde er doch vieler Stück vergessen, Und ist in Summa vnmüglich, das man diese edle Kunst gnugsam loben oder erheben könne oder möge. [6]ERstlichen aber, wenn man die Sache recht betrachtet, So befindet man, das diese Kunst von anfang der Welt allen vnd jglichen Creaturen von Gott gegeben, vnd von Anfang mit allen geschaffen, [7]den da ist nichten nichts in der Welt, das nicht ein Schall vnd Laut von sich gebe, Also auch, das auch die Lufft, welche doch an jr selbst vnsichtbarlich vnd vnbegreifflich, darinnen am aller wenigsten Musica, das ist, schönes Klangs vnd Lauts, vnd gantz stum vnd vnlautbar zu sein scheinet, Jedoch, wenn sie durch was beweget vnd getrieben wird, so gibt sie auch jre Musica, jren klang von sich, vnd die zuuor stum war, dieselbige sehet denn an, lautbar vnd eine Musica zu werden, das mans als den hören vnd begreiffen kan, die zuuor nicht gehöret noch begreifflich war, durch welches der Geist wunderbarliche vnd grosse Geheimnis anzeiget, dauon ich itzund nicht sagen wil. [8]ZUm andern, ist der Thieren vnd sonderlich der Vogel Musica, Klang vnd Gesang, noch viel wunderbarlicher, Wie denn der König Dauid, der köstliche Musicus, welcher auff seinem Psalter vnd Seitenspiel lauter Göttlichen Gesang singet vnd spielet, selbs bezeuget vnd mit grosser verwunderung vnd freidigen Geist von dem wunderbarlichen Gesang der

TABLE 3 Luther's Preface to the *Symphoniae Iucundae* (*cont.*)

| **Martinvs Lvther mvsicae stvdiosis** | **Martin Luther to students of music** |
| --- | --- |
| mysteria, de quibus hic non est locus dicendi. [8]Sed mirabilior est Musica in animantibus, praesertim volucribus, ut Musicissimus ille Rex et diuinus psaltes Dauid cum ingenti stupore et exultante spiritu praedicit mirabilem illam volucrum peritiam et certitudinem canendi, dicens Psalmo centesimo tertio, 'Super ea volucres coeli habitant, de medio ramorum dant voces.' | marvellous mysteries of which this is not the place to speak. [8]But more marvellous is music in living beings, especially birds, as that most musical king and divine harpist David, with great amazement and exultant spirit proclaims that wondrous skill and assurance birds have in singing, saying in Ps. 103 [104: 12]:[b] 'By them shall the fowls of the heaven have their habitation, which sing among the branches.' |
| 2. [1]Verum ad humanam vocem omnia sunt prope immusica, tanta est optimi Creatoris in hac vna re supereffusa et incompraehensibilis munificentia et sapientia. [2]Sudarunt Philosophi, vt intelligerent hoc mirabile artificium vocis humanae, quo modo tam leui motu linguae leuiorique adhuc motu gutturis pulsus aer funderet illam infinitam varietatem et articulationem vocis et verborum, pro arbitrio animae gubernantis, tam potenter et vehementer, ut per tanta interualla locorum circulariter ab omnibus distincte non solum audiri, sed et intelligi possit. [3]Sed sudant tantum, nunquam inueniunt, et cum admiratione desinunt in stuporem, [4]Quin nulli adhuc reperti sunt, qui | 2. [1]But beside the human voice all things are almost unmusical, so great are the excellent Creator's superabundant and incomprehensible munificence and wisdom in this one matter. [2]Philosophers have laboured to understand this miraculous artifice of the human voice: how the air, struck with so slight a motion of the tongue and an even slighter motion of the throat, pours fourth that infinite variety and articulation of voice and words at the will of the governing soul, so powerfully and vigorously that through such great distances of the area all around it can not only be heard distinctly by all, but understood. [3]But they merely labour, never find, and end up in wonderment and amazement. |

b Writing in Latin, Luther uses the numeration of the Vulgate; the German version gives that of the Masoretic Hebrew text and of Protestant versions such as his own and the Authorised Version (quoted here).

**Vorrede des Heiligen Tewren man Gottes Doctoris Martini Lutheri, von der Himlischen Kunst Musica, vormals nie Deudsch im Druck ausgangen**

Vogel am 104. Psalm weissaget vnd singet, da er also spricht: 'Auff denselben sitzen die Vogel des Himels vnd singen vnter den Zweigen.'

2. [1]WAs sol ich aber sagen von des Menschen Stimme, gegen welcher alle andere Gesenge, Klang vnd Laut gar nicht zu rechnen sind, denn dieselbigen hat Gott mit einer solchen Musica begnadet, das auch in dem einigen seine vberschwengliche vnd vnbegreiffliche Güte vnd Weisheit nicht kan noch mag verstanden werden. [2]Den es haben sich wol die Philosophi vnd gelerten Leut hart beulissen vnd bemühet, dieses wunderbarlich Werck vnd Kunst der Menschlichen Stimme zu erforschen vnd begreiffen, wie es zugieng das die Lufft durch eine solche kleine vnd geringe bewegung der Zungen, vnd darnach auch noch durch eine geringere bewegung der kelen oder des halses, also auff mancherley art vnd weise, nach dem, wie es durch das gemüt geregieret vnd gelencket wird, auch also krefftig vnd gewaltig Wort, Laut, Gesang vnd Klang von sich geben könne, das sie so fern vnd weit, geringes herumb, von jederman vnterschiedlich nicht allein gehört, sondern auch verstanden vnd vernomen wird. [3]Sie haben sich aber das zu erforschen allein vnterstanden, aber doch nicht erforschet, [4]Ja es ist auch noch keiner nicht komen welcher hette könen sagen vnd anzeigen, wo von das Lachen des Menschen (denn vom Weinen wil ich nichts sagen) kome, vnd wie es zugehe, das der Mensch lachet, des verwundern sie sich, darbey bleibts auch, vnd könnens nicht erforschen. [5]Das aber, von der vnmesslichen weisheit Gottes in dieser einigen Creatur, wollen wir den, so mehr zeit, denn wir haben, zu bedencken befehlen, ich habs allein kürtzlich wollen anzeigen.

TABLE 3 Luther's Preface to the *Symphoniae Iucundae* (*cont.*)

| **Martinvs Lvther mvsicae stvdiosis** | **Martin Luther to students of music** |
|---|---|
| definire et statuere potuerint, quid sit ille sibilus et alphabetum quoddam vocis humanae, seu materia prima, nempe Risus (de fletu nihil dicam). Mirantur, sed non complectuntur. [5]Verum haec speculabilia de infinita sapientia Dei in hac vna creatura relinquamus melioribus et ociosioribus, nos vix gustum attingimus. | [4]Indeed, none have yet been found who could determine and establish the nature of that hiss and as it were alphabet or prime matter of the human voice, namely laughter (of weeping I will say nothing). They wonder, but do not comprehend. [5]But let us leave these speculations on God's infinite wisdom in this one creature to better men with more time on their hands; we hardly touch even on a taste of the question. |
| 3. [1]De vsu tantae rei dicere hic oportuit. [2]Sed et ille ipse sua infinita varietate et vtilitate longe superat omnium eloquentissimorum eloquentissimam eloquentiam. [3]Hoc vnum possumus nunc afferre, [4]Quod experientia testis est, Musicam esse vnam, quae post verbum Dei merito celebrari debeat, domina et gubernatrix affectuum humanorum (de bestiis nunc tacendum est) quibus tamen ipsi homines, ceu a suis dominis, gubernantur et saepius rapiuntur. [5]Hac laude Musicae nulla maior potest (a nobis quidem) concipi. [6]Siue enim velis tristes erigere, siue laetos terrere, desperantes animare, superbos frangere, amantes sedare, odientes mitigare, et quis omnes illos numeret dominos cordis humani, scilicet affectus et impetus seu spiritus, impulsores omnium vel virtutum vel vitiorum? [7]Quid inuenias efficatius | 3. [1]I ought to speak now on the use of something so great; [2]but that too in its infinite variety and utility far surpassed the most eloquent eloquence of the most eloquent. [3]This one thing I can contribute for the moment, [4]that experience bears witness to music's being the one thing that, after God's Word, deserves and ought to be celebrated, which rules and governs the human passions (at the moment I must say nothing of beasts) by which men themselves are governed as if by their masters and quite often carried away. [5]Than this praise of music none greater can be imagined, at least by us. [6]For whether you wish to cheer the miserable, or deter the cheerful, encourage the despairing, break the proud, calm the lovers, soothe the haters—and who shall count all those masters of the human heart, the affections and impulses or |

**Vorrede des Heiligen Tewren man Gottes, Doctoris Martini Lutheri, von der Himlischen Kunst Musica, vormals nie Deudsch im Druck ausgangen**

3. [1]NU solte ich auch von dieser edlen Kunst nutz sagen, [2]welcher also gros ist, das jn keiner, er sey so beredt, als er wolle, gnugsam erzelen mag, das einige kan ich jtzt anzeigen, [3]welchs auch die erfarung bezeuget, [4]das nach dem heiligen wort Gottes nichts nicht so billich vnd so hoch zu rhümen vnd zu loben, als eben die Musica, nemlich aus der vrsach, das sie aller bewegung des Menschlichen hertzen (den von den vnuernünfftigen Thieren wil ich jtzt nichts sagen) ein Regiererin, jr mechtig vnd gewaltig ist, durch welche doch offtmals die Menschen, gleich als von jrem Herren, regiert vnd vberwunden werden. [5]DEnn nichts auff Erden krefftiger ist, [6]die Trawrigen frölich, die Frölichen trawrig, die Verzagten hertzenhafftig zu machen, die Hoffertigen zur demut zu reitzen, die hitzige vnd vbermessige Liebe zu stillen vnd dempffen, den neid vnd hass zu mindern, vnd wer kan alle bewegung des Menschlichen hertzen, welche die Leute regieren, vnd entweder zu tugend oder zu laster reitzen vnd treiben, erzelen, diesselbige bewegung des gemüts im zaum zu halten vnd zu regieren, [7]sage ich, ist nichts krefftiger denn die Musica. [8]Ja der heilige Geist lobet vnd ehret selbs diese edle Kunst als seines eigenen ampts Werckzeug, in dem, das er in der heiligen Schrifft bezeuget, das seine Gaben, das ist, die bewegung vnd anreitzung zu allerley tugend vnd guten wercken, durch die Musica den Propheten gegeben werden, Wie wir den im Propheten Elisa sehen, welcher, so er weissagen sol, befihlt er, das man jm ein Spielman brengen sol, Vnd da der Spielman auff der Seiten spielet kam die Hand des HERRN auff jn etc. Widerumb zeuget die Schrifft, das durch die Musica der Sathan, welcher die Leute zu aller vntugend vnd laster treibet, vertrieben werde, Wie denn im Könige Saul angezeigt wird, vber

TABLE 3 Luther's Preface to the *Symphoniae Iucundae* (*cont.*)

| **Martinvs Lvther mvsicae stvdiosis** | **Martin Luther to students of music** |
|---|---|
| quam ipsam Musicam? [8]Honorat eam ipse Spiritus sanctus, ceu sui proprii officii organum, dum in scripturis suis sanctis testatur, dona sua per eam Prophetis illabi, id est omnium virtutum affectus, vt in Eliseo videre est, Rursus per eandem expelli Satanam, id est omnium vitiorum impulsorem, vt in Saule rege Israel monstratur. | spirits that drive all virtues or vices?—[7]what could you find more efficacious than music herself? [8]Even the Holy Ghost honours her as the instrument of his own function, bearing witness in Holy Scripture, that his gifts are instilled into the prophets through music, as may be seen in the case of Elisha [2 Kgs. 3: 15], and again that she drives out Satan, that is the instigator of all vices, as is shown in the case of Saul king of Israel [1 Sam. 16: 23] |
| 4. [1]Vnde non frustra Patres et Prophetae verbo Dei nihil voluerunt esse coniunctius quam Musicam. [2]Inde enim tot Cantica et Psalmi in quibus simul agunt et sermo et vox in animo auditoris, dum in caeteris animantibus et corporibus sola musica sine sermone gesticulatur. [3]Denique homini soli prae caeteris sermo voci ipsos homines, videbis quam multiplex et varius sit Creator gloriosus in donis Musicae dispertitis, quantum differat homo ab homine in voce et verbo, vt alius alium mirabiliter excellat, negant enim posse duos homines inueniri similis per omnia vocis et loquelae, etiam si saepius imitari alii alios videantur, velut alii aliorum simiae. | 4. [1]It was therefore not in vain that the fathers and prophets chose nothing to be more closely linked to God's Word than music. [2]That was the cause of all those canticles and Psalms, in which words and song [literally 'voice'] act together on the listener's mind, whereas in the case of other living beings and bodies music expresses itself alone without words. [3]Then again man alone apart from the rest was given the gift of words combined with song, so that he should know that he ought to praise God, that is with loud preaching and words combined with sweet melody. [4]And if you compare human beings themselves you will see how manifold and varied the glorious Creator is in distributing the gifts of music, how much they differ from each other in song and speech, so that one marvellously excels another, for they say that no two persons can be found |

**Vorrede des Heiligen Tewren man Gottes Doctoris Martini Lutheri, von der Himlischen Kunst Musica, vormals nie Deudsch im Druck ausgangen**

welchen, wenn der Geist Gottes kam, so nam Dauid die Harffen vnd spielet mit seiner Hand, so erquicket sich Saul, vnd ward besser mit jm, vnd der böse Geist weich von jm.

4. [1]Darumb haben die heiligen Veter vnd die Propheten nicht vergebens das wort Gottes in mancherley Gesenge, [2]Seitenspiel gebracht, dauon wir denn so mancherley köstliche Gesenge vnd Psalm haben, welche beide mit worten vnd auch mit dem gesang vnd klang die hertzen der Menschen bewegen. In den vnuernünfftigen Thieren aber, Seitenspielen vnd andern Instrumenten, da höret man allein den gesang, laut vnd klang, one rede vnd wort, [3]Dem Menschen aber ist allein vor den andern Creaturen die stimme mit der rede gegeben, das er solt künnen vnd wissen, Gott mit Gesengen vnd worten zugleich zu loben, Nemlich mit dem hellen, klingenden predigen vnd rhümen von Gottes güte vnd gnade, darinnen schöne wort vnd lieblicher klang zugleich würde gehöret. [4]WEnn aber einer die Menschen gegen einander helt vnd eines jglichen stimme betrachtet, So befindet er, wie Gott so ein herrlicher vnd manchfeltiger Schöpffer ist, in den stimmen der Menschen aus zu teilen, wie so eine grosse vnterscheid der stimme vnd sprache halben vnter den Menschen ist, wie hierinnen einer dem andern also weit vberlegen ist. Denn man sagt, das man nicht zween Menschen künne finden, welche gantz gleiche stimme, sprach vnd ausrede haben möchten, Vnd ob gleich einer sich auff des andern weise mit hohem vleis gibet, vnd jm gleich sein vnd wie der Aff alles nach thun wil.

TABLE 3 Luther's Preface to the *Symphoniae Iucundae* (*cont.*)

| Martinvs Lvther mvsicae stvdiosis | Martin Luther to students of music |
|---|---|
| | alike in all respects of song and speech, even though some are often seen to imitate others as if they were their apes. |
| 5. [1]Vbi autem tandem accesserit studium et Musica artificialis, quae naturalem corrigat, excolat et explicet. [2]Hic tandem gustare cum stupore licet (sed non comprehendere) absolutam et perfectam sapientiam Dei in opere suo mirabili Musicae, in quo genere hoc excellit, quod vna et eadem voce canitur suo tenore pergente, pluribus interim vocibus circum circa mirabiliter ludentibus, exultantibus et iucundissimis gestibus eandem ornantibus, et velut iuxta eam diuinam quandam choream ducentibus, vt iis, qui saltem modice afficiuntur, nihil mirabilius hoc seculo extare videatur. [3]Qui vero non afficiuntur, nae illi vere amusi et digni sunt, qui aliquem Merdipoetam interim audiant vel porcorum Musicam. | 5. [1]But when in time there are added the study and technical knowledge of music to correct, enhance, and develop natural ability, [2]then at last we may relish with amazement (but not understand) God's absolute and perfect wisdom in his marvellous work of music, in which field the greatest excellence is that, while one and the same voice continues in its course, several voices play, exult, and adorn it with the most delightful gestures all round it in wondrous ways, and so to speak lead a kind of divine dance, so that those who are even moderately affected by it think there is nothing more wonderful in this world. [3]But those who are not affected by it are truly without the Muses, and worthy to listen to some shit-poet or the music of pigs. |
| 6. [1]Sed res est maior, quam vt hac breuitate vtilitates eius describi queant. [2]Tu, iuuenis optime, commendatam hanc nobilem, salutarem et laetam creaturam tibi habeas, qua et tuis affectibus interim medearis contra turpes libidines et prauas societates. [3]Deinde assuescas in hac creatura Creatorem agnoscere et laudare, [4]Et deprauatos animos qui hac pulcherrima et natura et arte | 6. [1]But music is too great a thing for its benefits to be described in this brief compass. [2]May you, excellent young man, accept the commendation of this noble, salutary, and happy creature, to be on occasion medicine for your passions against shameful lusts and evil company. [3]Then may you become accustomed in this creature to recognize and praise the Creator; [4]and with the greatest care shun and avoid the depraved minds that abuse |

**Vorrede des Heiligen Tewren man Gottes Doctoris Martini Lutheri, von der Himlischen Kunst Musica, vormals nie Deudsch im Druck ausgangen**

5. [1]Wo aber die natürliche Musica durch die Kunst gescherfft vnd polirt wird, [2]da sihet vnd erkennet man erst zum teil (denn gentzlich kans nicht begrieffen noch verstanden werden) mit grosser verwunderung die grosse vnd volkomene weisheit Gottes in seinem wunderbarlichen werck der Musica, in welcher vor allem das seltzam vnd wol zu verwundern ist, das einer eine schlechte weise oder Tenor (wie es die Musici heissen) her singet, neben welcher drey, vier oder fünff andere stimmen auch gesungen werden, die vmb solche schlechte weise oder Tenor, gleich als mit jauchtzen gerings herumbher, vmb solchen Tenor spielen vnd springen vnd mit mancherley art vnd klang dieselbige weise wunderbarlich zieren vnd schmücken vnd gleich wie einen Himlischen Tantzreien füren, Also das die jenigen, so solches ein wenig verstehen vnd dadurch bewegt werden, sich des hefftig verwundern müssen vnd meinen, das nichts seltzamers in der Welt sey, denn ein solcher Gesang mit viel stimmen geschmückt. [3]Wer aber dazu kein lust noch liebe hat vnd durch solch lieblich Wunderwerck nicht beweget wird, das mus warlich ein grober Klotz sein, der nicht werd ist, das er solche liebliche Musica, sondern das wüste, wilde Eselgeschrey des Chorals, oder der Hunde oder Sewe Gesang vnd Musica höre.

6. [1]WAs sol ich aber viel sagen. Es ist die sach vnd der nutz dieser edlen Kunst viel grösser vnd reicher, denn das es also in einer kürtze möge erzelt werden, [2]Darumb wil ich jederman, vnd sonderlich den jungen Leuten, diese Kunst befohlen vnd sie hiemit vermanet haben, das sie jnen diese köstliche, nützliche vnd fröliche Creatur Gottes tewr, lieb vnd werd sein lassen, durch welcher erkentnis vnd vleissige vbung sie zuzeiten böse gedancken vertreiben vnd auch böse Geselschafft vnd andere vntugend vermeiden können, [3]Darnach das sie sich auch gewehnen, Gott den Schöpffer in dieser Creatur zu erkennen, zu loben vnd preisen, [4]vnd die jenigen, so durch vnzucht verderbet vnd dieser schönen Natur vnd Kunst (wie denn die vnzüchtigen Poeten auch mit jrer Natur vnd Kunst thun) zu schendlicher, toller, vnzüchtiger liebe missbrauchen, mit allem vleis fliehen vnd vermeiden vnd gewis

TABLE 3 Luther's Preface to the *Symphoniae Iucundae* (*cont.*)

| **Martinvs Lvther mvsicae stvdiosis** | **Martin Luther to students of music** |
|---|---|
| abutuntur, ceu impudici poetae, ad suos insanos amores, et summo studio caueto et vitato, certus, quod Diabolus eos rapiat contra naturam, vt quae hoc dono vult et debet Deum solum laudare autorem, isti adulterini filii, rapina ex dono Dei facta, colunt eodem hostem Dei et aduersarium naturae et artis huius iucundissimae. [5]Bene in Domino vale. | this most beautiful thing, both art and nature, like indecent poets, for their own mad loves, certain that the devil seizes them against nature, so that she who wishes and ought by this gift to praise only God its author, is developed by those bastard sons, the raiders of God's gift, as an enemy of God and an adversary of this most delightful nature and art.[c] [5]Farewell in the Lord. |

c To make sense of this passage it is necessary to read neither *eodem* nor *eadem* but *eandem*, and take *colunt* as an error for the consecutive subjunctive *colant*. But the German exhibits a similar anacoluthon: *welche Natur* is a subject without a predicate.

**Vorrede des Heiligen Tewren man Gottes, Doctoris Martini Lutheri, von der Himlischen Kunst Musica, vormals nie Deudsch im Druck ausgangen**

wissen sollen, das solche der Teuffel, wider die Natur, also treibet, welche Natur, dieweil sie allein Gott, den Schöpffer aller Creaturn, mit solcher edlen Gabe sol vnd wil ehren vnd loben, so werden diese vngeratene Kinder vnnd Wechselbelge durch den Satan dazu getrieben, das sie solche Gabe Gott dem HERRN nemen vnd rauben vnd damit den Teuffel, welcher ein Feind Gottes, der Natur vnd dieser lieblichen Kunst ist, ehren vnd damit dienen. [5]Hiemit will ich euch alle Gott dem HERRN befohlen haben. Geben zu Wittemberg. Im 1538. Jare. Vorrede des Heiligen tewren Man Gottes, Doctoris Martini Lutheri, von der Himlischen Kunst Musica, Vormals nie Deudsch im Druck ausgangen.

APPENDIX 2

# Comparing 'Law and Grace' (1529–1550)

In Chapter 4, we compare a cross sample of versions of Lucas Cranach's image *Law and Grace* that include biblical references and quotations or paraphrases:

- Lucas Cranach the Elder, 1529, painting with textual gloss in German script, 82.2 cm × 118 cm, Herzogliches Museum Gotha (FR no. 221), sometimes called 'Damnation and Redemption' or simply the 'Gotha painting'
- Lucas Cranach the Elder, 1530, woodcut with textual gloss in German type, 23.3 cm × 32.4 cm, The British Museum, London (KF no. 353)
- Lucas Cranach the Younger, 1550, painting with textual gloss in Latin type, 19 cm × 25.5 cm, Brod Gallery, London (KF no. 355).

The images, the glosses, the exact wording of the glosses, and whether the glosses are in Latin or German varies slightly across three versions.

In the 1530 version, the images are divided into subsections with headings: 'Vom Regenbogen und Gericht' ('Of the Rainbow and Judgment'); 'Vom Teufel und Tode' ('Of the Devil and Death'); 'Von Mose und den Propheten' ('Of Moses and the Prophets'); 'Vom Menschen' ('Of People'); 'Vom Täufer' ('Of the Baptist'); 'Vom Tod und Lamm' ('Of Death and the Lamb'). These divisions help the viewer to parse individual icons within the narrative and theological structure.

The table below provides a listing of the biblical iconography used across these versions of *Law and Grace*, compared with their biblical references and textual glosses.

 | DOI:10.1163/9789004527430_011

TABLE 4 Iconography, biblical references and textual glosses for *Law and Grace* (1529, 1530, and 1550)

| **Bible iconography** | **Biblical reference and paraphrase of glosses** |
|---|---|
| *After the Flood* | |
| 1. Christ rules in heaven. Gen. 1.1–31, John 1.1–31 | 1. Rom. 1.18. From heaven, God revealed his wrath on unrighteous people |
| 2. In the Garden of Eden, Adam and Eve are tempted by the snake and eat the apple from the Tree of Knowledge (the Fall). Gen. 2.1–3.24 | 2. Rom. 3.23. We are all sinners and live sinfully |
| *Devil and Death* | |
| 3. During their Exodus from their slavery in Egypt the people of Israel are plagued in the desert by serpents as a punishment, so a bronze serpent is raised up and the people are told to look at the serpent to be healed. Num.21.4–9, John 3.14. | 3. 1 Cor. 15.3, 15–28. Failure to live by the law brings death |
| 5. Adam, now clothed in a loincloth, is sent into the flames fiery hell. Gen. 3.24, Mt. 13.42 | 5. Rom. 4.15. Failure to live by the law brings wrath of God |
| *Moses and the Prophets* | |
| 4. Moses is granted the tablets of the law. Deut. 5.1–23 | 4. Rom. 3.1–3, 27–30. Jews and circumcision |
| 6. The commandments, the law, history and the prophets (Torah, Prophets) of the Old Testament are gathered. A group of patriarchs stand together. The Old Testament, passim | 4. Mt. 11.8–15. The prophets foretold John the Baptist |
| *Humanity* | |
| 7. Adam stands looking at Christ. (Not in the Bible, but implied in 1 Cor. 15.20–22) | 7. Rom. 1.17 (1529, 1530). The righteous will live by faith<br>Gal. 5.6 (1550). We are saved by grace alone |
| 7a. The shepherds with their flock (Gotha, 1530 only). Lk. 2.8–17 | 7a. Rom. 3.28. People are justified by faith |
| 7a. The Annunciation. The Holy Spirit in heaven shines a light at the Virgin Mary (1530 and 1550 only). Lk. 1.26–38 | 7b. Isa. 7.14. A virgin will conceive |

TABLE 4 Iconography, biblical references and textual glosses for *Law and Grace* (*cont.*)

| Bible iconography | Biblical reference and paraphrase of glosses |
| --- | --- |
| *Salvation* | |
| 8. John the Baptist points to Jesus and identifies him as the Messiah. John 1.6–36 | 8. John 1.36. This is the Lamb of God |
| 9. Christ is crucified on the cross. John 19.16–37 | 9. 1 Pet. 1.2 (1530 only, no text 1550). Christ's blood and sacrifice takes away the sins of the world |
| *Death and the Lamb* | |
| 10. While in the tomb, Christ harrows Hell and slays the dragon and tramples death. (1530, the Lamb of God, holding a resurrection pennant, does the trampling). Eph. 4.7–10, 1 Cor. 15.55 The stone is rolled away from the entrance to the tomb. John 20.1–2 | 10. 1 Cor. 15.54–55, 57. Death has been defeated by Jesus Christ |
| 10a. Christ ascends to heaven. (1529 shows the Ascension, 1530 and 1550 show Christ the King, image 1). Acts 1.6–11 | No gloss 1529. See Image 1 for 1530, 1550 |

# Bibliography

## Primary Sources

### *Archival Primary Sources*


*Annaberger Schulordnung*, Stadtbibliothek Leipzig.

Bayerische Staatsbibliothek, clm 10277, fos. 2$^r$–56$^v$.

Berlin, Staatsbibliothek Preußischer Kulturbesitz, MS lat. Quarto 479, fos. 1–37.

*Compendium de Discantu Mensurabili*, Erfurt, Bibliotheca Amploniana, MS 94.

Maastricht, Regionaal Historisch Centrum Limburg MS Collection 14B.002A: Kapittel van St Servaas te Maastricht, 980–1.

*Visitationsakten der Superintendatur Eilenburg* 1574, Landeshauptarchiv Sachsen-Anhalt Abteilung Merseburg, Rep. 47, Kap. II, Nr. 43, BL 99.

*Visitationsbericht des Meißnischen Kreises: Visitationsabschied für die Stadt Döbeln*, Hauptstaatsarchiv Dresden, Loc. 1987, XVI.


### *Printed Primary Sources*


Becker, Cornelius, *Der Psalter Davids Gesangweis* (Leipzig: Apel Lantzenberger, 1602).

Birck, Sixt, *Beel: Ain Herrliche Tragedi wider die Abgötterey auß dem Propheten Daniel darinn angezaigt wirt durch was mittel ain rechte Religion in ainem Regiment oder Policey mög angericht werden* (Augsburg: Philipp Ulhart the Elder, 1539).

Bugenhagen, Johannes, *Die Historia des leydens vnd der Aufferstehung vnsers Herrn Jhesu Christi aus den vier Evangelien, durch Johannem Bugenhagen Pomer vleyssig zusammen bracht* (Wittenberg: Hans Weiß, 1526).

Bullinger, Heinrich, *Warhaffte Bekanntnuß Warhaffte Bekanntnuß der dieneren der kirchen zu Zürych: was sy vß Gottes wort, mit der heyligen allgemeinen Christenlichen Kirchen glaubind vnd leerind, in sonderheit aber von dem Nachtmal vnsers herren Jesu Christi: mit gebürlicher Antwort vff das vnbegründt ergerlich schmähen, verdam[m]en vnd schelten D. Martin Luthers* (Zürich: Christoph Froschauer, 1545).

Burmeister, Joachim, *Hypomnematum musicae poeticae* (Rostock: Reusner, 1599).

*Effigies Monvmenti in Reproborvm Rebinorvm Iudæorvm Apostatrvm Confvsionem et Ignominiam. Ad VVitebergensis Templi oppidani murum, versus ortum antiquitus positi* (VVitebergæ: Excusa typis VVolffgangi Meissneri, M. D. XCVI).

*Etlich Cristlich lider / Lobgesang / vnd Psalm / dem rai-/nen wort Gottes gemeß / auf der / heyligen schrifft / durch mancher-/ley hochgelerter gemacht / in der Kirchen zum singen / wie es dann / zum ttayl berayt zu Wittenberg / in übung ist* ('Wittenberg' [Nürnberg: Jobst Gutknecht], M.D.X.iiij [1524]).

*Eyn Enchiridion oder Handbüchlein. / eynem ytzlichen Christen fast nutzlich bey sich zuhaben / zur stetter vbung vnd trachtung geystlicher gesenge vnd Psalmen / Rechtschaffen vnd kunstlich verteutscht* (Erfurt: In der Permenter Gasse, zum Ferbefaß, 1524).

Fabricius, Laurentius, *De Schemhamphorasch usu et abusu apud Iudaeos orations duae* (Wittenberg: Johann Dörfler, 1596).

Finck, Hermann, *Practica musica Hermanni Finckii, exempla variorum signorum, proportionum et canonum, iudicium de tonis, ac quaedam de arte suaviter et artificiose cantandi continens* (Wittenberg: Georg Rhau, 1556).

Foppens, Jean-François, *Bibliotheca Belgica, sive Virorum in Belgio vita, scriptisque illustrium* (Brussels: Petrus Foppens, 1739).

Gesner, Conrad, *Pandectae* (Zürich: Christoph Froschauer, 1548).

Greff, Joachim, *Ein lieblich vnd nutzbarlich spil von dem Patriarchen jacob und seinen zwelff Sönen. Aus dem Ersten Buch Mosi gezogen, und zu Magdeburg auf dem Schützenhoff ym 1534. jar gehalten* (Magdeburg: Michael Lotter, 1534).

Greff, Joachim, *Tragoedia des Buchs Iudith jnn Deudsche Reim verfasset durch Joachim Greff von Zwickaw nützlich zu lesen* (Wittenberg: Georg Rhaw, 1536).

Greff, Joachim, *Das Leiden vnd Aufferstehung vnsers Herrn Jhesu Christi, aus den vier Euangelisten durch D. Johan Bugenhagen Pomern vleissig zusamen gebracht, vnd nachmals durch Joachimum Greff vo[n] Zwickau jnn Deutsch Reim verfasset, seliglich vnd tröstlich zu lessen* (Wittenberg: Nickel Schirlentz, 1538).

Greff, Joachim, *Ein Geistliches schönes newes spil auff das heilige Osterfest gestellet* (Magdeburg: Michael Lotter, 1542).

Greff, Joachim, *Lazarus: Vom Tode durch Christum am vierden tage erwecket* (Wittenberg: [Rhau(?) Frischmut(?)], 1545).

Hoë von Hoënegg, Matthias, *Chur Sächsische Evangelische Jubel Frewde: In der Churfürstlichen Sächsischen Schloß Kirchen zu Dreßden, theils vor, theils bey wehrendem, angestalten Jubelfest, neben andern Solenniteten, auch mit Christlichen Predigten [...] gehalten. Nach der Vorrede, findet der Christliche Leser, mit was für Solenniteten das Evangelische Jubelfest, in [...] Dreßden, seye gehalten worden* (Leipzig: Lamberg und Kloseman, 1617).

Jacobi, John [Johann] Christian, *Psalmodia Germanica: Or, A Specimen of Divine Hymns, Translated from the High Dutch. Together with Their Proper Tunes and Thorough Bass* (London: J. Young in St Paul's Churchyard, 1722).

Karlstadt, Andreas Bodenstein von, *Von Abtuhung der Bilder und Das Keyn Bedtler undther den Christen seyn sollen* (Wittenberg: [n. pub.], 1522).

*Klug'sches Gesangbuch*, 2nd edn (Wittenberg: Klug, 1533).

Krüger, Bartholomäus, *Historia unseres Herrn und Heilandes Jesu Christi* (Augsburg: Matthäus Franck, 1580).

Lacher, Ambrosius, *Euclides Elementorum libri VI sumptu et opera Ambrosii Lacher de Merspurgk excussa* (Frankfurt an der Oder: Magister Ambrosius, 1506).

Lacher, Ambrosius, *Epytoma Johannis de Muris in musicam Boecii* (Frankfurt an der Oder: Magister Ambrosius, 1508).

Lampadius, Auctor, *Compendium Musices* (Bern: Samuel Apiarius, 1554).

Lippius, Johannes, *Synopsis musicae novae omnino verae atque methodicae universae, in omnis sophiae praegustum [Parergon] inventae disputatae et propositae omnibus philomusis* (Strassburg: Paulus Ledertz typis Carolus Kieffer, 1612).

Luther, Martin, *Eyn Sermon von dem Wucher Doct. Mar. Luther Augustiner zu Witte[n] bergk* (Wittenberg: Johann Rhau-Grunenbeg, 1520).

Luther, Martin, *Von Kauffshandlung vnd wucher* (Wittenberg: Hans Lufft, 1522).

Luther, Martin, *Eine Heerpredigt widder den Tuercken* (Wittenberg: Nickel Schirlenz, 1529).

Luther, Martin, *Libellus de Ritv et Moribvs Turcorum Ante LXX. Annos Aeditus VVittemberge apud Iohannem Lufft* (Wittenberg: Hans Lufft, 1530).

Luther, Martin, *Geistliche lieder auffs new gebessert zu Wittemberg* (Wittenberg: Klug, 1535).

Luther, Martin, *Der XXIX. Psalm Davids [...] Mit einer vorrede D. Martini Luthers* (Wittenberg: Hans Lufft, 1536).

Luther, Martin, *Symphoniae iucundae atque adeo breves quatuor vocum* (Wittenberg: Walther, 1538).

Luther, Martin, *Eine Heerpredigt Wider den Türcken* (Wittenberg: George Rhau, 1541).

Luther, Martin, *Verlegung des Alcoran Bruder Richardi Prediger Ordens Anno 1300 verdeutscht durch D. Martin Luther* (Wittenberg: Hans Lufft, 1542).

Luther, Martin, *Von den Jüden und jren Lügen D. M. Luther, Gedrückt zu Wittemberg Durch Hans Lufft* (Wittenberg: Hans Lufft, 1543).

Luther, Martin, *Die Propheten alle Deudsch. D. Mart[in] Lut[her] Gedruckt zu Wittemberg Durch Hans Lufft M.D.XLIII* (Wittenberg: Hans Lufft, 1544).

Luther, Martin, *Biblia: das ist; Die gantze Heilige Schrifft: Deudsch Auffs new zugericht D. Mart[in]. Luth[er]. Begnadet mit Kurfürstlicher zu Sachsen Freiheit. Gedruckt zu Wittemberg Durch Hans Lufft M.D.XLV* (Wittenberg: Hans Lufft, 1545).

Luther, Martin, *Abbildung des Bapstum durch Mart[in] Luth[er] D. Wittemberg* (Wittenberg: [Hans Lufft], 1545).

Luther, Martin, *De usuris taxanda, ad pastores Ecclesiarum Commonefactio* (Frankfurt [a.M.]: Peter Br[a]ub[ach], 1554).

Margarita, Anton, *Der gantz Jüdisch glaub, sampt ainer gründtlichen und warhafften anzaygunge aller Satzungen, Ceremonien, Gebethen, haymliche und offentlichen Gebreuch deren sich dye Juden halten, durch das gantz Jar. Mit schönen und gegründten Argumenten wyder jren Glauben* (Augsburg: Heinrich Steiner, 1530).

Mathesius, Johann Balthasar, *Herrn Magister Johannes Mathesii weyland berühmten und frommen Pfarrers im Joachimsthal Lebens-Beschreibung* (Dresden: Zimmermann, 1705).

Mathesius, Johannes, *Historien von deß Ehrwürdigen in Gott seligen theuren Manns Gottes, D. Martin Luthers, Anfang, Lehre, Leben* (Nürnberg: Kauffmann, 1608).

Melanchthon, Philipp, *Loci Communes, das ist die furnehmsten Artikel Christlicher lere Philippi Melanch[thonis] Aus dem Latin verdeudscht durch Justum Jonam* (Wittenberg: Rhaw, 1536).

Melanchthon, Philipp, *Loci Commvnes Theologici Recens Collecti et Recogniti a Philippo Melanthone [sic], Vitebergae M.D.XXXVI* (Wittenberg: Peter Seitz, 1536).

Melanchthon, Philipp, *Loci Communes, das ist die furnehmsten Artikel Christlicher lere Philipp. Melanch[thons] Aus dem Latin verdeudscht durch Justum Jonam* (Wittenberg: Peter Seitz, 1539).

Monro, Robert, *Monro His Expedition vvith the vvorthy Scots Regiment (called Mac-Keyes Regiment)* (London: William Jones, 1637).

Petri, Olaus, *Swenske songer eller wisor nw på prentade / förökade* [...] *utsatte* (Stockholm: Kungliga Tryckeriet, 1536).

Porchetus, Salvaticus, *Victoria Porcheti aduersus impios, in quia ex sacris literis, tum ex dictis Talmud, ac Caballistarum, et aliorum omnium authorum, quos Hebraei recipient, monstratur veritas catholicae fidei* (Paris: François Regnault, 1520).

Rebhun, Paul, *Ein Geistlich Spiel von der Gotfurchtigen und keuschen Frauen Susannen, gantz lustig und fruchtbarlich zu lesen* (Zwickau: Meyerpeck, 1536).

Reuchlin, Johann, *De Arte Cabbalistica Libri Tres* (Hagenau: Thomas Anshelmus, 1517).

Sachs, Hans, *Die Wittembergisch Nachtigall, die man yetz höret uberall* (Bamberg: Georg Erlinger, 1523).

Sachs, Hans, *Ein Epitaphium / oder klagred ob der leich / D. Martini Luthers* (Nürnberg: Georg Wächter, 1546).

Sachs, Hans, *Der Narrenfresser. Mehr das Narren Bad* (Nürnberg: Georg Merckel, 1553).

Sachs, Hans, *Die ganz Passio*, in Hans Sachs, *Sehr herrliche schöne und warhaffte Gedicht geistlich unnd weltlich allerley Art* (Nürnberg: Christoff Heußler, 1558).

Sachs, Hans, *Ein Faßnacht Spil / Die fünff Elenden wandrer / mit sechs personen / kůrtz-weylig zu hőren* (Nürnberg: George Merkel, 1560).

Sachs, Hans, 'Ein lustig Faßnachtsspiel / mit drey Personen / Das Narrenschneiden', in Hans Sachs, *Das erste Buch, Sehr herrliche schöne & warhaffte Gedicht. Sehr Herrliche, Schöne vnd Warhaffte Gedicht Geistlich vnd Weltlich allerley art, als ernstliche Tragödien, liebliche Comödien* (Augsburg: Hans Kruger, 1612), pp. 938–46.

Sapidus, Johannes, *Anabion sive Lazarus redividus* (Köln: Gymnich, 1539).

Saur, Abraham, *Theatrum Urbium: Warhafftige Contrafeytung und Summarische Beschreibung vast aller Vornehmen und namhafftigen Stätten, Schlössern und Klöster* (Frankfurt a.M.: Nicolaus Bassaeus, 1595).

Schelhorn, Johann Georg, *Amoenitates Literariae: Quibus Variae Observationes, Scripta item quaedam anecdota & rariora Opuscula exhibentur* (Frankfurt a.M. and Leipzig: Daniel Bartholomaei und Sohn, 1725).

Schwenck, Lorenz, *Lob vnd Preis, Der Himlischen Kunst MVSICA: Mit einer herrlichen, schönen Vorrede, des seligen, tewren, hochbegabten Mannes, Doctoris Martini Lutheri, vormals deudsch im Drucke nihe ausgegangen durch Johan Walther* (Wittenberg: Lorenz Schwenck, 1564).

Selnecker, Nikolaus, *Historica Oratio: Vom Leben und Wandel des Ehrwirdigen Herrn vnd thewren Mannes Gottes D. Martini Lutheri* (Leipzig: H. & V. Werdenstein, 1576).

Seydel, Matthäus, *Evangelia auffs einfeltigste in gemeine Teutsche reime gebracht* (Nürnberg: Christoff Heußler, 1565).

Sleidanus, Johannes, *Warhafftige Beschreibunge allerley fürnemer Hendel, so sich in Glaubens vnnd anderen Weltlichen sachen, bey Regierung des Großmechtigsten Keyser Carls des Fünfften, mehrerntheyls in Teutscher Nation zugetragen* (Frankfurt a.M.: [Sigmund Feyerabend], 1565).

Slüter, Joachim, *Geystlike leder vppt nye gebetert tho Wittenberch / dorch D. Martin Luther* (Rostock: Ludwig Ovetz, 1531).

Spangenberg, Cyriacus, *Eine Christliche Comoedia Von dem Cananeischen Weiblein, Matthei am 15. Capittel* (Schmalkalden: Michel Schmück, 1589).

Spangenberg, Cyriacus, *Comoedia: Ein geistlich Spiel Vom Euangelio am Sontage Oculi, von dem besessenen, tauben vnd stummen Menschen, Luce am 11.* (Schmalkalden: Michel Schmück, 1590).

*Summarie von königlichen und keyserlichen darzu landt und lehen rechten, genannt Der Schwabenspiegel* (Augsburg: Zeyner, 1473).

Wild, Sebastian, *Die Passion und Auffersteehung Christi*, in Sebastian Wild, *Schöner Comedien und Tragedien zwölff: Auß heiliger Göttlicher schrift und auch auß etlichen Historien gezogen* (Augsburg: Matthäus Franck, 1566).

Zapf, Georg Wilhelm, *Über das Leben und die Verdienste Johann von Dalbergs* (Augsburg: [n. pub.], 1789).

### *Edited Primary Sources*

Afflighen, Johannes of, *De Musica cum Tonario*, ed. by J. Smits van Waesberghe, Corpus Scriptorum de Musica [CSM], 1 (Rome: American Institute of Musicology, 1950).

Aquinas, St Thomas, *Summa Theologiae*, ed. by Thomas Gilby, 60 vols [ST] (London: Blackfriars, 1963–66).

Augustine, *De diversis quaestionibus octoginta tribus. De octo Dulcitii quaestionibus*, ed. by A. Mutzenbecher, Corpus Christianorum Series Latina [CCSL], 44A (Tournhout: Brepols, 1975).

Boethius, Anicius Manlius Severinus, *De institutione musica libri quinque*, ed. by Gottfried Friedlein, Bibliotheca scriptorum Graecorum et Romanorum Teubneriana (Leipzig: Teubner, 1867).

Boethius, Anicius Manlius Severinus, *Commentum Oxoniense in musicam Boethii*, ed. by Matthias Hochadel, Veröffentlichungen der Musikhistorischen Kommission der Bayrischen Akademie der Wissenschaften, 16 (München: Beck, 2002).

Burmeister, Joachim, *Joachim Burmeister: Musical Poetics*, trans. and ed. by Benito V. Rivera (New Haven, CT: Yale University Press, 1993).

Carlyle, Thomas, *Critical and Miscellaneous Essays in Five Volumes*, II (London: Chapman and Hall, 1899).

Coverdale, Myles, *Remains of Myles Coverdale, Bishop of Exeter*, ed. by George Pearson, Parker Society, 14 (Cambridge: Cambridge University Press, 1846).

De Muris, Johannes, *Musica speculativa secundum Boetium*, ed. by Christoph Falkenroth, Beihefte zum Archiv für Musikwissenschaft, 34 (Stuttgart: Steiner, 1992).

De Wette, Wilhelm Martin Leberecht, *Dr Martin Luthers Briefe, Sendschreiben und Bedenken*, 6 vols (Berlin: Reimer, 1828), v.

Denecker, T., B. Janssens, and L. Jocqué, eds, *Corpus Christianorum Continuatio Mediaevalis* [CCCM] (Turnhout: Brepols, 1967–).

*Die Musik in Geschichte und Gegenwart: Allgemeine Enzyklopädie der Musik* [MGG], ed. by Friedrich Blume, 17 vols (Kassel: Bärenreiter, 1949–68).

Durand, Guillaume, *Rationale divinorum officium* I–IV, ed. by Anselme Davril OSB and Timothy M. Thibodeau, CCCM, 140 (Turnhout: Brepols, 1995).

Erasmus, Desiderus, *Moriae encomium (1509)* [*The Praise of Folly*], trans. by Clarence Miller (New Haven, CT: Yale University Press, 2003).

Gerbert, Martin, ed., *Scriptores ecclesiastici de musica sacra potissimum ex variis Italiae, Galliae et Germaniae codicibus manuscriptis collecti et nunc primum publica luce donati* [GS], 3 vols (St Blasien: Typis San Blasianis, 1784; repr. Hildesheim: Georg Olms, 1963).

Gess, Felician, ed., *Akten und Briefe zur Kirchenpolitik Herzog Georgs von Sachsen* (Leipzig: Teubner, 1905).

Gregory the Great, *S. Gregorii Magni registrum epistularum libri VII–XIV*, ed. by D. Norberg, CCSL, 104A (Tournhout: Brepols, 1982).

Helt, Georg, *Georg Helts Buchwechsel*, ed. by Otto Clemen, Archiv für Reformationsgeschichte Ergänzungsband, 2 (Leipzig: Verlag von M. Heinsius Nachfolger, 1907).

Herbenus, Matthäus, *De natura cantus ac miraculis vocis*, ed. by Joseph Smits van Waesberghe, Beiträge zur Rheinischen Musikgeschichte, 22 (Köln: Arno Volk, 1957).

Janssens, B., ed., *Corpus Christianorum Series Graeca* (Turnhout: Brepols, 1957–).

Liège, Jacques de, *Jacobi Leodiensis Speculum musicae*, ed. by Roger Bragard, CSM, 3, 7 vols (Rome: American Institute of Musicology, 1955–73).

Luther, Martin, *D. Martin Luthers sowol in Deutscher als Lateinischer Sprache verfertigte und aus der letztern in die erstere übersetzte Sämtliche Schriften* [W1], ed. by Johann George Walch (Halle: Johann Justinus Gebauer, 1740–53).

Luther, Martin, *D. Martin Luthers Werke: Kritische Gesamtausgabe* [WA], ed. by Joachim Karl Friedrich Knaake and others (Weimar: Hermann Böhlau, 1883–1985).

Luther, Martin, *Luthers geistliche Lieder und Kirchengesänge*, ed. by Markus Jenny, Archiv zur Weimarer Ausgabe der Werke Martin Luthers [AWA], 4 (Köln: Böhlau, 1985).

Luther, Martin, *Geist aus Luther's Schriften*, ed. by Friedrich Wilhelm Lomler and others (Darmstadt: Verlag Karl Wilhelm Leske, 1830).

Luther, Martin, *Luther's Works: American Edition* [LW], ed. by Jaroslav Pelikan, Helmut T. Lehmann, and others (St Louis, MO: Concordia, 1955–).

Luther, Martin, *Luther's Works, Volume 53: Liturgy and Hymns*, ed. by Ulrich S. Leupold (Minneapolis: Fortress, 1965).

Maimonides, Moses, *The Guide of the Perplexed*, ed. by Shlomo Pines, 3 vols (Chicago: University of Chicago Press, 1963).

Melanchthon, Philipp, *Corpus Reformatorum* [CR], ed. by Karl Gottlob Bretschneider and others (Braunschweig: C. A. Schwetschke & Sohn, 1834–1946).

Melanchthon, Philipp, *Melanchthoniana Paedagogica: Eine Ergänzung zu den Werken Melanchthons im Corpus Reformatorum*, ed. by Karl Hartfelder (Leipzig: Teubner, 1892).

Migne, Jacques-Paul, ed., *Patrologiae Cursus Completus, Series Graeca* [PG], 161 vols (Paris: Imprimerie Catholique, 1857–88).

Mirandola, Giovanni Pico della, *Über die Würde des Menschen*, trans. by Norbert Baumgarten, ed. by August Buck, Philosophische Bibliothek, 427 (Hamburg: Felix Meiner, 1990).

Müller, Nikolaus, ed., *Die Wittenberger Bewegung 1521 und 1522* (Leipzig: Heinsius, 1911).

Narhamer, Johan[n], *Historia Jobs: 1546*, ed. by Barbara Könneker and Wolfgang Michael, Arbeiten zur mittleren deutschen Sprache und Literatur, 12 (Bern: Peter Lang, 1983).

Neumann, Werner, and Hans-Joachim Schulze, eds, *Bach-Dokumente*, 7 vols (Kassel: Bärenreiter, 1963–79), II (1969).

Pallas, Karl, ed., *Die Registraturen der Kirchenvisitationen im ehemals sächsischen Kurkreise*, I: *Die Ephorien Wittenberg, Kemberg und Zahna* (Halle: Otto Hendel, 1906).

Pralle, Ludwig, and Gregor Richter, eds, *Die Fuldaer Stadtpfarrei*, II: *Urkunden der Fuldaer Stadtpfarrei*, Veröffentlichungen des Fuldaer Geschichtsvereins, 32 (Fulda: Parzeller, 1952).

Pseudo-Aquinas, *Ars musice*, ed. by Mario di Martino (Naples: Eugenio de Simone, 1933).

Rhau, Georg, *Symphoniae jucundae 1538*, ed. by Hans Albrecht, Georg Rhau Musikdrucke, 3 (Kassel: Bärenreiter, 1959).

Sachs, Hans, *Hans Sachs: Fastnachtsspiele und Gedichte. Mit einem Nachwort von Rudolf Mirbt*, ed. by Reinhard Barth (München: Christian Kaiser Verlag, 1988).

Sycamber, Rutgerus de Venray, *Dialogus de musica*, ed. by Fritz Soddemann, Beiträge zur Rheinischen Musikgeschichte, 54 (Köln: Arno Volk, 1963).

Tinctoris, Johannes, *Complexus effectuum musices* (*c.* 1474–5), in *Johannes Tinctoris Opera theoretica*, ed. by Albert Seay, CSM, 22, II, 165–77.

Von Rosheim, Joseph, *The Historical Writings of Joseph of Rosheim Leader of Jewry in Early Modern Germany*, ed. by Chava Fraenkel-Goldschmidt, Studies in European Judaism, 12 (Leiden: Brill, 2006).

Vormbaum, Reinhold, ed., *Evangelische Schulordnungen, I: Die evangelischen Schulordnungen des Sechzehnten Jahrhunderts* [ES] (Gütersloh: Bertelsmann, 1860).

Weissenborn, J. C. Hermann, ed., *Acten der Erfurter Universität*, Historische Commission der Provinz Sachsen, 3 vols (Halle: Hendel, 1881–99).

Wollick, Nicolaus, *Die Musica Gregoriana des Nicolaus Wollick*, ed. by Klaus Wolfgang Niemöller, Beiträge zur Rheinischen Musikgeschichte, 11 (Köln: Arno Volk, 1955).

Wollick, Nicolaus, *Nicolaus Wollick, 1480–1541, und sein Musiktraktat*, ed. by Klaus Wolfgang Niemöller, Beiträge zur Rheinischen Musikgeschichte, 13 (Köln: Arno Volk, 1956).

## Secondary Sources

### *Books*

Alt, Heinrich, *Theater und Kirche in ihrem gegenseitigen Verhältniß historisch dargestellt* (Berlin: Verlag der Plahnschen Buchhandlung, 1846).

Anderson, Benedict, *Imagined Communities: Reflections on the Origin and Spread of Nationalism* (London: Verso, 2006).

Anton, Karl, *Luther und die Musik: Eine Gabe an das deutsche Volk zum Reformations-Jubiläum* (Zwickau: Verlag Johannes Herrmann, 1916).

Arend, Sabine, Gerald Dörner, and others, eds, *Ordnungen für die Kirche—Wirkungen auf die Welt: Evangelische Kirchenordnungen des 16. Jahrhunderts* (Tübingen: Mohr Siebeck, 2015).

Aue-Ben-David, Irene, Aya Elyada, Moshe Sluhovsky, Christian Wiese, and others, eds, *Jews and Protestants: From the Reformation to the Present* (Berlin: de Gruyter, 2020).

Aylett, Robert, and Peter N. Skrine, eds, *Hans Sachs and Folk Theatre in The Late Middle Ages: Studies in The History of Popular Culture* (Lampeter: Edwin Mellen Press, 1995).

Ayres, Lewis, *Nicaea and Its Legacy* (Oxford: Oxford University Press, 2004).

Bacon, Thomas, *Martin Luther and the Drama*, Amsterdamer Publikationen zur Sprache und Literatur, 25 (Amsterdam: Rodopi, 1976).

Barth, Hans-Martin, *Der Teufel und Jesus Christus in der Theologie Martin Luthers* (Göttingen: Vandenhoek und Ruprecht, 1967).

Bechter, Barbara, *St. Nicolaikirche Döbeln*, DKV-Kunstführer, Nr. 598/2 (München: Deutscher Kunstverlag, 2002).

Bell, Dean Phillip, and Stephen G. Burnett, eds, *Jews, Judaism, and the Reformation in Sixteenth-Century Germany*, Studies in Central European Studies (Leiden: Brill, 2006).

Belting, Hans, *Bild-Anthropologie: Entwürfe für eine Bildwissenschaft* (München: Hans Fink Verlag, 2001).

Bering, Dietz, *War Luther Antisemit? Das deutsch-jüdische Verhältnis als Tragödie der Nähe* (Berlin: Berlin University Press, 2014).

Bethge, Ernst Heinrich, and others, eds, *Ein gute Wehr und Waffen: Vortragsbuch für Reformationsfeiern* (Leipzig: Strauch, [1917]).

Bienert, Walther, *Martin Luther und die Juden: Ein Quellenbuch mit zeitgenössischen Illustrationen* (Berlin: de Gruyter, 1982).

Bietenholz, Peter, and Thomas Deutscher, eds, *Contemporaries of Erasmus: A Biographical Register of the Renaissance and Reformation* (Toronto: University of Toronto Press, 1987).

Bildhauer, Bettina, and Robert Mills, eds, *The Monstrous Middle Ages* (Cardiff: University of Wales Press, 2003).

Bland, Kalman P., *The Artless Jew: Medieval and Modern Affirmations and Denials of the Visual* (Princeton, NJ: Princeton University Press, 2000).

Block, Johannes, *Verstehen durch Musik: Das gesungene Wort in der Theologie—Ein hermeneutischer Beitrag zur Hymnologie am Beispiel Martin Luthers*, Mainzer Hymnologische Studien, 6 (Tübingen/Basel: Francke, 2002).

Bloom, Harold, *A Map of Misreading* (New York: Oxford University Press, 1976).

Bloom, Harold, *The Anxiety of Influence* (New York: Oxford University Press, 1997).

Boersma, Gerald P., *Augustine's Early Theology of Image: A Study in the Development of Pro-Nicene Theology* (Oxford: Oxford University Press, 2016).

Bornkamm, Heinrich, *Luther und das Alte Testament* (Tübingen: Mohr, 1948).

Bornkamm, Heinrich, *Luther and the Old Testament*, trans. by Eric and Ruth Gritsch (Minneapolis: Fortress, 1969).

Brecht, Martin, *Martin Luther*, 3 vols (Stuttgart: Calver Verlag, 1981–83).

Brecht, Martin, *Martin Luther*, trans. by James Schaaf, 3 vols (St Louis, MO: Augsburg Fortress, 1985–99).

Brecht, Martin, *Ausgewählte Aufsätze I: Reformation* (Stuttgart: Calver Verlag, 1995).

Brown, Christopher, *Singing the Gospel: Lutheran Hymns and the Success of the Reformation* (Cambridge, MA: Harvard University Press, 2005).

Buchwald, Georg, ed., *Von den Juden und ihren Lügen. Im Auszuge mitgeteilt von D. Georg Buchwald*, Luthers Flugschriften für unsere Zeit, 3 (Dresden: Verlag Landesverein für Innere Mission, [1931]).

Buchwald, Reinhard, *Joachim Greff: Untersuchungen über die Anfänge des Renaissancedramas in Sachsen*, Probefahrten: Erstlingsarbeiten aus dem deutschen Seminar in Leipzig, 11 (Leipzig: R. Voigtländers Verlag, 1907).

Burba, Klaus, *Die Christologie in Luthers Liedern*, Schriften des Vereins für Reformationsgeschichte, 175 (Gütersloh: Bertelsmann, 1956).

Burnett, Stephen G., *Christian Hebraism in the Reformation Era (1500–1660): Authors, Books, and the Transmission of Jewish Learning* (Leiden: Brill, 2012).

Butt, John, *Music Education and the Art of Performance in the German Baroque* (Cambridge: Cambridge University Press, 1994).

Byvanck, Alexander W., *De beeldende Kunst in den Tijd van Plato*, Mededelingen der Koniklijke Nederlandse Akademie van Wetenschappen, Afdeling Letterkunde, Nieuwe Reeks d. 18, no. 16 (Amsterdam: Noord-Hollandsche Uitgevers Maatschappij, 1955).

Carrasco, Julia, and Timo Trümer, eds, *Bild und Botschaft: Cranach im Dienst von Hof und Reformation—anlässlich der Ausstellung 'Bild und Botschaft. Cranach im Dienst von Hof und Reformation'* (Heidelberg: Morio Verlag, 2015).

Chadwick, *Boethius: The Consolations of Music, Logic, Theology and Philosophy* (Oxford: Clarendon Press, 1990).

Cheyette, Bryan, *The Construction of 'the Jew' in English Literature and Society* (Cambridge: Cambridge University Press, 1994).

Cohen, Jeffrey Jerome, ed., *Monster Theory* (Minneapolis: University of Minnesota Press, 1996).

Covington, Sarah, and Kathryn Reklis, eds, *Protestant Aesthetics and the Arts* (Abingdon: Routledge, 2020).

Creizenach, Wilhelm, *Geschichte des neueren Dramas: Renaissance und Reformation*, 3/2 (Halle: Max Niemeyer, 1903).

Curths, Karl, *Die Schlacht bei Breitenfeld unweit Leipzig am 7ten September 1631 und die Schlacht bei Lützen am 7ten November 1631* (Leipzig and Altenburg: Brockhaus, 1814).

Detering, Nicolas, Michael Fischer, and Aibe-Marlene Gerdes, eds, *Populäre Kriegslyrik im Ersten Weltkrieg*, Populäre Kultur und Musik, 7 (Münster: Waxmann, 2013).

Dingel, Irene, Günther Wartenberg, and Michael Beyer, *Georg Major (1502–74): Ein Theologe der Wittenberger Reformation* (Leipzig: Evangelische Verlagsanstalt, 2005).

Doyle-Anderson, Ann, and Girancarlo Maiorino, *The Figino, or On the Purpose of Painting: Art Theory in the Late Renaissance* (Toronto: University of Toronto Press, 2001).

Dülmen, Richard van, and others, eds, *Volkskultur: Zur Wiederentdeckung des vergessenen Alltags* (Frankfurt a.M.: Fischer, 1984).

Edwards, Mark U., Jr, *Luther's Last Battles: Politics and Polemics 1531–46* (Leiden: Brill, 1983).

Edwards, Mark U., Jr, *Printing, Propaganda and Martin Luther* (Berkeley: University of California Press, 1994).

Ehrstine, Glenn, *Theater, Culture, and Community in Reformation Bern, 1523–55*, Studies in Medieval and Reformation Thought, 85 (Leiden: Brill, 2001).

Eisenstein, Elizabeth, *The Printing Press as an Agent of Change* (Cambridge: Cambridge University Press, 1980).

*Encyclopedia of Comparative Iconography: Themes Depicted in Works of Art*, ed. by Helene E. Roberts, 2 vols (Chicago: Fitzroy Dearborn, 1998).

Eusterschulte, Anne, and others, eds, *Anthropological Reformations: Anthropology in the Era of Reformation* (Göttingen: Vandenhoek & Ruprecht, 2015).

Fabre-Vassas, Claudine, *The Singular Beast: Jews, Christians, and the Pig* (New York: Columbia University Press, 1997).

Falb, Alfred, *Luther und die Juden* (Munich: Boepple, 1921).

Falk, Gerhard, *The Jew in Christian Theology: Martin Luther's Anti-Jewish Vom Schem Hamphoras, Previously Unpublished in English, and Other Milestones in Church Doctrine Concerning Judaism* (Jefferson, NC: McFarland & Co., 1992).

Fenlon, Iain, ed., *The Renaissance from the 1470s to the End of the Sixteenth Century* (Englewood Cliffs, NJ: Prentice Hall, 1989).

Fischer, Michael, *Religion, Nation, Krieg: Der Lutherchoral Ein feste Burg ist unser Gott zwischen Befreiungskriegen und Erstem Weltkrieg*, Populäre Kultur und Music, 11 (Münster: Waxmann, 2014).

Fitschen, Klaus, Marianne Schröter, Christopher Spehr, and Ernst-Joachim Watschke, eds, *Kulturelle Wirkungen der Reformation—Cultural Impact of the Reformation. Kongressdokumentation Lutherstadt Wittenberg August 2017*, 1 (Leipzig: Evangelische Verlagsanstalt Leipzig, 2019).

Fleck, Miriam Verena, *'Ein tröstlich gemelde'. Die Glaubensallegorie 'Gesetz und Gnade' in Europa zwischen Spätmittelalter und Früher Neuzeit*, Studien zur Kunstgeschichte des Mittelalters und der Frühen Neuzeit, 5 (Korb: Didymos-Verlag, 2010).

Francisco, Adam S., *Martin Luther and Islam: A Study in Sixteenth-Century Polemics and Apologetics*, The History of Christian-Muslim Relations, 8 (Leiden: Brill, 2007).

Frank, Günter, and H. J. Selderhuis, eds, *Philosophie der Reformierten*, Melanchthon-Schriften der Stadt Bretten, 12 (Stuttgart-Bad Cannstadt, Frommann-Holzboog Verlag, 2012).

Freise, Dorothea, *Spiele und Spielinitiativen in spätmittelalterlichen Städten*, Veröffentlichungen des Max-Plancks-Instituts für Geschichte, 178 (Frankfurt a.M.: Vandenhoeck und Ruprecht, 2002).

Freitag, Werner, and others, eds, *Mitteldeutsche Lebensbilder, Menschen im Zeitalter der Reformation* (Weimar and Köln: Böhlau Verlag, 2004).

Freud, Sigmund, *Totem and Taboo: Resemblances between the Psychic Lives of Savages and Neurotics* (New York: Moffat, Yard and Co., 1919).

Friedländer, Max J. and Jakob Rosenberg, *Die Gemälde von Lukas Cranach* [FR], rev. by G. Schwartz (Basel: Birkhäuser Verlag, 1979).

Friedman, John Block, *The Monstrous Races in Medieval Life and Thought* (Cambridge, MA: Harvard University Press, 1981).

Fritsch, Theodor ['Frey, Thomas'], *Antisemiten-Katechismus. Eine Zusammenstellung des wichtigsten Materials zum Verständniß der Judenfrage* (Leipzig: Verlag von Theodor Fritsch, 1887).

Fritsch, Theodor ['Frey, Thomas'], *Handbuch der Judenfrage. Die wichtigsten Tatsachen zur Beurteilung des jüdischen Volkes* (Leipzig: Hammer-Verlag, 1931).

Fritsch, Theodor ['Frey, Thomas'], *Der falsche Gott. Beweis-Material gegen Jahwe* (Leipzig: Hammer-Verlag, 1933).

Fritz, Johann Michael, and others, eds, *Die bewahrende Kraft des Luthertums: mittelalterliche Kunstwerke in evangelischen Kirchen* (Regensburg: Schnell & Steiner, 1997).

Ganz, David, and Thomas Lentes, eds, *Sehen und Sakralität in der Vormoderne*, Kultbild, 4 (Berlin: Reimer Verlag, 2011).

Gasch, Stefan, and others, eds, *Senfl Studien I*, Wiener Forum für ältere Musikgeschichte, 4 (Tutzing: Hans Schneider, 2012).

Gaul, Otto, and Ulf-Dietrich Korn, eds, *Die Stadt Lemgo* (Münster: Aschendorff, 1983).

Goedecke, Karl, and Julius Tittmann, eds, *Deutsche Dichter des sechzehnten Jahrhunderts: Schauspiele aus dem sechzehnten Jahrhundert* (Leipzig: Brockhaus, 1868).

Göllner, Theodor, ed., *Deutsche Musiktheorie des 15. bis 17. Jahrhunderts, I: Von Paumann bis Calvisius* (Darmstadt: Wissenschaftliche Buchgesellschaft, 2003).

Gombrich, Ernst Hans, *Art and Illusion: A Study in the Psychology of Pictorial Representation* (New York: Pantheon Books, 1961).

Gombrich, Ernst Hans, *Symbolic Images: Studies in the Art of the Renaissance* (London: Phaidon, 1985).

Grayzel, Solomon, and Kenneth R. Snow, eds, *The Church and the Jews in the XIIIth Century: Volume II, 1254–1314* (New York: The Jewish Theological Seminary Press, 1989).

Grisar, Hartmann, and Franz Heege, *Luthers Kampfbilder*, 4 vols (Freiburg im Breisgau: Herder, 1921–1923).

Gritsch, Eric W., *Martin Luther's Anti-Semitism: Against His Better Judgment* (Grand Rapids: Eerdmans, 2012).

Groll, Karin, *Das Passional Christi und Antichristi von Lucas Cranach d. Ä.* (Frankfurt a.M.: Peter Lang, 1990).

Groos, Arthur, and others, eds, *Topographies of the Early Modern City*, Transatlantic Studies on Medieval and Early Modern Literature and Culture, 3 (Göttingen: Vandenhoek and Ruprecht, 2008).

Hahn, Gerhard, *Evangelium als literarische Anweisung. Zu Luthers Stellung in der Geschichte des deutschen kirchlichen Liedes*, Münchener Texte und Untersuchungen zur deutschen Literatur des Mittelalters, 73 (München and Zürich: Artemis, 1981).

Hall, James, *Dictionary of Subject and Symbols in Art* (London: John Murray, 1979).

Hause, Stefan, *Das Lutherhaus—Eine Museumsgeschichte*, Schriften der Stiftung Luthergedenkstätten Sachsen-Anhalt, 3 (Leipzig: Evangelische Verlagsanstalt, 2003).

Haustein, Jörg, *Martin Luthers Stellung zum Zauber- und Hexenwesen*, Münchener Kirchenhistorische Studien, 2 (Stuttgart: Kohlhammer, 1990).

Heal, Bridget, *A Magnificent Faith: Art and Identity in Lutheran Germany* (Oxford: Oxford University Press, 2017).

Heilmann, Anja, *Boethius' Musiktheorie und das Quadrivium* (Göttingen: Vandenhoek und Ruprecht, 2007).

Helm, Claudia, and Jost Hausmann, eds, *1495—Kaiser, Reich, Reformen: Der Reichstag zu Worms. Ausstellung des Landeshauptarchivs Koblenz in Verbindung mit der Stadt Worms zum 500jährigen Jubiläum des Wormser Reichstags von 1495* (Koblenz: Landesarchivverwaltung Rheinland-Pfalz, 1995).

Heng, Geraldine, *The Invention of Race in the European Middle Ages* (Cambridge: Cambridge University Press, 2018).

Hentschel, Frank, *Sinnlichkeit und Vernunft in der mittelalterlichen Musiktheorie* (Stuttgart: Frank Steiner Verlag, 2000).

Hentschel, Frank, ed., *Musik und die Geschichte der Philosophie und Naturwissenschaften im Mittelalter: Fragen zur Wechselwirkung von 'Musica' und 'Philosophia' im Mittelalter*, Studien und Texte zur Geistesgeschichte des Mittelalters, 62 (Leiden: Brill, 1998).

Herl, Joseph, *Worship Wars in Early Lutheranism: Choir, Congregation and Three Centuries of Conflict* (New York: Oxford University Press, 2004).

Hertel, Gustav, and others, eds, *Die Chroniken der niedersächsischen Städte: Magdeburg*, Die Chroniken der deutschen Städte vom 14. bis 16. Jahrhundert, 27, 2 vols (Leipzig: Verlag von S. Hirtzel, 1869–99).

Herzog, Emil, *Geschichte des Zwickauer Gymnasium: Eine Gedenkschrift zur Einweihungsfeier des neuen Gymnasialgebäudes* (Zwickau: Richtersche Buchhandlung, 1869).

Heschel, Susannah, *The Aryan Jesus: Christian Theologians and the Bible in Nazi Germany* (Princeton, NJ: Princeton University Press, 2010).

Hess, Solomon, *Lebensgeschichte M. Heinrich Bullingers, Antistes der Kirche Zürich* (Zürich: Friedrich Schultheß, 1828).

Hirta, Markus, ed., *Mit dem Schwert oder festem Glauben: Luther und die Hexen*, Katalog Mittelalterliches Kriminalmuseum Rothenburg (Darmstadt: Wissenschaftliche Buchgesellschaft/Theiss, 2017).

Holley, Michael Ann, and Keith Moxey, eds, *Art History Aesthetics: Visual Studies* (Williamstown, MA: Sterling and Francine Clark Arts Institute, 2001).

*Hollstein's German Engravings, Etchings and Woodcuts 1400–1700, 52: J. S. Schott—L. Schultes* (Amsterdam: M. Hertzberger, 2000).

Holstein, Hugo, *Die Reformation im Spiegelbilde der dramatischen Literatur des 16. Jahrhunderts*, Schriften des Vereins für Reformationsgeschichte, 14/15 (Halle: Verein für Reformationsgeschichte, 1886).

Hübner, Erich, and Renate Steiger, eds, *Kirche und Musik: Gesammelte Aufsätze zur Geschichte der gottesdienstlichen Musik* (Göttingen: Vandenhoek und Ruprecht, 1979).

'Islebensis', *Dr Martin Luther und das Judenthum* (Berlin: O. Lorenz, 1879).

Janota, Johannes, *Studien zu Funktion und Typus des deutschen geistlichen Liedes im Mittelalter*, Münchner Texte und Untersuchungen zur deutschen Literatur des Mittelalters, 23 (München: Beck, 1968).

Junghans, Helmar, *Martin Luther und Wittenberg* (München: Koehler & Amelang, 1996).

Katznelson, Ira, and Miri Rubin, eds, *Religious Conversion: History, Experience and Meaning* (London: Routledge, 2016).

Kaufmann, Thomas, *Konfession und Kultur: lutherischer Protestantismus in der zweiten Hälfte des Reformationsjahrhunderts* (Tübingen: Mohr Siebeck, 2006).

Kaufmann, Thomas, *Luthers 'Judenschriften': Ein Beitrag zu ihrer historischen Kontextualisierung* (Tübingen: Mohr Siebeck, 2011).

Kaufmann, Thomas, *Luthers Juden* (Stuttgart: Reclam Verlag, 2014).

Kaufmann, Thomas, *Luther's Jews: A Journey into Anti-Semitism*, trans. by Lesley Sharpe and Jeremy Noakes (Oxford: Oxford University Press, 2017).

Kern, Margit, *Tugend versus Gnade. Protestantische Bildprogramme in Nürnberg, Pirna, Regensburg und Ulm*, Berliner Schriften zur Kunst, 16 (Berlin: Gebrüder Mann Verlag, 2002).

Kinzig, Wolfram, and Cornelia Kück, *Judentum und Christentum zwischen Konfrontation und Faszination* (Stuttgart: Kohlhammer, 2002).

Klein, Theodor, *Die Prozessionsgesänge der Mainzer Kirche aus dem 14. bis 18. Jahrhundert*, Quellen und Abhandlungen zur mittelrheinischen Kirchengeschichte, 7 (Speyer: Verlag der Jaegerschen Buckdruckerei, 1962).

Koch, Joseph, ed., *Artes Liberales: Von der Antiken Bildung zur Wissenschaft des Mittelalters* (Leiden: Brill, 1976).

Koepplin, Dieter, and Tilman Falk, *Lukas Cranach: Gemälde, Zeichnung, Druckgraphik* [KF], 2 vols (Basel: Birkhäuser, 1974–76).

Koerner, Joseph Leo, *The Moment of Self-Portraiture in German Renaissance Art* (Chicago: University of Chicago Press, 1993).

Koerner, Joseph Leo, *The Reformation of the Image* (Chicago: University of Chicago Press, 2003).

König, Andrea, *Medienethik aus theologischer Perspektive. Medien und Protestantismus. Chancen, Risiken, Herausforderungen und Handlungskonzepte* (Marburg: Tectum, 2006).

Könneker, Barbara, *Wesen und Wandlung der Narrenidee im Zeitalter des Humanismus: Brant-Murner-Erasmus* (Wiesbaden: Steiner, 1966).

Kristeva, Julia, *Powers of Horror: An Essay on Abjection*, trans. by Leon S. Rodiez (New York: Columbia University Press, 1980; repr. 1982).

Kühebacher, Egon, and others, eds, *Tiroler Volksschauspiel: Beiträge zur Theatergeschichte des Alpenraumes*, Schriftenreihe des Südtiroler Kulturinstitutes, 3 (Bozen: Athesia, 1976).

Kunz, Tobias, ed., *Baugestalt und Bildfunktion. Texte zur Architektur- und Kunstgeschichte* (Berlin: Lukas-Verlag, 2006).

Kunzle, David, *The Early Comic Strip, Narrative Strips and Picture Stories in the European Broadsheet from c. 1450 to 1825* (Berkeley: University of California Press, 1973).

Lähnemann, Henrike, *Hystoria Judith: Deutsche Judithdichtungen vom 12. bis zum 16. Jahrhundert*, Scrinium Friburgense, 20 (Berlin: Walter de Gruyter, 2006).

Landesverband Jüdischer Gemeinden Sachsen-Anhalt, Magdeburg, ed., *Geschichte jüdischer Gemeinden in Sachsen-Anhalt: Versuch einer Erinnerung* (Wernigerode: Oemler-Verlag, 1997).

Leaver, Robin, A., *Luther's Liturgical Music: Principles and Implications*, Lutheran Quarterly Books (Grand Rapids: Eerdmans, 2007).

Lewy, Max, *Schloss Hartenfels bei Torgau: Von der K[öni]gl[ichen] Technischen Hochschule zu Dresden genehmigte Doktordissertation*, Beiträge zur Bauwissenschaft, 10 (Berlin: Ernst Wasmuth, 1908).

Linden, Walter, *Luthers Kampfschriften gegen das Judentum* (Berlin: Klinckhardt und Biermann, 1936).

Line, Johannes, *Wann wurde das Lutherlied Ein feste Burg ist unser Gott verfaßt? Historische kritische Untersuchung* (Leipzig: Rautenstrauch, 1886).

Lipton, Sara, *Dark Mirror: The Medieval Origins of Anti-Jewish Iconography* (New York: Metropolitan, 2014).

Löcher, Kurt, ed., *Martin Luther und die Refiormation in Deutschland. Vorträge zur Ausstellung im Germanischen Nationalmuseum Nürnberg 1983* (Schweinfurt: Weppert, 1983).

Loehr, Johanna, and others, eds, *Dona Melanchthoniana: Festgabe für Heinz Scheible zum 70. Geburtstag* (Stuttgart-Bad Cannstatt: Frommann-Holzboog, 2001).

Loewe, Jost Andreas, *Richard Smyth and the Language of Orthodoxy: Re-imagining Tudor Catholic Polemicism*, Studies in Medieval and Reformation Traditions, 96 (Leiden: Brill, 2003).

Loewe, Jost Andreas, *Johann Sebastian Bach's St John Passion (BWV 245): A Theological Commentary with a New Study Translation by Katherine Firth and a Foreword by N. T. Wright*, Studies in the History of Christian Traditions, 168 (Leiden: Brill, 2014).

Löwe, Hartmut, and Claus-Jürgen Roepke, eds, *Luther und die Folgen. Beiträge zur sozialgeschichtlichen Bedeutung der lutherischen Reformation* (München: Christian Kaiser Verlag, 1983).

Lüthy, Christoph, Claudia Swan, Paul Bakker, Claus Zittel, and others, eds, *Image, Imaginination, and Cognition: Medieval and Early Modern Theory and Cognition*, Intersections, 55 (Leiden: Brill, 2008).

Marsh, William M., *Martin Luther on Reading the Bible as Christian Scripture: The Messiah in Luther's Biblical Hermeneutic and Theology*, Princeton Theological Monograph Series, 223 (Eugene, OR: Pickwick, 2017).

Matheus, Michael, Arnold Nesselrath, and Arnold Wallraff, eds, *Martin Luther in Rom: Die Ewige Stadt als kosmopolitisches Zentrum und ihre Wahrnehmung*, Bibliothek des historischen Instituts in Rom, 134 (Berlin: de Gruyter, 2017).

Maurer, Wilhelm, *Kirche und Synagoge: Motive und Formen der Auseinandersetzung der Kirche mit dem Judentum* (Stuttgart: Kohlhammer, 1953).

McGrath, Alister E., *Iustitia Dei: A History of the Christian Doctrine of Justification. The Beginnings to the Reformation* (Cambridge: Cambridge University Press, 1986).

Mellinkoff, Ruth, *Outcasts: Signs of Otherness in Northern European Art of the Late Middle Ages* (Berkeley: University of California Press, 1993).

Melloni, Alberto, ed., *Martin Luther: A Christian between Reforms and Modernity (1517–2017)*, 3 vols (Berlin: de Gruyter, 2017).

Merback, Mitchell B., ed. *Beyond the Yellow Badge: Anti-Judaism and Antisemitism in Medieval and Early Modern Visual Culture*, Brill's Series in Jewish Studies, 37 (Leiden: Brill, 2007).

Merriman, John, *A History of Modern Europe: From the Renaissance to the Age of Napoleon* (New York: W. W. Norton & Company, 2010).

Metz, Detlef, *Das protestantische Drama: Evangelisches geistliches Theater in der Reformationszeit und im konfessionellen Zeitalter* (Weimar and Köln: Böhlau, 2013).

Meyer, Almut Agnes, *Heilsgewissheit und Endzeiterwartung im deutschen Drama des 16. Jahrhunderts: Untersuchungen über die Beziehungen zwischen geistlichem Spiel, bildender Kunst und den Wandlungen des Zeitgeistes im lutherischen Raum*, Heidelberger Forschungen, 18 (Heidelberg: Carl Winter Universitätsverlag, 1976).

Michael, Wolfgang Friedrich, *Das deutsche Drama der Reformationszeit* (Bern: Peter Lang, 1984).

Michels, Norbert, *Cranach in Anhalt: Vom Alten zum Neuen Glauben* (Petersberg: Michael Imhof Verlag, 2015).

Mommsen, Wolfgang J., and others, eds, *Stadtbürgertum und Adel in der Reformation*, Studien zur Sozialgeschichte der Reformation in England und Deutschland, 5 (Stuttgart: Klett-Cotta, 1979).

Müller, Georg Gottfried, *Das kursächsische Schulwesen beim Erlaß der Schulordnung von 1580* (Dresden: Jahresbericht des Wettiner Gymnasiums zu Dresden, 1888).

Müller, Harald, *Habit und Habitus: Mönche und Humanisten im Dialog* (Tübingen: Mohr Siebeck, 2006).

Müller-Heuser, Franz, *Vox humana: Ein Beitrag zur Untersuchung der Stimmästhetik des Mittelalters*, Kölner Beiträge zur Musikwissenschaft, 196 (Regensburg: Gustav Bosse, 1997).

Nettl, Paul, *Luther and Music* (Philadelphia: Muhlenberg Press, 1948; repr. New York: Russell & Russell, 1967).

Neumann, Bernd, *Geistliches Schauspiel im Zeugnis der Zeit: Zur Aufführung mittelalterlicher religiöser Dramen im deutschen Sprachgebiet*, Münchner Texte und Untersuchungen zur deutschen Literatur des Mittelalters, 84/85 (München: Artemis Verlag, 1987).

Noble, Bonnie J., *Lucas Cranach the Elder: Art and Devotion of the German Reformation* (Lanham, MD: University Press of America, 2009).

Oberman, Heiko Augustinus, *Luther: Mensch zwischen Gott und Teufel* (Berlin: Severin und Siedler, 1981).

Oberman, Heiko Augustinus, *Luther: Man between God and the Devil*, trans. by Eileen Walliser-Schwartzbart (London: Harper Collins, 1993).

Oberman, Heiko Augustinus, *Wurzeln des Antisemitismus. Christenangst und Judenplage im Zeitalter von Humanismus und Reformation* (Berlin: Severin und Siedler, 1981).

Oberman, Heiko Augustinus, *The Roots of Anti-Semitism in the Age of Renaissance and Reformation*, trans. by James Porter, (Philadelphia: Fortress, 1984).

Oberman, Heiko Augustinus, and Thomas A. Brady Jr, eds, *Itinerarium Italicum: The Profile of the Italian Renaissance in the Mirror of its European Transformations, Dedicated to Paul Oskar Kristeller on the Occasion of his 70th Birthday* (Leiden: Brill, 1975).

Ocker, Christopher, *Luther, Conflict, and Christendom: Reformation Europe and Christianity in the West* (Cambridge: Cambridge University Press, 2018).

Oelke, Harry, and Wolfgang Kraus, eds, *Martin Luthers 'Judenschriften'. Die Rezeption im 19. und 20. Jahrhundert* (Göttingen: Vandenhoeck & Ruprecht 2016).

Oesterreich, Peter, and Thomas Sloane, eds, *Rhetorica Movet: Studies in Historical and Modern Rhetoric in Honour of Heinrich F. Plett* (Leiden: Brill, 1999).

Ohly, Friedrich, *Gesetz und Evangelium. Zur Typologie bei Luther und Lucas Cranach. Zum Blutstrahl in der Gnade der Kunst* (Münster: Aschendorff, 1985).

Opitz, Peter J., *The Myth of the Reformation*, Refo500 Academic Studies, 9 (Göttingen: Vandenhoeck & Ruprecht, 2013).

Ozment, Steven, *The Serpent and the Lamb: Cranach, Luther, and the Making of the Reformation* (New Haven, CT: Yale University Press, 2011).

Page, Christopher, *The 'Summa musice': A Thirteenth-Century Manual for Singers* (Cambridge: Cambridge University Press, 1991.

Pangritz, Andreas, *Theologie und Antisemitismus: Das Beispiel Martin Luthers* (Frankfurt a.M.: Peter Lang, 2017).

Parente, James A., Jr, *Religious Drama and the Humanist Tradition*, Studies in the History of Christian Traditions, 39 (Leiden: Brill, 1987).

Petersen, Nils Holger, and others, eds, *The Arts and the Cultural Heritage of Martin Luther: Special Issue of Transfiguration: Nordic Journal for Christianity and the Arts* (Copenhagen: Museum Tusculanum Press, 2002).

Pettegree, Andrew, *Reformation and the Culture of Persuasion* (Cambridge: Cambridge University Press, 2005).

Pettegree, Andrew, ed., *The Early Reformation in Europe* (Cambridge: Cambridge University Press, 1992).

Pettegree, Andrew, ed., *The Reformation World* (London: Routledge, 2002).

Pinkwart, Wolfgang, ed., *Genetische Ansätze in der Kulturlandschaftsforschung. Festschrift für Helmut Jäger*, Würzburger geographische Arbeiten, 60 (Würzburg: Institut für Geographie der Julius-Maximilians-Universität, 1983).

Plett, Heinrich F., ed., *Renaissance-Rhetorik* (Berlin: de Gruyter, 1993).

Pöpper, Thomas, Susanne Wegmann, and others, eds, *Das Bild des neuen Glaubens: das Cranach-Retabel in der Schneeberger St. Wolfgangkirche* (Regensburg: Schnell & Steiner, 2011).

Preuß, Hans, *Martin Luther, der Künstler* (Gütersloh: Bertelsmann, 1931).

Probst, Christopher J., *Demonizing the Jews: Luther and the Protestant Church in Nazi Germany*, published in association with the United States Holocaust Museum (Bloomington: Indiana University Press, 2012).

Rautenstrauch, Johannes, *Luther und die Pflege der kirchlichen Musik in Sachsen: Ein Beitrag zur Geschichte der katholischen Brüderschaften, der vor- und nachreformatorischen Kurrenden, Schulchöre und Kantoreien Sachsens* [KS] (Leipzig: Breitkopf und Härtel, 1907).

Reinitzer, Heimo, *Gesetz und Evangelium. Über ein reformatorisches Bildthema, seine Tradition, Funktion und Wirkungsgeschichte*, 2 vols (Hamburg: Christians, 2006).

Richter, Karl, ed., *August Hermann Francke: Schriften über Erziehung und Unterricht*, Pädaogische Bibliothek: eine Sammlung der wichtigsten pädagogischen Schriften älterer und neuerer Zeit, 5 (Leipzig: Siegismund und Volkening, 1872).

Röcke, Werner, and others, eds, *Die Literatur im Übergang vom Mittelalter und früher Neuzeit*, Hansers Sozialgeschichte der deutschen Literatur, 1 (München and Wien: Hanser Verlag, 2004).

Romano, Giovanni, ed. *Fermo Stella e Sperindio Cagnoli seguaci di Gaudenzio Ferrari: una bottega d'arte nel Cinquecento Padano*, Quaderni del Museo Bernareggi, Museo Adriano Bernareggi Bergamo, x (Milano: Silvana, 2006).

Roper, Lyndal, *Martin Luther: Renegade and Prophet* (New York: Random House, 2017).

Roper, Lyndal, *Living I Was Your Plague: Martin Luther's World and Legacy* (Princeton, NJ: Princeton University Press, 2021).

Rous, Anne-Simone, ed., *Martin Luther—Aufbruch in eine neue Welt* (Dresden: Sandstein, 2016).

Rowe, Nina, *The Jew, the Cathedral and the Medieval City: Synagoga and Ecclesia in the Thirteenth Century* (Cambridge: Cambridge University Press, 2011).

Rubin, Miri, *Corpus Christi: The Eucharist in Late Medieval Culture* (Cambridge: Cambridge University Press, 1991).

Rupp, E. Gordon, *Martin Luther and the Jews: Robert Waley Cohen Memorial Lecture* (London: The Council for Christians and Jews, 1972).

Sasse, Martin, *Martin Luther über die Juden: Weg mit ihnen!* (Freiburg im Breisgau: Sturmhut Verlag, 1938).

Sasse, Martin, *Martin Luther over de Joden'* (Eisenach: [n. pub.], 1938).

Sasse, Martin, *Martin Luther on the Jews* (Freiburg im Breisgau: Bar & Bartosch, 1939).

Schade, Richard Erich, *Studies in Early German Comedy 1500–1650*, Studies in German Literature, Linguistics and Culture, 24 (Columbia, SC: Camden House, 1988).

Schalk, Carl F., *Luther on Music: Paradigms of Praise* (St Louis, MO: Concordia, 1988).

Schillinger, Jean, and others, eds, *Der Narr in der deutschen Literatur im Mittelalter und in der frühen Neuzeit*, Jahrbuch für internationale Germanistik, Reihe A, 96 (Bern: Peter Lang, 2009).

Schlüter, Marie, *Musikgeschichte Wittenbergs im 16. Jahrhundert: Quellenkundliche und sozialgeschichtliche Untersuchungen* (Göttingen: Vandenhoek und Ruprecht, 2010).

Schramm, Brook, and Stjerna, Kirsi I., eds, *Martin Luther, the Bible, and the Jewish People: A Reader* (Minneapolis: Fortress, 2012).

Scribner, Robert W., *Popular Culture and Popular Movements in Reformation Germany* (London: Hambledon Press, 1987).

Scribner, Robert W., *For the Sake of Simple Folk: Popular Propaganda for the German Reformation* (Oxford: Clarendon Press, 1994).

Scribner, Robert W., ed., *Bilder and Bildertum in Spätmittelalter und in der frühen Neuzeit*, Wolfenbütteler Forschungen, 46 (Wiesbaden: Otto Harrassowitz, 1990).

Sehling, Emil, ed., *Die Evangelischen Kirchenordnungen des XVI. Jahrhunderts*: Sachsen und Thüringen, nebst anliegenden Gebieten (Leipzig: O. R. Reisland, 1902).

Seiferth, Wolfgang, *Synagoge und Kirche im Mittelalter: Historische und theologische, literarische und kunstgeschichtliche Dokumentation zur Geschichte der Juden im Mittelalter* (München: Kösel Verlag, 1964).

Shachar, Isaiah, *The 'Judensau': A Medieval Anti-Jewish Motif and its History*, Warburg Institute Surveys, 5 (London: Warburg Institute, 1974).

Sintenis, Friedrich, *Zur Geschichte des Zerbster Schulwesens: Einladungsschrift zur Feier des fünfzigjährigen Bestehens des Herzoglichen Francisceums zu Zerbst 18. und 19. Mai 1853* (Zerbst: Friedrich Römer, 1853).

Smith, Kathryn A., *Art, Identity and Devotion in Fourteenth-Century England*, The British Library Studies in Medieval Culture (Toronto: University of Toronto Press, 2003).

Sonnen, Max von, *Die Weserrenaissance: Die Bauentwicklung um die Wende des XVI. und XVII. Jahrhunderts an der oberen und mittleren Weser und in den angrenzenden Landesteilen* (Münster: Aschendorff, 1969).

Spiewok, Wolfgang, *Das deutsche Fastnachtspiel: Ursprung, Funktionen, Aufführungspraxis* (Greifswald: Reineke, 1997).

Spinks, Jennifer Susan, *Monstrous Births and Visual Culture in Sixteenth-Century Germany* (London: Pickering & Chatto, 2009).

Spinks, Jennifer Susan, Dagmar Eichberger, and others, eds, *Religion, the Supernatural and Visual Culture in Early Modern Europe: An Album Amicorum for Charles Zika*, Studies in Medieval and Reformation Traditions, 191 (Leiden: Brill, 2015).

Spitta, Friedrich, *Ein feste Burg ist unser Gott: Das Lied Luthers in ihrer Bedeutung für das evangelische Kirchenlied* (Göttingen: Vandenhoek und Ruprecht, 1905).

Spitz, Lewis W., ed., *Humanismus und Reformation in der deutschen Geschichte. Ein Tagungsbericht*, Veröffentlichungen der historischen Kommission zu Berlin, 51 (Berlin: De Gruyter, 1981).

Steche, Richard, *Amtshauptmannschaft Borna*, Beschreibende Darstellung der älteren Bau- und Kunstdenkmäler des Königreichs Sachsen, 15 (Dresden: C. C. Meinhold & Söhne, 1891).

Steiger, Johann Anselm, ed., *Reformation Heute: Band IV—Reformation und Medien: Zu den intermedialen Wirkungen der Reformation* (Leipzig: Evangelische Verlagsanstalt, 2018).

Stern, Selma, *Josel von Rosheim: Befehlshaber der Judenschaft im Heiligen römischen Reich deutscher Nation* (Stuttgart: Deutsche Verlagsanstalt, 1959).

Stern, Selma, *Josel of Rosheim: Commander of Jewry in the Holy Roman Empire of the German Nation*, trans. by Gertrude Hirschler (Philadelphia: Jewish Publication Society of America, 1965).

Steude, Wolfram, *Untersuchungen zur mitteldeutschen Musiküberlieferung und Musikpflege im 16. Jahrhundert* (Leipzig: Peters, 1978).

Stirm, Margarete, *Die Bilderfrage in der Reformation*, Quellen und Forschungen zur Reformationsgeschichte, 45 (Gütersloh: Gütersloher Verlagshaus Mohn, 1977).

Strickland, Debra Higgs, *Saracens, Demons and Jews: Making Monsters in Medieval Art* (Princeton, NJ: Princeton University Press, 2003).

Strings, Sabrina, *Fearing the Black Body: The Racial Origins of Fat Phobia* (New York: New York University Press, 2019).

Stuplich, Brigitte, *Zur Dramentechnik des Hans Sachs* (Stuttgart-Bad Cannstatt: Frommann-Holzboog, 1998).

Suhle, Hermann, *Beiträge zur Geschichte der fürstlichen Schule zu Dessau, I: 1536–1628*, Sechster Jahresbericht des Herzoglichen Friedrichs-Realgymnasiums (Dessau: C. Dünnhaupt, 1888).

Tyler, Imogen, *Revolting Subjects: Social Abjection and Resistance in Neoliberal Britain* (London: Bloomsbury [ZED Books], 2013).

Untermann, Matthias, and others, eds, *Religiosität in Mittelalter und Neuzeit*, Mitteilungen der Deutschen Gesellschaft für Archäologie des Mittelalters und der Neuzeit, 23 (Heidelberg: Neumann, 2011).

Veit, Patrice, *Das Kirchenlied in der Reformation Martin Luthers*, Veröffentlichungen des Instituts für Europäische Geschichte Mainz (Stuttgart: F. Steiner, 1986).

Wackernagel, Philipp, *Bibliographie zur Geschichte des deutschen Kirchenliedes im XVI. Jahrhundert* (Frankfurt a.M.: Heyder & Zimmer, 1855).

Wackernagel, Philipp, *Das deutsche Kirchenlied von der ältesten zeit bis zu Anfang des 17. Jahrhunderts: mit Berücksichtigung der deutschen kirchlichen Lieddichtung im weiteren Sinne und der lateinischen von Hilarius bis Georg Fabricius und Wolfgang Ammonius* (Leipzig: Teubner, 1870).

Wagner Oettinger, Rebecca, *Music as Propaganda in the German Reformation* (Aldershot: Ashgate, 2001).

Weber, Arno, *Geschichte der Kantorei-Gesellschaften im Gebiete des ehemaligen Kurfürstentums Sachsen*, Publikationen der Internationalen Musikgesellschaft: Beihefte IX [*KG*] (Leipzig: Breitkopf und Härtel, 1902).

Weimer, Christoph, *Luther, Cranach und die Bilder: Gesetz und Evangelium—Schlüssel zum reformatorischen Bildgebrauch* (Stuttgart: Calwer Verlag, 1999).

Wenzel, Horst, and others, eds, *Typus und Individuät im Mittelalter*, Forschungen zur Geschichte der älteren deutschen Literatur, 4 (München: Wilhelm Fink Verlag, 1983).

Whitford, David, *Martin Luther in Context* (Cambridge: Cambridge University Press, 2018).

Wiesenfeldt, Christiane, and Stefan Menzel, eds, *Musik und Reformation—Politisierung, Medialisierung, Missionierung*, Beiträge zur Geschichte der Kirchenmusik im Auftrag der Görres-Gesellschaft, 22 (Paderborn: Ferdinand Schoenigh, 2020).

Wiessner, Heinz, ed., *Die Bistümer der Kirchenprovinz Magdeburg, Bistum Naumburg: Die Diözese*, Max-Planck-Institut für Geschichte: Germania Sacra Neue Folge, 35, 1/1 (Berlin: de Gruyter, 1996).

Williams, Christopher John Fardo, *Aristotle's De Generatione et Corruptione* (Oxford: Clarendon Press, 2002).

Willis, Jonathan P., *Church Music and Protestantism in Post-Reformation England: Discourses, Sites and Identities* (Farnham: Ashgate, 2010).

Wimböck, Gabriele, Karin Leonhard, and Markus Friedrich, eds, *Evidentia. Reichweiten visueller Wahrnehmung in der Frühen Neuzeit*, Pluralisierung & Autorität, 9 (Berlin: LIT, 2007).

Wolbe, Eugen, *Geschichte der Juden in Berlin und in der Mark Brandenburg* (Berlin: Kedem, 1937).

Wolff, Christoph, *Bach: Essays on His Life and Music* (Cambridge, MA: Harvard University Press, 1991).

Wolff, Christoph, *Johann Sebastian Bach: The Learned Musician* (Oxford: Oxford University Press, 2000).

Wolfram, Georg, *Ein feste Burg ist unser Gott: Die Entstehungszeit und der ursprüngliche Sinn des Lutherliedes* (Berlin and Leipzig: de Gruyter, 1936).

Wright, William J., *Martin Luther's Understanding of God's Two Kingdoms: A Response to the Challenge of Skepticism*, Texts and Studies in Reformation and pre-Reformation Thought (Grand Rapids: Baker Academic, 2010).

Wuttke, Dieter, ed., *Fastnachtsspiele des 15. und 16. Jahrhunderts* (Stuttgart: Reclam, 2006).

### *Unpublished Dissertations*

Champagne, Marie Therese, 'The relationship between the papacy and the Jews in twelfth-century Rome: papal attitudes toward biblical Judaism and contemporary European Jewry' (unpublished doctoral dissertation, Louisiana State University, 2005).

Guster, Holger, 'Die Hostienmonstranzen des 13. und 14. Jahrhunderts in Europa' (unpublished doctoral dissertation, University of Heidelberg, 2009).

Lorenz, Ralph, 'Pedagogical Implications of Musica practica in Sixteenth-Century Wittenberg' (unpublished doctoral dissertation, Indiana University, 1995).

Rosebrock, Matthew, 'The Highest Art: Martin Luther's Visual Theology in *Oratio, Meditatio, Tentatio*' (unpublished doctoral dissertation, Fuller Theological Seminary, 2017).

Roth, Christine, 'Traditionsbindungen in der lutherischen Musikkultur des 16. und frühen 17. Jahrhunderts: Studien zu Repertoire und Kontexten' (unpublished doctoral dissertation, Universität Zürich, 2019).

Schneider, Annette, 'Studie zu Kinderfesten an Martini und Nikolaus. Untersucht am Beispiel ausgewählter Orte des Mansfelder Landes' (unpublished doctoral dissertation, Martin-Luther-Universität Halle-Wittenberg, 1994).

Seidel, Andrea, 'Joachim Greff und das protestantische Schauspiel' (unpublished doctoral dissertation, Martin-Luther-Universität Halle-Wittenberg, 1994).

Slemon, Peter, 'Adam von Fulda on musica plana and compositio: De musica, Book II, a translation and commentary' (unpublished doctoral dissertation, University of British Columbia, 1994).

Stirm, Margarete, 'Die Bilderfrage bei den Reformatoren' (unpublished doctoral dissertation, Kirchliche Hochschule Berlin, 1973).

Wölbing, Walter, 'Der Drucker und Musikverleger Georg Rhau: Ein Beitrag zur Drucker- und Verlegertätigkeit im Zeitalter der Reformation' (unpublished doctoral dissertation, Friedrich-Wilhelms-Universität Berlin, 1922).

Zeunert, Susanne, 'Bilder in Martin Luthers Tischreden: Argumente und Beispiele gegen die Laster Hochmut, Abgötterei und Betrug' (unpublished doctoral dissertation, University of Trier, 2016).

### *Articles*

Altenburg, Detlef, 'Die Musik in der Fronleichnamsprozession des 14. und 15. Jahrhunderts', *Musica Disciplina*, 38 (1984), 5–24.

Ameln, Konrad, 'Die älteste Überlieferung der Weise "Ein feste Burg ist unser Gott"', *Jahrbuch für Liturgik und Hymnologie*, 1 (1955), 110–12.

Ameln, Konrad, 'Das Klugsche Gesangbuch, Wittenberg 1529: Versuche einer Rekonstruktion', *Jahrbuch für Liturgik und Hymnologie*, 16 (1971), 159–62.

Ameln, Konrad, and Karol Hławiczka, 'Eine niederländische Psalm-Weise, Vorlage oder Nachbildung der Melodie von "Ein feste Burg"? Eine Diskussion', *Jahrbuch für Liturgik und Hymnologie*, 18 (1973), 189–95.

Andersson, Christiane, 'Religiöse Bilder Cranachs im Dienste der Reformation', in *Humanismus und Reformation in der deutschen Geschichte. Ein Tagungsbericht*, ed. by Lewis W. Spitz, Veröffentlichungen der historischen Kommission zu Berlin, 51 (Berlin: De Gruyter, 1981), pp. 43–79.

Andersson, Christiane, 'Protestant paintings: Artworks by Lucas Cranach and his workshop', in *Protestant Aesthetics and the Arts*, ed. by Sarah Covington and Kathryn Reklis (Abingdon: Routledge, 2020), pp. 41–56.

Badstübner, Ernst, '"Gesetz und Gnade". Über einige Veröffentlichungen im vergangenen Jahrzehnt zur lutherischen Rechtfertigungslehre im Bild', in *Baugestalt und Bildfunktion. Texte zur Architektur- und Kunstgeschichte*, ed. by Tobias Kunz (Berlin: Lukas-Verlag, 2006), pp. 252–66.

Bartelink, G. J. M., 'Bemerkungen über die Quellen der Schrift "De natura cantus ac miraculis vocis" von Herbenus Traiectensis', *Humanistica Lovaniensia*, 21 (1972), 51–64.

Bautz, Friedrich Wilhelm, 'Cornelius Becker', in *Biographisch-Bibliographisches Kirchenlexikon* [*BBKL*] (Hamm: Traugott Bautz, 1990), I, 449–50.

Bautz, Friedrich Wilhelm, 'Hausmann, Nikolaus', in *BBKL* (Hamm: Traugott Bautz, 1990), II, 607–10.

Bell, Dean Phillip, 'Martin Luther and the Jews: Context and Content', *Theology Today*, 74.3 (2017), 215–24.

Benjamin, Walter, 'L'œuvre d'art à l'époque de sa reproduction méchanisée', *Zeitschrift für Sozialforschung*, 5 (1936), 40–68.

Bergmann, Rosemarie, 'A "tröstlich pictura": Luther's Attitude in the Question of Images', *Renaissance and Reformation/Renaissance et Réforme*, n.s., 5.1 (1981), 15–25.

Bernhard, Michael, 'La *Summa musice* du Ps.-Jean de Murs: Son auteur et sa datation', *Revue de musicologie*, 84 (1998), 19–25.

Bernstein, Lawrence F., 'The Bibliography of Music in Conrad Gesner's *Pandectae* (1548)', *Acta Musicologica*, 45 (1973), 119–63.

Bildhauer, Bettina, 'Blood, Jews and Monsters in Medieval Culture', in *The Monstrous Middle Ages*, ed. by Bettina Bildhauer and Robert Mills (Toronto: University of Toronto Press, 2003), pp. 75–96.

Bildhauer, Bettina, and Robert Mills, 'Conceptualizing the Monstrous', in *The Monstrous Middle Ages*, ed. by Bettina Bildhauer and Robert Mills (Cardiff: University of Wales Press, 2003), pp. 1–27.

Blankenburg, Walter, 'Luther, Martin', in *MGG*, ed. by Friedrich Blume, 17 vols (Kassel: Bärenreiter, 1949–68), VIII, 1334–46.

Blankenburg, Walter, 'Überlieferung und Textgeschichte von Martin Luthers "Encomion musices"', *Lutherjahrbuch*, 39 (1972), 80–104.

Bohde, Daniela, 'Schräge Blicke—exzentrische Kompositionen: "Kreuzigungen und Beweinungen" in der altdeutschen Malerei und Graphik', *Zeitschrift für Kunstgeschichte*, 75 (2012), 193–222.

Brecht, Martin, 'Zum Verständnis von Martin Luthers Lied "Ein feste Burg"', *Archiv für Reformationsgeschichte*, 70 (1979), 106–21.

Bremer, Kai, 'Bekenntnis und Bekehrung. Überlegungen zu Text und Kontext von Luthers "Eyn newes lied"', in *Musik und Reformation—Politisierung, Medialisierung, Missionierung*, ed. by Christiane Wiesenfeldt and Stefan Menzel, Beiträge zur Geschichte der Kirchenmusik im Auftrag der Görres-Gesellschaft, 22 (Paderborn: Ferdinand Schoenigh, 2020), pp. 175–86.

Breuer, Wilhelm, 'Zur Aufführungspraxis vorreformatorischer Fronleichnamsspiele in Deutschland', *Zeitschrift für deutsche Philologie*, 94 (Sonderheft 1975), 50–71.

Brown, Christopher, 'Devotional Life in Hymns, Liturgy, Music and Prayer', in *Lutheran Ecclesiastical Culture 1550–1675*, ed. by Robert Kolb and others, Brill Companion to the Christian Tradition, 11 (Leiden: Brill, 2008), pp. 205–58.

Brown, Christopher Boyd, 'Art and the Artist in the Lutheran Reformation: Johannes Mathesisus and Joachimsthal', *Church History*, 86.4 (2017), 1081–1120.

Bubenheimer, Ulrich, 'Luthers Stellung zum Aufruhr in Wittenberg 1520–1522 und die frühreformatorischen Wurzeln des landesherrlichen Kirchenregiments', *Zeitschrift der Savigny-Stiftung für Rechtsgeschichte—Kanonistische Abteilung*, 102 (1985), 147–214.

Buchwald, Georg, *Theologische Studien und Kritiken*, 59 (1886), 563–72.

Burnett, Stephen G., 'Jews and Judaism', in *Martin Luther in Context*, ed. by David Whitford (Cambridge: Cambridge University Press, 2018), pp. 179–88.

Buszin, Walter, 'Luther on Music', *Musical Quarterly*, 32 (1946), 80–97.

Bynum, Caroline Walker, 'Are Things "Indifferent"? How Objects Change Our Understanding of Religious History', *German History*, 34.1 (2016), 88–112.

Campenhausen, H. von, 'Die Bilderfrage in der Reformation', *Zeitschrift für Kirchengeschichte*, 68 (1957), 96–128.

Casey, Paul F., '"Start spreading the News": Martin Luther's first published song', in *In laudem Caroli: Renaissance and Reformation Studies for Charles Garfield Nauert*, ed. by James V. Mehl and others (Kirksville: Thomas Jefferson University Press, 1998), pp. 75–94.

Cashion, Debra Taylor, 'The Art of Nikolaus Glockendon: Imitation and Originality in the Art of Renaissance Germany', *Journal of Historians of Netherlandish Art*, 2.1–2 (2010).

Cohen, Jeffrey Jerome, 'The Use of Monsters and the Middle Ages', *SELIM: Journal of the Spanish Society for Medieval English Language and Literature*, 2 (1992): 48–71.

Cohon, Samuel S., 'The Name of God, A Study in Rabbinic Theology', *Hebrew Union College Annual*, 23.1 (1950–51), 579–604.

De Bom, Erik, '"Homo ipse ludus ac fabula": Vives's Views on the Dignity of Man as Expressed in his *Fabula de Homine*', *Humanistica Lovaniensia*, 57 (2008), 91–114.

Denecke, Dietrich, 'Wege und Städte zwischen Wittenberg und Rom um 1500. Eine historisch-geographische Studie zur Romreise Martin Luthers', in *Genetische Ansätze in der Kulturlandschaftsforschung. Festschrift für Helmut Jäger*, ed. by Wolfgang Pinkwart, Würzburger geographische Arbeiten, 60 (Würzburg: Institut für Geographie der Julius-Maximilians-Universität, 1983), pp. 77–106.

Dittmann, Lorenz, 'Die Kunst der Reformationszeit', in *Martin Luther 1483–1983: Ringvorlesung der Philosophischen Fakultät Sommersemester 1983*, ed. by P. Erdmann (Saarbrücken: Universität des Saarlandes), 1983, pp. 141–72.

Dyer, Joseph, 'The Place of Musica in Medieval Classifications of Knowledge', *Journal of Musicology*, 24 (2007), 3–71.

Dyer, Joseph, 'Speculative "Musica" and the Medieval University of Paris', *Music & Letters*, 90 (2009), 177–204.

Ehresmann, Donald L., 'The Brazen Serpent, a Reformation Motif in the Works of Lucas Cranach the Elder and His Workshop', *Marsyas*, 12 (1967), 32–47.

Eisenstein, Elizabeth, Anthony Grafton, and Adrian Johns, 'The Forum: How Revolutionary Was the Print Revolution?', *American Historical Review*, 107 (2002), 84–12.

Eusterschulte, Anne, 'Der reformulierte Bilderstreit—Grundlagen einer reformierten Theorie der Imago', in *Philosophie der Reformierten*, ed. by Günter Frank and H. J. Selderhuis, Melanchthon-Schriften der Stadt Bretten, 12 (Stuttgart-Bad Cannstadt: Frommann-Holzboog, 2012), pp. 113–67.

Fabian, Ernst, 'Fürstenbesuche und Volksbelustigungen in Zwickau im 16. Jahrhundert', *Mitteilungen des Altertumsvereins für Zwickau*, 10 (1910), 119–28.

Fellerer, Karl Gustav, 'Die Musica in den Artes Liberales', in *Artes Liberales: Von der Antiken Bildung zur Wissenschaft des Mittelalters*, ed. by Joseph Koch and others (Leiden: Brill, 1976), pp. 33–49.

Ferand, Ernest T., '"Sodaine and Unexpected" Music in the Renaissance', *Musical Quarterly*, 37 (1951), 10–27.

Firth, Katherine, '"Bright flower breaks from charnel bough": The arts of peace and the 1953 Coronation', *The Finzi Journal* (2014), 90–118.

Fischer, Michael, 'Zur lyrischen Rezeption des Lutherliedes 'Ein feste Burg ist unser Gott' im Ersten Weltkrieg', *Populäre Kriegslyrik im Ersten Weltkrieg*, ed. by Nicolas Detering, Michael Fischer, and Aibe-Marlene Gerdes, Populäre Kultur und Musik, 7 (Münster: Waxmann, 2013), pp. 67–97.

Fleischer, Manfred P., 'Melanchthon as Praeceptor of Late-Humanist Poetry', *The Sixteenth Century Journal*, 20.4 (1989), 559–580.

Franke, Birgit, 'Mittelalterliche Wallfahrt in Sachsen—ein Arbeitsbericht', *Arbeits- und Forschunsgberichte zur sächsischen Bodendenkmalspflege*, 44 (2002), 105–16.

Friedrich, Markus, 'Das Hör-Reich und das Sehe-Reich. Zur Bewertung des Sehens bei Luther und im frühneuzeitlichen Luthertum', in *Evidentia. Reichweiten visueller Wahrnehmung in der Frühen Neuzeit*, ed. by Gabriele Wimböck, Karin Leonhard, and Markus Friedrich, Pluralisierung & Autorität, 9 (Berlin: LIT, 2007), pp. 425–50.

Gawthrop, Richard, and Richard Strauss, 'Protestantism and Literacy in Early Modern Germany', *Past and Present*, 104 (1984), 31–55.

'German Student', 'On Luther's Love for and Knowledge of Music', *Musical Times*, 1.11 (1845), 82–87.

Gillet, Joseph Eugene, 'Das Ziel des Dramas in Deutschland vor Gottsched', *Modern Philology*, 12.8 (1915), 481–87.

Gillet, Joseph Eugene, 'Über den Zweck des Dramas in Deutschland im 16. und 17. Jahrhundert', *Publications of the Modern Languages Association*, 32.3 (1917), 430–67.

Gillet, Joseph Eugene, 'Über den Zweck des Schuldramas in Deutschland im 16. und 17. Jahrhundert', *The Journal of English and Germanic Philology*, 17.1 (1918), 69–78.

Gillet, Joseph Eugene, 'The German Dramatist of the Sixteenth Century and his Bible', *Publications of the Modern Languages Association*, 34.3 (1919), 465–93.

Gombrich, Ernst Hans, 'Icones Symbolicae: The Visual Image in Neo-Platonic Thought', *Journal of the Warburg and Courtauld Institutes*, 11 (1948), 163–92.

Gonzaga, Alessandro, *De Victorini Feltrensis Vita*, in *Il pensiero pedagogico dell'Umanesimo*, ed. by Eugenio Garin (Florence: Guintine & Sansoni, 1958), p. 552–67.

Grislis, Egil, 'Martin Luther and the Jews', *Consensus*, 27.1 (2001), 63–84.

Groote, Inga Mai, 'Musikalische Katechismen und "kunstreiche Componisten" für Schule und Haus—eine "Sozialisierung" von Musik in lutherischen Kontexten?', in *Musik und Reformation—Politisierung, Medialisierung, Missionierung*, ed. by Christiane Wiesenfeldt and Stefan Menzel, Beiträge zur Geschichte der Kirchenmusik im Auftrag der Görres-Gesellschaft, 22 (Paderborn: Ferdinand Schoenigh, 2020), pp. 201–220.

Grosse, Sven, 'Renaissance-Humanismus und Reformation: Lorenzo Valla und seine Relevanz für die Kontroverse über die Willensfreiheit in der Reformationszeit', *Kerygma und Dogma*, 48 (2002), 276–300.

Grün-Oesterreich, Andrea, and Peter Oesterreich, '*Dialectica docet, rhetorica movet*: Luthers Reform der Rhetorik', in *Rhetorica Movet: Studies in Historical and Modern Rhetoric in Honour of Heinrich F. Plett*, ed. by Peter Oesterreich and Thomas Sloane (Leiden: Brill, 1999), pp. 25–42.

Gutjahr, Mirko, 'Wie protestantisch ist Luthers Müll: Die Konfessionalisierung und ihre Auswirkungen auf die materielle Alltagskultur des 16. Jahrhunderts', in *Religiosität in Mittelalter und Neuzeit*, ed. by Matthias Untermann and others, Mitteilungen der Deutschen Gesellschaft für Archäologie des Mittelalters und der Neuzeit, 23 (Heidelberg: Neumann, 2011), pp. 43–50.

Haberkern, Philip, '"After me there will come braver men": Jan Hus and Reformation Polemics in the 1530s', *German History*, 27.2 (2009), 177–95.

Heal, Bridget, 'The Catholic Eye and the Protestant Ear: The Reformation as a Non-Visual Event?', in *The Myth of the Reformation*, ed. by Peter J. Opitz, Refo500 Academic Studies, 9 (Göttingen: Vandenhoeck & Ruprecht, 2013), pp. 321–55.

Heal, Bridget, 'Church Space and Religious Change in Reformation Germany', in *Religious Conversion: History, Experience and Meaning*, ed. by Ira Katznelson and Miri Rubin (London: Routledge, 2016), pp. 80–98.

Heidrich, Jürgen, 'Zur Frühgeschichte des Liedes *Ein feste Burg ist unser Gott* im 16. Jahrhundert', in *Kulturelle Wirkungen der Reformation—Cultural Impact of the Reformation. Kongressdokumentation Lutherstadt Wittenberg August 2017*, ed. by Klaus Fitschen, Marianne Schröter, Christopher Spehr, and Ernst-Joachim Watschke, I (Leipzig: Evangelische Verlagsanstalt Leipzig, 2019), pp. 285–96.

Heine, Heinrich, 'Zur Geschichte der Religion und Philosophie in Deutschland, 1834', in *Der Salon: Zweiter Band* (Hamburg: Hoffmann und Campe, 1834), pp. 79–80.

Herlinger, Jan W., 'A Fifteenth-Century Italian Compilation of Music Theory', *Acta Musicologica*, 53 (1981), 90–105.

Hirtler, Eva, 'Die Musik im Übergang von der scientia mathematica zur scientia media', in *Musik und die Geschichte der Philosophie und Naturwissenschaften im Mittelalter: Fragen zur Wechselwirkung von 'Musica' und 'Philosophia' im Mittelalter*, ed. by Frank Hentschel, Studien und Texte zur Geistesgeschichte des Mittelalters, 62 (Leiden: Brill, 1998), pp. 19–38.

Hoppe, Hans, 'Musikalische Renaissance in der alten Hansestadt Lemgo und am Hofe Simons VI. zu Brake', *Heimatland Lippe*, 57 (1964), 93–97.

Hüschen, Heinrich, 'Herbenus (Herben), Matthaeus', in *MGG*, VI, 190, rev. by Klaus-Jürgen Sachs (2002), *MGG*², VIII, 1359–60.

Hüschen, Heinrich, 'Susato, Johannes de', in *Rheinische Musiker*, ed. by Karl Gustav Fellerer (Köln: Volk, 1966), 4: 165–67.

IJsewijn, J., 'The Coming of Humanism to the Low Countries', in *Itinerarium Italicum: The Profile of the Italian Renaissance in the Mirror of its European Transformations*,

*Dedicated to Paul Oskar Kristeller on the Occasion of his 70th Birthday*, ed. by Heiko Augustinus Oberman and Thomas A. Brady Jr (Leiden: Brill, 1975), pp. 193–301.

Israëls, Machtelt, 'Altars on the Street: The Wool Guild, the Carmelites and the Feast of Corpus Domini in Siena (1356–1456)', *Renaissance Studies*, 20.2 (2006), 180–200.

Jacobs, Eduard, 'Bemerkungen zur Geschichte des Schauspiels und der Sitten am Harz im 16. und 17. Jahrhundert', *Zeitschrift des Harz-Vereins für Geschichte und Altertumskunde*, 1 (1868), 77–117.

Jenny, Markus, 'Neue Hypothesen zur Entstehung und Bedeutung von "Ein feste Burg"', *Jahrbuch für Liturgik und Hymnologie*, 9 (1964), 143–52.

Jung, Jaqueline E., 'The Passion, the Jews and the Crisis of the Individual', in *Beyond the Yellow Badge: Anti-Judaism and Anti-Semitism in Medieval and Early Modern Visual Culture*, ed. by Mitchell B. Merback, Brill's Series in Jewish Studies, 37 (Leiden: Brill, 2007), pp. 145–77.

Kade, Otto, 'Die "Inventio" des Luther-Codex und der deutsche Kulturprotestantismus', in *Kulturelle Wirkungen der Reformation—Cultural Impact of the Reformation. Kongressdokumentation Lutherstadt Wittenberg August 2017*, ed. by Klaus Fitschen, Marianne Schröter, Christopher Spehr, and Ernst-Joachim Watschke, I (Leipzig: Evangelische Verlagsanstalt Leipzig, 2019), pp. 317–26.

Kanarfogel, Ephraim, 'Ashkenazic Talmudic Interpretation and the Jewish-Christian Encounter', *Medieval Encounters*, 22 (2016), 72–94.

Kaufmann, Thomas, 'Das Judentum in der frühreformatorischen Flugschriften-publizistik', *Theologie und Kirche*, 95.4 (1998), 429–61.

Kaufmann, Thomas, 'Luther and the Jews', *Antisemitism Studies*, 3.1 (2019), 46–65 (first publ. in *Jews, Judaism, and the Reformation in Sixteenth-Century Germany*, ed. by Dean Phillip Bell and Stephen G. Burnett, Studies in Central European Studies (Leiden: Brill, 2006), pp. 69–104).

Kaufmann, Thomas, 'Türckenbüchlein', Zur christlichen Wahrnehmung 'türkischer Religion' in Spätmittelalter und Reformation, Forschungen zur Kirchen- und Dogmengeschichte, 97 (Göttingen: Vandenhoek & Ruprecht, 2008).

Kaufmann, Thomas, 'Antisemitische Lutherflorilegien: Hinweise und Materialien zu einer fatalen Rezeptionsgeschichte', *Zeitschrift für Theologie und Kirche*, 112.2 (2015), 192–228.

Kessler, Herbert, 'Pictorial Narrative and Church Mission in Sixth-Century Gaul', *Studies in the History of Art*, 16 (1985), 75–91.

Kirn, Paul, 'Friedrich der Weise und Jacopo de' Barbari', *Jahrbuch der Preußischen Kunstsammlungen*, 46 (1925), 130–34.

Kitchen, Martin, 'The Antisemite's *Vade Mecum*: Theodor Fritsch's *Handbuch der Judenfrage*', *Antisemitism Studies*, 2.2 (2018), 199–234.

Klän, Werner, 'Der "vierte Mann". Auf den Spuren von Nikolaus Selneckers (1530–1592), Beitrag zu Entstehung und Verbreitung der Konkordienformel', *Lutherische Theologie und Kirche*, 17 (1993), 145–74.

Kloeden, Wolfdietrich von, 'Selnecker, Nikolaus', in *BBKL*, IX, 1376–79.

Koepplin, Dieter, 'Kommet her zu mir alle. Das tröstliche Bild des Gekreuzigten im Verständnis Luthers', in *Martin Luther und die Refiormation in Deutschland. Vorträge zur Ausstellung im Germanischen Nationalmuseum Nürnberg 1983*, ed. by Kurt Löcher (Schweinfurt: Weppert, 1983), pp. 153–99.

Kolb, Robert, 'Georg Major as Controversialist: Polemics in the Late Reformation', *Church History*, 45.4 (1976), 455–68.

Kongsted, O., 'Ludwig Senfl's Luther-Motetter: en forskningsberetning', *Fund og Forskning*, 39 (2000), 7–41.

Könneker, Barbara: '"Wold ihrs den nicht schir gleuben do?" Joachim Greffs protestantisches Osterspiel', *Daphnis*, 23 (1994), 309–44.

Laforge, Danielle, 'Wechselbeziehungen zwischen Narrheit und Weisheit: Abgrenzung des Narrenbegriffs und epochale Bewertung', in *Der Narr in der deutschen Literatur im Mittelalter und in der frühen Neuzeit*, ed. by Jean Schillinger and others, Jahrbuch für internationale Germanistik, Reihe A, 96 (Bern: Peter Lang, 2009), pp. 310–11.

Leaver, Robin A., 'The Lutheran Reformation', in *The Renaissance from the 1470s to the End of the Sixteenth Century*, ed. by Iain Fenlon (Englewood Cliffs, NJ: Prentice Hall, 1989), pp. 263–85.

Leppin, Volker, 'Kirchenausstattungen in territorialen Kirchenordnungen bis 1548', in *Ordnungen für die Kirche—Wirkungen auf die Welt: Evangelische Kirchenordnungen des 16. Jahrhunderts*, ed. by Sabine Arend, Gerald Dörner, and others (Tübingen: Mohr Siebeck, 2015), pp. 137–55.

Liliencron, Rochus von, 'Die Chorgesänge des lateinisch-deutschen Schuldramas im XVI. Jahrhundert', *Vierteljahrsschrift für Musikwissenschaft*, 6 (1890), 309–87.

Livingston, Ernest, 'The Place of Music in German Education around 1600', *Journal of Research in Music Education*, 19.2 (1971), 144–67.

Loewe, Jost Andreas, 'Proclaiming the Passion: Popular Drama and the Passion Tradition in Luther's Germany', *Renaissance and Reformation Review*, 12.2 (2010), 235–82.

Loewe, Jost Andreas, '"Musica est optimum": Martin Luther's Theory of Music', *Music and Letters*, 94.4 (2013), 573–605.

Loewe, Jost Andreas, 'Why do Lutherans Sing? Lutherans, Music and the Gospel in the First Century of the Reformation', *Church History*, 82 (2013), 69–89.

Loewe, Jost Andreas, 'Martin Luther, Music, and the Seven Liberal Arts', *Oxford University Press: OUP Blog*, 2 (2014): <https://blog.oup.com/2014/02/martin-luther-music-seven-liberal-arts/> [accessed 28 June 2022].

Loewe, Jost Andreas, and Katherine Firth, 'Luther's "Mighty Fortress"', *Lutheran Quarterly*, 32.2 (2018), 125–45.

Lohfert Jørgensen, Hans Henrik, 'Live Matter and Living Images: Towards a Theory of Animation in Material Media', *Konsthistorisk tidskrift/Journal of Art History*, 86.3 (2017), 251–70.

Lohmann, Martin J., 'The Wittenberg Circle', in *Martin Luther in Context*, ed. by David Whitford (Cambridge: Cambridge University Press, 2018), pp. 249–56.

Mager, Inge, 'Martin Luthers Lied "Ein feste Burg ist unser Gott" und Psalm 46', *Jahrbuch für Liturgik und Hymnologie*, 30 (1986), 87–96.

Manchinu OSB, Paola, 'Sperindio Cagnoli, una creatura di Gaudenzio Ferrari', in *Fermo Stella e Sperindio Cagnoli seguaci di Gaudenzio Ferrari: una bottega d'arte nel Cinquecento Padano*, ed. by Giovanni Romano, Quaderni del Museo Bernareggi, Museo Adriano Bernareggi Bergamo, x (Milano: Silvana, 2006), pp. 59–74.

Manzon, Tommaso, 'Bridging Heaven and Earth: An Investigation in the Metaphysics of Martin Luther's Theory of Music, in Continuous Dialogue with Florensky', *Aisthema*, 5.1 (2018), 37–54.

*Martin Luther and Antisemitism*, ed. by Daniel Maoz (= *Consensus*, 41.2 (2020)).

Meding, Wichmann von, 'Ein feste Burg ist unser Gott: Martin Luthers christliche Auslegung des Psalms 46', *Zeitschrift für Theologie und Kirche*, 90.1 (1993), 25–56.

Menzel, Stefan, '"Eine feste burgk ist unser got". Otto Kade, die "Inventio" des Luther-Codex und der deutsche Kulturprotestantismus', in *Kulturelle Wirkungen der Reformation—Cultural Impact of the Reformation. Kongressdokumentation Lutherstadt Wittenberg August 2017*, ed. by Klaus Fitschen, Marianne Schröter, Christopher Spehr, and Ernst-Joachim Watschke, I (Leipzig: Evangelische Verlagsanstalt Leipzig, 2019), pp. 317–26.

Mertens, Volker, 'Das Fastnachtspiel zwischen Subversion und Affirmation', in *Topographies of the Early Modern City*, ed. by Arthur Groos and others, Transatlantic Studies on Medieval and Early Modern Literature and Culture, 3 (Göttingen: Vandenhoek and Ruprecht, 2008), pp. 43–60.

Meserve, Margaret, 'A Roman Monster in the Humanist Imagination', in *Et Amicorum: Essays on Renaissance Humanism and Philosophy*, ed. by Margaret Meserve and Anthony Ossa-Richardson, Brill's Studies in Intellectual History, 273 (Leiden: Brill, 2018), pp. 118–43.

Mielke, Ursula, 'Erhard Schön', in *Hollstein's German Engravings, Etchings and Woodcuts 1400–1700, 52: J. S. Schott—L. Schultes* (Amsterdam: M. Hertzberger, 2000), pp. 47–48.

Millen, Rochelle L., 'On the Jews and the Lutherans: the ELCA Confronts History', in *Remembering for the Future: The Holocaust in an Age of Genocide*, ed. by J. K. Roth, E. Maxwell, M. Levy, and W. Whitworth (London: Palgrave Macmillan, 2001), pp. 587–602.

Miller, B. Lodes M., '"Hic jacet Ludevicus Fenfflius": Neues zur Biographie von Ludwig Senfl', *Die Musikforschung*, 58 (2005), 260–66.

Moeller, Bernd, 'Stadt und Buch: Bemerkungen zur Struktur der reformatorischen Bewegungen in Deutschland', in *Stadtbürgertum und Adel in der Reformation*, ed. by Wolfgang J. Mommsen and others, Studien zur Sozialgeschichte der Reformation in England und Deutschland, 5 (Stuttgart: Klett-Cotta, 1979), pp. 29–39.

Moeller, Bernd, 'Religious Life in Germany on the Eve of the Reformation', in *Pre-Reformation Germany*, ed. by Gerald Strauss (New York: Harper and Row, 1972), pp. 14–30.

Möller, Eberhard, 'Joachim Greff und die musikalische Gestaltung des Schuldramas in Mitteldeutschland', *Musikgeschichte in Mittel- und Osteuropa*, 6 (2000), 201–20.

Moser, Hans, 'Die Innsbrucker Spielhandschrift in der geistlichen Spieltradition Tirols', in *Tiroler Volksschauspiel: Beiträge zur Theatergeschichte des Alpenraumes*, ed. by Egon Kühebacher and others, Schriftenreihe des Südtiroler Kulturinstituts, 3 (Bozen: Athesia, 1976), pp. 178–89.

Nebelsick, Louis D., and Tomoko Emmerling, '"Finding Luther": Toward an Archaeology of the Reformer and the Earliest Reformation', *Church History*, 86.4 (2017), 1155–1207.

Niemöller, Klaus Wolfgang, 'Die musikalische Rhetorik und ihre Genese in Musik und Musikanschauung der Renaissance', in *Renaissance-Rhetorik*, ed. by Heinrich F. Plett (Berlin, 1993), pp. 285–311.

Niemöller, Klaus Wolfgang, 'Deutsche Musiktheorie im 16. Jahrhundert: Geistes- und institutionsgeschichtliche Grundlagen', in *Deutsche Musiktheorie des 15. bis 17. Jahrhunderts*, 1: *Von Paumann bis Calvisius*, ed. by Theodor Göllner (Darmstadt, 2003), pp. 69–98.

Nipperday, Thomas, 'Luther und die Bildung der Deutschen', in *Luther und die Folgen. Beiträge zur sozialgeschichtlichen Bedeutung der lutherischen Reformation*, ed. by Hartmut Löwe and Claus-Jürgen Roepke (München: Christian Kaiser Verlag, 1983), pp. 13–27.

Noble, Bonnie J., '"A Work in Which the Angels Are Wont to Rejoice": Lucas Cranach's "Schneeberg Altarpiece"', *The Sixteenth Century Journal*, 34.4 (2003), 1011–37.

Noble, Bonnie J., '"Law and Gospel" and the Strategies of Pictorial Rhetoric', in Bonnie J. Noble, *Lucas Cranach the Elder: Art and Devotion of the German Reformation* (Lanham, MD: University Press of America, 2009), pp. 27–66 (first publ. as '*Law and Gospel*: Scripture, Truth, and Pictorial Rhetoric', *Southeastern College Art Conference Review*, 14.4 (2004), 314–32).

Olson, Oliver K., 'Theology of Revolution: Magdeburg, 1550–1551', *The Sixteenth Century Journal*, 3.1 (1972), 56–79.

Pettegree, Andrew, '"The Law and the Gospel": The Evolution of an Evangelical Pictorial Theme in the Bibles of the Reformation', in *The Bible as Book: The Reformation*, ed.

by Orlaith O'Sullivan and Ellen N. Herron (London: The British Library & Oak Knoll Press, 2000), pp. 123–36.

Pettegree, Andrew, 'Books, Pamphlets and Polemic', in *The Reformation World*, ed. by Andrew Pettegree (London: Routledge, 2002), pp. 109–26.

Pettegree, Andrew, and Matthew Hall, 'The Reformation and the Book: A Reconsideration', *The Historical Journal*, 47.4 (2004), 785–808.

Pietschmann, Klaus, and Steven Rozenski, Jr, 'Singing the Self: The Autobiography of the Fifteenth-Century German Singer and Composer Johannes von Soest', *Early Music History*, 29 (2010), 119–59.

Pouelle, Emmanuel, 'John of Murs', in *Dictionary of Scientific Biography*, ed. by Charles Goulston Gillispie (New York: Scribner, 1973), VII, 128–33.

Posset, Franz, 'Martin Luther on "Deësis." His Rejection of the Artistic Representation of "Jesus, John, and Mary"', *Renaissance and Reformation/Renaissance et Réforme*, n.s., 20.3 (1996), 57–76.

Puff, Helmut, 'Martin Luther, the Sexual Reformation and Same-Sex Sexuality', in *Martin Luther: A Christian between Reforms and Modernity (1517–2017)*, ed. by Alberto Melloni, 3 vols (Berlin: De Gruyter, 2017), I, pp. 663–78.

Purcell, Christina, and Carolyn Kagan, 'Joy at work: the impact of non-professional singing workshops on employee well-being', in *Report of the Joy at Work Singing Workshops included as part of the RIHSC Annual Conference, Manchester 2007* (Manchester: Research Institute for Health and Social Change Manchester Metropolitan University, 2008), pp. 2–15.

Ragotzky, Hedda, 'Der Bauer in der Narrenrolle: zur Funktion "Verkehrter Welt" im frühen Nürnberger Fastnachtsspiel', in *Typus und Individuät im Mittelalter*, ed. by Horst Wenzel and others, Forschungen zur Geschichte der älteren deutschen Literatur, 4 (München: Wilhelm Fink Verlag, 1983), pp. 77–101.

Rambaran-Olm, Mary, M. Breann Leake, and Micah James Goodrich, 'Medieval studies: the stakes of the field', *postmedieval: a journal of medieval cultural studies*, 11 (2020), 356–70.

Richter, Rainer G., 'Sächsische Ofenkacheln der Reformationszeit', *Keramos*, 227 (2015), 1–29.

Riegel, Martin, 'Paul Eber (1511–1569)', *Fränkische Lebensbilder*, 21 (2006), 103–17.

Roch, Eckhard, 'Zwischen Geist und Materie: Grundlagen des musikalischen Materialbegriffes in Philosophie und Rhetorik', *Archiv für Musikwissenschaft*, 59 (2002), 136–64.

Röcke, Werner, 'Literarische Gegenwelten: Fastnachtspiele und karnivaleske Festkultur', in *Die Literatur im Übergang vom Mittelalter und früher Neuzeit*, ed. by Werner Röcke and others, Hansers Sozialgeschichte der deutschen Literatur, 1 (München and Wien: Hanser Verlag, 2004), pp. 420–45.

Rohls, Jan, '"... unser Knie beugen wir doch nicht mehr": Bilderverbot und bildende Kunst im Zeitalter der Reformation', *Zeitschrift für Theologie und Kirche*, 81.3 (1984), 332–51.

Roper, Lyndal, 'Witchcraft and the Western Imagination', *Transactions of the Royal Historical Society* 16, (2006), 117–47.

Roper, Lyndal, 'Luther Relics', in *Religion, the Supernatural and Visual Culture in Early Modern Europe: An Album Amicorum for Charles Zika*, ed. by Jennifer Spinks, Dagmar Eichberger, and others, Studies in Medieval and Reformation Traditions, 191 (Leiden: Brill, 2015), pp. 330–53.

Rosen, Valeska von, 'Gibt es "das reformatorische Bild"? Zur Revision essentialistischer und dichotomer Medienvorstellungen in der deutschen und niederländischen Reformation', in *Reformation Heute: Band IV—Reformation und Medien: Zu den intermedialen Wirkungen der Reformation*, ed. by Johann Anselm Steiger (Leipzig: Evangelische Verlagsanstalt, 2018), pp. 9–34.

Rößler, Martin, '"Helft mir Gotts Güte preise": Der Wittenberger Liederdichter Paul Eber', in *Dona Melanchthoniana: Festgabe für Heinz Scheible zum 70. Geburtstag*, ed. by Johanna Loehr and others (Stuttgart-Bad Cannstatt: Frommann-Holzboog, 2001), pp. 339–80.

Roth, Christine, 'Das Lied Ein feste Burg im Schaffen des Michael Praetorius: Von der Aktualisierung musikalischer Traditionen', in *Kulturelle Wirkungen der Reformation—Cultural Impact of the Reformation. Kongressdokumentation Lutherstadt Wittenberg August 2017*, ed. by Klaus Fitschen, Marianne Schröter, Christopher Spehr, and Ernst-Joachim Watschke, 1 (Leipzig: Evangelische Verlagsanstalt Leipzig, 2019), pp. 345–54.

Rowe, Nina, 'Idealization and Subjection at The South Façade of Strasbourg Cathedral', in *Beyond the Yellow Badge: Anti-Judaism and Anti-Semitism in Medieval and Early Modern Visual Culture*, ed. by Mitchell B. Merback, Brill's Series in Jewish Studies, 37 (Leiden: Brill, 2007), pp. 179–202.

Rublack, Ulinka, 'Grapho-relics: Lutheranism and the materialization of the word', in *Relics and remains*, ed. by Alexandra Walsham, special issue supplement, 5 (= *Past and Present*, 206 (2010)), pp. 144–66.

Rudnik, Ursula, 'Early Modern Hate Speech—Martin Luther's Antisemitism, Responses and Reactions', *Cross Currents*, 67.2 (2017), 421–30.

Sabar, Shalom, 'Between Calvinists and Jews: Hebrew Script in Rembrandt's Art', in *Beyond the Yellow Badge: Anti-Judaism and Anti-Semitism in Medieval and Early Modern Visual Culture*, ed. by Mitchell B. Merback, Brill's Series in Jewish Studies, 37 (Leiden: Brill, 2007), pp. 371–404.

Sachs, Klaus-Jürgen, 'Zur Funktion der Berufungen auf das achte Buch von Aristoteles "Politik" in Musiktraktaten des 15. Jahrhunderts', in *Musik und die Geschichte der Philosophie und Naturwissenschaften im Mittelalter: Fragen zur Wechselwirkung von*

*'Musica' und 'Philosophia' im Mittelalter*, ed. by Frank Hentschel, Studien und Texte zur Geistesgeschichte des Mittelalters, 62 (Leiden: Brill, 1998), pp. 269–90.

Schilling, Johannes, 'Martin Luther and the Arts: Music, Poetry, and Hymns', in *Oxford Research Encyclopedia of Religion* <https://doi.org/10.1093/acrefore/9780199340378.013.293> [accessed 28 June 2022].

Schilling, Johannes, 'Musik', in *Luther Handbuch*, ed. by Albrecht Beutel (Tübingen: Mohr Siebeck, 2005), pp. 236–243.

Schmidt, Thomas, 'Ein feste Burg ist unser Gott? Der Choral in der Instrumentalmusik des 19. Jahrhunderts zwischen Sakralem Andachtstopos und konfessionellen Statement', in *Kulturelle Wirkungen der Reformation—Cultural Impact of the Reformation. Kongressdokumentation Lutherstadt Wittenberg August 2017*, ed. by Klaus Fitschen, Marianne Schröter, Christopher Spehr, and Ernst-Joachim Watschke, I (Leipzig: Evangelische Verlagsanstalt Leipzig, 2019), pp. 307–16.

Schneider, Hans, 'Luthers Romreise', in *Martin Luther in Rom: Die Ewige Stadt als kosmopolitisches Zentrum und ihre Wahrnehmung*, ed. by Michael Matheus, Arnold Nesselrath, Martin Wallraff, Bibliothek des historischen Instituts in Rom, 134 (Berlin: de Gruyter: 2017), pp. 3–32.

Schramm, Brooks, 'Luther's Schem Hamphoras', *Dialog: A Journal of Theology*, 56.2 (2017), 151–55.

Scribner, Robert W., 'Flugblatt und Analphabetentum', in *Flugschriften als Massenmedium der Reformationszeit, Beiträge zum Tübinger Symposion 1980*, ed. by Hans-Joachim Köhler and others, Spätmittelalter und frühe Neuzeit, 13 (Stuttgart: Klett-Cotta, 1981), pp. 65–76.

Scribner, Robert W., 'Reformation, Karneval und die "verkehrte Welt"', in *Volkskultur: Zur Wiederentdeckung des vergessenen Alltags*, ed. by Richard van Dülmen and others (Frankfurt a.M.: Fischer, 1984), pp. 117–52.

Scribner, Robert W., 'Incombustible Luther: The Image of the Reformer in Early Modern Germany', *Past and Present*, 110 (1986), 36–68.

Scribner, Robert W., 'Demons, Defecation and Monsters: Luther's "Depiction of the Papacy" (1545)', in R. W. Scribner, *Popular Culture and Popular Movements in Reformation Germany* (London: Hambledon Press, 1987), pp. 277–99.

Scribner, Robert W., 'Das Visuelle in der Volksfrömmigkeit', in *Bilder and Bildertum in Spätmittelalter und in der frühen Neuzeit*, ed. by R. W. Scribner, Wolfenbütteler Forschungen, 46 (Wiesbaden: Otto Harrassowitz, 1990), pp. 9–20.

Seidel, Andrea, 'Joachim Greff: Dramatiker im Dienste der Reformation', in *Mitteldeutsche Lebensbilder, Menschen im Zeitalter der Reformation*, ed. by Werner Freitag (Köln, Weimar, Wien: Böhlau Verlag, 2004), pp. 11–31.

Silver, Larry, 'Luther's Artists', in *Martin Luther in Context*, ed. by David Whitford (Cambridge: Cambridge University Press, 2018), pp. 187–203.

Simon, Eckehard, 'Staging the Reformation in the Nuremberg Carnival', in *Topographies of the Early Modern City*, ed. by Arthur Groos, and others, Transatlantic Studies on Medieval and Early Modern Literature and Culture, 3 (Göttingen: Vandenhoek and Ruprecht, 2008), pp. 61–96.

Slotemaker, John T., 'The Trinitarian House of David: Martin Luther's Anti-Jewish Exegesis of 2 Samuel 23.1–7', *Harvard Theological Review*, 104:2 (2011), 233–54.

Smith, Jeffrey Chipps, 'Graduate Seminar "Art, Reformation, and the Cult of Martin Luther", Herzog August Bibliothek, Wolfenbüttel, Germany,' *The Sixteenth Century Journal*, 48.4 (2017), 991.

Sólyom, Jenő, '"Das Reich muß uns doch bleiben": Zur letzten Zeile des Liedes "Ein feste Burg"', *Jahrbuch für Liturgik und Hymnologie*, 20 (1976), 166–71.

Spelman, Leslie, 'Luther and the Arts', *The Journal of Aesthetics and Art Criticism*, 10.2 (1951), 166–75.

Spinks, Jennifer, 'After Luther: Visual Culture, Materiality and the Legacy of 1517', *Journal of Ecclesiastical History*, 72.4 (2021), 822–27.

Staats, Reinhart, '"Ein feste Burg ist unser Gott": Die Entstehung des Lutherliedes im Abendmahlsstreit 1527', *Theologische Literaturzeitschrift*, 123 (1998), 115–26.

Stammler, Wolfgang, 'Greff, Joachim', in *Neue Deutsche Biographie* (Berlin: Duncker & Humblott, 1966), VII, 18–19.

Stewart, Alison, 'Paper Festivals and Popular Entertainment: The Kermis Woodcuts of Sebald Beham in Reformation Nuremberg', *The Sixteenth Century Journal*, 24.2 (1993), 301–50.

Strickland, Debra Higgs, 'The Jews, Leviticus, and the Unclean in Medieval Bestiaries', in *Beyond the Yellow Badge: Anti-Judaism and Anti-Semitism in Medieval and Early Modern Visual Culture*, ed. by Mitchell B. Merback, Brill's Series in Jewish Studies, 37 (Leiden: Brill, 2007), pp. 203–32.

Tacke, Andreas, '"Ich het euch vil zuschreiben, hab aber vil zuschaffen": Cranach der Ältere als "Parallel Entrepreneur". Auftragslage und Marktstrategien im Kontext des Schneeberger Altares von 1539', in *Das Bild des neuen Glaubens: das Cranach-Retabel in der Schneeberger St. Wolfgangkirche*, ed. by Thomas Pöpper, Susanne Wegmann, and others (Regensburg: Schnell & Steiner, 2011), pp. 71–84.

Tacke, Andreas, 'Gleich dem Kaninchen vor der Schlange: Altgläubige und die Wittenberger Bildpropaganda', in *Bild und Botschaft: Cranach im Dienst von Hof und Reformation—anlässlich der Ausstellung "Bild und Botschaft. Cranach im Dienst von Hof und Reformation*, ed. by Julia Carrasco and Timo Trümer (Heidelberg, Morio: 2015), pp. 82–87.

Tacke, Andreas, 'Hier liege ich … Perspektivwechsel für die bildende Kunst der Reformationszeit', in *Martin Luther—Aufbruch in eine neue Welt*, ed. by Anne-Simone Rous (Dresden: Sandstein, 2016), pp. 222–29.

Tacke, Andreas, and Birgit Ulrike Münch, 'Bildende Kunst und Reformation', in *Musik und Reformation—Politisierung, Medialisierung, Missionierung*, ed. by Christiane Wiesenfeldt and Stefan Menzel, Beiträge zur Geschichte der Kirchenmusik im Auftrag der Görres-Gesellschaft, 22 (Paderborn: Ferdinand Schoenigh, 2020), pp. 131–44.

Tarry, Joe E., 'Music in the Educational Philosophy of Martin Luther', *Journal of Research in Music Education*, 21 (1973), 355–65.

Thomke, Hellmut, 'Das Wort sie sollen lassen stahn! Überlegungen zur Sprache und zur poetischen Form von Luthers Liedern am Beispiel des Reformationsliedes "Ein feste Burg ist unser Gott"', *Jahrbuch für Liturgik und Hymnologie*, 29 (1985), 79–89.

Thust, Karl Christian, 'Luthers Lied "Ein feste Burg ist unser Gott". Nationalhymne des deutschen Protestantismus', *Deutsches Pfarrerblatt*, 112 (11/2012), 643–48.

Van Stam, Frans Pieter, 'Luthers Lied "Ein feste Burg": Mitten aus dem Abendmahlsstreit mit Zwingli entstanden—1527', *Church History/NAKG*, 82.1 (2002), 35–60.

Völker, Karl, "Die historischen Hintergründe von 'Ein feste Burg'," *Deutsches Pfarrerblatt*, 40 (1936), 768–88.

Wade, Erik, 'The Beast with Two Backs: Bestiality, Sex Between Men, and Byzantine Theology in the Paenitentiale Theodori', *Journal of Medieval Worlds*, 2.1–2 (2020), 11–26.

Walter, Peter, 'Johannes von Dalberg und der Humanismus', in *1495—Kaiser, Reich, Reformen: Der Reichstag zu Worms. Ausstellung des Landeshauptarchivs Koblenz in Verbindung mit der Stadt Worms zum 500jährigen Jubiläum des Wormser Reichstags von 1495*, ed. by Claudia Helm and Jost Hausmann (Koblenz: Landeshauptarchivverwaltung Rheinland-Pfalz, 1995), pp. 139–71.

Wegmann, Susanne, 'Der reformatorische Blick. Sehen oder Hören—welche Sinneswahrnehmung führt zu Gott?', in *Sehen und Sakralität in der Vormoderne*, ed. by David Ganz and Thomas Lentes, Kultbild, 4 (Berlin: Reimer Verlag, 2011), pp. 292–301.

Weigel, Maria Lucia, 'Bekenntnisbilder—Bekenntnisse im Bild', in *Bekennen und Bekenntnis im Kontext der Wittenberger Reformation*, ed. by Daniel Gehrt, Johannes Hund, Stefan Michel, and others (Göttingen: Vandenhoek & Ruprecht, 2019), pp. 259–78.

Weimar, Christoph, 'Luther and Cranach on Justification in Word and Image', *Lutheran Quarterly*, 18 (2004), 387–405.

Weinstein, Roni, 'Jews and Lutheranism: An Ambiguous Silence', in *Martin Luther: A Christian between Reforms and Modernity* (*1517–2017*), ed. by Alberto Melloni, 3 vols (Berlin: De Gruyter, 2017), I, pp. 635–48.

Weisheipl, James, 'Curriculum of the Faculty of Arts at Oxford in the Early Fourteenth Century', *Medieval Studies*, 26 (1964), 143–85.

Wengert, Timothy J., 'Philip Melanchthon and the Jews: A Reappraisal', in *Jews, Judaism, and the Reformation in Sixteenth-Century Germany*, ed. by Dean Phillip Bell and Stephen G. Burnett, Studies in Central European Studies (Leiden: Brill, 2006), pp. 105–135.

Werner, Elke Anna, 'Feindbild', in *Handbuch der politischen Ikonographie*, ed. by Uwe Fleckner, Martin Warnke, and Hendrik Ziegler (München: Beck, 2011), I, pp. 301–305.

Werner, Elke Anna, 'Pictorial Concepts of Law and Grace: Relations between the Lutheran Reformation and the Anthropology of the Image', in *Anthropological Reformations: Anthropology in the Era of Reformation*, ed. by Anne Eusterschulte and others (Göttingen: Vandenhoek & Ruprecht, 2015), pp. 134–53.

Werner, Elke Anna, 'Martin Luther and Visual Culture', in *Oxford Research Encyclopedia, Religion* (Oxford: Oxford University Press, 2016).

Wiedemann, Konrad, 'Rutgerus Sycamber', in *Contemporaries of Erasmus: A Biographical Register of the Renaissance and Reformation*, ed. by Peter Bietenholz and Thomas Deutscher (Toronto: University of Toronto Press, 1987), III, pp. 301–2.

Wiese, Christian, 'Luther's Shadow: Jewish and Protestant Interpretations of the Reformers Writings on the Jews, 1917–33', in *Jews and Protestants: From the Reformation to the Present*, ed. by Irene Aue-Ben-David, Aya Elyada, Moshe Sluhovsky, Christian Wiese, and others (Berlin: de Gruyter, 2020), pp. 161–88.

Wolf, Johannes, 'Ein Beitrag zur Diskantlehre des 14. Jahrhunderts', *Sammelbände der Internationalen Musikgesellschaft*, 15 (1914), 504–34.

Wouters, H. H. E., 'Mattheus Herbenus Trajectensis, een humanist van het eerste uur', in *Miscellanea Trajectensia: Bijdragen tot de geschiedenis van Maastricht*, ed. by Gerard Willem Augustinus Panhuysen (Maastricht: Limburgs Geschied- en Oudheidkundig Genootschap, 1962), pp. 263–329.

Žak, Sabine, 'Die Gründung der Hofkapelle in Heidelberg', *Archiv für Musikwissenschaft*, 50 (1993), 145–63.

# Index